What Reading Research Tells Us About Children With Diverse Learning Needs

Bases and Basics

The LEA Series on Special Education and Disability
John Wills Lloyd, Series Editor

What Reading Research Tells Us About Children With Diverse Learning Needs

Bases and Basics

Edited by

DEBORAH C. SIMMONS
EDWARD J. KAMEENUI
University of Oregon

 LAWRENCE ERLBAUM ASSOCIATES, PUBLISHERS
1998   Mahwah, New Jersey   London

Lawrence Erlbaum Associates, Inc., Publishers
10 Industrial Avenue
Mahwah, New Jersey 07430

Cover design by Kathryn Houghtaling Lacey

Library of Congress Cataloging-in-Publication Data

What reading research tells us about children with diverse learning
    needs : bases and basics / edited by Deborah C. Simmons, Edward J.
    Kameenui.
        p. cm.
    Includes bibliographical references and indexes.
    ISBN 0-8085-2515-0 (cloth : alk. paper). -- ISBN 0-8058-2516-9
(pbk. : alk. paper)
    1. Reading disability. 2. Reading--Research. 3. Reading-
-Remedial teaching. I. Simmons, Deborah C. II. Kameenui, Edward
J.
LB1050.5.W47   1998
372.43--dc21   98-25644
                                                        CIP

Books published by Lawrence Erlbaum Associates are printed on acid-free paper,
and their bindings are chosen for strength and durability.

Printed in the United States of America
10 9 8 7 6 5 4

Contents

CHAPTER

1

Introduction

Deborah C. Simmons
Edward J. Kameenui
University of Oregon

ISSUES AND CHALLENGES
IN READING ACHIEVEMENT

Professional educators and the public at large have long known that reading is an enabling skill that traverses academic disciplines and translates into meaningful personal, social, and economic outcomes for individuals. It is common knowledge that reading is the fulcrum of academics, the pivotal ability that stabilizes and leverages children's opportunities to learn and to become reflective, independent learners. Despite society's long recognition of the importance of successful reading, only recently have we begun to understand the profound and enduring consequences of not learning to read and the new-found evidence of the critical and abbreviated period in which we have to alter reading trajectories (California Department of Education, 1995; Juel, 1988; Lyon & Chhabra, 1996).

One need not look beyond the school dropout data, prison rosters, or recipients of federal public assistance to find that poor reading ability is pervasive and common to many who are not succeeding in today's society—a society whose literacy demands continue to galvanize the distinctions between the "haves and have nots." Studies of individuals who are resilient to personal and societal adversity indicate that the ability to read has powerful and far-reaching positive effects and, likewise, the converse. Literacy level is both negatively associated with lower annual earnings and higher unemployment. The absence of proficient reading skills is a considerable risk factor associated not only with academic failure and school dropout but unemployment and adjudication (Cornwall & Bawden, 1992; Werner, 1993). Stanovich (1986) drew parallels between a biblical proverb and the domain of reading noting that the rich get richer and the poor get poorer. In that parallel, he observed that readers who read early and successfully not only reap the advantage of early literacy but accumulate experiences with print that continue to differentiate and discriminate between good and poor readers throughout their academic careers. Unfortunately, the rich get richer phenomenon has been verified not only in academic but also in economic domains. Individuals who test in the "least proficient" literacy levels are often unemployable as even low-skilled jobs demand adequate reading abilities (Whitman, 1995). According to a survey of more than 3,000 employers in Atlanta, Boston, Detroit, and Los Angeles, economist Harry Holzer found that "only 5 to 10 percent of the low-skilled job openings in these cities were available to applicants" (p. 31) with low literacy skills (cited in Whitman, 1995). If the relation between reading and other desirable outcomes is so strong, trends from national data suggest we have just cause for concern.

Reports on progress toward the National Education Goals reported by the Department of Education (National Center for Education Statistics, 1993) found that 90 million of America's 191 million adults (47%) either are illiterate or can perform only simple literacy tasks. Findings from the 1994 National Assessment of Educational Progress (NAEP), a federally supported program that monitors the progress of students in core academic areas, indicated that 25% of the 38 states participating in both the 1992 and 1994 fourth-grade assessments showed a significant decrease in reading proficiency over the 2-year period. On average, fourth graders in the 1994 assessment scored only one point above the basic level of 212 with the proficient (243) and advanced (275) levels far out of reach. Four of 10 fourth graders (42%) among schools surveyed were reading at a "below basic" level (National Center for Educational Statistics, 1996).

An increasing number of children are failing to learn how to unlock the meaning and opportunities that printed words can avail. The NAEP 1992 and 1994 data found that children who are Black or Hispanic, are poor, born to parents who are less educated, and do not live in two-parent family structures are more likely to have low literacy skills than children who are White, wealthy, have educated parents, and hail from Norman Rockwell-type families. Nevertheless, the overall decline in 1994 NAEP Reading Assessment was not restricted to particular subgroups of students. Rather, a broad range of subgroups showed significant decreases in reading proficiency, including male and female students; White, Black, and Hispanic students; and students from the northeast, central, and west regions of the country (National Center for Educational Statistics, 1996, p. xi).

Findings from national data suggested a second notable trend: Performance of 12th-grade students in the advanced level of reading achievement showed little change from 1992 to 1994 with 4% of students scoring in this category. Instead, the decline in reading scores was largely attributable to a greater percentage of children who scored in the proficient (average) range and most notably the increased number of children who performed at the bottom of the achievement scale (National Center for Education Statistics, 1996). Just what does an increase in the number of children who score at the bottom of the achievement scale mean? How does it translate into actual children who are having difficulty learning to read in classrooms? Findings from national longitudinal studies indicate that one in six children "will encounter a problem in learning to read" (p. 2) and that this problem emerges during the first 3 years of school (National Center to Improve the Tools of Educators, 1996).

These statistics paint a particularly bleak picture for America's future when considered in the context of the impending societal changes expected in the advent of the 21st century. Peter Drucker (1993) noted that the rise of a "knowledge" society in the 21st century will replace our industrial society. In the *knowledge* society, Drucker notes that *knowledge* workers will replace blue-collar workers as the dominant class in the 21st century. According to Drucker, the skills society will require of the worker are much more sophisticated, print-oriented skills than those currently required of the U.S. workforce. U.S society in general will be greatly challenged to develop competitive knowledgeable workers.

Particularly challenged will be those students we refer to as *diverse learners;* that is, those children who by virtue of their instructional, socioeconomic, experiential, physiological, and neurological characteristics bring different and oftentimes additional requirements to instruction and curriculum. Children with diverse learning needs reflect the range of inter- and intraindividual differences that are prevalent in all learners. Nevertheless, many fail to benefit from conventional educational practices. This failure to benefit often translates concretely and explicitly into low reading ability and in a cumulative and more intractable inability to achieve in a range of academic subjects.

Although national statistics may mask their faces and names, we know these children by label and reading levels. Some we know as students with specific learning disabilities and language disorders, others are identified as at risk, and still others may have no identified disability yet consistently struggle to translate the printed word into meaningful language. Although we use a variety of labels to identify these children and a variety of characteristics to describe their behaviors, the common denominator is their performance in reading, and more specifically, their reading failure.

We know that a significant proportion of children in today's schools fail to learn to read adequately and that the seriousness of the problem has garnered national attention (Lyon & Chhabra, 1996; National Center to Improve the Tools of Educators, 1996). Furthermore, we know that this failure to read proficiently emerges early in children's academic lives, endures in the absence of strategic instruction and opportunities to learn, and exacts long-term consequences for a range of learners. Fortunately, the field of reading and related disciplines are at a point in their research and professional knowledge bases to prevent and intercept reading failure for many children. Significant progress has been made in identifying cognitive, psychological, behavioral, and neurological characteristics of learners that relate to successful reading acquisition. Noteworthy advances have likewise been evidenced in curricular and instructional interventions to offset the effects of within- and outside-the-learner variables (Lipson & Wixson, 1986).

The purpose of this book is to communicate findings of a research synthesis investigating the bases of reading failure and the curricular and instructional basics to help guide the design and advancement of children's reading performance. The synthesis, completed by the National Center to Improve the Tools of Educators (NCITE) and sponsored by the U.S. Department of Education's Office of Special Education Programs, was conducted as part of NCITE's mission to improve the quality of educational tools that largely shape practice in American schools. Consistent with that mission, we are privileged to share with you the synthesis outcomes with the hope of advancing the role and utility of research for improving reading outcomes for children. In the remainder of this chapter, we describe the purpose of the original research syntheses and book, frameworks that guided our research analysis and synthesis, methodology for locating and reviewing research, and (d) organization and conventions of the book.

PURPOSE, PARAMETERS, AND GUIDING FRAMEWORKS

The purpose of NCITE's reading research synthesis was to examine recent secondary and primary sources that had as their main objective the review or summary of evaluative and integrative reading research focused primarily on students with reading or learning disabilities or readers identified as low-achieving, dyslexic, poor, less-skilled, and low-performing. In addition, students without identified disabilities sometimes identified as average achievers, skilled readers, normal achieving, and good readers were often participants in the research reviewed and provided important comparison groups. Six general areas of the reading research were reviewed: emergent literacy, phonological awareness, word recognition, vocabulary knowledge, text organization and structure, and metacognitive strategies.

The primary goals of the research synthesis were to (a) survey a fairly representative sample of relevant primary and secondary research, (b) identify themes and patterns of corroborating evidence, (c) summarize a set of propositions related to the "design" of reading instruction for students with diverse learning and curricular needs, and (d) examine the alignment between the findings of the research synthesis and a pedagogical framework comprised of six "architectural principles" for *designing* reading instruction for students with diverse learning and curricular needs.

Orienting Framework for Synthesizing Research

The following questions were used to frame the search and research synthesis:

1. Is there converging evidence regarding the characteristics of students who experience delays and difficulties in reading?
2. Does research provide converging evidence regarding the processes of reading acquisition and development for skilled readers?
3. Is there convergence in the research literature regarding the instructional implications and interventions for students who experience reading delays and difficulties?
4. What implications for designing instruction can be derived from these these areas of converging evidence?
5. To what extent do these implications align with a set of six general architectural principles for designing instruction in general, and reading instruction in particular, for students who experience reading delays and difficulties?

Arguably, the review and synthesis of this voluminous body of research involving learners whose predominant characteristic is reading failure is an ambitious task. We, no doubt, have omitted important studies that would ostensibly strengthen the overall findings and conclusions of our synthesis. We recognize the limitations of a "representative review of research"; nevertheless, the area of reading research is ripe and replete with validated and valuable information that the field can bring to bear in understanding and intervening in the domain of reading. The potential congruence between this and other reviews may serve to strengthen the conclusions of our nonquantitative synthesis.

These limitations notwithstanding, the first intent of our reading research synthesis and this book is to summarize what reading research tells us about children with diverse learning needs by examining research findings and organizing them into areas of convergence. An area of convergence is defined as a finding of evidence that recurs across multiple sources, across multiple researchers, and within and between multiple samples of learners. An area of convergence might focus on a common learner characteristic, a particular reading process, or a principle for intervention. We took a conservative stance in designating a set of findings as an area of convergence; consequently, one might view these points of educational intersection as common knowledge and well established. It is important to recall that the purpose of our synthesis was not to generate new knowledge, but to analyze and integrate existing evidence into reliable tenets and principles to guide our understanding and advancement of reading instruction.

Our second objective was to outline a framework of principles to guide the design and application of research-based principles into reading instruction for students with diverse learning needs. Despite the quantity and quality of converging evidence to guide reading instruction and practice, history documents that such knowledge does not find its way into classrooms; therefore, the effects of knowledge are never fully realized (Malouf & Schiller, 1995). Specifically, we examined the alignment between a six-principle framework and the curricular and instructional implications for reading instruction derived from our review of the literature.

Six-Principle Curriculum and Instructional Design Framework

Our framework for reviewing instructional and curricular practices was determined a priori and is based on a set of six principles consolidated by researchers at the National Center to Improve the Tools of Educators at the University of Oregon (Dixon, Carnine, & Kameenui, 1992). The curriculum design principles were derived from "numerous studies and investigations [that] have identified features of high quality educational tools for diverse learners" (Carnine, 1994, p. 345). The instructional and curricular implications of each area of reading (e.g., phonological awareness, vocabulary acquisition) are developed within these six pedagogical principles. These principles are central to designing reading instruction that responds to the acute instructional needs of diverse learners—those who are vulnerable and need intensive and systematic methods to achieve the complex rules and strategies required of reading. The framework and curricular implications are essential for children "for whom simply keeping pace with their peers amounts to losing more and more ground" (Kameenui, 1993, p. 379). NCITE associates (Dixon et al., 1992) identified the following six principles that traverse a range of academic contents and are sufficiently encompassing, sensitive, and flexible to capture the distinct and critical features of varying academic domains and cognitive constructs (e.g., phonological awareness, metacognition): *big ideas, mediated scaffolding, conspicuous strategies, strategic integration, primed background knowledge,* and *judicious review.* A brief description of each principle follows with each developed more fully in the respective areas of reading.

Big Ideas. Big ideas are concepts and principles that facilitate the most efficient and broadest acquisition of knowledge across a range of examples in a domain (Carnine, 1994). Big ideas make it possible for students to learn the most as efficiently as possible and serve as anchoring concepts by which "small" ideas can often be understood. In instructional curricula, big ideas serve to emphasize what is important. The growing amount of information to be learned is a source of heavy pressure on educators. Daniel Bell of Harvard University estimated that by the late 1990s the quantity of available information will double every 24 months. In effect, this means that learners in today's schools could be exposed to more information in a year than their grandparents were in a lifetime (Longstreet & Shane, 1993).

The principal assumptions of big ideas are that not all curriculum objectives and related instructional activities contribute equally to academic development, and more important information should be taught more thoroughly than less important information (Brophy, 1992; Carnine, 1994). Particular information is fundamental while other ideas are simply *not* essential, especially for diverse learners who face the "tyranny of time and must catch up with their peers" (Kameenui, 1993, p. 379). For these learners, in particular, it is important that big ideas are prominent features of instructional tools in the respective content areas. Big ideas should be the instructional anchors of programs for students with diverse learning needs. It doesn't suggest other information should not be taught, simply that it should not have equal weight or equal time. Big ideas are identified in each of the six areas of reading reviewed.

Conspicuous Strategies. Strategies are a general set of steps experts follow to solve problems. Many students induce the steps in a strategy on their own. Inducing learning strategies, however, may require a considerable amount of time before the student identifies the optimum strategy. For students with diverse learning needs, such an approach is highly problematic because instructional time is a precious commodity and these learners may not induce an effective or efficient strategy. Learning is most efficient when strategies are made explicit. Strategies that are of medium breadth, generalizable, and conspicuous facilitate the most efficient learning for students with learning disabilities (Kameenui & Carnine, 1998).

When applied to a content area such as reading comprehension and a specific skill such as determining the main idea, a conspicuous strategy is the set of steps that lead to effective and efficient comprehension and identification of the main idea. They are the steps a reader takes to identify and comprehend the main idea. Unfortunately, many students with diverse learning needs do not intuit or figure out that the main idea tells about the whole paragraph or story until much time has passed and many opportunities for learning have been exhausted. Moreover, published curricula may not make explicit the strategic steps necessary for teachers to communicate the process adequately.

Mediated Scaffolding. Mediated scaffolding refers to the personal guidance, assistance, and support that teachers, peers, materials, or tasks provide a learner. Rosenshine (1995) classified versions of scaffolds as "procedural prompts" that range from key words that help children generate questions as they read "who, what, when" to frameworks for concept maps. Scaffolds can be seen as temporary support to assist the learner during initial learning and have a history of empirical support (Vygotsky, 1978).

On new or difficult tasks, scaffolding may be substantial and then systematically and gradually removed as learners acquire knowledge and skills. Scaffolding can be achieved through the careful selection of examples that progress from less difficult to more difficult, the purposeful separation of highly similar and potentially confusing facts and concepts (e.g., /p/ and /b/ in early letter-sound correspondence learning), the strategic sequencing of tasks that require learners to recognize then produce a response, or the additional information that selected and well-sequenced examples provide. Scaffolds will parallel the type of reading skill and strategy being taught, and a variety of these instructional supports are described in this book.

Strategic Integration. Strategic integration involves the careful combination of new information with what the learner already knows to produce a more generalizable, higher order skill. Integrating new information with existing knowledge increases the likelihood that new information will be understood at a deeper level. The integration must be strategic so that new information does not become confused with what the learner already knows. Likewise, it must be parsimonious, emphasizing critical connections.

For new information to be understood and applied, it should be integrated with what a learner already knows and understands. For example, in narrative composition, there appears to be a logical for strategically integrating story grammar elements across reading comprehension and written composition based on identification, application, and generation activities. In beginning reading, once learners can hear sounds in words and recognize letter-sound correspondences those skills can be integrated to recognize words. It is these powerful and oftentimes logical connections that comprise strategic integration.

Judicious Review. Successful learning also depends on a review process to reinforce the essential building blocks of information within a content domain. According to Dempster (1991), the pedagogical jingle of "practice makes perfect" is simply not a reliable standard to ensure successful learning. Simple repetition of information will not ensure efficient learning.

Kameenui and Carnine (1989) identified four critical dimensions of judicious review: (a) sufficient to enable a student to perform the task without hesitation, (b) distributed over time, (c) cumulative with less complex information integrated into more complex tasks, and (d) varied to illustrate the wide application of a student's understanding of the information. So how does a teacher select information for review, schedule review to ensure retention, and design activities to extend a learner's understanding of the skills, concepts, or strategies? Answers to these questions are addressed in the respective chapters by area of reading.

Primed Background Knowledge. Successful acquisition of new information depends largely on the knowledge the learner brings to a task, the accuracy of that information, and the degree to which the learner accesses and uses that information. For students with diverse learning needs, priming background knowledge is critical to success as it is designed to foster success on tasks by addressing the memory and strategy deficits they bring to beginning reading tasks. Priming is a brief reminder or exercise requiring the learner to retrieve known information.

For example, if learners are facile in hearing and manipulating sounds in words and can reliably identify letter-sound correspondences, they are prepared to learn how to apply that information to identify words. However, students with diverse learning needs may not access information in memory efficiently and effectively or may not consistently rely on effective strategies to identify unknown words. In such cases, the task of priming background knowledge is paramount to subsequent reading success. Therefore, a teacher would prime the critical letter-sound correspondences that are to be used in a word or set of words before presenting the word recognition task.

OVERVIEW AND ORGANIZATION
OF THE BOOK

Currently, we have no easy or fully specified answers for how to optimize academic learning for the increasingly large number of children who fail to learn to read satisfactorily in order to fulfill personal, economic, and vocational goals. However, there is an extensive knowledge base that informs us of both the characteristics and needs of learners and provides the basis for curriculum and instruction to preempt and ameliorate the predictable consequences of early reading failure. This book provides in-depth analyses and discussion of six areas of reading summarizing what the research tells us about students with diverse learning needs. As already noted, the book is principle-oriented in that it attempts to identify samenesses from the body of knowledge in reading and abstracts those common findings into guidelines (not prescriptions) for understanding reading failure and reading practices.

The volume is organized into six sections corresponding to the six areas of reading reviewed. Each section consists of two chapters. The first chapter in each section is the research synthesis for the respective area and focuses on (a) identification of the problems and characteristics of diverse learners and in most cases typically developing readers, (b) definition of educational terminology relevant to the chapter, and (c) development of the research base and conclusions for the respective areas of convergence. The second chapter in each section is the instructional and curricular implications analysis corresponding to the specified area of reading. Within each section, a similar format is used to assist the reader and maintain continuity. In addition, a graphic organizer is provided to introduce the reader to the main ideas of each chapter along with summary tables that highlight critical research variables.

The length of chapters varies according to the amount of research for the respective areas. For example, phonological awareness and its implications for children who have difficulty reading has been the focus of numerous empirical studies in recent years, thus this topic received more extensive coverage than others. In contrast, the area of emergent literacy enjoys less robust research efforts and as a result, the empirical research convergence is less extensive. Following, we describe the specific methodology used to identify and analyze the research reviewed.

METHODOLOGY

General Areas of Review

To establish reasonable parameters for this review, we delimited our efforts to six general areas of reading research: emergent literacy, phonological awareness, word recognition, vocabulary knowledge, text organization and structure, and metacognitive strategies. These areas were selected because they represented a range of important topics in reading and allowed sufficient redundancy across areas to ensure a wide but manageable review and analysis of the literature. For example, reading comprehension was not included as a general area of review because the dimensions of text structure, vocabulary knowledge, and metacognitive strategies were examined. It was assumed that review of these three areas would yield an adequate analysis of research in reading comprehension. Likewise, it was predicted that the systematic redundancy across the areas of phonological awareness, word recognition, and emergent literacy would render a representative review of the research on early reading instruction, decoding, phonic analysis, and other processes (e.g., phonological recoding) acquired during early phases of reading.

Data Sources for Original
Research Synthesis

Three secondary sources were included in the literature review in each of the six areas: books and book chapters, journal articles and technical reports in the Education Resources Information Center (ERIC), and journal articles found in *Psychological Abstracts*. In each of these sources, research summaries, summative reviews, meta-analyses, best-evidence syntheses, and other descriptive, integrative research reviews were identified. In addition, the bibliographies of research reviews, books, book chapters, journal articles, and technical reports were also examined to locate reviews and studies meeting the criteria.

Principal secondary sources were included in the research review if they were:

- published between 1985 and 1993,
- included subjects with disabilities (e.g., learning disabled, dyslexic, reading disabled, language delayed) or readers identified as "garden variety poor readers" (e.g., poor, at-risk, low-achievers, less skilled, unskilled),
- included students of preschool age through Grade 8,

- employed criterion measures that involved the process of reading (e.g., naming letters, comprehension monitoring, manipulating linguistic symbols), and
- summarized studies involving experimental and control group comparisons (e.g., experimental, quasiexperimental, single subject).

Based on these criteria, research reviews that employed qualitative analyses and anecdotal data and reports were not reviewed. Selected chapters from secondary sources were used for context and background information.

The process of locating and identifying research reviews in each of the principal secondary sources (e.g., books, journal articles in ERIC), varied according to the source. For example, to search the principal secondary source of books, a subject search using the descriptors, "Reading Research," yielded 12 entries. A key word search using "Reading and Research," yielded 131 entries. These entries were scrutinized and references clearly unrelated or published before 1985 were eliminated.

This list of references was cross-referenced with other principal secondary sources, such as a publication edited by Sam Weintraub and published by the International Reading Association that is a compilation of abstracts (800–1,000 words) on research in reading. The cross-referencing yielded a preliminary set of references that were individually located by hand. For example, a major secondary source was the *Handbook of Reading Research* (Vol. II). An examination of this source yielded reference lists from chapters of varying topics (e.g., emergent literacy, conditions of vocabulary, teachers' instructional actions). To ascertain whether references would be appropriate for the review, the following decision rules were followed: (a) the title of the reference included descriptors such as diverse learners, low performers, special education, reading disability, disability, specific reading disability, or learning disability; (b) the title indicated it was a research review or other secondary source; and (c) the title focused on reading or a related topic.

The procedures for locating references in the *Psychological Literature* computerized database for the years 1985 to 1993 included using the *Psychological Literature Thesaurus* to obtain key word descriptors. Three key words were used in conjunction with the descriptors "literature review": reading achievement, which resulted in 16 references of which 9 were selected; reading disabilities, which yielded 46 references, of which 34 were selected; and reading ability, which generated 31 references, of which 8 were selected.

To supplement the review of principal secondary sources and incorporate evaluative research not represented in secondary sources, electronic searches of computerized databases (i.e., *ERIC, Psychological Abstracts)*, and a hand search of research journals for *primary* sources were also conducted. The criteria used to conduct the electronic and hand searches were the same as for principal secondary sources, but limited to journals published from Winter 1990 to the Spring 1993. The hand search was conducted on a range of journals that included, for example, *Reading Research Quarterly, American Educational Research Journal, Journal of Educational Psychology, Exceptional Children, Journal of Experimental Child Psychology, Journal of Learning Disabilities, Learning Disability Quarterly, The Journal of Special Education, Remedial and Special Education, Education and Treatment of Children,* and *Journal of Reading Behavior.*

The procedures for conducting the hand search of primary research sources published from 1990 to 1993, included: (a) searching the library shelves for the major research journals listed previously; (b) skimming each journal to locate appropriate articles; (c) recording the journal name, title of the article, author name, volume number, and page numbers of each article; and (d) copying the abstract of the articles. The list of articles located by hand search was then shared with the research team who identified the articles most appropriate for review. The articles were then copied and reviewed by two independent reviewers.

In total, 129 sources were reviewed; 61 secondary and 68 primary. Table 1.1 presents the number of sources categorized by type (i.e., primary or secondary) and area of reading.

TABLE 1.1
Sources Categorized by Type and Dimension of Reading

	Type		
Dimensions of Reading	*Primary*	*Secondary*	*Total*
Emergent literacy	13	11	24
Phonological awareness	13	15	28
Word recognition	10	14	24
Vocabulary development	16	7	23
Text organization	7	7	14
Strategies/metacognition	9	7	16
Total	68	61	129

Data Analysis and Organization

All sources were read by at least two independent reviewers and analyzed for two general classes of information, descriptive and pedagogical. Descriptive information classified sources by author(s) name, publication date, publication source, type of research, participant characteristics (e.g., age, grade level, type of learner—reading disability, poor reader, language deficient), and scope of research (i.e., the number of studies reviewed or summarized).

Pedagogical information involved a more elaborate coding of data central to the concepts in the orienting questions previously described: learner characteristics, processes of reading acquisition and development, and intervention strategies or procedures. Initial reviewers extracted information relevant to these three orienting foci and recorded their entries on standardized review forms. Each review form was then coded independently by two reviewers to ensure reliability of data categorization.

Information from the literature review was organized and analyzed by dimensions of reading and orienting question. Following a methodology employed by Spear and Sternberg (1986), findings within category were reviewed to determine areas of replication and converging evidence. Undoubtedly, conclusions drawn on degree of replication are controversial. The validity of our findings relies heavily on the integrity of the information published in primary and secondary sources. Our intent was to integrate research, not scrutinize the rigor or quality of published research. The operating assumption is an obvious constraint that must be recognized. Nonetheless, we consider the pattern of sameness and differences across researchers, research methodology, and sources useful to addressing the questions we posed earlier.

Addendum to Original Research Sources

The depth and breadth of reading research published since our original review of the literature required that we supplement our original sources with research published from December 1993 through May 1996. Our purpose in this addendum was to survey recent research to provide a representative sample of contemporary conclusions and to examine their alignment with previously established areas of convergence. Similar search and review procedures were used with the exception that the primary author of this book served as the second reviewer of all updates and additions to areas of convergence. Ninety-two articles were reviewed for the addendum--69 primary sources and 23 secondary sources (see Table 1.2). The majority of these sources were in phonological awareness.

TABLE 1.2
Additional Sources Categorized by Type and Dimension of Reading

	Type		
Dimensions of Reading	Primary	Secondary	Total
Emergent literacy	3	0	3
Phonological awareness	55	18	73
Word recognition	2	1	3
Vocabulary development	1	2	3
Text organization	3	1	4
Strategies/metacognition	5	1	6
Total	69	23	92

At the end of each respective synthesis, a figure delineates the primary and secondary sources studied and assessed and documents the authors, date of publication, dimension(s) of reading research, participants, and purpose of the research.

SUMMARY

More than a decade since the publication *Becoming a Nation of Readers* (Commission on Reading, 1985) chronicled the importance of reading, increasing numbers of children in the United States are failing to achieve levels of reading proficiency necessary to succeed in today's and tomorrow's knowledge-based society. We offer this book as evidence and testimony to the rich and deep research-based knowledge available to guide the design of effective reading instruction and practices for children who fail to learn from conventional methods and contexts. Although our research base is necessarily incomplete, it is substantial and applicable. We trust this book makes this information more accessible to those committed to a cause worthy of society's investment.

CONTRIBUTORS TO THE BOOK

This volume reflects the unified scholarship and true grit of a cadre of faculty and students committed to the advancement of reading research and practice. Those who were students at the time of authorship have assumed positions of responsibility in universities and educational research institutes throughout the nation. All contributed generously as the synthesis requirements exceeded all anticipated estimations of time and effort. In addition to authors, the conceptual guidance of Douglas Carnine cannot be overstated. Through his insightful analyses and development of principles to guide the design of curriculum tools to his broader mission to improve learning for all children, we benefit daily. Lastly, a special thank you to Katie Tate and Josh Wallin, who managed, manipulated, and mastered the technology to compile the infinite bits of data and information used in the construction of the synthesis.

ACKNOWLEDGMENTS

The contents of this book were developed for the Office of Special Education Programs, U.S. Department of Education under Contract Number HS96013001. This material does not necessarily represent the policy of the U.S. Department of Education, nor is the material necessarily endorsed by the federal government.

REFERENCES

Brophy, J. (1992). Probing the subtleties of subject-matter teaching. *Educational Leadership,* *49*(7), 4–8.

California Department of Education. (1995). *Every child a reader: The report of the California reading task force.* Sacramento: Bureau of Publications, California Department of Education.

Carnine, D. (1994). Introduction to the mini-series: Diverse learners and prevailing, emerging, and research-based educational approaches and their tools. *School Psychology Review,* *23*(3), 341–350.

Carnine, D. W. (1996). Strengthening the profession. In S. C. Cramer & W. Ellis (Eds.), *Learning disabilities: Lifelong issues* (pp. 113–118). Baltimore, MD: Paul H. Brookes.

Commission on Reading. (1985). *Becoming a nation of readers: The report of the commission on reading.* Washington, DC: The National Institute of Education.

Cornwall, A., & Bawden, H. (1992). Reading disabilities and aggression: A critical review. *Journal of Learning Disabilities, 25,* 281–288.

Dempster, F. N. (1991). Synthesis of research on reviews and tests. *Educational Leadership, 4,* 71–76.

Dixon, R., Carnine, D. W., & Kameenui, E. J. (1992). *Research synthesis in mathematics: Curriculum guidelines for diverse learners* (Monograph for National Center to Improve the Tools of Educators). Eugene: University of Oregon.

Drucker, P. F. (1993). The rise of the knowledge society. *The Wilson Quarterly, 17,* 52–72.

Juel, C. (1988). Learning to read and write: A longitudinal study of fifty-four children from first through fourth grade. *Journal of Educational Psychology, 80,* 437–447.

Kameenui, E. J. (1993). Diverse learners and the tyranny of time: Don't fix blame; fix the leaky roof. *The Reading Teacher, 46*(5), 376–383.

Kameenui, E. J., & Carnine, D. W. (Eds.). (1998). *Effective teaching strategies that accommodate diverse learners.* Columbus, OH: Merrill–Prentice Hall.

Lipson, M. J., & Wixson K. K. (1986). Reading disability research: An interactionist perspective. *Review of Educational Research, 56,* 111–136.

Longstreet, W. S., & Shane, H. G. (1993). *Curriculum for a new millennium*. Boston: Allyn & Bacon.

Lyon, G. R., & Chhabra, V. (1996). The current state of science and the future of specific reading disability. *Mental Retardation and Development Disabilities Research and Reviews, 2*, 2–9.

Malouf, D. B., & Schiller, E. P. (1995). Practice and research in special education. *Exceptional Children, 61*, 414–424.

National Center for Educational Statistics. (1993). *Adult literacy in America: A first look at the results of the National Adult Literacy Survey* (Stock No. 065-000-00588-3). Washington DC: U.S. Government Printing Office.

National Center for Educational Statistics. (1996). *NAEP 1994 Reading Report Card for the Nation and the States: Findings from the National Assessment of Educational Progress and Trial State Assesment* (Stock No. 065-000-00854-9). Washington DC: U.S. Government Printing Office.

National Center to Improve the Tools of Educators. (1996). *Learning to read/reading to learn information kit*. Reston, VA: Council for Exceptional Children.

Rosenshine, B. (1995). Advances in research on instruction. *The Journal of Educational Research, 88*(5), 262–268.

Spear, L. D., & Sternberg, R. J. (1986). An information procession framework for understanding reading disability. In S. Ceci (Ed.), *Handbook of cognitive, social, and neuropsychological aspects of learning disabilities* (Vol. 1, pp. 3–31). Hillsdale, NJ: Lawrence Erlbaum Associates.

Stanovich, K. E. (1986). Matthew effects in reading: Some consequences of individual differences in the acquisition of literacy. *Reading Research Quarterly, 21*, 360–407.

U.S. Department of Education. (1993). Dropout rates in the United States. *National Center for Educational Statistics*. Washington, DC: Author.

U.S. Department of Education. (1994). Digest of Education Statistics. *National Center for Educational Statistics*. Washington, DC: Author.

Vygotsky, L. S. (1978). *Mind in society*. Cambridge, MA: Harvard University Press.

Werner, E. (1993). Risk, resilience, and recovery: Perspectives from the Kauai longitudinal study. *Development and Psychopathology, 5*, 503–515.

Whitman, D. (1995, January 16). U.S. news: Cover story: Welfare: The myth of reform. *U.S. News & World Report, 118*, 30–33, 36–39.

CHAPTER

2

Emergent Literacy:
Research Bases

Barbara K. Gunn
Deborah C. Simmons
Edward J. Kameenui
University of Oregon

Although most preschool-age children cannot read and write in the conventional sense, their attempts at reading and writing show steady development during this stage (Hiebert, 1988). Typically, reading research during this preschool developmental period has focused on discrete skills that are prerequisite to reading, such as letter-sound correspondences and letter naming. By highlighting the processes and products of initial reading instruction, however, this research has largely excluded the role that writing (van Kleeck, 1990) and early childhood literacy learning play in facilitating reading and writing acquisition. In contrast, the emergent literacy perspective, which emanated from cognitive psychology and psycholinguistics, takes a broader view of literacy and examines children's literacy development before the onset of formal instruction (Hiebert & Papierz, 1990; Mason & Allen, 1986; McGee & Lomax, 1990; Sulzby & Teale, 1991).

From an emergent literacy perspective, reading and writing develop concurrently and interrelatedly in young children, fostered by experiences that permit and promote meaningful interaction with oral and written language (Sulzby & Teale, 1991), such as following along in a big book as an adult reads aloud or telling a story through a drawing (Hiebert & Papierz, 1990). Through the concept of emergent literacy, researchers have expanded the purview of research from reading to literacy, based on theories and findings that reading, writing, and oral language develop concurrently and interrelatedly in literate environments (Sulzby & Teale, 1991). Thus, this contemporary perspective stresses that developmental literacy learning occurs during the first years of a child's life (Mason & Allen, 1986) and is crucial to literacy acquisition (McGee & Lomax, 1990; Scarborough & Dobrich, 1994).

This chapter identifies and discusses areas of emerging evidence on the relationship between early childhood literacy experiences and subsequent reading acquisition. We do not wish to minimize the role of oral language in early literacy development, for it serves as a companion to the development of reading and writing. However, our focus is on aspects of literacy acquisition that are related to awareness and knowledge of print. First, dimensions of literacy knowledge and literacy experiences are discussed, based on data from recent primary studies and reviews of emergent literacy research. Then, areas of emerging evidence are examined for instructional implications for children entering school with diverse literacy experiences.

METHODOLOGY

Sources

We reviewed 27 sources including 15 primary studies (Brown & Briggs, 1991; Bus & van IJzendoorn, 1995; Crain-Thoreson & Dale, 1992; Dickinson & Tabors, 1991; Ehri & Sweet, 1991; Hiebert & Papierz, 1990; Hildebrand & Bader, 1992; Katims, 1991, 1994; Morrow, 1990; Morrow, O'Connor, & Smith, 1990; Roberts; 1992; Scarborough, Dobrich, & Hager, 1991; Snow, 1991; Stewart, 1992). Secondary sources included 10 overviews of research (Copeland & Edwards, 1990; Hiebert, 1988; Mason & Allen, 1986; McGee & Lomax, 1990; Pellegrimi & Galda, 1993; Smith, 1989; Sulzby & Teale, 1991; Teale & Sulzby, 1987; van Kleeck, 1990; Weir, 1989), one nonquantitative synthesis (Scarborough & Dobrich, 1994) and one quantitative synthesis (Stahl & Miller, 1989; see Table 2.1 at end of chapter).

Participant Characteristics

Participants in the research reviewed included children identified as normally achieving, at-risk, linguistically diverse, and, in two studies (Katims, 1991, 1994), children identified with cognitive, physical, emotional, behavioral, learning, and developmental disabilities. Due to the emergent literacy focus, the age of the participants ranged from preschoolers to 7-year-olds, with the majority being preschool and kindergarten children.

Summarization of Methodology

Two independent reviews of each source were conducted. Responses were grouped under three categories: general conclusions, learner characteristics, and instructional implications. Convergence within categories was achieved through a multiple-step process. Reliability was achieved through a process that combined independent reviews, intercoder comparisons of data categorization, coding clarification, and refinement with reliability checks on all sources. General areas of convergence were derived from the responses within category in conjunction with a second examination of each source.

Measures

Morrow et al. (1990) observed that the measures selected for a study influence the findings and conclusions of that study. Measure selection is a significant consideration in any research design, but is particularly important in emergent literacy where researchers address issues raised by other researchers and relate data across studies to consolidate existing research (Sulzby & Teale, 1991).

Measures in the research reviewed reflected the observational–descriptive nature of emergent literacy investigations and included direct observation of literacy behaviors, parent–child questionnaires about home literacy activities, and researcher-developed measures to assess listening comprehension and letter and word knowledge. Other, less frequently used measures included Clay's *Concepts about Print Test*, the *School-Home Early Language and Literacy Battery Kindergarten* (SHELL–K), and standardized measures such as the *Peabody Picture Vocabulary Test*–Revised (PPVT–R) and the *California Achievement Test* (subtests of visual and auditory discrimination, sound recognition, vocabulary, and oral comprehension).

Overview of Emergent Literacy Research

Definitions of Emergent Literacy. Our review of research revealed numerous but complementary definitions of emergent literacy. Researchers agreed that emergent literacy begins during the period before children receive formal reading instruction, (Stahl & Miller, 1989; Teale & Sulzby, 1987; van Kleeck, 1990); encompasses learning about reading, writing, and print prior to schooling (Sulzby & Teale, 1991); is acquired through informal as well as adult-directed home and school activities; and facilitates acquisition of specific knowledge of reading. Emergent literacy differs from conventional literacy as it examines the range of settings and experiences that support literacy, the role of the child's contributions (i.e., individual construction), and the relation between individual literacy outcomes and the diverse experiences that precede those outcomes.

Definitions of Emergent Literacy Terms

The term *emergent* denotes the developmental process of literacy acquisition and recognizes numerous forms of early literacy behavior. Although frequently discussed in the research we reviewed, these early literacy behaviors (or areas of knowledge) are characterized by terms defined in different ways by different authors. The following definitions of emergent literacy terms represent the most commonly used meanings, and will facilitate understanding of the review of emergent literacy.

> *Conventional literacy:* reading, writing, and spelling of text in a conventional manner.
> *Conventions of print:* knowledge of the semantic and visual structure of text.
> *Purpose of print:* knowledge that words convey a message separate from pictures or oral language.
> *Functions of print:* awareness of the uses of print from specific (e.g., making shopping lists, reading street signs, looking up information) to general (e.g., acquiring knowledge, conveying instructions, maintaining relationships).
> *Phonological awareness:* conscious ability to detect and manipulate sound (e.g., move, combine, and delete), access to the sound structure of language, awareness of sounds in spoken words in contrast to written words.

Dimensions of Emergent Literacy

Children begin school with diverse experiences and understandings of print: what it is, how it works, and why it is used. These experiences and understandings give rise to general literacy-related knowledge, as well as specific print skills and oral language competencies (Dickinson & Tabors, 1991; Mason & Allen, 1986). Our review revealed that through exposure to written language (e.g., storybook reading and daily living routines) many children develop an awareness of print, letter naming, and phonemic awareness. Additionally, through exposure to oral language, preschool children develop listening comprehension, vocabulary, and language facility. These initial understandings about print are particularly important considering that children who are behind in their literacy experiences upon entering school become "at risk" in subsequent years (Copeland & Edwards, 1990; Mason & Allen, 1986; Smith, 1989). For example, Scarborough et al. (1991) examined the relation of preschool development to later school accomplishment using parental reports about literacy activities in children's homes during their preschool years and assessments of reading achievement. They found that by the time poor readers entered school they had accumulated substantially less experience with books and reading than those who became better readers. Similarly, Ferreiro and Teberosky (cited in Mason & Allen, 1986) found that children who entered school without understanding the link between their oral language experiences and formal instruction did not advance at the same rate in learning to read and write as children who did make the connection.

Chapter Overview

In this chapter, we focus first on converging themes in emergent literacy research and examine what is known about five areas of emergent literacy: awareness of print, relationship of print to speech, text structure, phonological awareness, and letter naming and writing. Next, we present conclusions about general areas of literacy experiences that facilitate that knowledge, including cultural communication practices and community / home literacy experiences. Finally, we examine the specific contributions of interactive dialogue, storybook reading, and symbolic play to literacy knowledge. Figure 2.1 represents a graphic representation of the chapter's structure.

GENERAL AREAS OF EMERGENCE

Our review of the emergent literacy literature suggested that early childhood literacy experiences affect successful reading acquisition along several dimensions. These literacy experiences are, in turn, influenced by social contexts and conditions as diverse as the individual literacy outcomes they help to shape. The challenge for the preschool or elementary classroom teacher is clear: They are charged with designing and delivering reading instruction that not only builds on what the individual child knows, but also accommodates the myriad individual literacy backgrounds present in the classroom.

To summarize, five areas of emerging evidence have implications for addressing those differences and making a closer match between a child's literacy background and classroom instruction:

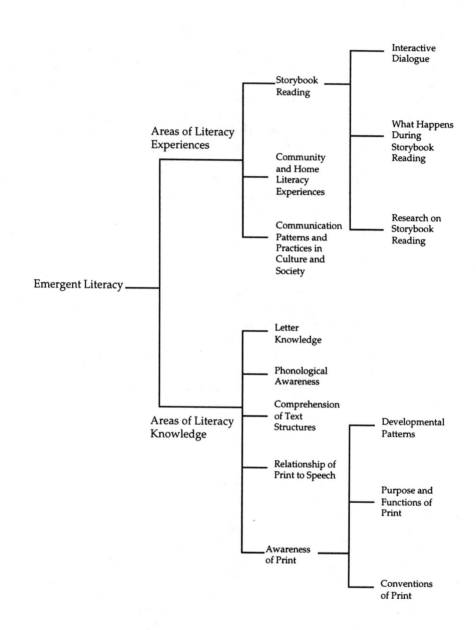

FIG. 2.1. Overview of chapter on emergent Literacy.

- Experiences with print (through reading and writing) help preschool children develop an understanding of the conventions, purpose, and functions of print.
- Children learn how to attend to language and apply this knowledge to literacy situations by interacting with others who model language functions.
- Phonological awareness and letter recognition contribute to initial reading acquisition by helping children develop efficient word-recognition strategies (e.g., detecting pronunciations and storing associations in memory).
- Socioeconomic status does not contribute most directly to reading achievement. Rather, other family characteristics related to context are more explanatory such as academic guidance, attitude toward education, parental aspirations for the child, conversations in the home, reading materials in the home, and cultural activities.
- Storybook reading, as well as the nature of the adult–child interactions surrounding storybook reading, affects children's knowledge about, strategies for, and attitudes toward reading.

To understand the implications of emergent literacy for initial reading acquisition, it is helpful to examine the characteristics of the research in this area. The next section describes methodologies employed in emergent literacy research and identifies three specific foci.

Characteristics of Emergent Literacy Research

To date, emergent literacy research is comprised of more descriptive and correlational studies than experimental investigations (Mason & Allen, 1986; Teale & Sulzby, 1987). This emphasis on descriptive research is not atypical of an area of emerging interest as such a phase is important for identifying the features and dimensions of the phenomenon of interest. One area, phonological awareness, has been the subject of extensive experimental research, and has garnered much attention and examination at the experimental level. This is reflected in both the level of sophistication and the detail of findings, and as such, we only review phonological awareness in relation to emergent literacy research. A comprehensive review of phonological awareness research is located later in this text.

Studies of emergent literacy have multiple foci (Sulzby & Teale, 1991; van Kleeck, 1990). To learn about the role of family environment and literacy development, researchers have relied on descriptive research in the form of naturalistic observations. Ethnographic studies, for example, have described literacy artifacts in preschool children's environment and provided details about the literacy events to which they are exposed and in which they participate. Such studies are useful as they provide information about the literacy experiences of children from various cultures and backgrounds. Examples of ethnographic observation were found in Hiebert's (1988) overview of emergent literacy research, including studies examining the role of word games (e.g., Tobin, cited in Hiebert, 1988), storybook reading (e.g., Snow & Ninio, cited in Hiebert, 1988), and chalkboards (Durkin, cited in Hiebert, 1988) in familiarizing children with the functions of literacy.

A second type of naturalistic observation has looked more specifically at the nature of adult–child interactions surrounding literacy events (Bus & van IJzendoorn, 1995; Mason & Allen, 1986; Scarborough et al., 1991; Snow, 1991; Teale & Sulzby, 1987) to discern how adults foster literacy development. One example is a longitudinal study of the relation between preschool literacy development and later school achievement. Here Scarborough et al. (1991) interviewed middle-class parents about adult reading, parent–child reading, and children's solitary book activities in the home. Similarly, Hildebrand and Bader (1992) investigated the family literacy-related activities of 59 parents of children ages 3 to 5 1/2 to determine the contributions parents make to the home literacy environment.

A third type of research has moved beyond descriptive methodologies to determine which aspects of preschool literacy experience best predict reading achievement. For example, Dickinson and Tabors (1991) administered the *School–Home Early Language and Literacy Battery Kindergarten* (SHELL–K) to a sample of 5-year-olds to identify the components of their language and literacy development and the experiences that contributed to those components.

Descriptive, correlational methodologies and experimental designs are beginning to be used in complement to examine factors associated and causally linked with early literacy acquisition (Mason & Allen, 1986; Scarborough & Dobrich, 1994; Sulzby & Teale, 1991). As researchers continue to investigate factors that influence preconventional reading and writing, measures of effectiveness and methods of assessment should become more refined and validated across studies, which should result in a more consistent examination of data. Moreover, as findings from descriptive studies are used to plan interventions and as the effects of those interventions on literacy development are examined, the emergent literacy knowledge base will grow. To date, experimental interventions examining causal relations are limited; therefore, areas of emerging evidence should be interpreted with caution.

AREAS OF LITERACY KNOWLEDGE

Numerous frameworks have been set forth for categorizing areas of literacy knowledge (Mason & Allen, 1986; Morrow et al. 1990; Stahl & Miller, 1989; van Kleeck, 1990). Although these frameworks differ in structure, certain areas of literacy knowledge are common across the emergent literacy literature. The following structure, adapted from van Kleeck (1990) reflects those areas: awareness of print, knowledge of the relationship between speech and print, text structure, phonological awareness, and letter naming and writing. Each of these areas develops concurrently and interrelatedly, and continues to develop across the preschool and kindergarten period. Moreover, acquisition of these skills is an important part of early childhood literacy development, and substantially affects the ease with which children learn to read, write, and spell (Hiebert, 1988; van Kleeck, 1990; Weir, 1989).

Awareness of Print

Experiences with print (through reading and writing) give preschool children an understanding of the conventions, purpose, and function of print—understandings that have been shown to play an integral part in learning to read. Because certain terms are used differently across the emergent literacy research, the way we use a term may differ slightly from the way a particular author uses it; nonetheless the gist of the concept is retained. Generally, *awareness of print* refers to a child's knowledge of the forms and functions of print. For this review, we define *forms* as knowledge of the conventions of print, and *functions* as the purposes and uses of print. In this section, each of these types of print awareness is discussed in relation to the contribution it makes to a child's literacy knowledge.

Conventions of Print. Children learn about print from a variety of sources, and in the process come to realize that although print differs from speech, it carries messages just like speech (Morrow et al., 1990). Eventually, children learn that print—not pictures—carries the story. As preschool children listen to stories they learn not only how stories are structured semantically in terms of ideas but also visually in terms of their appearance on the printed page. That is, text begins at the top of the page, moves from left to right, and carries over to the next page when it is turned (Ehri & Sweet, 1991).

Attention to conventions of print is also seen in the development of written language. Children begin writing even before they can form letters, and this early writing reveals children's early attention to the conventions of written language (van Kleeck, 1990). Hiebert (1988) characterized this as a developmental progression in which early attempts at messages may take the form of scribbles that take on characteristics of the writing system, such as linearity. Eventually, the scribbling is superseded by letter-like forms that, in turn, are replaced by letters, generally familiar ones such as those in the child's name.

Functional and varied experiences in reading and writing print help children develop specific print skills, which appear to play an integral part in the process of learning to read (Dickinson & Tabors, 1991; Mason & Allen, 1986; Scarborough & Dobrich,1994).Because of differences in parental support for literacy, however, children do not come to school with the same range of print-related experiences (Mason & Allen, 1986). The failure of some children to pick up on physical cues to the nature of reading (e.g., sounds are arranged temporally, whereas writing is arranged permanently in space) means that teachers may need to assess children's level of understanding about print concepts and, when necessary, plan instruction to develop such understanding (Jagger & Smith-Burke, cited in Mason & Allen 1986). This may be accomplished by extending opportunities for children to interact with oral and written language in meaningful contexts such as story reading sessions in which book-handling skills are discussed (Weir, 1989).

Purpose and Functions of Print. Children understand the purpose of print when they realize that words convey a message; they understand the function of print when they realize that messages can serve multiple purposes (van Kleeck, 1990). While knowledge about the conventions of print enables children to understand the physical structure of written language, the conceptual knowledge that printed words convey a message—that is, the printed words contain meaning independent of the immediate social context—also helps young children bridge the gap between oral and written language. Additionally, as a result of interacting with and observing adults in their environment using print, preschool children also understand the vocabulary of reading in instructional contexts such as read, write, draw, page, and story (Morgan, cited in Weir, 1989; van Kleeck, 1990). When formal instruction begins, the child who has this vocabulary about print-related phenomena is more likely to understand the basic vocabulary in the classroom.

Print serves a broad variety of functions. The scope of print functions ranges from very specific (e.g., making shopping lists, reading product labels, writing checks, reading street signs, looking up information) to very general (e.g., acquiring knowledge, conveying instructions, and maintaining relationships). Because all preschool children are not exposed to the same range of print-related experiences, their knowledge of these functions varies considerably. This variation in knowledge of the functions of print is related to daily routines in the child's home; it is developed more fully in a subsequent section on the role of family environment.

Developmental Patterns. Our review of research revealed that conclusions about factors promoting the development of awareness of print (i.e., knowledge of the purposes and processes of reading and the ability to recognize print embedded in environmental contexts) are limited. Lomax and McGee (cited in Hiebert, 1988; Weir, 1989) analyzed developmental patterns of children ages 3 to 6 on a hierarchy of reading-related skills and the ability to recognize print embedded in environmental contexts. According to their model of developmental patterns, awareness of print preceded graphic awareness, followed by phonemic awareness, grapheme–phoneme correspondence knowledge, and word reading.

Specifically, prekindergarten children demonstrated facility with only the early developing capabilities (e.g., awareness of print and graphic awareness), whereas gains by older children with succeeding capabilities (e.g., word reading) were reported to depend on proficiency with earlier skills. It appears that levels of preschool literacy competency do exist, and furthermore, these competencies may play a role in facilitating subsequent reading-related skills (Weir, 1989).

Relationship of Print to Speech

The ability to map oral language onto print is important for early reading and writing experiences. Through interaction with others who model language functions, children learn to attend to language and to apply this knowledge to literacy situations. In English, the relationship between oral language (speech) and written language (print) uses the equivalence between phonemes and graphemes. However, because talking and reading are different processes and produce different outcomes (Akinnaso, cited in Mason & Allen, 1986), we cannot assume that children learn this equivalence solely by mapping their knowledge of oral language onto written language (Mason & Allen, 1986). Typically, it has been viewed as a developmental process, rather than an accumulation of discrete skills. Letter knowledge and phonological awareness are constituent skills in children's ability to realize this relationship (Ehri & Sweet, 1991; van Kleeck, 1990), but even before progressing to that level of knowledge, children may participate in less conventional forms of reading and writing that reflect their initial ideas about the relationship between speech and print (Hiebert, 1988; van Kleeck, 1990). For example, children may initially adopt a strategy in which they use one grapheme to represent one sound in an entire syllable or word, such as "Sio" to represent Santiago (Ferreiro, cited in van Kleeck, 1990). This may be followed by invented spelling that although not yet conventional, does adhere to the correspondence in the English orthography (van Kleeck, 1990).

Although the communicative function of oral language might make the acquisition of written language a natural process (Goodman & Goodman, cited in Mason & Allen, 1986), research suggests that written language acquisition can be problematic—due in part to basic differences between the linguistic properties of oral and written language.

Citing Perera's framework, Mason and Allen (1986) summarized the physical, situational, functional, form, and structural differences between oral and written language, and considered the impact of those differences on language instruction in the classroom.

For example, certain *physical differences* exist between written and spoken language. Print is processed by eye whereas speech is processed by ear (Kavanagh & Matingly, cited in Mason & Allen, 1986). This means, for example, that it may take 6 minutes to write a paragraph from a speech, but only 1 minute to read it.

Because of differences in early literacy experiences, children may come to school with varying concepts about the distinctions between the physical cues of reading and the aural cues of spoken language. For example, Ferreiro and Teberosky (cited in Mason & Allen, 1986) found that children varied in their ability to distinguish between oral conversation and a fairy tale or a news item when a researcher "read" to them from a storybook or a newspaper. Such failure to pick up on physical cues that differentiate written from spoken language can be problematic for beginning readers. To help children succeed in relating oral language to print, teachers may need to assess children's knowledge about the differences between speech and print, then clarify and expand their understanding (Jagger & Smith-Burke, cited in Mason & Allen, 1986).

Situational differences between oral and written language are apparent. Oral language most often occurs in a face-to-face context where the listener has the opportunity to ask for clarification or information. In written language or text, however, readers and writers are usually separated. Consequently, the writer must assume that the reader has the knowledge to process and comprehend the text. The reader in turn, must move backward or forward in the print to clarify information (Mason & Allen, 1986).

The multiple *functions* of language children use depends on the context and the desired function of a given communication. Whereas oral language is generally used to express, explore, and communicate, written language is used as a means for expanding one's own thinking, by prompting comparisons and analysis (Mason & Allen, 1986). If children have not had extensive interaction with adults who model these language functions before coming to school, then the teacher must incorporate opportunities into the curriculum.

When English is seen in print *form*, each letter is a distinct visual form, and each word is distinct due to the spaces between the words (Mason & Allen, 1986). Other physical characteristics include indentation, punctuation, and capitalization. By contrast, in speech the boundaries between words and even phonemes may be obscured as Ehri (cited in Mason & Allen, 1986) illustrated in comparing the written "Give me a piece of candy" with the spoken "Gimme a pieca candy" (p. 6).

Finally, spoken and written language differ in *structure*. For example, speakers tend to be more redundant than writers, and speech is also more informal than writing, as evidenced by the greater frequency of incomplete sentences, slang expressions, and meaningless vocalizations that function as place holders for thought in spoken language (Perera, cited in Mason & Allen, 1986). For children who come to school with differing exposures to the written and spoken discourse structures, awareness of the structural differences between spoken and written language may not be evident and, therefore, may negatively affect the transfer from listening to reading comprehension.

Given the differences between oral and written language, what are the instructional implications for children who have difficulty making the link between their oral language experiences and formal instruction in reading and writing? Several studies have suggested that when text is designed to resemble speech, beginning readers can process it more readily. Allen (cited in Mason & Allen, 1986) found that primary-grade children performed better on inferential comprehension tasks when the texts were closely linked to the children's oral language. Seventy children of varied reading ability read dictated, peer-written, and textbook stories. Allen observed that even the least able readers inferred well when reading their own texts, and they inferred somewhat better on peer stories than textbook stories. Similarly, Amstersam (cited in Mason & Allen, 1986) reported that children who repeated and later recalled natural language versus primerese versions of fables gave more complete recalls and fewer unnecessary repetitions of the text than children who used the language of the text.

These general manipulations of beginning reading instruction designed to lessen the differences between speech and print may be helpful for at-risk children. However, further research is needed to determine the specific sources of difficulty that at-risk populations experience in transferring speech to print, and how those children might best be helped (Mason & Allen, 1986).

Comprehension of Text Structures

As the ability to map oral language onto print is important for early reading and writing experiences, awareness of story grammar or text structures is important in facilitating children's comprehension of spoken and written language (Just & Carpenter; Perfetti, cited in van Kleeck, 1990). Children come to school with differing exposures to grammatical and discourse structures (Mason & Allen, 1986). Those who have had exposure to oral or written texts through storybook reading dialogue in the home may be sensitive to the schematic structure of stories from a very young age (Applebee, cited in van Kleeck, 1990). In fact, children recognize such features as formal opening and closing phrases (e.g., "Once upon a time") as early as 2 years of age. They also abstract a structure for the organization of stories and use this structure in their own comprehension and writing.

In their analysis of the writing of 16 kindergarten children, Brown and Briggs (1991) found that age, prior knowledge, level of social interaction, and environmental experiences influenced the participants' awareness of story elements. Moreover, repeated reading activities as well as reading a wide variety of discourse structures can influence the content and organization of children's stories by facilitating comprehension and developing story knowledge (Brown & Briggs, 1990; Mason & Allen, 1986; van Kleeck, 1990).

Although comprehension of text structures facilitates children's comprehension, few empirical investigations have been conducted in this area with young children, thus limiting converging evidence.

Phonological Awareness

Phonological awareness is reviewed extensively in another chapter; however, in this chapter we review its role and integral relation to emergent literacy.

In an alphabetic writing system such as English, beginning readers must use the alphabetic code to understand the link between the sounds of speech and the signs of letters (Mason & Allen, 1986; Sulzby & Teale, 1991). Phonological awareness, or the ability to perceive spoken words as a sequence of sounds, is a specific auditory skill that is of crucial importance to reading ability in an alphabetic system. Because research has established a correlational, if not causal relation between phonological awareness and reading (Ehri & Sweet, 1991; Mason & Allen, 1986; Sulzby & Teale, 1991; van Kleeck, 1990), phonological awareness is often raised in discussions of early childhood literacy education (Sulzby & Teale, 1991). Indeed, of all the areas of literacy knowledge developed during the preschool years, none has been studied as extensively or related as directly to early reading as phonological awareness (van Kleeck, 1990).

However, Sulzby and Teale (1991) noted that although phonological awareness has long been tied to research and practice in the teaching of phonics and other decoding skills, it has been neglected in emergent literacy due to the tendency to view phonological awareness research as traditional and bottom–up in theory. Despite this perspective, some researchers have argued that the ability to deal with the codes of alphabetic language does not automatically arise out of environmental print awareness. Instead, they suggested that young children must be helped to notice that words encode sounds as well as meaning (Dickinson & Snow; Mason; Masonheimer, Drum, & Ehri, cited in Sulzby & Teale, 1991).

Precursory phonological awareness skills such as rhyming and alliteration can emerge in informal contexts before school, and are seen in young children who can neither read nor spell (Snow, 1991; van Kleeck, 1990). A general order for the emergence of other phonological awareness abilities typically begins when children divide sentences into semantically meaningful word groups. According to Fox and Routh (cited in van Kleeck, 1990), the ability to segment sentences into words emerges next, followed by the more phonologically based skill of segmenting words into syllables. The ability to segment words into phonemes comes last (in their study, one fourth of words were segmented into phonemes by age 3). This general order of emergence has been supported in other investigations; however, the children in those studies tended to be older (Ehri; Holden & MacGinitie; Huttenlocher; Liberman; Liberman, Shankweiler, Fisher, & Carter, cited in van Kleeck, 1990).

In contrast to the informal context in which they acquire other emergent literacy skills, most children require specific instruction to acquire the phonological awareness skill of segmentation, or the ability to segment words into their component phonemes, and often master it later than other foundations for print literacy (van Kleeck, 1990). It has also been suggested that general phonological awareness skills be taught in conjunction with letter-sound knowledge to facilitate reading acquisition. Based on their review of research on instruction in phonological awareness, Ehri and Wilce (cited in Sulzby & Teal, 1991) reported that young children can be taught phonological awareness prior to formal reading instruction if they have a certain amount of letter knowledge. Training studies reviewed by Mason and Allen (1986) also revealed the advantages of knowledge of letter-sound principles for reading and spelling. They reported that when children understand that words contain discrete phonemes and that letters symbolize these phonemes, they are able to use more efficient word recognition strategies than when they rely on nonphonetic strategies.

Mason and Allen (1986) summarized their review of phonological awareness research by noting that instructional studies have led to improved outcomes in reading, but questions remain about how to employ information about word-and-letter recognition strategies to improve instruction. The authors concluded that although it is important for children to learn about letter-sound relationships, it should not be at the expense of reading comprehension opportunities or independent reading activities. Similarly, Sulzby and Teale (1991) proposed that without fundamental understandings of the functions and uses of literacy (e.g., storybook reading, language play, written language use in everyday practices), children may not profit from phonological awareness instruction. They suggested future investigations of phonological awareness combine rigorous classroom-based research on phonological awareness training and its relation to overall early childhood curriculum.

Letter Knowledge

Both phonological awareness and letter recognition contribute to initial reading acquisition by helping children develop efficient word-recognition strategies such as detecting pronunciations and storing associations in memory. Letter knowledge, like phonological awareness, may be acquired either through formal instruction or incidentally. Through incidental learning, for example, many children gain at least some concepts and skills related to the formal aspects of print prior to school (Hiebert & Papierz, 1990). They learn about the functions of written language in storybooks and poems while they learn about the forms (e.g., letter naming and visual discrimination) of written language (Hiebert, 1988).

Letter knowledge, which provides the basis for forming connections between the letters in spellings and the sounds in pronunciations, has been identified as a strong predictor of reading success (Ehri & Sweet, 1991) and has traditionally been a very important component of reading readiness programs (van Kleeck, 1990). Knowing the alphabet and its related sounds is associated with beginning literacy. In fact, letter knowledge measured at the beginning of kindergarten was one of two best predictors of reading achievement at the end of kindergarten and first grade; the other predictor was phonemic segmentation skill (Share, Jorm, Maclean, & Matthews, cited in Ehri & Sweet 1991). Furthermore, an analysis of the relationship between literacy development and participation in literacy activities at home revealed that children's exposure to letter names and sounds during the preschool years was positively associated with linguistically precocious performance on selected literacy measures (Crain-Thoreson & Dale, 1992).

Within the scope of this review, several reasons were offered for the effect of letter knowledge in reading acquisition. Based on observations of

5-year-old children in New Zealand, Clay (cited in Mason & Allen, 1986) concluded that:

> before children learn to decode words in and out of context, they become able to use some letter-sound information to recognize, remember, and spell words. This is possible even if they are not taught the letter sounds, because the names of the alphabet letters provide clues to the phonemic representations in words. (p. 18)

Ehri and Wilce (cited in Ehri & Sweet, 1991) hypothesized that letter knowledge enables beginning readers to adapt to the task of pointing to words as they read them and figure out how printed words correspond to spoken words. It may also enable them to remember how to read the individual words they encounter in the text. "This knowledge of letters provides the basis for forming connections between the letters seen in spellings and the sounds detected in pronunciations, and for storing these associations in memory in order to remember how to read those words when they are seen again" (p. 446).

Although letter knowledge may be a strong component in preschool programs, children may also learn these skills at home. In a study of 59 parents of preschool children, Hildebrand and Bader (1992) found that children who performed high on three emergent literacy measures, including writing letters of the alphabet, were more likely to have parents who provided them with alphabet books, blocks, and shapes. The authors suggested that as children exhibit behaviors indicative of emergent literacy, parents and teachers can seize the teachable moments, and provide developmentally appropriate materials and interactions to further literacy development.

Whether letter knowledge is learned at home or at school, through word games or letters on the refrigerator, it appears to foster the development of subsequent reading strategies. However, further research is needed to provide more precise information about the kinds of instruction that are appropriate for children at varying stages of development and ability levels.

In this section, we focused on emerging evidence in emergent literacy research and examined what is known about five areas of emergent literacy knowledge: awareness of print, relationship of print to speech, text structures, phonological awareness, and letter naming and writing. We also identified the following three areas of emerging evidence that have instructional implications for preschool and early elementary children:

1. Experiences with print (through reading and writing) help preschool children develop an understanding of the conventions, purpose, and functions of print. These understandings have been shown to play an integral part in the process of learning to read.
2. Children learn how to attend to language and apply this knowledge to literacy situations by interacting with others who model language functions.
3. Phonological awareness and letter recognition contribute to initial reading acquisition by helping children develop efficient word recognition strategies (e.g., detecting pronunciations and storing associations in memory).

AREAS OF LITERACY EXPERIENCES

Development of literacy knowledge cannot be fully understood without understanding the contexts in which literacy is experienced (Mason & Allen, 1986; Scarborough & Dobrich, 1994; Sulzby & Teale, 1991). Some studies of emergent literacy have focused on the print-literacy environment of young children, others have been interested in children's early literacy skills, whereas some investigations have focused on the nature of literacy interactions between parent and child. Findings from these studies inform researchers about the role of contexts (i.e., culture, community, and family) in early literacy development and the kind of literacy knowledge children typically acquire during preschool years (Bus & van IJzendoorn, 1995; van Kleeck, 1990). In the following section, we examine the social contexts that facilitate this knowledge, beginning with the larger context of culture, and then narrowing the focus to community–home environments, and finally family interactions.

Communication Patterns and
Practices in Culture and Society

"The purposes for literacy vary both within and across countries, and those purposes affect literacy practices and achievement" (Mason & Allen, 1986, p. 5). For example, in Israel, Jewish children learn to read Hebrew in order to read the Bible, even though they do not speak Hebrew (Downing, cited in Mason & Allen, 1986). Similarly, in Japanese reading instruction, story selection is used to emphasize moral development (Sakamoto & Makita, cited in Mason & Allen, 1986), as in India where cultural values and socialization are stressed in reading primers. Therefore, "we cannot consider the literacy of a child or an adult without also considering the context and perspective or purpose in their culture" (Mason & Allen, 1986, p. 5).

Literacy acquisition is also influenced by societal expectations, and the value a culture places on literacy for its members (Mason & Allen, 1986). For example, in Nepal, lower caste children, particularly girls, are not encouraged to learn to read and write (Junge & Shrestha, cited in Mason & Allen, 1986). Similarly, minority cultures in the United States as in other countries have often received inadequate reading and writing instruction. Feitelson (cited in Mason & Allen, 1986) cautioned that in societies such as Israel that have accepted large numbers of families from underdeveloped countries, the literacy traditions of the main culture may be missing among immigrants. Yet, research on well-educated parents in mainstream cultures whose children make the transition to literacy does not inform educators about how to work with children from less-literate immigrant families (Mason & Allen, 1986).

Literacy values can also influence how children view the significance and function of written language and may provide a basis for their interest and success in reading and writing (Clay, cited in Copeland & Edwards, 1990). In observations of Maori and Samoan children in New Zealand, Clay noted that although the two groups were about equal in oral language development at age 7, the Samoan children had made significantly better progress in reading than the Maori children—progress that was equal to that of the Pakehas (the Maori word for New Zealand Whites). Clay suggested that a critical difference was . . ."the parental attitudes of Samoans favoring education and their influence as models for reading [at church] and writing letters home [to Samoa]" (cited in Mason & Allen, 1986, p. 6).

These studies reveal the impact of social expectations and context on literacy learning. What families and communities believe and value about literacy is reflected in the level of preparation children bring to formal instruction, and affects the role of schools in providing literacy experiences and instruction.

Community and Home Literacy Experiences

Literacy activities in the more immediate environments of home and community largely influence a child's literacy development (Morrow, 1990; Scarborough & Dobrich, 1994). Thus, a number of studies have documented the positive relation between children's literacy experiences at home and the ease with which children transition to school (Copeland & Edwards, 1990; Mason & Allen 1986; van Kleeck, 1990). However, family literacy environments differ along several dimensions. For example, although some development of print awareness seems to be common across cultures, significant differences exist in the quantity of exposure children have with written language, particularly storybook reading (Stahl & Miller, 1989). Furthermore, parents' perceptions of the roles they can play in their child's literacy experiences also vary. In Heath's ethnographic study of Roadville (cited in Copeland & Edwards, 1990), a White working-class community, and Trackton, a Black working-class community, parents wanted their children to achieve in school, yet parents in both communities did not know they could help foster that success by writing extended pieces of prose or enriching their children's oral language experiences.

Research cautions against using group membership as a yardstick for measuring children's literacy preparation. In a meta-analysis of nearly 200 studies, White (cited in van Kleeck, 1990) concluded that it was not socioeconomic status that contributed most directly to reading achievement, but rather other family characteristics related to context such as academic guidance, attitude toward education, parental aspirations for the child, conversations and reading materials in the home, and cultural activities. In the next section, we examine more specific research on literacy experiences in the context of the family: parent–child interactions, and the role of imaginative play and storybook reading.

Storybook Reading

Throughout the literature, storybook reading or reading aloud to children emerges as a key component in facilitating early literacy acquisition (Hiebert, 1988; Mason & Allen, 1986; Morrow et al., 1990; Teale & Sulzby, 1987). For example, Morrow et al. (1990) noted that numerous correlational studies have documented the relationship between reading to children and subsequent success on reading readiness tasks (citing Burrough, 1972; Chomsky, 1972; Durkin, 1974–1975; Fodor, 1966; Irwin, 1960; Moon & Wells, 1979). Further, substantial evidence documents that children who are read to acquire concepts about the functions of written language in books (Hiebert, 1988; Mason & Allen, 1986). Children also learn that print differs from speech (Morrow et al., 1990; Smith, 1989) and that print, not pictures, contains the story that is being read. Mason and Allen (1986) observed that "... while additional research is needed to identify factors on the causal chain, a reasonable conjecture is that story reading at home makes important, if not necessary, contributions to later reading achievement" (p. 29).

Storybook reading takes on additional significance when one considers findings indicating that most successful early readers are children who have had contact at home with written materials (Hiebert, 1988; Hildebrand & Bader, 1992; Smith, 1989; Teale & Sulzby, 1987). Although demographic, attitudinal, and skill differences have also been implicated in the contribution that storybook reading makes to reading (Scarborough & Dobrich, 1994), it is evident that by the time poor readers enter school, they have had substantially less experience with books and reading than those who become better readers. Scarborough et al. (1991) asked parents of preschoolers about the frequencies of adult reading, parent–child reading, and children's solitary book activities in the home, and compared those responses to the children's reading achievement in second grade. Their findings indicated that the children who became poorer readers had less experience with books and reading than children who became better readers. Moreover, children entering school with meager literacy experiences, or less exposure to books and reading, had much to learn about print and were easily confused if they could not map words onto their oral language or could not recognize or distinguish letters (Dyson, cited in Mason & Allen, 1986).

An investigation of the effects of a storybook reading program on the literacy development of urban at-risk children focused on how school instructional programs might address meager literacy experiences (Morrow et al., 1990). Children in four experimental classes followed a daily program of literature experiences that included reading for pleasure, story retelling, repeated reading of favorite stories, interactive story reading, and recreational reading; while students in four control groups followed the district prescribed reading readiness program emphasizing letter recognition and letter-sound correspondence. The experimental groups scored significantly higher than the control groups on story retells, attempted reading of favorite stories, and comprehension tests. However, no significant differences existed between the groups on standardized measures of reading readiness.

Based on these findings, Morrow et al. (1990) suggested that a blend of approaches, coupling some elements of more traditional reading readiness programs with a strong storybook reading component, may be a sound choice for development of literacy instruction package. These findings have implications for preliterate children, in general, and at-risk learners, in particular. Without sufficient storybook reading experience in early childhood—whether at home or at school—students may be missing a key part of the initial foundation of reading. In the following section, we look at the nature of the research on these print experiences, the activities that comprise storybook reading, and the role of interactive dialogue.

Research on Storybook Reading. Sulzby and Teale (1991) noted that historically, storybook reading has received more research attention than any other aspect of young children's literacy experiences. Although it continues to be a significant area of study, they suggested that storybook reading research has evolved in at least four significant ways. First, the methodology has become descriptive in an effort to analyze what goes on during the activity. That is, researchers have moved toward methods that analyze the language and social interaction of storybook reading to gain clues about causal as well as correlational relationships. Second, much of the early storybook reading research focused on the one-to-one or one-to-few readings that typifies parent–child readings at home. By including group storybook reading sessions simulating classroom settings, several studies have examined the similarities and differences between home and school literacy situations. A third change has been the focus on children's independent reading attempts in addition to the focus on adult–child interactions in order to infer what concepts the child is using in reading situations.

Finally, descriptive methodologies and experimental designs are being used in a complementary manner. Information from descriptive studies is being used to design intervention studies and to examine the effects of those interventions on children's literacy development. For example, Katims (1994) investigated the effectiveness of classroom daily readings combined with structured scaffolding techniques in developing print concepts among children with mild to moderate disabilities. These shifts in storybook reading research expand on previously reported data and serve to inform us about how storybook reading contributes to children's writing, intellectual, emotional, and oral language development (Sulzby & Teale, 1991).

What Happens During Storybook Reading? Storybook reading practices are characterized by routines that help explain how storybook reading contributes to literacy learning (Scarborough & Dobrich, 1994; Sulzby & Teale, 1991). These routines appear to have developmental properties, with the adult acting as a scaffold—initially controlling those elements of the task that are beyond the child's ability, then gradually guiding and confirming the child's independent reenactments and attempts at decoding (Mason & Allen, 1986; Sulzby & Teale, 1991).

Based on their review of literacy acquisition in early childhood, Sulzby and Teale (1991) described these developmental properties in the context of parent–child reading sessions: labeling and commenting on items in discrete pictures; weaving an oral recount of the pictures in order; creating a story with the prosody and wording of written language; and attending to and decoding the actual printed story. More specifically, they highlighted several studies that clarified the applicability of the scaffolding concept for describing changes in storybook reading. In an examination of the structure and content of picture book interactions of 30 mothers and their 6-, 12-, or 18-month-old infants, DeLoache and DeMendoza (cited in Sulzby & Teale, 1991) observed that the content of mother–child interactions varied as a function of age; the older children's input became increasingly verbal, and the information supplied by the mother became increasingly complex. Sulzby and Teale (1991) found similar changes in the patterns of parent–child readings in eight Hispanic and Anglo families. The parent would frequently focus the very young child on specific objects or characters in the pictures of the books as opposed to the entire story. Then, as the children became toddlers, the parents would expand by telling the main points or reading selected parts of a story (Teale & Sulzby, 1987).

Similarly, in their analysis of emergent literacy research, Mason and Allen (1986) reviewed descriptive studies reporting on parent–child reading routines. Harkness and Miller (cited in Mason & Allen, 1986) also observed mother–child interactions during storybook reading. Although questions or comments to initiate book reading interactions continued throughout book reading sessions, mothers gradually increased the length of time between each interchange by reading longer text sections. Likewise, Ninio and Bruner (cited in Mason & Allen, 1986) analyzed mothers' dialogues that accompanied picturebook reading to young children. They found that mothers directed their children's attention to particular features in a book, asked questions, provided labels, and gave feedback by repeating or extending children's remarks. These findings are consistent with those of Scarborough and Dobrich (1994) in their review of the efficacy of shared book reading, in which observations of mother and child behavior revealed systematic patterns of parental feedback and child response during reading.

In sum, the scaffolded routines of storybook reading create predictable formats that help children learn how to participate in and gradually take more responsibility for storybook reading activities. These routines, as well as the language and social interactions that surround the text, appear to explain what makes storybook reading such a powerful influence in literacy development (Sulzby & Teale, 1991).

Interactive Dialogue. Although access to print in storybook reading may facilitate literacy acquisition, it has been suggested that how the parent reads to the child is also important (Bus & van IJzendoorn, 1995; Morrow et al., 1990; Teale & Sulzby, 1987). General consensus has been reached on the key role that adult mediation appears to play in literacy growth (Mason & Allen, 1986; Morrow, 1990; Morrow et al., 1990; Stahl

& Miller, 1989; Sulzby & Teale, 1991; Teale & Sulzby, 1987). Thus, the language and social interaction between a parent (or older sibling) and child during shared book experiences may aid in developing language skills (Snow, 1991); familiarizing the child with conventions of print (Dickinson & Tabors, 1991; Stahl & Miller, 1989); and serving as a model of reading (Morrow et al., 1990).

In a review of recent studies on the importance of verbal interactions during storybook reading, Mason and Allen (1986) found that the quality and quantity of interactions, not just the presence of reading materials and a story time routine shaped early reading development. They described the effects of verbal interactions in a study comparing early readers with nonearly readers (Thomas, cited in Mason & Allen, 1986). Early readers talked more frequently about literacy with family members, their interactions contained more instances of extending a topic, and they exhibited more accountability (requiring the completion of a language interjection). Because storybook reading is a social activity, children encounter an interpretation of the author's words, which is subsequently shaped by the interpretation and social interaction of the child and the adult reader (Morrow et al., 1990).

The ways in which adults mediate storybooks for children are as varied as the range of settings in which this activity takes place. Parents of early readers (Thomas, cited in van Kleeck, 1990) and parents of children who are successful in school (Heath; Wells, cited in van Kleeck, 1990) do more than read books and elicit labels, objects, and details of events. They guide children to relate information in books to other events, and engage them in discussing, interpreting, and making inferences (Bus & van IJzendoorn, 1995; Sulzby & Teale, 1991; van Kleeck, 1990).

These representations of storybook reading as a scaffolded activity are consonant with Hiebert's (1988) premise that during story reading, adults act as scaffolds for children by connecting story elements with what the child already knows, by asking questions, and by encouraging the children to ask questions. Vygotsky's (1966) theory (cited in Morrow, 1990) that children learn higher psychological processes through their social environment and specifically with adult guidance within a child's "zone of proximal development" also reinforces the idea that children acquire literacy behaviors by interacting–collaborating with an adult aided by their encouragement and assistance (Morrow, 1990).

In this section, we examined the social contexts that facilitate literacy knowledge, beginning with the larger context of culture, then narrowing the focus to community–home environments, and family interactions. We also identified the following two broad areas of emerging evidence:

1. Socioeconomic status does not contribute most directly to reading achievement. Rather, other family characteristics related to context are more explanatory such as academic guidance, attitude toward education, parental aspirations for the child, conversations in the home, reading materials in the home, and cultural activities. *

2. Storybook reading, as well as the nature of the adult–child interactions surrounding storybook reading, affects children's knowledge about, strategies for, and attitudes toward reading.

SUMMARY

Our review of the emergent literacy literature suggests that early childhood literacy experiences affect successful reading acquisition along several dimensions. These literacy experiences are, in turn, influenced by social contexts and conditions as diverse as the individual literacy outcomes they help to shape. The challenge for the preschool or elementary classroom teacher is clear: They are charged with designing and delivering reading instruction that not only builds on what the individual child knows, but also accommodates the myriad individual literacy backgrounds present in the classroom.

To summarize, five areas of emerging evidence have implications for addressing those differences and making a closer match between a child's literacy background and classroom instruction:

- Experiences with print (through reading and writing) help preschool children develop an understanding of the conventions, purpose, and functions of print.
- Children learn how to attend to language and apply this knowledge to literacy situations by interacting with others who model language functions.
- Phonological awareness and letter recognition contribute to initial reading acquisition by helping children develop efficient word-recognition strategies (e.g., detecting pronunciations and storing associations in memory).
- Socioeconomic status does not contribute most directly to reading achievement. Rather, other family characteristics related to context are more explanatory such as academic guidance, attitude toward education, parental aspirations for the child, conversations in the home, reading materials in the home, and cultural activities.

---

*This conclusion was derived by White from his 1982 meta-analysis [cited in van Kleeck, 1990], and has been reinforced by recent literature on socioeconomic status and academic achievement.

- Storybook reading, as well as the nature of the adult–child inter-actions surrounding storybook reading, affects children's know-ledge about, strategies for, and attitudes toward reading.

TABLE 2.1
Description of Emergent Literacy Sources

Secondary Sources

Author	Emergent Literacy Dimension	Participants	Purpose
Copeland & Edwards (1990)	Writing	Studies reflected varied populations of preschool to primary-age children	Examine the social aspects of young children's writing development
Hiebert (1988)	Preschool literacy experiences	Studies reflected varied populations of preschool to primary-age children	Provide an overview of emergent literacy research and its importance for beginning reading programs
Mason & Allen (1986)	Social/linguistic contexts of literacy, oral and written language, and early reading and writing skills	Studies reflected varied populations of preschool to primary-age children	Review emergent literacy research and studies on reading acquisition
McGee & Lomax (1990)	Beginning reading instruction	Studies reflected varied populations of preschool to primary-age children	Response to Stahl and Miller's (1989) meta-analysis of reading instruction approaches
Pellegrini & Galda (1993)	Symbolic play and literacy	Studies reflected varied populations of preschool to primary-age children	Review research on the ways in which symbolic play is related to emergent literacy
Scarborough & Dobrich (1994)	Preschool literacy experiences	Focus on preschool children	Review research on preschool reading experiences and literacy development

(Continued)

45

TABLE 2.1
CONTINUED

Author	Emergent Literacy Dimension	Participants	Purpose
Smith (1989)	Preschool literacy experiences	Focus on preschool children	Discuss the concept of emergent literacy
Stahl & Miller (1989)	Beginning reading instruction	Studies reflected varied populations of preschool to primary-age children	Meta-analysis of reading instruction approaches
Sulzby & Teale (1991)	Storybook reading, writing, metalinguistic awareness, phonemic awareness	Studies reflected varied populations of preschool to primary-age children	Review recent research on emergent literacy
Teale & Sulzby (1987)	Storybook reading	Studies reflected varied populations of preschool to primary-age children	Discuss recent research on the role of access and mediation in storybook reading
van Kleek (1990)	Preschool literacy experiences	Studies reflected varied populations of preschool to primary-age children	Discuss implications of recent research on emergent literacy for pre-kindergarten programs

Primary Sources

Author	*Emergent Literacy Dimension*	*Participants*	*Purpose*
Brown & Briggs (1991)	Story writing/text structure	Kindergarten students; $N = 16$	Examine kindergarten literacy development through writing

Study	Focus	Sample	Purpose
Bus & van IJzendoorn (1995)	Story reading/role of mother-child attachment	Dyads of 3-year-old children and their mothers; $N = 45$	Examine mother-child attachment relationships and differences in storybook reading
Crain-Thoreson & Dale (1992)	Story reading/letter names and sounds	Linguistically precocious children; $N = 25$ (studied from 20 months to 4.5 years)	Examine relation between language and literacy skills
Dickinson & Tabors (1991)	Impact of settings and experiences on early literacy development	5-year-old children; $N = 3$	Use multiple measures to assess early language and literacy development
Ehri & Sweet (1991)	Print knowledge and fingerpoint-reading	Children proficient in English; $N = 36$, $M = 5.1$ years	Investigate kinds of print-related knowledge needed for fingerpoint-reading
Hiebert & Papierz (1990)	Emergent literacy focus in reading basal activities	N/A	Examine reading instruction in the early childhood component of basal reading activities
Hildebrand & Bader (1992)	Home literacy environments	Parents of preschool children; $N = 59$	Examine relation between parents involvement in literacy activities and their child's emerging literacy behaviors
Katims (1991)	Development of emergent literacy behaviors in young children with disabilities	Children identified with disabilities; $N = 21$, $M = 5.3$ years	Determine if exposure to structured, print-rich environments would develop preliterate behaviors in children with disabilities
Katims (1994)	Development of emergent literacy behaviors in young children with disabilities	Children with mild to moderate disabilities; $N = 14$, $M = 5.2$ years	Examine influence of classroom curriculum and procedures on literacy development

(Continued)

47

TABLE 2.1
CONTINUED

Morrow (1990)	Role of physical environment in classroom learning experiences	Preschool children; $N = 170$	Determine the effects of physical design changes in preschool classroom play centers on children's literacy behaviors during play time
Morrow, O'Connor, & Smith (1990)	Storybook reading	At-risk Chapter I kindergarten students; $N = 62$	Effects of a storybook reading program on the literacy development of urban at-risk children
Roberts (1992)	Development of the concept of *word* as a unit of spoken and written language	K–second-grade students, $N = 32$	1. Describe development of concept of *word* related to beginning reading 2. To investigate relation between cognitive development and acquisition of concept of word
Scarborough, Dobrich, & Hager (1991)	Preschool literacy activities on the home	Poor and normal readers; $N = 56$ (studied from preschool to Grade 2)	Examine the relation between preschool literacy experience and later reading achievement
Snow (1991)	Role or oral language development and reading acquisition	Low-income families with preschoolers; $N = 80$	Describe environmental supports for literacy development in the home and at school for children from low-income families
Steward (1992)	Children's awareness of learning to read	Kindergarten students; $N = 56$	Investigate children's awareness of how they are learning to read

REFERENCES

Brown, D. L., & Briggs, L. D. (1991). Becoming literate: The acquisition of story discourse. *Reading Horizons, 32*(2), 139–153.

Bus, A. G., & van IJzendoorn, M. H. (1995). Mothers reading to their 3-year-olds: The role of mother–child attachment security in becoming literate. *Reading Research Quarterly, 30,* 998–1015.

Clay, M. (1979). *Stones—The concepts about print test.* Portsmouth, NH: Heinemann.

Copeland, K. A., & Edwards, P. A. (1990). Towards understanding the roles parents play in supporting young children's development in writing. *Early Child Development and Care, 56,* 11–17.

Crain-Thoreson, C., & Dale, P. S. (1992). Do early talkers become early readers? Linguistic precocity, preschool language, and emergent literacy. *Developmental Psychology, 28*(3), 421–429.

Dickinson, D. K., & Tabors, P. O. (1991). Early literacy: Linkages between home, school, and literacy achievement at age five. *Journal of Research in Childhood Education, 6*(1), 30–46.

Ehri, L. C., & Sweet, J. (1991). Fingerpoint-reading of memorized text: What enables beginners to process the print? *Reading Research Quarterly, 26,* 442–462.

Hiebert, E. H. (1988). The role of literacy experiences in early childhood programs. *The Elementary School Journal, 89,* 161–171.

Hiebert, E. H., & Papierz, J. M. (1990). The emergent literacy construct and kindergarten and readiness books of basal reading series. *Early Childhood Research Quarterly, 5,* 317–334.

Hildebrand, V. L., & Bader, L. A. (1992). An exploratory study of parents' involvement in their child's emerging literacy skills. *Reading Improvement, 29*(3), 163–170.

Katims, D. S. (1991). Emergent literacy in early childhood special education: Curriculum and instruction. *Topics in Early Childhood Special Education, 11,* 69–84.

Katims, D. S. (1994). Emergence of literacy in preschool children with disabilities. *Learning Disabilities Quarterly, 17,* 58–69.

Mason, J., & Allen, J. B. (1986). A review of emergent literacy with implications for research and practice in reading. *Review of Research in Education, 13,* 3–47.

McGee, L. M., & Lomax, R. G. (1990). On combining apples and oranges: A response to Stahl and Miller. *Review of Educational Research, 60,* 133–140.

Morrow, L. M. (1990). Preparing the classroom environment to promote literacy during play. *Early Childhood Research Quarterly, 5,* 537–554.

Morrow, L. M., O'Connor, E. M., & Smith, J. K. (1990). Effects of a story reading program on the literacy development of at-risk kindergarten children. *Journal of Reading Behavior, 22,* 255–275.

Pelligrini, A. D., & Galda, L. (1993). Ten years after: A reexamination of symbolic play and literacy research. *Reading Research Quarterly, 28,* 163–175.

Perera, K. (1984). *Children's writing and reading: Analyzing classroom language.* Oxford, England: Blackwell.

Roberts, B. (1992). The evolution of the young child's concept of word as a unit of spoken and written language. *Reading Research Quarterly, 27,* 125–138.

Scarborough, H. S., & Dobrich, W. (1994). On the efficacy of reading to preschoolers. *Developmental Review, 14,* 245–302.

Scarborough, H. S., Dobrich, W., & Hager, M. (1991). Preschool literacy experience and later reading achievement. *Journal of Learning Disabilities, 24,* 508–511.

Smith, C. B. (1989). Emergent literacy—an environmental concept. *The Reading Teacher, 42*(7), 528.

Snow, C. E. (1991). The theoretical basis for relationships between language and literacy in development. *Journal of Research in Childhood Education, 6*(1), 5–10.

Stahl, S. A., & Miller, P. D. (1989). Whole language and language experience approaches for beginning reading: A quantitative research synthesis. *Review of Educational Research, 59*(1), 87–116.

Stewart, J. (1992). Kindergarten students' awareness of reading at home and in school. *Journal of Educational Research, 86,* 95–104.

Sulzby, E., & Teale, W. (1991). Emergent literacy. In R. Barr, M. L. Kamil, P. B. Mosenthal, & P. D. Pearson (Eds.), *Handbook of reading research* (Vol. 2, pp. 727–757). New York: Longman.

Teale, W. H., & Sulzby, E. (1987). Literacy acquisition in early childhood: The roles of access and mediation in storybook reading. In D. A. Wagner (Ed.), *The future of literacy in a changing world* (pp. 111–130). New York: Pergamon Press.

van Kleeck, A. (1990). Emergent literacy: Learning about print before learning to read. *Topics in Language Disorders, 10*(2), 25–45.

Weir, B. (1989). A research base for pre kindergarten literacy programs. *The Reading Teacher, 42,* 456–460.

3

Emergent Literacy: Instructional and Curricular Basics and Implications

Barbara K. Gunn
Deborah C. Simmons
Edward J. Kameenui
University of Oregon

REVIEW OF EMERGING EVIDENCE

The seemingly simple tasks associated with beginning formal reading instruction can be problematic for the child who enters school with meager literacy experiences. Moreover, the teacher charged with developing beginning reading skills will likely face significant challenges—children with varied literacy experiences, diverse languages, competing literacy approaches. For child and teacher alike, this challenge is compounded by the relatively brief time available for optimal reading acquisition.

In our review of the emergent literacy literature, we identified areas of emerging evidence that have instructional implications for teaching beginning reading to students with diverse literacy experiences and learning needs. These areas represent a consolidation of current research and discourse on the aspects of emergent literacy knowledge that affect reading acquisition and the contexts that facilitate literacy knowledge.

The identified critical areas of emergent literacy knowledge are neither new nor revolutionary. Rather, they reflect consistent findings related to effective classroom practices and confirm the validity of literacy activities that have been practiced for years. Furthermore, the areas of literacy knowledge that affect reading acquisition complement and overlap.

In the following section, we highlight emerging evidence on those literacy practices that impact reading acquisition and development. In addition, we draw instructional implications for students with diverse literacy backgrounds and introduce major ideas that reflect the collective foci and content of the emerging evidence. Our goal is to point out how literacy practices can be aligned with a set of curriculum design principles to develop a better match between individual literacy experiences and the design of beginning reading instruction. We attempt to connect research and practice by responding to two focal questions: What are the research-based "big ideas," or instructional priorities, for emergent literacy? and, For those instructional priorities, what is the existing research evidence regarding curriculum design?

AREAS OF EMERGING EVIDENCE

- *Experiences with print (through reading and writing) help preschool children develop an understanding of the conventions, purpose, and functions of print.*

Children learn about print from a variety of sources and in the process come to realize that print—not pictures—carries the story. They also learn how text is structured visually (i.e., text begins at the top of the page, moves from left to right, and carries over to the next page when it is turned). Although knowledge about the conventions of print enables children to understand the physical structure of language, the conceptual knowledge that printed words convey a message also helps children bridge the gap between oral and written language.

Ideally, teachers observe and evaluate what primary-age children know about reading and writing in order to plan instruction and monitor learning throughout the year. This is particularly important with beginning reading, where classroom expectations and experiences should match appropriately individual levels of literacy experiences.

- *Children learn how to attend to language and apply this knowledge to literacy situations by interacting with others who model language functions.*

The multiple functions of language that children use depend on the context and the desired function of a given communication. If children have not interacted extensively with adults who model language functions (e.g., dialogue to entertain, give information, maintain relationships) before coming to school, it is particularly important to incorporate opportunities into the curriculum that distinguish the various uses of language and show the link between oral and written language.

- *Phonological awareness and letter recognition contribute to initial reading acquisition by helping children develop efficient word recognition strategies (e.g., detecting pronunciations and storing associations in memory).*

In addition to rich and varied experiences with print, phonological awareness and knowledge of print–speech relations play an important role in facilitating reading acquisition. Therefore, phonological awareness instruction should be an integral component of early reading programs. Within the emergent literacy research, viewpoints diverged on whether acquisition of phonological awareness and letter recognition are preconditions of literacy acquisition or whether they develop interdependently with literacy activities such as story reading and writing. However, moderate support was found for a systematic approach to teaching children the relation between sounds and letters in the context of reading authentic literature and writing using invented spellings.*

- *Storybook reading, as well as the nature of the adult–child interactions surrounding storybook reading, affects children's knowledge about, strategies for, and attitudes toward reading.*

Of all the strategies intended to promote growth in literacy acquisition, none is as commonly practiced, nor as strongly supported across the emergent literacy literature as storybook reading. Reading to children and interacting with them about text can have a significant influence on their literacy development. Children in different social and cultural groups have differing degrees of access to storybook reading. For example, it is not unusual for a teacher to have students who have experienced thousands of hours of story reading time, along with other students who have had little or no such exposure. This difference is further compounded by the type of adult–child interactions that occurs during storybook reading, such as the degree to which the adult engages the child's attention or encourages the child to take on parts of the story reading task.†

- *Socioeconomic status does not contribute most directly to reading achievement. Rather, other family characteristics related to context are more explanatory such as academic guidance, attitude toward education, parental aspirations for the child, conversations in the home, reading materials in the home, and cultural activities.*

In addition to the degree and type of interaction students experience during storybook reading, it is necessary for teachers to consider family

---

*Phonological awareness is covered extensively in another chapter and therefore is not discussed in detail here.

†This conclusion was derived by White from his 1982 meta-analysis [cited in van Kleck, 1990], and has been reinforced by recent literature on socioeconomic status and academic achievement.

characteristics. Variance in family background as well as in literacy experiences indicates a need to consider differences between family environments and ethnic groups when planning reading instruction.

In the following section, we discuss these areas of emerging evidence in relation to a framework of curriculum design principles. We derived two big ideas from the areas of emerging evidence and now use the principles of *conspicuous strategies, mediated scaffolding, strategic integration, primed background knowledge,* and *judicious review* to render those ideas more explicit and employable. The procedural design principles in combination with the big ideas illustrate how to translate research into practice. The following section should not be viewed as a prescription, but rather as an application of principles that can be used to make tangible these aspects of instruction that are important for students who lack literacy experiences.

RESEARCH-BASED INSTRUCTIONAL PRIORITIES IN EMERGENT LITERACY: BIG IDEAS

- *Children need to develop knowledge of and facility with multiple dimensions of early literacy knowledge (e.g., conventions, purpose, and functions of print, link between oral and written language, phonological awareness and letter-sound correspondence).*

- *Social contexts and conditions influence early literacy knowledge.*

Understanding the multiple dimensions of early literacy knowledge does not ensure that a child will learn how to read; however, this early knowledge of the functions and uses of oral and written language is important to successful literacy acquisition. By recognizing the influence of social contexts and conditions, teachers can develop strategies and structures for reading instruction that are accepting of children and their varied literacy experiences. In tandem, these two "big ideas" frame the content of the curriculum design principles and guide the focus of instruction.

EVIDENCE OF CURRICULUM DESIGN IN EMERGENT LITERACY

In this section, we focus on five curriculum design principles: conspicuous strategies, mediated scaffolding, strategic integration, primed background knowledge, and judicious review, while addressing the question: For the instructional priorities of emergent literacy, what is the existing research evidence regarding curriculum design?

Conspicuous Strategies

As an instructional priority, *conspicuous strategies* are a sequence of teaching events and teacher actions used to help students learn new literacy information and relate it to their existing knowledge. Because emergent literacy focuses on the development of general, diffused literacy knowledge rather than specific components of instruction, our review found limited applications for this design principle. However, conspicuous strategies can be incorporated in beginning reading instruction to ensure that all learners have basic literacy concepts. For example, during storybook reading teachers can show students how to recognize the fronts and backs of books, locate titles, or look at pictures and predict the story, rather than assume children will learn this through incidental exposure. Similarly, teachers can teach students a strategy for holding a pencil appropriately or checking the form of their letters against an alphabet sheet on their desks or the classroom wall.

In addition to teaching the physical aspects of literacy, conspicuous strategies can be used to help children understand the symbolic aspects of literacy. Roberts (1992) suggested that children's concept of a word proceeds along a developmental continuum from awareness of words in spoken language to awareness of words in written language. Although children eventually learn the abstract characteristics of a word through experiences with print, teachers can use a conspicuous strategy to focus the child's attention on the definitional attributes of words. By making explicit the connection between speech and print and discussing the featural and relational characteristics of words, teachers can help children acquire the abstract concept of word and accommodate their schemata to new information (Roberts, 1992).

Mediated Scaffolding

Children who have had limited exposure to print often lack the language experience, background knowledge, and awareness of print–speech relations that many children from the broader school population already possess upon entering school. Moreover, it cannot be assumed that these children will acquire this conceptual knowledge incidentally. Through the use of *mediated scaffolding*, teachers can provide guidance and support to help students (based on individual needs and current levels of ability) acquire the literacy concepts that will support initial reading acquisition and help reduce the likelihood of future academic failure.

Mediated scaffolding can be accomplished in a number of ways to meet the needs of students with diverse literacy experiences. To link oral and written language, for example, teachers may use texts that simulate speech by incorporating oral language patterns or children's writing. Or teachers can use daily storybook reading to discuss book-handling skills and directionality—concepts that are particularly important for children who are unfamiliar with printed texts. Teachers can also use repeated readings to give students multiple exposures to unfamiliar words or extended opportunities to look at books with predictable patterns, as well as provide support by modeling the behaviors associated with reading (Katims, 1994). Teachers can act as scaffolds during these storybook reading activities by adjusting their demands (e.g., asking increasingly complex questions or encouraging children to take on portions of the reading) or by reading more complex text as students gain knowledge of beginning literacy components.

Mediated scaffolding can also be used to address the social contexts and conditions that influence individual literacy knowledge by making the work and social contexts of the classroom compatible with those of the home and community. This can be done by organizing environments that match children's cultural experiences (e.g., parental attitudes toward literacy) with their instructional experiences, and by helping children see the connection between their literacy values and the act of reading.

The literature on classroom literacy environments supports the instructional value of mediated scaffolding, in keeping with Vygotsky's theory (cited in Morrow, 1990) that children learn higher psychological processes with adult guidance within a child's "zone of proximal development." Indeed, Morrow (1990) found that classrooms in which teachers provided guidance to students produced more literacy behaviors than classes where no guidance was given. In the adult-guided classrooms, teachers provided scaffolding by introducing literacy materials in the play centers and discussing with children how to use the materials (e.g., reading to dolls, writing notes to friends, making shopping lists, and taking telephone messages). The students in those classrooms, in turn, used more printed materials with attention to their printed aspects and produced more printed materials than students in classrooms with no specific teacher guidance.

Strategic Integration

Many children with diverse literacy experiences have difficulty making connections between old and new information. *Strategic integration* can be applied to help link old and new learning. For example, in the classroom, strategic integration can be accomplished by providing access to literacy materials in classroom writing centers and libraries. Teachers can also develop thematic play centers—such as a grocery store or doctor's office —where primary-age students can act out reading and writing behaviors. Students should also have opportunities to integrate and extend their literacy knowledge by reading aloud, listening to other students read aloud, and listening to tape recordings and videotapes in reading corners.

Instruction that integrates students' existing literacy knowledge with new learning can also help children become efficient at constructing meaning from text. However, as Stahl and Miller (1989) noted, instructional approaches that emphasize the construction of meaning alone may not be the most efficient means of helping children comprehend text. These authors observed that children need to develop word recognition abilities in order to read with understanding. Stahl and Miller (1989) suggested integrating effective components of beginning reading programs regardless of philosophy—an approach they observed in first-grade classrooms where teachers implemented reading programs that integrated direct instruction of phonics with children's literature and individual opportunities to write.

Morrow, O'Connor, and Smith (1990) offered further support for the importance of integrating effective components of reading programs. They found that a story reading program in an urban district with at-risk kindergarten children appeared to improve free and probed recall comprehension, attempted readings of favorite stories, children's concepts about books and print, and children's awareness of learning to read. However, in terms of developing auditory and visual discrimination or letter identification it did not appear to be superior to a readiness program. The authors concluded that a blend of approaches, that is, a strong storybook reading program coupled with instruction in letter recognition and letter–sound correspondence may be a reasonable instructional strategy, particularly for children with meager literacy experiences.

Primed Background Knowledge

All children bring some level of *background knowledge* (e.g., how to hold a book, awareness of directionality of print) to beginning reading. Early literacy contexts of home and community provide opportunities for children to learn about print through encounters in meaningful, real-life social interactions (van Kleeck, 1990). Background knowledge is important because it gives students a conceptual foundation for further learning. For example, Ehri and Sweet (1991) found that children's success with fingerpoint reading was influenced by what they already knew about print (e.g., letter names, phonemic segmentation).

Teachers can utilize children's background knowledge to help children link their personal literacy experiences to beginning reading instruction, while also closing the gap between students with rich and students with impoverished literacy experiences. Activities that draw on background knowledge include incorporating oral language activities (which discriminate between printed letters and words) into daily read-alouds, as well as frequent opportunities to retell stories, look at books with predictable patterns, write messages with invented spellings, and respond to literature through drawing (Hiebert & Papierz, 1990).

Judicious Review

Design principles serve as a framework for organizing effective, efficient instruction. However, even high-quality instruction falls short of its ultimate goal if not accompanied by opportunities for students to apply what they have learned. *Judicious review* suggests that proficiency occurs through frequent, diverse, purposeful, and meaningful practice. For the general knowledge forms encompassed by emergent literacy, this means that students should be offered repeated opportunities to engage in emergent literacy activities, and practice what they have learned. Review activities need not be highly controlled rehearsal sessions. Appropriate activities could include alphabet games, repetitive rhyming activities, re-reading of favorite stories, and regular opportunities to engage in literacy talk with teacher and peers.

CONCLUSION

Emergent literacy research examines early literacy knowledge and the contexts and conditions that foster that knowledge. Despite differing viewpoints on the relation between emerging literacy skills and reading acquisition, strong support was found in the literature for the important contribution that early childhood exposure to oral and written language makes to the facility with which children learn to read.

The typical variation in literacy backgrounds that children bring to reading can make teaching more difficult. Often a teacher has to choose between focusing on the learning needs of a few students at the expense of the group, or focusing on the group at the risk of leaving some students behind academically. This situation is particularly critical for children with gaps in their literacy knowledge who may be at risk in subsequent grades for becoming "diverse learners."

The primary purpose of this section was to discuss how literacy practices can be aligned with a set of curriculum design principles to develop a better match between individual literacy experiences and the design of beginning reading instruction. Emergent literacy knowledge provides a necessary and important (but not sufficient) foundation on which to build. A secondary purpose was to reconcile the emerging evidence on emergent literacy with the demands and limitations of beginning reading for the purpose of suggesting feasible, effective and efficient instruction that ensures that all students will obtain the necessary literacy background to support successful reading acquisition.

REFERENCES

Ehri, L. C., & Sweet, J. (1991). Fingerpoint-reading of memorized text: What enables beginners to process the print? *Reading Research Quarterly, 26,* 442–462.

Hiebert, E. H., & Papierz, J. M. (1990). The emergent literacy construct and kindergarten and readiness books of basal reading series. *Early Childhood Research Quarterly, 5,* 317–334.

Katims, D. S. (1994). Emergence of literacy in preschool children with disabilities. *Learning Disabilities Quarterly, 17,* 58–69.

Morrow, L. M. (1990). Preparing the classroom environment to promote literacy during play. *Early Childhood Research Quarterly, 5,* 537–554.

Morrow, L. M., O'Connor, E. M., & Smith, J. K. (1990). Effects of a story reading program on the literacy development of at-risk kindergarten children. *Journal of Reading Behavior, 22,* 255–275.

Roberts, B. (1992). The evolution of the young child's concept of word as a unit of spoken and written language. *Reading Research Quarterly, 27,* 125–138.

Stahl, S. A., & Miller, P. D. (1989). Whole language and language experience approaches for beginning reading: A quantitative research synthesis. *Review of Educational Research, 59,* 87–116.

van Kleeck, A. (1990). Emergent literacy: Learning about print before learning to read. *Topics in Language Disorders, 10*(2), 25–45.

CHAPTER

4

Phonological Awareness: Research Bases

Sylvia B. Smith
Deborah C. Simmons
Edward J. Kameenui
University of Oregon

Research of more than two decades has affirmed the importance of phonological awareness and its relation to reading acquisition. Thus, recent reviews of the literature (Hurford et al., 1993; Mann, 1993) indicated that the presence of phonological awareness is a hallmark characteristic of good readers while its absence is a consistent characteristic of poor readers.

Findings from a large body of research converge to suggest that students who enter first grade with little phonological awareness experience less success in reading than peers who enter school with a conscious awareness of the sound structure of words and the ability to manipulate sounds in words (Adams, 1990; Liberman & Shankweiler, 1985; Mann & Brady, 1988; Spector, 1995; Stanovich, 1985, 1986, 1988a, 1988b; Wagner, 1988). Many of the points made in this chapter are supported by multiple sources; therefore, we do not provide comprehensive lists of support for every assertion and conclusion. We do, however, provide representative sources to substantiate the magnitude of the evidence.

Two lines of research provide strong support that phonological awareness is part of a larger construct in coding and retrieving verbal information known as *phonological processing* (Hurford et al., 1993; Vellutino & Scanlon, 1987a, 1987b; Wagner, 1986, 1988; Wagner & Torgesen, 1987). Results from phonological processing research further indicate that deficits in processing the phonological features of language explain a significant proportion of beginning reading problems and correlated difficulties in reading comprehension, background knowledge, memory, and vocabulary differences (Liberman &

Shankweiler, 1985; Mann & Brady, 1988; Rack, Snowling, & Olson, 1992; Torgesen, Wagner, Simmons, & Laughon, 1990; Wagner & Torgesen, 1987).

In short, difficulties with awareness, coding, and retrieval of verbal sounds have powerful and long-reaching effects in reading. However, the most encouraging lines of research give strong evidence that significant gains in phonological awareness can be achieved with teaching and that the gains in phonological awareness directly affect the ease of reading acquisition and subsequent reading achievement.

METHODOLOGY

Overview of the Chapter

In this chapter, we identify areas of convergence in reading research regarding the importance, dimensions, and effects of phonological awareness on the reading acquisition of normal achievers and diverse learners. Over the last decade, phonological awareness has attracted extensive research and discussion. Because of the substantive research devoted to this topic and its validated relation to reading, the specificity of this chapter is unlike the scope of other chapters in this volume. Our rationale for a specific focus on phonological awareness is based on the importance of accounting for this extremely large body of research examining the relation between reading disability and phonological deficits. This importance stems from many sources and clusters around two areas of convergence: Phonological awareness is an underlying and critical dimension to early reading success; and phonological awareness explains significant differences between good and poor readers. The areas of convergence align with our overriding purpose: to identify areas of research convergence in reading, and to highlight the similarities and differences in convergence between normal achievers and diverse learners.

Phonological awareness has been heavily researched because of its direct relation with the ability to read unfamiliar words independently with relative ease (Bowey, 1994; Cornwall, 1992; Lenchner, Gerber, & Routh, 1990; Mann & Brady, 1988; Rack et al., 1992; Snowling, 1991; Stanovich, 1985, 1986; Torgesen, 1985; Vellutino & Scanlon, 1987a, 1987b; Wagner, 1988; Wagner & Torgesen, 1987). In addition, the ability to hear and consciously use sounds in language can be manifested in many processes fundamental to reading. The characteristics, contexts, and conditions of learners and learning are discussed based on conclusions and data from a research synthesis. The points of convergence provide instructionally relevant findings and were derived from the following sources of information and through the following process. Figure 4.1 presents a graphic depiction of the chapter's structure.

Phonological Awareness Chapter

Introduction
Methodology

Areas of Converging Evidence

The Phonological Processing Ability Explains Significant Differences Between Good and Poor Readers

- Components of Phonological Processing
- Phonological Processing Models
- Relations Between Phonological Processing and Learner Characteristics
- Summary

Phonologial Awareness May Be a Group of Highly Related, Independent Phonological Abilities or a General Ability with Multiple Dimensions

- Dimensions of Phonological Awareness
- Prominent Hypotheses Regarding Phonological Awareness
- Summary

Phonological Awareness Has a Reciprocal Relation to Reading Acquisition

- Hypothesized Relations
- Causal Relation
- Phonological Awareness as a Consequence of Reading Instruction and Practice
- Reciprocal Relation
- Limited Importance of Relation
- Summary

Phonological Awareness Is Necessary but Not Sufficient for Reading Acquisition

- Phonological Awareness and Alphabetic Understanding
- Instruction in Phonological Awareness and Letter-sound Correspondences
- Coding and Automaticity
- Phonological Awareness, Reading, and Spelling Instruction
- Summary

Phonological Awareness Deficits and Delays Can Be Reliably Identified in Young Children

- Best Predictors of Decoding and Word Identification
- Accuracy of Predictions
- Summary

Phonological Awareness is Teachable and Promoted by Attention to Instructional Variables

- Overview of Studies
- Effects of Phonological Awareness Instruction
- Components of Instruction
- Components with Limited Evidence
- Interaction of Instructional Variables and Learner Characteristics
- Summary

Conclusion

- Areas of Convergence
- Relation Between Phonological Awareness and Reading
- Construct Validity of Phonological Processing and Awareness
- Instructional Implications

FIG. 4.1. Overview of chapter on phonological awareness.

Sources

In the original synthesis, we reviewed 28 sources including 13 primary studies (Ball & Blachman, 1991; Byrne & Fielding-Barnsley, 1989; Cornwall, 1992; Cunningham, 1990; Hurford et al., 1993; Lenchner et al., 1990; Lie, 1991; Lundberg, Frost, & Petersen, 1988; Mann, 1993; O'Connor, Jenkins, & Slocum, 1995; Swanson & Ramalgia, 1992; Vellutino & Scanlon, 1987b; Yopp, 1988). To provide a representative but manageable portrait of research, we limited our search to studies and reviews published between 1985 and 1993. The 15 secondary sources included 7 descriptive narratives (Liberman & Shankweiler, 1985; Mann & Brady, 1988; Snowling, 1991; Spector, 1995; Stanovich, 1985, 1986; Torgesen, 1985; Torgesen et al., 1990), 3 descriptive analyses (Vellutino, 1991; Vellutino & Scanlon, 1987a; Wagner & Torgesen, 1987), 1 deficit model (Stanovich, 1988), 2 reviews (Rack et al., 1992; Wagner, 1986), one meta-analysis (Wagner, 1988), and 1 book (Adams, 1990).

Furthermore, the 13 primary studies included 7 intervention studies that examined the effect of phonological awareness intervention on phonological awareness, reading, and reading and spelling (Ball & Blachman, 1991; Byrne & Fielding-Barnsley, 1989; Cunningham, 1990; Lie, 1991; Lundberg et al., 1988; O'Connor et al., 1995; Vellutino & Scanlon, 1987b). Five of the primary studies were correlational and examined the relations among phonological awareness and memory, spelling, rapid naming, and prediction of future reading ability (Cornwall, 1992; Hurford et al., 1993; Lenchner et al., 1990; Mann, 1993; Swanson & Ramalgia, 1992). Finally, the last study examined the validity and reliability of existing phonological awareness measures (Yopp, 1988). Table 4.1, at the end of the chapter, provides a summary of the sources reviewed. In the 1993–1996 update, we reviewed 73 additional sources, 55 primary sources and 18 secondary sources.

Participant Characteristics

Participants in the research reviewed included students identified as normally achieving, general low performers, learning and reading disabled, remedial readers not identified as learning disabled, high achievers, culturally disadvantaged, language delayed, and linguistically diverse. Normal achievement was examined in 50 of the 66 primary studies and was the focus of 20 studies. In contrast, 22 studies compared normal and diverse learners whereas 13 studies focused only on diverse learners.

Participants' ages ranged from preschoolers to students in the sixth grade, except for reviews that included participants from preschool to adult age. However, the majority of sources focused on kindergarten and first-grade children. With the exception of two primary studies conducted in Scandinavian countries (Lie, 1991; Lundberg et al., 1988), one in Spain (Defior & Tudela, 1994), and one in Portugal (Cary & Verhaeghe, 1994) and studies included in literature reviews, all the sources targeted English-speaking participants.

Summary of Methodology

For the original review, two independent reviews were conducted for each source. Responses were grouped under three categories: general conclusions, learner characteristics, and instructional implications. Convergence within the categories was achieved through a multistep process. Reliability was achieved through independent reviews, intercoder comparisons of data categorization, coding clarification and refinement, and independent coding with reliability. To identify areas of convergence, the primary author of this chapter used the conclusions derived from the review and the coding process in concert with a second careful examination of each source. For the update, Deborah Simmons served as the second reviewer of all updates and additions to the areas of convergence.

Definitions

The research literatures of phonological processing and phonological awareness entail highly technical language. We offer the following definitions as a guide for the subsequent discussion of these complex concepts. In addition, we embed selected definitions in the chapter to facilitate understanding.

Phonological awareness. Conscious ability to detect and manipulate sounds (e.g., move, combine, and delete), access to the sound structure of language (e.g., Liberman & Shankweiler, 1985; Wagner & Torgesen, 1987), awareness of sounds in spoken words in contrast to written words.

Alphabetic understanding. Understanding that letters represent sounds and that whole words have a sound structure consisting of individual sounds and patterns of groups of sounds, the combination of alphabetic understanding and phonological awareness becomes the larger construct, alphabetic principle.

Automaticity. Quality of fluency; implies automatic level of response with various tasks, such as speed of retrieving the sound for a specific letter.

Grapheme. Written symbols or letters of the alphabet; arbitrary, abstract, and usually without meaning; the written equivalent of phonemes.

Phonemes. Individual sounds, smallest unit of sound.

Coding. *Translating* stimuli from one form to another (e.g., from auditory to written or from written to auditory); *encoding* is the first translation which involves coding auditory sound to phonological codes for use and storage; *recoding* involves the second-level translation that involves going from written symbols to their phonological equivalents (e.g., discrete graphemes to phonemes or written words to their pronunciations); retrieval represents the accessing step of coding.

Decoding. Translating individual letters or groups of letters into sounds to access the pronunciation of a word.

Letter-sound correspondence. Linkages between discrete phonemes and individual letters or graphemes.

Lexical access. Access to internal dictionary in memory.

Retrieval. Accessing coded information from short-term or long-term memory.

Memory. Not a unitary ability; types are short-term and long-term; memory processes relevant to reading include encoding, storage, and retrieval (Torgesen, 1985).

Metacognitive. Self-awareness of intellectual processes.

Phonological processing. The use of phonology or sounds of language to process verbal information in oral or written form in short- and long-term memory (Wagner & Torgesen, 1987). Components include awareness and coding (i.e., coding sounds for storage in memory and retrieval of sounds from memory codes) of verbal information only (Cornwall, 1992; Hurford et al., 1993; Torgesen et al., 1990; Vellutino & Scanlon, 1987a; Wagner & Torgesen, 1987).

Phonological coding. "The representation of information about the sound structure of verbal stimuli in memory" (Torgesen et al., 1990, p. 236).

Phonological recoding. Translation from either oral or written representation into a sound-based system to arrive at the meaning of words in the lexicon (stored vocabulary) in long-term memory (Wagner & Torgesen, 1987).

Phonetic recoding. Translation of verbal information into a sound-based system for temporary storage in working memory for processes such as decoding unfamiliar words in fluent reading, or during the beginning reading processes of blending and segmenting (Wagner & Torgesen, 1987).

Onset-rime. Two-part division of words into units that are smaller than syllables; onset is the first division of a single phoneme or consonant cluster (e.g., /br/ in bright), rime is the last division with multiple phonemes (e.g., /ight/ in bright).

Phonological units. Refers to the size of the sound units (e.g., phonemes, onset-rimes, syllables, word).

Phonemic awareness. Awareness of phonemes, discrete individual sounds that correspond to individual letters. Spector (1995) pointed out that many terms have been proffered for this ability, including *phonemic awareness, phonetic analysis, auditory analysis, phonological reading, phonological processing, and linguistic awareness.* We use *phonological awareness* as a general term and phonemic awareness when specifically referring to awareness at the phoneme level. The distinction between the two terms is based on the size of the phonological unit.

Representation. Use of arbitrary symbols (oral or written) to represent experience or concepts (e.g., words or graphic symbols like "$").

Word features. Semantic (meaning), syntax (use in sentence or phrase), graphic (letter correspondence to phonemes), and phonologic (sound). Features are used for coding and retrieval.

Chapter Structure

This chapter presents six areas of convergence and the varying degrees of support for each area. The six areas of convergence from the studies reviewed for this chapter are:

1. Phonological processing ability explains significant differences between good and poor readers.
2. Phonological awareness may be a group of highly related, independent phonological abilities or a general ability with multiple dimensions.
3. Phonological awareness has a reciprocal relation to reading acquisition.
4. Phonological awareness is necessary but not sufficient for reading acquisition.
5. Phonological awareness deficits and delays can be reliably identified in young children.
6. Phonological awareness is teachable and promoted by attention to instructional variables.

When the research differentiates processes, characteristics, or findings between normal achieving and diverse learners, we address these distinctions. We conclude with a summary of the areas of convergence and discussion of issues, limitations, and extensions of findings.

AREA OF CONVERGENCE 1:
Phonological Processing Ability Explains
Significant Differences Between Good and Poor Readers

One of the most salient findings of the research review was the substantial evidence from numerous lines of research that converged to support phonological processing as the basis for many of the differences in learner characteristics (Adams, 1990; Fletcher et al., 1994; van Ijzendoorn & Bus, 1994; Hurford et al., 1993; Liberman & Shankweiler, 1985; Lyon & Chhabra, 1996; Mann & Brady, 1988; Rack et al., 1992; Spector, 1995; Stanovich, 1985, 1986, 1988a; Swank & Catts, 1994; Torgesen, 1985; Torgesen et al., 1990; Vellutino & Scanlon, 1987a, 1987b; Wagner, 1986, 1988; Wagner & Torgesen, 1987). The multiple perspectives represented by these lines of research (e.g., assessment for early identification of reading problems, causal relations between phonological processing and reading acquisition, longitudinal correlational studies, training of phonological awareness) further support the strength of the convergence.

In this section, we delineate the components of phonological processing and discuss their differential relation to normally achieving and diverse learners. Because of the highly technical language, selective definitions are embedded to facilitate understanding.

Components of Phonological Processing

Extensive research has examined whether phonological processing is a general ability or a compilation of correlated independent abilities (e.g., O'Connor et al., 1995; Wagner & Torgesen, 1987; Wagner, Torgesen, Laughon, Simmons, & Rashotte, 1993). Based on their review of phonological processing research, Wagner and Torgesen (1987) proposed a partial answer: To some degree, phonological ability is general across tasks. This conclusion is based on significant interrelations among the component abilities. However, Wagner and Torgesen (1987) also concluded that there is an empirical basis for separating one component, awareness, from another component, coding (i.e., coding and retrieval). Similarly, several lines of research provide strong support that phonological processing includes two broad dimensions, coding and awareness (Ackerman & Dykman, 1993; Hurford et al., 1993; Liberman & Shankweiler, 1985; Mann & Brady, 1988; Wagner & Torgesen, 1987), each with multiple dimensions. See Fig. 4.2 for a summary of the dimensions of phonological processing and respective components.

Coding. Researchers have isolated two dimensions of coding: *phonetic* and *phonological* (Liberman & Shankweiler, 1985; Swank, 1994; Vellutino & Scanlon, 1987a; Wagner & Torgesen, 1987). Both dimensions include multiple processes that require memory and coding from one form of representation to another (e.g., written to sound units for memory). The distinction between the two coding dimensions is type of memory. That is, phonetic recoding takes place in short-term memory for such processes as

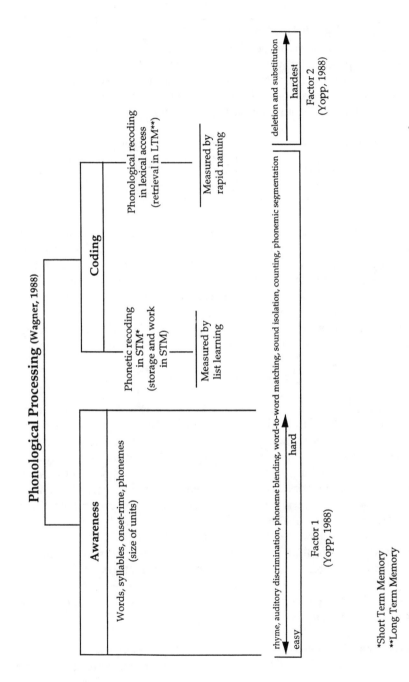

FIG. 4.2. Components of phonological processing and dimensions of phonological awareness.

69

sounding out unfamiliar words. In contrast, phonological recoding accesses the lexicon in long-term memory for known words in a three-step process. First, written symbols are recoded to the pronunciation of the written word. Second, the pronunciation of the written word is matched with the pronunciation of words in memory. Third, pronunciations of words in memory are linked with meaning for retrieval of meaning and pronunciation (Wagner & Torgesen, 1987). In examining reading disabilities, research looks at:

1. What features of words are used in different types of memory?
2. Is the quality of encoding different for normally achieving and diverse learners, and if so, in what way?
3. Which is problematic for diverse learners, storage capacity or quality of original encoding? (Torgesen, 1985)

Awareness. Phonological awareness is a general ability with multiple dimensions, which uses a single modality, auditory. Thus, it is the ability to hear sounds in spoken words in contrast to recognizing sounds in written words, which involves the other phonological processing dimension, coding. Phonological awareness is an inclusive term, referring to all sizes of sound units, such as words, syllables, onset-rimes, and phonemes. Phonemic awareness, however, refers only to the phoneme level. Awareness is less complex than coding in the demands it puts on memory and processing.

Phonological Processing Models

Torgesen and colleagues (Torgesen, Wagner, & Rashotte, 1994; Wagner, Torgesen, & Rashotte, 1994; Wagner et al., 1993) conducted a series of studies to compare alternative models of young children's phonological processing abilities in kindergarten through second-grade children. A major purpose of the studies was to determine whether phonological processing abilities are a general, overall ability or a group of independent, but highly related abilities. As a result of those studies, Torgesen and colleagues (Torgesen & Hecht, 1996; Torgesen et al., 1994; Wagner et al., 1993) concluded that phonological processing abilities are independent and highly correlated. Moreover, analyses from those studies indicated that phonological awareness and rapid naming bare unique causal relations to reading acquisition (Torgesen & Hecht, 1996).

Relations Between Phonological
Processing and Learner Characteristics

Several lines of research provide convincing evidence that phonological processing deficits cause differences in perceiving, coding, retaining phonological information in short-term memory, and retrieving verbal information between normal achievers and students with normal intelligence and reading disabilities (Adams & Gathercole, 1995; Hurford & Shedelbower, 1993; Liberman & Shankweiler, 1985; Lyon & Chhabra, 1996; Mann & Brady, 1988; Manis, Custodio, & Szeszulski, 1993; Rack et al., 1992; Stanovich, 1985, 1986, 1988a; 1994; Torgesen et al., 1990; Vellutino & Scanlon, 1987a; Wagner, 1988; Wagner & Torgesen, 1987). Characteristics of diverse learners who experience difficulties specific to reading that are not attributable to an overall lower level of achievement or cognitive ability were examined across all the studies cited. In contrast, comparisons of poor readers with normal intelligence and general lower cognitive ability were examined in few studies (e.g., Badian, 1994a; Fawcett & Nicolson, 1994; Hurford et al., 1993; Hurford et al., 1994; Hurford, Schauf, Bunce, Blaich, & Moore, 1994; Stanovich, 1988a). Therefore, much of our discussion is specific to students with normal intelligence and reading disabilities and good readers. In addition, the present chapter includes discussions of studies with language or speech-impaired children as representative studies of a specific subtype of reading disability (Catts, 1993; Swank, 1994).

In the second area of convergence, we discuss learner characteristics differences in phonological awareness; therefore, the discussion in the present section is limited to differences in coding in short-term and long-term memory, articulation rate, and general intelligence. Converging evidence supported the notion that the phonological features of language were problematic for a significant number of diverse learners (Blachman, 1994; Cornwall, 1992; Lyon & Chhabra, 1996; Torgesen et al., 1990; Vellutino & Scanlon, 1987a, 1987b; Wagner, 1986; Wagner et al., 1993). Four types of evidence indicated differences between normally achieving and diverse learners' skills in coding phonologic features that also affected memory: recall of verbal information (in contrast to recall of nonverbal items such as abstract figures); memory span (verbatim retention of new strings of verbal items); articulation rate (how quickly words are spoken after presented auditorially); and rapid naming of stimuli presented in isolation and simultaneously in a series (verbally labeling familiar material; Ackerman & Dykman, 1993; Adams & Gathercole, 1995; Cornwall, 1992; Fawcett & Nicolson, 1994; Korhonen, 1995; Leather & Henry, 1994; Torgesen, 1985; Torgesen et al., 1990).

Recall of Verbal Information. The finding that differences were specific to type of information suggested that learners were not different in memory capacity (Torgesen, 1985). Hypothesized explanations that short-term memory is limited for everyone suggested the importance of efficiency of processes because of limitations (Mann & Brady, 1988). No differences were found in recall of nonverbal items, such as drawings of figures, or in accuracy of nonverbal material, such as environmental sounds like frogs croaking (Mann & Brady, 1988; McDougall, Hulme, Ellis, & Monk, 1994; Torgesen, 1985).

However, differential use of word features for coding is suggested by tasks using phonological and semantic distracters, tasks measuring familiar and nonsense groups of letters, and error analysis for recall of lists of spoken words (Mann & Brady, 1988; Torgesen, 1985; Vellutino & Scanlon, 1987a, 1987b). In contrast to good readers, poor readers (a) were not more distracted by phonologically similar words implying less sensitivity to phonological features, (b) categorized words on the basis of semantic features more than phonological features, (c) performed equally on nonsense words in contrast to good readers who performed better on familiar words, and (d) did use phonetic codes in recalling lists of spoken words by attending to similar phonological features in adjacent words; however, they were less efficient than good readers (Mann & Brady, 1988, Torgesen, 1985; Vellutino & Scanlon, 1987a, 1987b). Thus, differences between normally achieving and diverse learners were specific to the linguistic material presented and their use of the phonological features of words in encoding, storage, recoding, and retrieval. Differences were not specific to syntax and comprehension; however, in addition, diverse learners did make more use of semantic features in categorizing words than phonological (Vellutino & Scanlon, 1987b).

Memory Span to Assess Short-Term Memory. The following differences suggested that the ability to code phonological features is problematic for diverse learners. For example, we know that newly presented information is encoded in short-term or working memory by phonological features (Torgesen, 1985). When asked to repeat strings of digits or objects that are new to them, diverse learners respond less quickly and accurately (Cornwall, 1992; Torgesen et al., 1990), suggesting problems with the initial coding process. The literature infers that poor recall indicates either an absence of coded material available for recall or a poor quality code (Mann & Brady, 1988; Torgesen, 1985).

Poor performance in short-term working memory is hypothesized to adversely affect productive vocabulary, length of utterance, and syntactic knowledge (Adams & Gathercole, 1995; Swank, 1994). In short, difficulties in coding phonological information for storage reduces or makes less accessible the amount of phonological information in various linguistic categories such as semantic, syntactic, and morphographic (Adams & Gathercole, 1995; Carlisle & Nomanbhoy, 1993; McCutchen & Crain-Thoreson, 1994; Vellutino, Scanlon, & Spearing, 1995).

Articulation Rate. In addition, diverse learners' slower rates of articulation draw attention to lack of fluency with phonological features of language (Torgesen et al., 1990). Adams and Gathercole (1995) hypothesized that articulation rate may affect amount of speech production and indirectly short-term memory. Similarly, Korhonen's (1995) results supported the hypothesis proposed by Catts and Torgesen (cited in Korhonen, 1995) that articulation rate offers partial explanation for naming problems. In contrast, Ackerman and Dykman (1993) offered a limitation to the role that slow rates of articulation may play by concluding their results offered no support for the hypothesis that slow articulation rate is the overarching deficit in reading disabilities. Researchers indicated the need for more research to delineate the role that articulation plays in reading disabilities.

Rapid Naming to Assess Lexical Access in Long-Term Memory. Rapid naming tests have indicated that even when students understood the material, diverse learners' rate of rapid naming was slower than other students; in other words, the problem was rate of naming familiar material not comprehension, which suggested either a problem in recoding information in long-term memory to its phonological features for pronunciation and/or problems in retrieving poorly coded material (Katz, cited in Mann & Brady, 1988). For example, error analysis found that students would incorrectly name a picture with a word similar in phonological structure to the correct word. Katz hypothesized that the object had been correctly identified and understood but that difficulty occurred in phonetically producing the word (Katz, cited in Liberman & Shankweiler, 1985). Serving as an extension to Katz's hypothesis is Fawcett and Nicolson's (1994) conclusion that slower naming rates for pictures in contrast to color, digit, or letter stimuli may indicate that the rapid naming deficit is a function of the number of possible responses and hence, the amount of processing required. Rapid-naming, independent of phonological awareness, was found significantly related to reading fluency in older readers (Bowers, 1993; Bowers & Wolf, 1993). Longitudinal and cross-sectional research indicated that rapid naming deficits were persistent and stable with only slight diminution with age (Blachman, 1994; Fawcett & Nicolson, 1994; Korhonen, 1995). Specifically, Wood (cited in Blachman, 1994) noted that whereas phonological awareness deficits may initially identify a child as reading disabled, it is naming deficits that keep a child needing remedial services.

Relation to Intelligence. In addition, our review indicated that phonological processing is relatively independent of overall intelligence, a finding of particular relevance for diverse learners (Fletcher et al., 1994;

Torgesen, 1985; Vellutino & Scanlon, 1987b; Wagner & Torgesen, 1987). However, three recent lines of research indicated that phonological processing may not be as independent of general intelligence as hypothesized in earlier research (Torgesen et al., 1994), particularly if intelligence is more broadly defined to include successive processing, or holding information in order (Das, Mishra, & Kirby, 1994; Naglieri & Reardon, 1993). Successive processing, a category of cognitive processes, is highly related to short-term memory and, therefore, may represent the same process involved in coding processes. Moreover, although Wagner and colleagues (1993) found substantial correlations between phonological processing and cognitive ability, they did not conclude that the correlations were in conflict with the specific phonological processing deficit theory of reading disabilities.

Summary

Phonological processing consists of two components, awareness and coding, each having multiple dimensions that are relevant to reading acquisition. Explanations for differences between normally achieving and diverse learners in the ability to code, retain in short-term memory, and retrieve verbal information suggested the following causal chain (Liberman & Shankweiler, 1985; Lyon & Chhabra, 1996; Mann & Brady, 1988; Swank, 1994; Torgesen, 1985; Wagner et al., 1993):

> IF *poor perception* THEN *poor quality of representation or coding*
> IF *poor coding* THEN poor *durability in storage*
> IF *poor durability in storage* THEN *poor retrieval*

The research indicated that differences between good and poor readers were specific to linguistic material. Our first area of convergence, that phonological processing (awareness, coding, and retrieval) is the basis for many differences in reading acquisition, has provided the larger context for our second area of convergence, where we explore the construct of phonological awareness.

AREA OF CONVERGENCE 2:
Phonological Awareness May Be a Group
of Highly Related, Independent Phonological
Abilities or a General Ability With Multiple Dimensions

As the study of phonological processing advances, research has moved to fine-grained examinations of the components of phonological processing. As indicated in the previous area of convergence, phonological processing includes phonological awareness and two types of coding (i.e., coding in short-term memory as measured by digit span or list-learning and in long-term memory as measured by rapid-naming). Converging evidence supports the notion that awareness and two types of coding are independent. We focus our discussion in this area of convergence on phonological awareness. The discussion to follow considers dimensions of phonological awareness, and prominent hypotheses regarding the construct of phonological awareness. The purpose for discussing the dimensions and prominent hypothesis of phonological awareness is to create a framework for understanding phonological awareness, its relation to reading, and the instructional implication of that relation which we will discuss in subsequent areas of convergence.

Dimensions of Phonological Awareness

Research has shown that phonological awareness dimensions can be validly and reliably measured through a variety of tasks (Wagner, 1986; Yopp, 1988). The following tasks have been used in recent research as indicators of phonological awareness: auditory discrimination, blending, counting, deletion, isolation, rhyme, segmenting, substitution, sound categorization, tapping, reversing order of sounds, and word-to-word matching (Ball & Blachman, 1991; Catts, 1993; Felton & Pepper, 1995; Lundberg et al., 1988; Majsterek & Ellenwood, 1995; O'Connor, Jenkins, Leicester, & Slocum, 1993; Spector, 1995; Swank, 1994; Yopp, 1988).

The dimensions appear to be a function of development and instructional experiences. Extant research has indicated that, for most children, phonological awareness of larger phonological units (e.g., compound words, syllables, onset-rimes) develops without formal systematic instruction (e.g., Liberman & Shankweiler, 1985). In contrast, phonemic awareness appears dependent upon concurrent acquisition of alphabetic understanding (Bowey, 1994; Stanovich, 1994). Recent conceptualizations of phonological awareness refer to this two-level developmental progression as a holistic sensitivity to phonological structures, and a fully explicit analytical awareness that includes the ability to manipulate spoken words at the phoneme level (Bowey, 1994; Stanovich, 1994; Torgesen & Davis, 1996).

For example, in groups of 4-year-old children, none could segment by phoneme (i.e., analytic awareness) whereas about 50% could segment by syllables (i.e., holistic sensitivity); in a group of 5-year-olds, 17% could segment by phoneme and about 50% could do so by syllable. Finally, in a group of 6-year-old children, 70% could segment by phoneme and 90% by syllable (Liberman & Shankweiler, 1985). Vandervelden and

Siegel's (1995) results were consistent with and extended Liberman and Shankweiler's results.

Vandervelden and Siegel (1995) found strong support for the hypotheses that partial segmentation is easier than complete segmentation (e.g., that kindergarten children in the second half of the kindergarten year can segment the initial phoneme but cannot perform sequential segmentation of all phonemes). However, research has not fully established how phonological awareness develops, particularly the relation between maturation in language development and instructional experiences.

A contrasting conceptualization of phonological awareness dimensions is found in Yopp's (1988) study and in Stahl and Murray's (1994) study that extended Yopp's work. These studies examined task characteristics that contributed to difficulty apart from development and instructional experiences. Participants in both studies were normally achieving children. Thus it is important to note the conclusions may be specific to normally achieving children. The conclusions from the two studies indicated that differences in performance may be explained more by memory load and the size of the phonological unit of the task than by phonological dimensions. For example, are sounds put together, taken apart, added, matched?

Yopp (1988) found that the similarity in cognitive requirements across the dimensions was manipulation of phoneme units. Difficulty appeared to be a function of the number of steps required for completion of the manipulation. Specifically, phonological awareness dimensions vary in the number of steps required for completion. Each step requires material to be held in memory. For example, phonemic awareness dimensions were divided into two categories based on the memory processes and operations required: one operation on verbal material followed by response, as in segmentation; and one operation followed by holding the response to that operation in memory while performing other operations before making the final response, as in deletion (Yopp, 1988). For example:

1. When asked what sounds are heard in cat (segmentation), the response requires one operation of pulling apart sounds: /c/ /a/ /t/.

2. When asked to delete the first sound from cat and say the word that remain, the response requires two operation. First, identify the beginning sound and segment the sounds. Second, the remaining sounds need to be held in memory and then blended.

/c/
/a/ /t/, at

Based on results from a factor analysis Yopp (1988) concluded that the

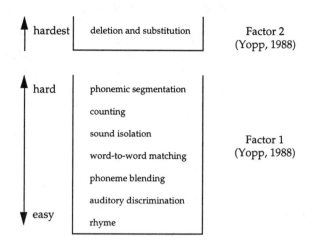

FIG. 4.3. Range of difficulty for phonological awareness dimensions based on the performace of normally achieving children (Yopp, 1988).

dimensions of phonological awareness represent a range of difficulty as evidenced by two factors. Dimensions in Factor 1 put less of a load on memory than dimensions in Factor 2. See Fig. 4.3.

Whereas Yopp's (1988) findings are specific to manipulation of sound units at the phoneme level, Stahl and Murray (1994) investigated the effect of varying the size of the phonological unit (e.g., syllable, onset-rime, phoneme) on the relative difficulty of dimensions. Stahl and Murray (1994) concluded that size of the phonological unit does contribute to difficulty and, moreover, that phonological awareness may be best conceptualized by the size of the phonological unit (e.g., onset-rime or phoneme) in contrast to a dimensions such as blending or segmenting. For example, onset-rime manipulations were easier than phoneme manipulations across dimensions, particularly within phoneme clusters. Consequently, we note that the size of the phonological unit may be as defining as differences among the dimensions in explaining the construct of phonological awareness.

Prominent Hypotheses Regarding
Phonological Awareness

The question whether phonological awareness is a general ability or a collection of independent but related abilities has received increasing attention over the last decade (e.g., Davidson & Jenkins, 1994; Lenchner et al., 1990; O'Connor et al., 1993; O'Connor et al., 1995; Slocum, O'Connor, & Jenkins, 1993; Stahl & Murray, 1994; Wagner et al., 1993). For example, whereas in 1990 Lenchner and colleagues drew attention to the relatively few studies focusing on whether or not dimensions measure an underlying single ability, several lines of research since 1990 have examined that question (e.g., O'Connor et al., 1995).

Our review of the available evidence provides moderate support for two hypotheses: Phonological awareness is either a general ability, or a group of highly related but independent abilities. The hypotheses have different instructional implications. The general ability hypothesis implies that learning one dimension will affect, either performance on additional dimensions, or understanding the whole notion of phonological awareness as evidenced in knowing how sounds relate to letter symbols. However, the independent abilities hypothesis implies that each dimension will need separate instruction.

General Ability Hypothesis. The general ability hypothesis is supported by studies that investigated the correlations among tasks used as indicators of phonological awareness dimensions, and levels of linguistic complexity. Support for a "general ability" hypothesis stems from the high degree of interrelatedness among dimensions of phonological awareness (e.g., Vellutino & Scanlon, 1987b; Wagner, 1986; Wagner & Torgesen, 1987; Yopp, 1988). This degree of interrelatedness may mean that the dimensions share significant commonalty and tap a similar construct (Yopp, 1988). Two related studies examined the construct of phonological awareness, Yopp (1988) and Stahl and Murray (1994) who extended Yopp's study.

Based on a correlation analysis, Yopp (1988) found that most phonological awareness dimensions (i.e., auditory discrimination, phoneme blending, phoneme counting, phoneme deletion, rhyme, phoneme segmentation, sound isolation, and word-to-word matching) were significantly interrelated. These strong interrelations indicated that the tests may be measuring a similar construct. Yopp's (1988) findings from a factorial analysis indicated that the tests loaded on two factors, except rhyme and auditory discrimination that minimally loaded on either factor. This means that rhyme and auditory discrimination may tap a similar but separate construct. See Fig. 4.3.

Stahl and Murray (1994) provided support with the explanation that differences in the size of the phonological unit (e.g., syllables, onset-rimes, phonemes), rather than differences in dimensions (e.g., blending and segmenting) best describe phonological awareness. In addition, a factor analysis indicated that the phonological awareness dimensions loaded on one factor which may provide support for the general ability theory.

Evidence from Yopp (1988) and Stahl and Murray (1994) suggest strong similarities across dimensions and that differences among dimensions may be a function of the size of phonological units and memory load.

Independent Abilities Hypothesis. Despite moderate support of phonological awareness as a general ability, a number of important issues remain unresolved. Research has investigated causal relations among phonological awareness dimensions and different measures of reading skill and the degree of generalization within and across dimensions. Wagner's (1988) meta-analysis indicated differential relations dependent on the measure of reading. Thus, Wagner found that two dimensions of awareness, blending and segmenting, did not have independent causal relations with word recognition (linking pronunciation with meaning) but did for word analysis (taking apart phonological units in words). Byrne and Fielding-Barnsley (1989) found that detection of common phonemes in words and segmenting are to some degree independent of each other or may have a hierarcheal relation, which, if that is the case, may support the general abilities hypothesis. In that study, all students who could detect could also segment; however, some could segment but not detect.

In contrast to the documented relations among segmenting, blending, and detection, rhyme is weakly related with other phonemic dimensions. Moreover, because of the less strong relation among rhyme and other phonemic awareness dimensions, Yopp (1988) concluded that rhyme may tap a different underlying ability and, therefore, cautioned against basing phonological awareness on rhyme.

A current line of research investigating generalization across classes of dimensions (e.g., does learning blending first help learning segmenting later?) offered support for the relative independence of analysis and synthesis abilities (Davidson & Jenkins, 1994; O'Connor et al., 1993; O'Connor et al., 1995; Slocum et al., 1993). Results from this line of research supported Wagner and colleagues' separate abilities theory (1993) by indicating that no transfer exists from synthesis to analysis and little to no transfer from analysis to synthesis.

Although the overall lack of generalization suggested relatively independent abilities, O'Connor and colleagues (1993) and Slocum and colleagues (1993) suggested an alternative explanation for lack of generalization. They hypothesized that lack of generalization may depend on the interaction among instructional design issues. Specifically, is lack of generalization due to inattention to size of the phonological unit, sufficient range of examples, and learner characteristics (O'Connor et al., 1993). Their alternative hypothesis aligns with the evidence provided for the general ability hypothesis. For example, Cary and Verhaeghe (1994) found that although training Portuguese kindergartners at the phoneme level generalized to the syllable level, training at the syllable level did not generalize to the phoneme level. However, if lack of generalization is a consequence of the independence of dimensions, rather than instructional design features, this means that each dimension important to reading must be directly taught.

Summary

In conclusion, our review of the available evidence provided moderate support for two viable hypotheses. First, phonological awareness is a general ability that has multiple dimensions varying in difficulty (Stahl & Murray, 1994; Wagner & Torgesen, 1987; Yopp, 1988). Second, phonological awareness abilities are highly correlated but independent (Davidson & Jenkins, 1994; O'Connor et al., 1993; Slocum et al., 1993; Torgesen et al., 1994; Wagner et al., 1993; Wagner, 1988). Figure 4.3 lists phonological awareness dimensions and diagrams the range of difficulty from easiest (rhyme) to hardest (deletion). Two factors that contribute to difficulty are the memory requirements and the size of the phonological units used in the dimension. Developmental studies indicated that the more difficult dimensions usually did not develop without instruction. Research has not yet conclusively established whether phonological awareness is a unitary construct or a group of high related, but independent abilities; and the relation between development, instructional experiences, and dimensions of phonological awareness. One reason for lack of convergence is that we do not fully understand the role instructional design can play in promoting generalization from one dimension to another. This understanding bears critical instructional implications for timing and efficiency of phonological awareness instruction. Unpacking the construct of phonological awareness has served as a framework for the next section in which we discuss the role that phonological awareness plays in beginning reading.

AREA OF CONVERGENCE 3:
Phonological Awareness Has a
Reciprocal Relation to Reading Acquisition

Hypothesized Relations

Our review indicated a range of hypothesized relations between phonological awareness and learning to read. Specifically, phonological awareness has been hypothesized to be a prerequisite for learning to read; influenced by reading instruction and practice; and both a cause and a consequence of reading acquisition (i.e., reciprocal). The importance of establishing the relation between phonological awareness and reading acquisition is the differential implications of each relation for the timing and content of instruction. For example, if evidence provides powerful support for a causal relation, then phonological awareness training prior to formal reading instruction is implied. However, if the evidence supports the hypothesis that formal reading instruction develops phonological awareness, the timing and instructional sequence issues are reversed. In addition, if phonological awareness develops as a consequence of reading, then the critical importance of phonological practice in connected text and the amount of reading in which each student engages is strongly implied. If evidence establishes that phonological awareness is necessary before reading instruction and that phonological awareness is also developed by specific types of instruction, emphasis on phonological awareness before and during beginning reading instruction is firmly established. Under both conditions, phonological awareness would foster reading acquisition.

In this area of convergence, we first review the strength of evidence for a causal relation between phonological awareness and reading acquisition. Next, we present evidence from studies with readers of varying ages and ability that phonological awareness also develops as a consequence of reading instruction. Then, we examine support for a reciprocal relation provided by causal and consequence of instruction evidence. Last, we consider limitations of the importance of the relation between phonological awareness and reading acquisition.

Causal Relation

Over the past decade, growing support for a causal relation between phonological awareness and reading acquisition has been evidenced in the language used in research conclusions. For example, articles appearing in 1985 used tentative language stating that phonological awareness *may* improve reading acquisition (Liberman & Shankweiler, 1985) and there is *mounting* evidence that the relationship is causal (Stanovich, 1985).

In contrast, more recent reviews specifically concluded that converging evidence is sufficiently strong to establish a causal relationship (Mann & Brady, 1988; Wagner, 1988; Wagner & Torgesen, 1987). Moreover, our review of secondary sources provided consistent evidence for a strong causal relation between phonological awareness and learning to read (e.g., Adams, 1990; Liberman & Shankweiler, 1985; Mann & Brady, 1988; Rack et al., 1992; Spector, 1995; Stanovich, 1985, 1986, 1988a, 1988b; Wagner, 1988).

We examine support for the causal relation by reviewing evidence from the following types of study: correlational, experimental intervention, and comparisons of good and poor readers.

Correlational Studies. Two general purposes categorize the correlation studies reviewed: predicting later reading achievement and understanding the relations among aspects of reading and dimensions of phonological awareness. First, predictive studies compared the relation between phonological awareness at an earlier age with subsequent reading achievement at a later age, for the purpose of discovering correlations between phonological awareness and reading. If consistent and strong correlation was found, then phonological awareness would predict later reading achievement.

Our review revealed that phonological awareness reliably predicted reading achievement across the age levels of participants from preschool through sixth grade (Cornwall, 1992; Hurford et al., 1993; Mann, 1993; Majsterek & Ellenwood, 1995; McGuinness, McGuinness, & Donohue, 1995; Swank & Catts, 1994). For example, McGuinness and colleagues (1995) found that a phonological awareness measure predicted the degree of success in acquiring alphabetic understanding, reading, and spelling skills. McGuinness and colleagues concluded that "effects of prior phonological awareness contribute to more rapid acquisition of the alphabetic principle" (1995, p. 851). Similarly, an investigation that focused on learning letter-sound correspondences (Mauer & Kamhi, 1996) indicated that performance on a short-term memory task and a phonological awareness dimension, sound categorization, predicted the overall performance on learning letter-sound correspondences.

Alone, the predictive evidence does not establish causal relation because other variables may be the explanatory factor. However, powerful evidence for a causal relation results when predictive findings with high validity are combined with highly significant effects of beginning reading measures in intervention studies prior to formal reading instruction (Wagner, 1988).

Second, research documenting the relation between phonological awareness and reading indicated that various dimensions of phonological awareness are related differentially to reading (Manis et al., 1993; Mauer & Kamhi, 1996; Vandervelden & Siegel, 1995). These lines of research are relatively new and, therefore, provide emerging evidence that does not have sufficient replication to support general conclusions. Consequently, we offer four examples of emerging evidence. First, initial phonemic recognition and partial segmentation are strongly correlated to letter-sound correspondence knowledge and beginning decoding skills (Bryne & Fielding-Barnsley, 1993a; Swank & Catts, 1994; Vandervelden & Siegel, 1995), whereas deletion and substitution are more strongly correlated to more advanced skills in reading and spelling (Swank & Catts, 1994; Vandervelden & Siegel, 1995). Third, limited phonemic inventories (e.g., encoding short vowels as the same sounds) that are caused by either discrimination problems or encoding problems may cause problems learning the direct mapping of speech sounds to letters (Swank, 1994). Fourth, evidence indicated that blending and segmenting phonemes are more highly related to reading than blending and segmenting syllables (Wagner, 1988; Wagner & Torgesen, 1987).

The significance of correlational studies are twofold: First, the power of phonological awareness to predict reading achievement enables early identification of students at risk for difficulty in learning to read (Hurford et al., 1993; Hurford et al., 1994; Majsterek & Ellenwood, 1995; Mann, 1993; McGuinness et al., 1995; Swank & Catts, 1994). Second, differential information about the interrelations among phonological abilities (i.e., awareness, coding, and retrieval), specific subskills for reading, and age of children teach us much about the nature of the reading process itself and reading disabilities (Stanovich, 1988a; Swank & Catts, 1994; Vandervelden & Siegel, 1995; Vellutino & Scanlon, 1987a).

Intervention Studies. Intervention studies with prereaders or novice readers provided a second source of support for a causal relation between phonological awareness and reading (Ball & Blachman, 1991; Brady, Fowler, Stone, & Winbury, 1994; Byrne & Fielding-Barnsley, 1989, 1993a; Cunningham, 1990; Davidson & Jenkins, 1994; Lie, 1991; Lundberg et al., 1988; O'Connor et al., 1993; O'Connor et al., 1995; Torgesen & Davis, 1996; Vellutino & Scanlon, 1987a). Wagner and Torgesen (1987) noted that if training in phonological awareness improves subsequent reading, it is reasonable to infer a causal relation.

In this type of study, the effect of phonological awareness instruction on subsequent phonological awareness development, reading, and possibly spelling achievement was assessed with pre- and posttest comparisons of achievement. Phonological awareness instruction had a significant influence on subsequent measures in all intervention studies reviewed; however, the strength of conclusions varied.

Comparisons of Good and Poor Readers Studies. Vellutino and Scanlon's work of more than a decade comparing poor second- and sixth-grade readers to good second- and sixth-grade readers (e.g., 1987a) is particularly noteworthy. Their work with good and poor readers indicated that the ability to grasp phonemic segmentation is a prerequisite for linking sounds to corresponding letters and subsequent word identification, and that poor readers were able to profit from phonemic segmentation training with positive effects on ability to identify words. These authors concluded that facility of phonemic segmentation is causally related and not simply a consequence of reading. Other researchers in our review who reviewed research or examined differences between good and poor readers reached the same conclusion across ages and various alphabetic languages (e.g., Adams, 1990; Lenchner et al., 1990; Rack et al., 1992; Stanovich, 1985, 1986, 1988a).

In summary, multiple research perspectives add converging evidence that strongly supports a causal relation between phonological awareness and reading acquisition. Next, we present evidence that phonological awareness is developed by reading instruction and reading.

Phonological Awareness As a Consequence of Reading Instruction and Practice

Establishing a causal relation between phonological awareness and reading acquisition does not preclude other directional relations (e.g., reading instruction causes phonological awareness development). Our review produced moderate but converging evidence that phonological awareness is developed by reading instruction and the act of reading. Evidence came from three sources: reviews of studies with skilled readers in nonalphabetic languages; reviews of studies with adult illiterates in alphabetic languages; primary intervention studies with normally achieving and low achieving readers.

First, studies that found skilled adult readers in nonalphabetic languages were deficient in phonemic segmentation (Adams, 1990; Mann & Brady, 1988) provided support for the hypothesis that phonological awareness is a consequence of reading instruction and practice because nonalphabetic languages do not include phonological awareness instruction. Second, studies in alphabetic languages that focused on adult illiterates indicated that those who successfully completed literacy programs had higher levels of phonological awareness than those who did not (Adams, 1990; Mann & Brady, 1988). Support for the consequence relation is inferred from the higher levels of phonological awareness among adults receiving more instruction and practice by finishing the program compared to those who did not finish.

Third, six primary studies in our review with normal achievers and diverse readers concluded that, in addition to instruction in reading and phonological awareness, that the process of reading increased reading and phonological awareness performance across ability (e.g., normally achieving, normal intelligence and reading disability, low intelligence and reading disability; Hatcher, Hulme, & Ellis, 1994; Hurford et al., 1993; Lovett, Borden, De Luca, Lacerenza, Benson, & Brackstone, 1994; Manis et al., 1993; McGuinness et al., 1995; Vandervelden & Siegel, 1995). Finally, although Wagner and Torgesen (1987) indicated that learning to read is a nontrivial cause in the development of phonological awareness; they indicated the effect of instruction and practice on phonological awareness has not received much research attention (see also Mann & Brady, 1988; Wagner, 1988). A longitudinal study that examined the development of phonological and orthographic skill in dyslexic children (Manis et al., 1993) is an exception to the evidence indicating that development of phonological awareness is the consequence of reading instruction and practice in reading. Manis and colleagues' (1993) results suggested that the phonological awareness skills of older children with dyslexia were persistent and lagged behind their reading ability.

Reciprocal Relation

Support for two hypotheses: that phonological awareness is a causal factor in reading acquisition, and that reading instruction and practice are causal factors in the development of phonological awareness suggests a reciprocal relation. In a reciprocal relation, causal relations occur in both directions— phonological awareness facilitates and is facilitated by reading acquisition The existence of a reciprocal relation means that phonological awareness is important prior to and during learning to read.

Understanding the role phonological awareness plays in reading acquisition has advanced with an increase in the number of phonological awareness studies with older readers. From Spring 1993 to Summer 1996, the number of studies with older readers increased from 4 to 14. In this chapter, we examined 13 primary studies with older readers (Ackerman & Dykman, 1993; Cornwall, 1992; Das et al., 1994; Eden, Stein, Wood, & Wood, 1995; Fawcett & Nicolson, 1994; Fletcher et al., 1994; Hatcher et al., 1994; Korhonen, 1995; Lenchner et al., 1990; Lovett et al., 1994; Manis et al., 1993; McCutchen & Crain-Thoreson, 1994; Naglieri & Reardon, 1993) and Vellutino and Scanlon's research with older readers (Vellutino, Scanlon, & Spearing, 1995; 1987a, 1987b). Besides the primary sources, reviews of the causes of reading disabilities generally referred to research across ages (e.g., Rack et al., 1992; Snowling, 1991).

The practical importance of the reciprocal relation between reading and phonological development has been argued extensively and passionately by several authors (e.g., Adams, 1990; Blachman, 1994; Stanovich, 1985; Vellutino & Scanlon, 1987a; Wagner & Torgesen, 1987). Similarly, our review found consistent recommendations for early identification of students at risk for reading failure (e.g., low ability in phonological awareness) and early, explicit instruction in phonological awareness prior to and in tandem with beginning reading instruction (e.g., Ball & Blachman, 1991; Cunningham, 1990; Felton & Pepper, 1995; O'Connor et al., 1993).

Limited Importance of Relation

Several authors pointed to heterogeneous causes for reading disabilities and the subsequent dangers of focusing on one intervention target such as phonological awareness (Blachman, 1994; Eden et al., 1995; Fletcher et al., 1994; Snowling, 1991; Wagner, 1986). The 25 intervention studies in our review indicated that instructional implications are inherent in the relations between phonological awareness and reading acquisition. In contrast, although differences in visual and phonological processing abilities appear to offer some explanations for reading disabilities, the instructional implication of those relations are not as clear as those of phonological awareness (Eden et al., 1995; Snowling, 1991; Torgesen, 1985; Wagner, 1988). Nevertheless, attention to a larger research focus (e.g., relations among awareness, phonetic recoding, phonological recoding, orthographic processing and their covariation with reading) is important because this research may help explain why not *all* children respond to phonological interventions (Wood, cited in Blachman, 1994; Vellutino & Scanlon, 1987a; Wagner & Torgesen, 1987).

For example, roughly one third of our primary studies included examinations of the relations between coding (i.e., coding in short-term and long-term lexical access memory) and reading acquisition (Ackerman & Dykman, 1993; Badian, 1994b; Brady et al., 1994; Bowey, 1994; Catts, 1993; Cornwall, 1992; Das et al., 1994; Eden et al., 1995; Fawcett & Nicolson, 1994; Felton, 1993; Fletcher et al., 1994; Hurford & Shedelbower, 1993; Korhonen, 1995; Leather & Henry, 1994; Mauer & Kamhi, 1996; McCutchen & Crain-Thoreson, 1994; McGuinness et al., 1995; Naglieri & Reardon, 1993; O'Connor et al., 1993; Torgesen & Davis, 1996; Torgesen et al., 1990; Vellutino & Scanlon, 1987b; Vellutino, Scanlon, & Spearing, 1995; Wagner et al., 1993). Conclusions from these studies pointed to the need for future research to examine instruction in rapid naming and list learning. For example, interaction of several independent processes (i.e., deletion, naming, and list learning) may determine the extent and severity of reading problems (Felton, 1993). Moreover, the interrelation of awareness and two types of coding (naming and list learning) may relate to automaticity (Cornwall, 1992). Similarly, emerging evidence is indicating that naming speed may be a critical component in learning to read successfully (Ackerman & Dykman, 1993; Fawcett & Nicolson, 1994; Korhonen, 1995; O'Connor et al., 1993; Torgesen et al., 1990). In short, Swank's (1994) summarization of the effect of coding deficits on reading acquisition implicated difficulties in development of alphabetic understanding, decoding, listening and reading comprehension, vocabulary development, and the lack of reading practice that come from lack of speed and efficiency in the various processes involved in reading.

Summary

The critical relation of phonological awareness to reading acquisition appears firmly established, the evidence for a causal relation being strong. Because fewer studies exist for older children, our evidence for the effect of learning to read on phonological awareness is more limited. Nevertheless, the combination of conclusions from primary studies with older children and from the secondary sources that indicated an effect of reading on phonological awareness development strongly suggests the existence of a reciprocal relation.

A causal relation implicates the timing and content of beginning reading instruction. It is critical, therefore, to understand the relative importance of instruction in phonological awareness throughout reading instruction. In the next area of convergence, we discuss evidence of the sufficiency of phonological awareness alone in learning to read.

AREA OF CONVERGENCE 4:
Phonological Awareness Is Necessary
But Not Sufficient for Reading Acquisition

A sizable body of research indicates causal and reciprocal relations between phonological awareness and reading acquisition. In this section, we review research that has examined the role and relation of phonological awareness to alphabetic understanding (Adams, 1990; Ball & Blachman, 1991; Bowey, 1994; Byrne & Fielding-Barnsley, 1989; Mauer & Kamhi, 1996; McGuinness et al., 1995; Rack et al., 1992; Spector, 1995; Stanovich, 1985; Vellutino, 1991; Vellutino & Scanlon, 1987a), and to coding linguistic material into phonological codes and automaticity (Ackerman & Dykman, 1993; Cornwall, 1992; Fawcett & Nicolson, 1994; Korhonen, 1995; Torgesen et al., 1990; Vellutino & Scanlon, 1987b).

In addition, our review indicated that despite phonological awareness interventions, approximately 10% to 30% of children with phonological deficits do not improve through traditional interventions—that deficits are persistent and stable. Therefore, we summarize studies with young and older readers that either included phonological awareness instruction concurrent with reading and spelling instruction or employed phonologically based reading instruction (Blachman, 1994; Castle, Riach, & Nicholson, 1994; Felton, 1993; Hatcher et al., 1994; Iverson & Tumner, 1993; Lovett et al., 1994; Weiner, 1994). Findings are described in terms of the relation among the characteristics of diverse learners and their subsequent needs in instruction.

Phonological Awareness
and Alphabetic Understanding

Phonological awareness involves the ability to hear and manipulate sounds. Though research has established its importance, the way phonological awareness relates to and promotes other processes of reading acquisition requires further unpacking. Specifically, what is the relation and role of phonological awareness in alphabetic understanding? *Alphabetic understanding* refers to understanding that letters represent sounds and that whole words embody a sound structure of individual sounds and patterns of groups of sounds. The alphabetic principle is the combination of alphabetic understanding and phonological awareness. The alphabetic principle facilitates reading because readers cannot access words in their own internal dictionaries (lexicon) if they are unable to pronounce the words. Thus, the alphabetic principle enables the reader to translate independently a visual symbol into a sound, or as Spector (1995) expressed, to be able to crack the code by "mapping letters to sound" (p. 7) or to decode. This independence is in contrast to beginning readers who may depend upon someone else saying the word that the letters represent (Adams, 1990; Spector, 1995).

Instruction in Phonological Awareness
and Letter-Sound Correspondences

Converging evidence provided strong support that a combination of *phonemic awareness and letter-sound correspondence* training is necessary to understand the alphabetic principle (Adams, 1990; Ball & Blachman, 1991; Byrne & Fielding-Barnsley, 1989, 1993a; Mann, 1993; Rack et al., 1992; Snowling, 1991; Spector, 1995; Stanovich, 1986; Vellutino, 1991). In the intervention studies reviewed, six included phonological awareness and letter-sound correspondence instruction (Ball & Blachman, 1991; Byrne & Fielding-Barnsley, 1989; Cunningham, 1990; Davidson & Jenkins, 1994; O'Connor et al., 1993; O'Connor et al., 1995), whereas five exclusively taught phonological awareness abilities (Brady et al., 1994; Foster, Erickson, Foster, Brinkman, & Torgesen, 1994; Lie, 1991; Lundberg et al., 1988; Slocum et al., 1993). We use three representative studies to illustrate the evidence.

First, the results of an intervention study with normally achieving kindergartners clearly indicated that phonemic awareness and letter-sound correspondence significantly enhanced later reading and spelling performance more so than training in letter-sound correspondence alone (Ball & Blachman, 1991). Similarly, in teaching young preliterate children to acquire the alphabetic principle, Byrne and Fielding-Barnsley (1989) found that only those who learned phonemic segmentation and phoneme identification skills and graphic symbols for initial sounds were able to correctly choose between mow and sow after they had been taught mat and sat.

A third study examined the effects of a metacognitive component on phonological awareness and letter-sound correspondence instruction with normally achieving kindergarten and first-grade children (Cunningham, 1990). The study compared two instructional approaches across kindergarten and first grade: letter-sound correspondence and skill training in phonemic awareness, and letter-sound correspondence, skill training, and instruction in strategic use of phonemic awareness skills in context of reading. Adding explicit instruction in strategic application of the skills to instruction in letter-sound correspondence and skill training in phonological awareness resulted in significant improvement in reading. Specifically, improvement was noted in letter-sound correspondence knowledge, word recognition, and reading comprehension. Cunningham (1990) concluded that the difference was explained by contextualized instruction that included instruction in and demonstration of conspicuous strategies; guided practice; and strategic and purposeful review of previous lessons in addition to the combination of phonemic awareness and letter-sound correspondence instruction.

Two additional studies compared the addition of a metacognitive component (Lovett et al., 1994; Weiner, 1994). Lovett et al. (1994) found that for older readers with reading disabilities that the metacognitive component was critical for broad-based generalization, supporting Cunningham's (1990) results. In contrast, Weiner (1994) found that low readers in the metacognitive approach did not perform as well on outcome measures as those in a phonological awareness skill and drill approach. However, Weiner's (1994) study was cut short and some of the instructional design features may have been comprised in the reduction.

Coding and Automaticity

Evidence is converging to establish that coding and automaticity are as necessary as phonological awareness and alphabetic understanding to reading acquisition. Coding involves translating stimuli from one form to another (e.g., from auditory to written or from written to auditory), whereas automaticity has to do with the quality (i.e., fluency) of the response, or the quality of coding. Our understanding of the relation between fluent coding (phonological processing) and reading acquisition is limited by the amount of the available phonological processing research, specifically training research. Wagner and Torgesen (1987) drew attention to the need for extending phonological awareness research to include phonological processing. Such an extension would attempt to better understand the interaction between processing and awareness for different reading ability levels.

Since 1987, a new line of research has been emerging that suggests *rapid letter naming* and *list learning* abilities may significantly affect ease of reading acquisition (Ackerman & Dykman, 1993; Cornwall, 1992; Fawcett & Nicolson, 1994; Korhonen, 1995; Torgesen et al., 1990; Vellutino & Scanlon, 1987b). Rapid letter naming and list learning are two tasks commonly used to measure ability to code material into phonological representations (refer to second area of convergence in this chapter for explanation of coding). We use primary studies with readers to illustrate the trend in research to examine the relations among awareness, coding, and reading acquisition.

First, three studies with children with reading disabilities, ages 7 to 18, indicated that rapid naming deficits are stable over time (Ackerman & Dykman, 1993; Fawcett & Nicolson, 1994; Korhonen, 1995). Nevertheless, in a 9-year follow-up study, Korhonen (1995) found that the naming deficits were not as prominent in older children as they were when the children were younger. This diminution of the deficit implies an effect of maturation or instruction. In support of this implication, one training study (Brady et al., 1994) reported gains in naming as a result of a phonological awareness intervention with young children; however, deficits in rapid naming were not a focus of intervention studies reviewed in this chapter.

Second, a study with older readers investigated the predictive relations of phonological awareness, naming speed (phonological recoding), and list learning (phonetic recoding) with reading and spelling (Cornwall, 1992). Students that had rapid rates of letter naming did better in word identification and prose passage reading speed and accuracy than students with lower rates of rapid naming. In contrast, list learning ability predicted only word identification.

Cornwall (1992) linked naming and list learning to automaticity. In addition, Cornwall suggested that relative differences in naming and list learning may impact ability to learn and recall alphabet letters. Thus, teaching skills of rapid naming of verbal material and memorizing lists (such as the alphabet) may be significant additions to instructional combinations. However, much remains to be known about the practical features of instruction.

Phonological Awareness, Reading, and Spelling Instruction

Phonological processing lines of research are documenting the persistence of reading disabilities despite instruction in phonological awareness. As a consequence, Wagner and colleagues (1993) and Blachman (1994) concluded that interventions gains will be hard won, more may be needed prior to reading instruction than phonological awareness, and the intensity and extent of phonological awareness and reading instruction may need to be more than is found in present research. This persistence of the deficits highlights the critical nature of beginning reading instruction (Blachman, 1994; Felton, 1993). Findings of four studies with beginning reading instruction (Castle et al., 1994; Hatcher et al., 1994; Iverson & Tumner, 1993; Weiner, 1994) and one study with remedial reading instruction (Lovett et al., 1994) demonstrated the benefit of phonological awareness in concert with reading and spelling instruction. Blachman (1994) and Felton (1993) argued that instruction for children with reading disabilities needs to be explicit at the phonological awareness, alphabetic understanding, and application to decoding levels to provide sufficient intensity for those children who may be resistant to instruction. Similarly, Lovett et al. (1994) concluded that explicit and intense instruction, practice, and feedback directly at the level of deficit, processing phonemes in printed and auditory form, produced the wide-spread generalization they had been unable to achieve in earlier studies.

Summary

The complexity of the reading process in the roles played by phonological awareness and coding in reading acquisition and disability is made clear by the range of studies. Findings suggest that a single approach to understanding the reading process is inadequate (e.g., Adams, 1990; Snowling, 1991; Stanovich, 1985; Vellutino & Scanlon, 1987a, 1987b). Vellutino's (1991) conclusion that research supports a comprehensive and balanced approach is echoed in the research we reviewed. Research supported combining phonological awareness instruction with letter-sound correspondence instruction and instruction that makes clear the utility of the alphabetic principle in the context of reading. Recent research suggests that instruction in rapid naming and list learning may be critical components of beginning reading instruction, specifically for diverse learners. Next, we conclude with evidence that phonological awareness can be taught with significant gains in subsequent reading and spelling achievement for all learners as our final area of convergence.

AREA OF CONVERGENCE 5:
Phonological Awareness Deficits and Delays
Can Be Reliably Identified in Young Children

Establishment of the causal relation between phonological awareness and reading acquisition (i.e., decoding and word identification as indicated by decoding real and nonsense words) highlighted the need for parsimonious means for identifying children at risk for reading difficulties. The result has been a growing area of research investigating the reliability and validity of measures for predicting and diagnosing reading disabilities. In this area, we discuss studies that investigated the best predictors of decoding and word identification for young children before or concurrent with beginning reading instruction and the accuracy of those predictions. The studies included eight primary sources (Badian, 1994b; Catts, 1993; Felton, 1993; Hurford, Johnston, et al., 1994; Hurford, Schauf, et al., 1994; Majsterek & Ellenwood, 1995; Mann, 1993; McGuinness et al., 1995; Swank & Catts, 1994) and one secondary source (Felton & Pepper, 1995).

Two types of correlational research investigated the best predictors of reading acquisition (i.e., as indicated by decoding and word identification). The first type studied phonological awareness in kindergarten or beginning first grade and subsequent decoding and word identification to identify variables that best predict differences in decoding and word identification. The performance on predictor variables could be used in identifying those children who may need intervention. A second type of correlational research classifies students by degree of risk at the younger age of testing and by reading ability at the older age. The two classifications are compared to determine the reliability of percentages for at-risk classification (e.g., Felton, 1993; Hurford, Johnston, et al., 1994; Hurford, Schauf, et al., 1994).

Best Predictors of Decoding
and Word Identification

Four variables predicted decoding and word identification in nonreaders and beginning readers: phonological awareness, phonological processing, orthographic processing, and letter-sound knowledge. Phonological awareness dimensions included deletion of syllables and phonemes in various positions, syllable tapping, phoneme identity, blending, and segmenting. Phonological processing tasks included rapid serial naming of colors, letters, digits, and objects. The measure of orthographic processing tested detection of either the reversal or correct orientation of letters and number. It is documented in only one study (Badian, 1994b) and therefore, has limited support as a predictor variable. Letter-sound knowledge tasks that predicted decoding and word identification included invented spelling, letter-sound correspondences, and letter-names. In concert with Mann's work (1993), Torgesen and Davis (1996) suggested that invented spelling may be the most sensitive indicator that children have had a range of instructional experiences sufficient for success in decoding and word identification.

The following combinations of predictor variables were recommended for screening batteries: phonological awareness, rapid naming, and letter and letter-sound knowledge. Three examples illustrate recommendations for screening procedures at the preschool level, identification procedures during the beginning of first grade, and a general recommendation for young prereaders with speech and language problems. First, a 3-year study was designed to develop and evaluate a preschool screening procedure (Majsterek & Ellenwood, 1995). Based on their results, Majsterek and Ellenwood (1995) recommended that blending be included in prekindergarten batteries and that letter-names and letter-sounds be added to the end of kindergarten and the beginning of first-grade batteries. During the beginning of first grade, Swank and Catts (1994) found deletion to be the most effective discriminator between good and poor first-grade readers on decoding and word identification. Third, Catts (1993) recommended that children with speech–language impairments be considered for early intervention programs that target prevention of reading disabilities. In addition, Felton and Pepper (1995) recommended that screening tests for early identification and intervention include measures of both phonological awareness and rapid naming. The following times were recommended for identifying children at risk of reading disabilities: in preschool or at the beginning of kindergarten; at the end of kindergarten or the beginning of first grade; and later as warranted by reading performance.

Two studies provided criteria for determining the severity and nature of reading disabilities (Felton, 1993; Felton & Pepper, 1995). *Severity* (i.e., extent) of reading disability could be conceptualized as the number of tests on which the student meet criteria as being at risk. The *nature of the disability* could be defined by the type of test on which the student met at-risk criteria (e.g., awareness or rapid naming; Felton, 1993; Felton & Pepper, 1995). Furthermore, a student meeting at-risk criteria on multiple tests and in multiple areas, such as phonological awareness and rapid naming, would be considered at high risk.

Accuracy of Predictions

Studies that compared identification at a younger age to later classification of reading ability found the following ranges of accuracy. Felton and Pepper

(1995) indicated that accuracy rates were higher for children who read well and for those with severe reading problems. It appears to be more difficult to predict those children who have moderate at-risk status. Their (1995) interpretation of lower accuracy rates for moderate reading difficulties is that other variables that are not being measured, such as qualitative variables like home literacy, may provide additional important information for intervention decisions. Hurford, Schauf, and colleagues (1994) compared discrepancies in percentages of accurate identification of at-risk students in two studies investigating identification of at-risk first graders. They concluded that the following factors affected degree of accuracy: stringent versus relaxed criteria of inclusion for being considered at risk, and differences in times of assessment according to relations among within-child developmental factors, tasks selected as indicators of specific abilities, and the instructional environment. Accuracy of identification ranged from approximately 80% to 98% in the studies reviewed (e.g., Felton & Pepper, 1995; Hurford, Johnston, et al., 1994; Hurford, Schauf, et al., 1994; Swank & Catts, 1994).

Technical adequacy and valid use of available tools also affects accuracy of identification. Byrne and Fielding-Barnsley (1993b) found that global similarity in words affected reliability. Global similarity involves a high degree of similarity among consonants and vowels in words used for discriminations, such as matching two of three words that begin with the same phoneme. For example, *coat* and *cone* share two common sounds (i.e., uncontrolled for global similarity), whereas, *coat* and *can* share only one common sound (i.e., controlled for global similarity). Byrne and Fielding-Barnsley (1993b) found that children received higher scores for uncontrolled (i.e., tests that included words with global similarity) than for controlled tests. Such overestimation of a child's phonological awareness ability resulted in not identifying as many as 50% of the children in the study who were considered at risk with the test controlling for global similarity.

Felton and Pepper (1995) indicated that presently too few tools are criterion-referenced, standardized, and normed because many measures were developed for specific studies. Consequently, the development of identification batteries is still in its infancy. Felton and Pepper (1995) listed commercially available tests with good technical adequacy. These tests measure phonological awareness and reading readiness skills (e.g., Kaufman Brief Survey of Early Academic and Language Skills, Lindamood's LAC test, Rosner's Test of Auditory Analysis, Torgesen and Bryant's Test of Phonological Awareness, German's Test of Word Finding, Torgesen's Comprehensive Test of Phonological Skills). In addition, Felton and Pepper (1995) noted that tools for identification of being at risk for reading disabilities have a different purpose than tools to determine eligibility for learning disability classification. At-risk tools assess relevant prerequisite skills for decoding and word identification.

Despite good accuracy rates of identification four current needs exist: development of specific norms for identification of at-risk population; identification of the most valid predictors of ability to read at single-word level (Stanovich, cited in Lyon & Chhabra, 1996; Swank & Catts, 1994); and convergence on the qualitative factors that may be effecting at-risk status for children with mild reading disabilities (Felton & Pepper, 1995).

Summary

Children at risk for reading disabilities can be reliably identified as early as prekindergarten through first-grade age within a range of approximately 80% to 90% accuracy. Children at the ends of the at-risk continuum (little or high risk) are more reliably identified than those in the middle range. Although reliable and valid test batteries for identification are available commercially, development of parsimonious batteries of predictors is still in its infancy. The following sequence summarizes recommendations from the studies reviewed. Screen children before or as they enter kindergarten on phonological awareness and rapid-naming. Screen again at the end of kindergarten or the beginning of first grade on phonological awareness, rapid-naming, letter-sound correspondences, decoding of real and nonsense words, and perhaps invented spelling. Last, provide appropriate diagnostic testing and interventions for as long as children are considered at risk.

AREA OF CONVERGENCE 6:
Phonological Awareness is Teachable
and Promoted by Attention to Instructional Variables

We frame our discussion of the sixth area of convergence with the following six-part structure. First, we give an overview of the 24 intervention studies and their effects. Then, we examine the components of effective instruction. In addition, we identify significant independent variables found in only one or two studies and, therefore, supported by limited evidence. Fifth, we discuss the interaction of variables with specific learner characteristics. Finally, our summary provides instructional implications of the fifth area of convergence.

Overview of Studies

Our review examined research published since 1985; therefore, this sixth area of convergence is from a selective, but nevertheless representative analysis and synthesis of 25 studies of the effects of phonological awareness interventions on the phonological awareness development, reading, and spelling acquisition of normally achieving students and diverse learners. In addition to primary studies, we included eight secondary sources.

Across the studies, age, student ability, and reading ability were frequently investigated as demographic and explanatory variables. Disabilities or delays were examined in 16 studies, unlike normal achievement which was the focus of 9 intervention studies. Fourteen of the 25 studies involved nonreaders, 8 focused on students in beginning reading instruction. A large gap exists in intervention studies for older readers (Lovett et al., 1994; Truch, 1994; Vellutino & Scanlon, 1987b). Therefore the instructional implications drawn from the intervention studies reviewed are most relevant for children prior to and concurrent with beginning reading instruction.

Participants' ages ranged from preschool through sixth grade; the average age group was kindergarten and first grade. However, Truch (1994) included the performance of learners from childhood through adult years in his analysis. Normally achieving children and children with identified intelligence, language, and phonological awareness disabilities or delays were studied in the 25 intervention studies. Twenty-one studies used English-speaking students. Non-English-speaking children in Portuguese, Spanish, and Scandinavian countries were participants in four studies (Cary & Verhaeghe, 1994; Defior & Tudela, 1994; Lie, 1991; Lundberg et al., 1988). These studies were included as representative intervention studies with non-English-speaking students in alphabetic languages.

The length of intervention interventions varied from a few days (e.g., 5 days) to a year. Length of sessions varied from 10 to 90 minutes and ranged in frequency from daily to twice a week. Roughly 85% of the studies had an average of 25 minutes of instruction three times a week for 11 weeks, or an average of 14 instructional hours. In one study (Lovett et al., 1994), the intervention involved 35 hours.

Effects of Phonological Awareness Instruction

The effects of teaching phonological awareness were among the most instructionally salient findings in our review of intervention studies. Thus, all studies reported positive short-term effects on reading, spelling, or phonological awareness development. Eighty-four percent of the studies looked at effects on reading; 100% looked at effects of phonological awareness instruction on subsequent phonological awareness development, whereas roughly 60% looked at effects on spelling. In addition to those short-term effects, seven studies reported positive long-term transfer effects on reading and spelling and long-term maintenance effects on phonological tasks from several months up to 2 years (Brady et al., 1994; Byrne & Fielding-Barnsley, 1993a; Iverson & Tunmer, 1993; Hatcher et al., 1994; Lie, 1991; Lundberg et al., 1988; Weiner, 1994).

Components of Effective Instruction

We found consistent attention to the following components across the intervention studies.

1. Student's mental manipulations of sounds were made overt with concrete representation of sound.
2. Individual sounds were orally modeled by the teacher and produced by student.
3. Explicit instruction was specifically recommended by researchers.
4. Letter-sound correspondence component was added to phonological awareness interventions.
5. The dimension of segmenting or combinations of segmenting, blending, and phoneme identity received focus.
6. Linguistic complexity was scaffolded.
7. Phonological awareness was either added to, or supplemented reading instruction for beginning readers or poor readers.

Concrete Representation. Utilization of concrete representation of sound was an instructional feature in approximately 80% of the studies. Concrete representation involves using neutral objects to represent a sound. For example, after students heard the teacher model a sound, the students then said the phoneme while simultaneously moving a marker representing the phoneme (Ball & Blachman, 1991).

Oral Production of Individual Sounds. Isolated individual sounds (phonemes) are orally produced by the teacher in a demonstration and by students in response and practice. For example, in Lie (1991) the first sound was taught by teacher modeling the isolation of the sound, students producing the sound, and teacher drawing attention to unique sound production features in the mouth (i.e., how the sound feels when you say it). See Table 4.2 for a summary of sound production and strategies for sound detection and manipulation (i.e., phonological awareness).

Five studies included an instructional focus on articulatory features as either part of the Lindamood ADD program or instructional features that were influenced by the Lindamood ADD program (Brady et al., 1994; Lie, 1991; McGuinness et al., 1995; Torgesen & Davis, 1996; Truch, 1994).

TABLE 4.2

Presentation Features: Isolated Sound Modeling, Student Sound Production, Strategies

Study	Ball & Blachman (1991)	Byrne & Fielding-Barnsley (1989)	Cunningham (1990)	Lie (1991)	Lundberg et al. (1988)	O'Connor et al. (1993)	Vellutino & Scanlon (1987b)
Teacher model isolated sound	yes	yes	yes	yes	yes	yes	—
Student produce isolated sound	yes	yes	yes	yes	—	yes	yes
Concrete representation	yes	yes	yes	yes	yes	yes	yes
Strategy or Activity	say it & move it	associate symbol with words. associate symbols with sounds. segmentation strategy	think-aloud strategy	feel the articulation and listen. segmentation strategy	clap, dance, march, move markers	touch and say	decoding, segmentation

Note. ___ indicates absence of information.   Concrete representation is also indicated as an activity or strategy

Moreover, Cary and Verhaeghe (1994) measured the effect of phonological awareness instruction on progress in awareness of articulatory features.

Explicit Instruction. The following features common across the studies suggested an explicit instructional characteristic: teacher modeling specific sounds; student production of specific sound; and direct teaching of phonological detection and manipulation. Direct teaching involved strategies (e.g., concrete representation) and scaffolding of difficult dimensions (i.e., providing graduated amounts of teacher, task, or materials assistance).

Letter-Sound Correspondence Instruction. In a previous section, we discussed the utility of letter-sound correspondence instruction combined with phonological awareness to help students understand how sounds relate to written symbols in alphabet languages (see Area of Convergence 4). Interventions that included letter-sound instruction with phonological instruction reported significant differences in reading and phonological awareness measures (Ball & Blachman, 1991; Blachman, Ball, Black, & Tangel, 1994; Byrne & Fielding-Barnsley, 1989; Castle et al., 1994; Cunningham, 1990; Davidson & Jenkins, 1994; Defior & Tudela, 1994; Hurford, Johnstone, et al., 1994; O'Connor et al., 1995; Torgesen & Davis, 1996).

However, phonological awareness instruction alone does produce reliable growth in phonological awareness and reading and spelling (Brady et al., 1994; Cary & Verhaeghe, 1994; Foster et al., 1994; Lie, 1991; Lundberg et al., 1988; Slocum et al., 1993). Nevertheless, the combination is more efficient in the relative effect on acquisition of alphabetic understanding (e.g., Ball & Blachman, 1991; Byrne & Fielding-Barnsley, 1989).

Dimensions. Segmentation was the most common phonological awareness dimension investigated. However, segmentation interventions focused on different sizes of phonological units. For example, in three studies (Brady et al., 1994; Hatcher et al., 1994; Lundberg et al., 1988), the segmentation task was scaffolded by beginning with larger and more natural phonological units (e.g., compound words and syllables) and ending with the smallest and most difficult unit (i.e., phoneme). Whereas instruction in segmentation was combined with other dimensions in 21 studies, segmentation was the single focus in Ball and Blachman's (1991) study. Conclusions from lines of research that extend Fox and Routh's (1984) work suggest that a combination of concurrent blending and segmenting instruction will produce optimum benefit for further development of phonological awareness, alphabetic understanding, and reading acquisition (O'Connor et al., 1993; O'Connor et al., 1995; Slocum et al., 1993; Torgesen, Morgan, & Davis, 1992).

Three studies did not include segmentation, but rather focused on identifying common phonemes in words by position (Byrne & Fielding-Barnsley, 1989; Cary & Verhaeghe, 1994; Defior & Tudela, 1994). Based on a line of research investigating the acquisition of alphabetic understanding, Byrne and Fielding-Barnsley (1989, 1993a) concluded that the ability to identify common phonemes in words is more important than the ability to segment sounds in words as prerequisite to alphabetic understanding. They concluded that, whereas identifying common phonemes in words subsumes segmenting, segmenting does not subsume identifying common phonemes.

Dimensions of Linguistic Complexity. Common and consistent attention to the following linguistics dimensions has an explanatory function for consistent significant effects: word length, size of phonological unit, relative difficulty of phoneme position in words, and relative difficulty of phonological properties of words (all studies).

Our reasons for highlighting linguistic complexity are fourfold. First, attention to linguistic complexity or difficulty is derived from theory that poor quality of perception and coding explain a large portion of differences in learning to read. Second, when instruction is scaffolded (e.g., gradational and intentional adjustment of task difficulty) by increasing the complexity of sound, the problematic aspect of reading (i.e., phonological features of language) is mediated. Thus, scaffolding linguistic complexity appears to meet specific needs of diverse learners. Last, significant effects of phonological awareness instruction on phonological development, reading, or spelling were found in all studies, implying that controlling linguistic complexity is helpful for all learners.

Throughout this chapter our discussion has focused on the smallest phonological unit, phonemes, for three reasons. First, our review indicated that the phoneme level bears a critical relation to beginning reading (Lyon, 1995; Wagner, 1988). Second, research indicated that the processes at the phoneme level did not develop naturally or easily without instruction (Bowey, 1994; Liberman & Shankweiler, 1985; Stanovich, 1994). Third, the relation between phonological processing characteristics of diverse learners and characteristics of the phoneme level is problematic (Cornwall, 1992; Rack et al., 1992; Spector, 1995; Stahl & Murray, 1994; Torgesen, 1985; Vellutino & Scanlon, 1987a, 1987b). In short, phonemes are difficult to perceive because they are the smallest phonological unit, not acoustically pure, and have no meaning in isolation.

Word length was a function of size of phonological unit. When instruction focused on the phoneme size of phonological units, usually words were restricted to one to three phonemes. Requiring attention to one to three phonemes is obviously less complex than requiring attention to longer strings of phonemes, as in longer words. Our summary of *size of phonological units* indicates that nearly all studies utilized the phoneme level and roughly 90% focused on the phoneme level and measured for effects on reading and spelling. Furthermore, onset-rime instruction usually focused on the initial phoneme (Byrne & Fielding-Barnsley, 1989; O'Connor et al., 1993). Comparisons of significant effects from instruction at the phoneme level, particularly when combined with instruction in letter-sound correspondences for each phoneme to nonsignificant effects for control groups, add support to the developmental literature, indicating that phonemic awareness does not develop naturally (Liberman & Shankweiler, 1985). Nevertheless, the effects of teaching at the phoneme level compared to teaching at larger levels or teaching in a specific developmental sequence remain largely undocumented. Although nearly all studies made reference to the critical importance of instruction at the phoneme level, only one study, Cary and Verhaeghe (1994) controlled for differences between size to examine differential effectiveness.

Relative *difficulty of phoneme position in words* was acknowledged in nine studies, such as Ball and Blachman (1991), Byrne and Fielding-Barnsley (1989), Cunningham (1990), Defior and Tudela, 1994; Lie (1991), Lundberg et al. (1988), and O'Connor et al. (1995). Initial position was taught first and significant attention to the *phonological properties* of words was an integral component in more than half the interventions. For example, continuous sounds were introduced before stop sounds because stop sounds are more difficult to elongate and, therefore, more difficult to isolate for detection and manipulation. Specifically, Ball and Blachman (1991) indicated that stop sounds in initial position (e.g., tap) were introduced last because of articulatory distortion that occurs in segmenting. For example, /t/ becomes attached to the vowel /a/ or to the /u/ sound because of the difficulty in only voicing the /t/. Similarly, Lie (1991) introduced consonant clusters toward the end of the intervention because consonant clusters are more difficult than continuants (e.g., /f/ in fish can become ffffish in contrast to /st/ in star which is impossible to elongate and difficult to isolate).

Phonological Awareness and Reading Instruction. Five studies documented the benefit of combining a metacognitive component (i.e., direct teaching of application of phonological awareness skills in context of reading) with phonological awareness instruction for students across ability (Castle et al., 1994; Cunningham, 1990; Hatcher et al., 1994; Iverson & Tunmer, 1993; Lovett et al., 1994). For example, Lovett and colleagues (1994) concluded that an optimum program for students with severe reading disabilities would combine both a skill and drill and a strategy approach based on differentially significant effects on reading for both approaches. The only exception was Weiner's study (1994) that found that low readers did better with phonological awareness instruction at a skill and drill level in contrast to an application level.

Components With Limited Evidence

The following independent variables effected significant improvement in only one or two studies. Even though these variables resulted in significant effects, they require replication to obtain convergence:

1. Cary and Verhaeghe (1994) compared the differential effectiveness of size of phonological units. They found progress in phonemic segmentation ability and transfer from one size of phonological unit to another size only for instruction at the phoneme level in contrast to instruction at the syllable or rime levels.
2. Teaching phonemic detection as the phonemes appear in words (i.e., sequential instruction in phonemic awareness) was more effective than instruction in phoneme position (initial, medial, final). In addition, an articulation component (i.e., attention was drawn to sound production) was part of both types of instruction (Lie, 1991).
3. Two studies taught a broad array of phonological awareness skills (e.g., rhyme, detection, and segmenting; Lundberg et al., 1988; O'Connor et al., 1993).
4. One study compared teaching a broad array of phonological awareness skills to segmenting and blending only and found comparable effects with both types of instruction (O'Connor et al., 1995).
5. Computer-aided instruction (CAI; Foster et al., 1994; Torgesen & Barker, 1995) may provide sufficient intensity of phonological awareness instruction for students low in phonological awareness.

Interaction of Instructional Variables and Learner Characteristics

The intervention studies in this review converged to provide strong support for phonological awareness instruction prior to reading instruction across abilities. In particular, three recommendations were made for the best time for teaching phonological awareness to specific ability groups, the length of treatment, and the intensity of treatment:

1. Instruct in phonological awareness before formal reading instruction for children with disabilities or phonological awareness delays (Blachman, 1994; O'Connor et al., 1993; O'Connor et al., 1995; Torgesen & Davis, 1996; Torgesen et al., 1994).

2. Begin phonological awareness instruction early in first grade or kindergarten for children with lower academic ability or difficulty in learning to read (Blachman, 1994; Hatcher et al., 1994; Iverson & Tumner, 1994; Lie, 1991).
3. Combine phonological awareness with reading instruction for older readers with reading disabilities. Directly intervene at the level of deficit, the phoneme (Lovett et al., 1994).

Thus, for diverse learners, strong effects across the studies underscored the critical nature of *when* diverse learners receive phonological awareness instruction. The effects add support to the third area of convergence, that phonological awareness has a causal relation to reading acquisition. Because phonological awareness has been established as one of the prerequisites for reading acquisition, the timing of phonological awareness instruction is obligatory, not optional.

Four studies provided three pieces of evidence relevant for diverse learners but without sufficient replication for convergence. First, Lie (1991) found that phonological awareness instruction improved the performance of diverse learners more than normally achieving students. In particular, in one study comparing effects by ability groups, effects were greater for diverse learners than for normal achievers; that is, diverse learners probably profited more from phonological awareness instruction (Lie, 1991).

Second, a study comparing diverse learners and normally achieving students found that phonological instruction significantly facilitated reading acquisition for both diverse learners and normally achieving children (Vellutino & Scanlon, 1987b). Third, a study with normal achievers indicated that a high degree of specificity may occur in initial learning. For example, /m/ may be detected in initial but not final positions (Byrne & Fielding-Barnsley, 1989), implying that if specificity occurs for normally achieving children it probably also applies to diverse learners. Last, positive effects for normally achieving students were found in all studies; phonological awareness instruction is efficient in that it is beneficial for all learners.

In addition, research with students with phonological processing or reading disabilities, in contrast to normally achieving students, calls for future research to identify optimum instructional variables and procedures. For example, multiple lines of research have indicated that reading disabilities are persistent (Blachman, 1994; Eden et al., 1995; Felton, 1993; Korhonen, 1995; Lovett et al., 1994; Stanovich, 1994; Torgesen et al., 1994). The persistence is particularly characteristic of children who may have multiple deficits such as phonological awareness, rapid naming, or orthographic processing deficits. Similarly, results from Torgesen and colleagues' work (1992, 1994, in press) indicated that not all children who need phonological awareness instruction are able to respond to that instruction sufficiently to make significant progress. Therefore, intervention research since 1993 has pointed to the following needs.

1. We need to investigate the benefits of long-term interventions across grades with more longitudinal research (Blachman, 1994; Felton, 1993).
2. We need to continue identifying what constitutes sufficiently intense and parsimonious instruction for those children who do not respond to instruction as presently designed in phonological awareness research (Torgesen et al., 1994).
3. The optimum integration of phonological awareness and reading instruction needs to be both identified and practiced (Felton, 1993; Lovett et al., 1994; Stanovich, 1994).
4. Continued investigation is needed on the capability of CAI to provide adequate individualized practice with immediate feedback for children needing more intense interventions (Lundberg, 1995; Foster et al., 1994; Torgesen & Barker, 1995). CAI may be more feasible than providing sufficient teacher-directed instruction for children with severe needs.

Summary

The presence of the following features in phonological awareness instruction appeared to produce the positive effects: letter-sound correspondence; instruction at the phoneme level of phonological units; segmenting and combination of segmenting with blending or phoneme identity; attention to linguistic complexity; and explicit instruction that includes oral production of isolated sounds.

The importance and potential feasibility of phonological awareness instruction in authentic settings are suggested by two factors: (a) phonological awareness instruction made a significant difference across ability; therefore, it is efficient; and (b) difference was achieved in roughly 85% of the studies in an average of 25 minutes of instruction three times a week for 11 weeks. The following conclusions supported the importance of applying phonological awareness to the sound–symbol system in two contexts. First, evidence documented the benefit of teaching letter-sound correspondences and applying phonological awareness skills in the letter-sound correspondence context. Second, an emerging line of research is indicating that adding phonological awareness to reading instruction by making explicit the application of phonological awareness to reading skills provides significant benefit to poor readers (Blachman, 1994; Hatcher et al., 1994; Iverson & Tumner, 1993).

Linguistic complexity, the instructional variable that received greatest differentiation and, therefore, multiple dimensions of attention, supports our thesis logically, theoretically, and empirically: A large portion of reading disabilities can be explained by difficulties in phonological processing, specifically, phonological awareness. The finding that difficulty in perceiving and manipulating sounds of our language not only explains a large number of reading problems but can be taught, and taught across abilities at a young age, has powerful implications for the possibility of reducing reading failure. Controlling linguistic difficulty with instructional design principles of strategies, scaffolding, and integration of sound and graphic features of words contributed to positive effects across studies. The evidence from our review of primary and secondary sources provides clear and astonishingly convergent evidence that phonological awareness can be taught and that attention to instructional variables makes a significant difference on ease of reading and spelling acquisition for all learners.

CONCLUSION

Our discussion is summarized in four sections: areas of convergence, relation between phonological awareness and reading, construct validity of phonological processing and awareness, and instructional implications. In this summary, we draw attention to degree of convergence, issues, and limitations of our review.

Areas of Convergence

Our review of the research affirmed the importance of phonological awareness for reading acquisition. Results indicated that deficits in processing the sounds of language explain a significant proportion of beginning reading problems and correlated problems with older readers. The most encouraging lines of research suggested that the phonological awareness deficit is amenable to instruction, with particular attention to instructional variables that result in significant improvement. Moreover, the gains in phonological awareness directly affect ease of reading and spelling acquisition and achievement. However, recent evidence is establishing that for some children, reading disabilities may be persistent and severe. For these children, the literature indicated need for long-term and intense interventions, coupled with long-term monitoring of progress (Lyon & Chhabra, 1996).

To summarize, six main areas of convergence establish the importance of the relation between phonological awareness and reading acquisition:

1. The phonological processing ability explains significant differences between good and poor readers.
2. Phonological awareness may be a group of highly related, independent phonological abilities or a general ability with multiple dimensions.
3. Phonological awareness has a reciprocal relation to reading acquisition.
4. Phonological awareness is necessary but not sufficient.
5. Phonological awareness deficits and delays can be reliably identified in young children.
6. Phonological awareness is teachable and promoted by attention to instructional variables.

Relation Between Phonological Awareness and Reading

Of the 100 sources reviewed, approximately 70% were primary studies that found significant relations between phonological awareness and reading. Roughly 50% of these primary studies included students with identified reading disabilities, and 50% of these studies involving students with reading disabilities were intervention studies. In the Spring of 1993, emphasis in phonological awareness intervention studies shifted from normally achieving students to students with reading disabilities. From Spring 1993 to 1996, the proportion of intervention studies involving students with reading disabilities increased from roughly one third of the intervention studies we reviewed in the 1986 through Winter, 1993 phase to two thirds. None of the studies disagreed with the hypothesis that phonological awareness plays a central role in the ease of reading acquisition. In considering the relation between phonological awareness and reading acquisition, we found strong support for the first and third areas of convergence:

1. Phonological processing appears to explain the greatest amount of variance between good and poor readers. (Phonological awareness is a component of phonological processing.)
3. Phonological awareness has a causal and a reciprocal relation to reading acquisition.

Issues surrounding the strength and direction of the relation between phonological awareness and reading continue to be investigated, with support for relations in both directions: Phonological awareness facilitates reading and is facilitated by reading instruction.

Our review was representative of the general area of phonological awareness. Therefore, we were limited in depth of articles for any one aspect of phonological awareness. In addition, our purpose was instructional rather than etiological. For example, because of our focus, we did not examine explanations of reading disability outside of phonological processing in depth and our depth mirrored awareness rather than processing literature. However, we reacknowledge that phonological deficits do not appear to explain all reading disabilities, only a great proportion.

Construct Validity of Phonological Processing and Awareness

Throughout the review, we raised questions about the degree of support for the second area of convergence:

> Phonological awareness may be a group of highly related, independent phonological abilities or a general ability with multiple dimensions.

The issues parallel similar issues about the larger construct of phonological processing. The questions are construct validity questions. For example, we found the following two questions continue to be examined: Does rhyme belong to the same construct as more difficult dimensions (e.g., segmentation); and are segmentation and blending independent skills? Whereas our review found emerging evidence that segmentation and blending may be independent skills, our review did not include research examining the place of rhyme in the construct. In addition, we found consistent convergence about strength of relations among the dimensions. Therefore, we acknowledge that our use of "unitary construct" and "dimensions" may receive other interpretations. Consequently, we note that our review does not provide conclusive evidence for either general ability or a group of highly related, independent abilities description of the construct.

The scope of our review did not provide an in-depth examination of any one dimension of phonological awareness. In addition, we draw attention to the need for future research with each phonological awareness dimension, relations among dimensions, and relations among dimensions and aspects of reading across age groups reiterated by several of the researchers. Recent research has begun to examine these very issues. Similarly, interrelations among the components of phonological processing (i.e., phonological awareness, coding in short-term, and retrieval from long-term memory) are examined in more recent studies. In our discussion, we struggled to separate the examination of phonological awareness from phonological processing. The research trend implies the reason for our struggle: Although phonological awareness deficits explain a large proportion of reading disabilities, all the components of phonological processing, including awareness, are significantly interrelated and their interrelation is significantly related to reading (Ackerman & Dykman, 1993; Felton, 1993; Torgesen et al., 1994). Moreover, evidence from recent correlational research is establishing the critical importance of rapid-naming deficits in many children with persistent reading disabilities.

Instructional Implications

We found consistent support in a growing body of research for the fourth, fifth, and sixth areas of convergence:

4. Phonological awareness is necessary but not sufficient for reading acquisition.
5. Phonological awareness deficits and delays are easily and reliably identified in young children.
6. Phonological awareness is teachable and promoted by attention to instructional variables.

We would like to emphasize that potential reading disability can be identified in young children and that diverse learners profit from phonological awareness instruction. In particular, researchers recommend that phonological awareness assessment be part of testing batteries for prereaders and that phonological awareness instruction be part of preschool and kindergarten curriculum. Moreover, it is important to test again at either the end of kindergarten or the beginning of first grade to assess whether children have had sufficient phonological awareness and letter-sound correspondence instruction to gain alphabetic understanding.

Finally, one important variable seemed to distinguish the studies in our review. Phonological awareness was taught. It was not left to develop in the absence of explicit instruction. We also discussed the increased effects on subsequent reading achievement gained by combining phonological awareness instruction with instruction in letter-sound correspondences and explicit teaching. The simple lesson is that instruction that makes explicit the connections between letters and sounds and the segmental nature of language produces significant effects on subsequent reading and spelling achievement across reader ability and age. We acknowledge that although our representative review was limited to eight studies with beginning readers and one with older readers, there appears to be emerging interest in including phonological awareness in remedial reading programs.

Even though recent research found phonological ability to be more closely related to general intelligence than found in earlier studies (Torgesen et al., 1994), it is appropriate to emphasize the consistency of improvement in reading and spelling acquisition across learners, particularly diverse learners. Similarly, even though the same research indicated that not all diverse learners achieve the significant gains reported for some groups (Torgesen et al., 1994), it is more appropriate to consider how design of instruction can be intensified for children who did not respond or benefit. We draw attention to synonymous use of intense and explicit by Torgesen et al. (1994) and the consistent recommendation for explicit instruction by the research reviewed. The available research produced emerging, yet inconclusive evidence of the optimal design of instruction across: age and ability groups, combinations of instructional variables, and scope and sequence of instruction.

Phonological awareness research is characterized by diverse studies from various disciplines, with multiple perspectives, and by solid convergence. That is, we know much about what causes a large proportion of reading disabilities, and we know how to identify students at-risk for, and those with reading disabilities. We are accumulating elements of instructional design that produce consistent and robust positive effects across ability. The result—we know much about how to prevent and ameliorate reading failure.

TABLE 4.1

Secondary and Primary Sources for the Synthesis of the Research on Phonological Awareness (PA) and Its Relation to Reading Acquisition

Secondary Sources

Author(s)	PA Dimension	Participant Characteristics	Purpose
Adams (1990)	All dimensions	Preschool-adult, all levels of ability	Synthesize reading research, specifically acquisition and disabilities.
Barinaga (1996)	Not PA. basic temporal processing	Language-learning impairments, grade-school	Discuss Tallal et al.'s (1996) training program with computer games to improve brain's response to fast-paced stimuli, such as stop consonants.
Blachman (1994)	General PA	Kindergarten through grade school	Respond to Torgesen et al.'s (1994) longitudinal study. Discuss stability of phonological processing deficits, training, variables that influence response to training.
Byrne & Fielding-Barnsley (1993a)	Phoneme identity	Normal achievement, preschool and end of first grade, $N = 119$	Evaluate training program in phoneme identity vs. control effects on PA, alphabetic understanding, decoding, spelling.
Felton (1993)	Rhyming, segmenting at syllable and phoneme levels, phoneme identity, manipulating sounds in sequence (LAC)	At-risk for reading problems in low PA and/or naming, kindergarten, $N = 81$	Evaluate differential effects of code-based, context-based, or control reading methods during Grades 1 and 2 on children with deficits in PA and/or naming with varying degrees of severity
Felton & Pepper (1995)	General		Review prediction/identification literature and make recommendations for interventions.
van Iizendoorn & Bus (1994)	General	All ages and ability.	Discuss results of a meta-analysis that examines support for core deficit theory.

Lenchner et al. (1990)	Rhyme, segmentation, all dimensions	Children–adults, normal development, reading disability	Examine phonological development and ability differences related to reading acquisition.
Liberman & Shankweiler (1985)	General	All ages and ability	Discuss research relating PA and learning to read and write successfully. Discuss phonological core deficit.
Lundberg (1995)	Phoneme segmentation	Dyslexia, grade-school	Provide guidelines for remediating dyslexia with computer-aided instruction that provides synthesized speech feedback. Discuss effects of quasi-experiments with CAI on reading and spelling.
Lyon (1995)	General and phoneme level	Reading disabilities	Report on current stage of reading disabilities research.
Lyon & Chhabra (1996)	General	Reading disabilities	Review critical advances in reading disabilities including etiologies, identification, developmental course, intervention. Propose new definition of dyslexia. Outline future research.
Mann & Brady (1988)	Phoneme level, rhyme, phonemic manipulation	Reading disabilities, all ages	Summarize role of language deficiencies in reading disability.
Rack et al. (1992)	General PA and segmentation	Reading disabilities, dyslexia, normal achievement, 7–14 years old	Review literature that examines what aspects of word recognition are problematic for readers with dyslexia.
Snider (1995)	All dimensions	Children	Summarize PA research including importance of PA, and instructional implication.
Snowling (1991)	Rhyme, segmentation, at onset-time and phoneme levels	Normal achievement, low performance, reading disabilities, language delays, illiterate, adults, families	Discuss cause of reading disability. Develop instructional implications.

(Continued)

TABLE 4.1
CONTINUED

Spector (1995)	General	Preschool-beginning reading	Summarize PA interventions and make recommendations for instruction.
Stanovich (1985)	General	Learning disabilities, remedial reading, normal achievement, children-adults	Summarize research convergence on causes of reading failure.
Stanovich (1986)	General, phoneme level	Reading disabilities, and poor reading ability	Discuss relation between reading and cognitive processes, what individual differences contribute to cascading reading problems.
Stanovich (1988a)	Rhyme, oddity	Beginning reading ability through Grade 7 skilled reading ability, reading disabilities, low performance	Discuss development of phonological core deficit model for reading disabilities.
Stanovich (1988b)	General	Good and poor reading ability	Discuss causal cognitive mechanisms underlying differences in learning to read. Discuss implications of reading failure on academic achievement and cognitive development.
Stanovich (1994)	General	At risk for reading disabilities, children.	Discuss constructivism and skill-based reading instruction in context of goals of instruction, needs of at-risk learners, research findings.
Swank (1994)	General	Good and poor reading ability	Explain theoretical construct of specific phonological coding ability.
Torgesen (1985)		Reading disabilities	Discuss causal relation between memory processes and specific reading disability.
Torgesen et al. (1990)	Phonological processing	Reading disabilities, young children	Discuss examination of assessment and diagnosis of phonological coding problems.

Study	Skill	Population	Description
Torgesen et al. (1994)	Blending, segmenting	Cohort of children from kindergarten age through Grade 2, $N = 244$	Discuss examination of PA skills before and after reading instruction, whether PA is a single skill or multiple skills, whether structure of PA changes as result of reading instruction and age.
Torgesen & Barker (1995)	General	Learning disabilities	Discuss CAI and practice as part of instructional model for children with learning disabilities.
Torgesen & Hecht (1996)	Phonological processing and awareness	Children at risk of reading disabilities	Discuss instructional variables that may be critical for children at risk of reading disabilities. Discuss intervention research.
Vellutino (1991)	General		Discuss convergent findings of code- vs. meaning-based beginning reading instruction.
Vellutino & Scanlon (1987a)	General, segmentation	Normal achievement, reading disabilities, Grades 2 and 6	Examine evidence for linguistic coding basis to reading disabilities.
Wagner (1986)	General, segmenting and blending	Reading disabilities	Review literature examining the causal relation between phonological processing and reading, training implication, and the components of phonological processing.
Wagner (1988)	Blending and segmenting	Beginning reading ability	Discuss a meta-analysis of literature examining the causal relations between phonological processing and reading acquisition.
Wagner & Torgesen (1987)	General	Young children	Discuss components of phonological processing and causal role in reading acquisition.

(Continued)

113

TABLE 4.1
CONTINUED

Primary Sources

Author	Dimension of PA	Participant Characteristics	Purpose
Ackerman & Dykman (1993)	Alliteration and rhyme oddity tasks	ADD and/or developmental reading disorder, low reading ability, ages 7–12, $N = 119$	Test multiple causation model of reading disabilities. Examine discriminatory and predictor variables.
Adams & Gathercole (1995)	No PA. phonological working memory	High and low phonological working memory, 3 yrs. old, $N = 38$	Investigate whether phonological working memory is related to spoken language development.
Badian (1993b)	Deletion at syllable and phoneme levels	Poor reading ability, ages 6–8 tested again 1–2 years later, $N = 86$	Examine whether performance on reading-related cognitive processes predicts reading progress in poor readers. Processes included orthographic, phonological rapid-naming.
Badian (1993a)	Deletion	Normal achievement, ages 6–10, $N = 170$	Examine effectiveness and reliability of PA, naming, and visual processing predictors to differentiate good and poor readers.
Badian (1994b)	Syllable tapping	All kindergarten children in a small district. Tested at kindergarten age, at fall of Grade 1, 1st spring of Grade 1, $N = 118$	Evaluate a screening battery, specifically PA, rapid serial naming, orthographic processing, Identify best predictors.
Badian (1994a)	Deletion at syllable and phoneme levels	Good, dyslexic, and readers, garden-variety poor reading ability, ages 6–10, $N = 110$	Examine whether there are cognitive differences that discriminate between reading ability groups.

Study	Task	Sample	Purpose
Ball & Blachman (1991)	Phoneme segmentation	Normal achievement, kindergarten age, $N = 151$	Examine effect of segmentation instruction on reading and spelling. Examine effect of segmentation + letter-sound instruction on reading and spelling.
Berninger et al. (1994)	Phoneme segmentation, phoneme identity, phoneme articulation	Grades 4, 5, 6 $N = 300$	Investigate relations among fine motor, orthographic, phonological, working memory, verbal intelligence, reading, and writing systems.
Blachman et al. (1994)	Phoneme segmentation	Normal achievement, low-income, inner-city public schools, kindergarten age, $N = 159$	Provide evaluation of phonological awareness interventions taught in the regular classrooms by the regular classroom teachers vs. control.
Bowers (1993)	Phoneme deletion	Average and poor reading ability, followed same children from Grade 2 to Grade 4, $N = 37$	Examine factors that determine fluency, specifically phoneme deletion and rapid digit naming.
Bowey (1994)	Rime oddity, onset oddity, phoneme oddity, phoneme identity	Normal achievement, age 5, $N = 96$	Examine notion that reading instruction promotes phonemic sensitivity by separating children into nonreader and novice reader groups and testing PA and AU, and digit span.
Brady et al. (1994)	Rhyme, segmentation, and categorization above the level of the phoneme; identity and segmentation at phoneme level	Normal achievement, in inner-city public schools, intact classes, kindergarten age, $N = 96$	Evaluate research-based instruction in regular classroom vs. control. Explore cognitive and linguistic learner characteristics that affect response to instruction. Explore effect of phonological awareness instruction of phonological processes.
Byrne & Fielding-Barnsley (1989)	Identity of initial phoneme, segmentation	Preliterate, ages 3–5 five experiments with, $N = 11–30$	Explore what conditions lead to alphabetic understanding.
Byrne & Fielding-Barnsley (1993b)	Phoneme identity	Normal achievement kindergarten age, $N = 27$	Investigate the possible confound of global similarity in test items and implications for identification of at risk.

(Continued)

TABLE 4.1
CONTINUED

Study	Task	Sample	Purpose
Carlisle & Nomanbhoy (1993)	Deletion at syllable and phoneme level	Multiple levels of ability, Grade 1, $N = 115$	Examine the relations among PA, morphological awareness, vocabulary, and word-reading.
Cary & Verhaeghe (1994)	Rhyme and segmentation at syllable, and phoneme levels	Preliterate, normal achievement, Portuguese-speaking kindergarten age, two experiments with, $N = 32, 47$	Compare phoneme vs. syllable level vs. control training effects.
Castle et al. (1994)	Phoneme segmentation, phoneme substitution, phoneme deletion, rhyme	Low phonological awareness, kindergarten age, two experiments with, $N = 30, 51$	Compare phonological awareness within whole language vs. whole language training effects on reading and spelling acquisition.
Catts (1993)	Blending, deletion	Normal achievement, speech-language-impairments, kindergarten–Grade 2, $N = 86$	Investigate predictors for children with speech-language impairments and relation between impairments and reading disabilities.
Cornwell (1992)	Phoneme deletion and blending	Learning disabled/severe reading disabilities, ages 7.5 to 12.3, $N = 54$	Explore relation of PA, naming speed, verbal memory on word attack identification, comprehension, and spelling to find predictors of achievement.
Cunningham (1990)	Phoneme segmentation and blending	Normal achievement kindergarten age, $N = 48$	Examine the effect of PA instruction on kindergarten and Grade 1 reading and meta-level instruction along with PA on Grade 1 reading.
Cunningham & Stanovich (1993)	Phoneme deletion, phoneme transposition	Normal achievement Grade 1, $N = 26$	Examine whether exposure to print as measured by home literacy environment is differentially related to PA, orthographic processing, and word recognition.
Das et al. (1994)	Phoneme segmentation	Normal IQ and normal reading ability; average IQ and dyslexia, high IQ and dyslexia, 9–11 yrs. old	Test hypothesis that children with dyslexia, identified by word decoding deficit, will be poor in successive processing and rapid articulation irrespective of IQ.

Davidson & Jenkins (1994)	Phoneme segmentation, phoneme blending	Preliterate, low phonological awareness, kindergarten, $N = 40$	Compare blending vs. segmenting vs. blending and segmenting vs. control on phonological awareness development and beginning reading and spelling training effects.
Defior & Tudela (1994)	Sound categorization by position	Normal achievement, 6 yr. old, Spanish, $N = 60$	Compare sound categorization vs. conceptual categorization vs. control training effects on reading and writing performance.
Eden et al. (1995)	Segmenting at syllable and phoneme level, "Pig Latin" task, addition, deletion, substitution, shift	Normal achievement, poor reading ability, reading disabilities, average age 11, $N = 93$	Compare children with and without reading disabilities on measures of phonological and visuospatial abilities.
Fawcett & Nicolson (1994)	No PA, rapid naming	Normal achievement, slow learning ability and dyslexia, ages 8–17, $N = 77$	Administer range of rapid-naming tests to range of ability learners. Examine if results provide theoretical basis of use of processing speed tests in development of diagnostic battery for persons with dyslexia aged 8 through adulthood.
Fletcher et al. (1994)	Phoneme deletion	LD ($SD = 1.5$ between achievement and IQ), low achievement in reading, ages 7.5–9.5, $N = 199$	Examine the validity of discrepancy and low-achievement definitions.
Foster et al. (1994)	Segmentation blending phoneme identity	Low phonological awareness, first-semester kindergarten, $N = 27$. Normal achievement second-semester kindergarten, $N = 69$	Compare and test two versions of a computer-aided phonological awareness programs vs. no training effects.
Hatcher et al. (1994)	Rhyme; segmentation; identity at word within sentence, syllable, and phoneme levels; blending; omission; substitution; transposition	Low reading ability, third year, 6 and 7 yr. old, British, $N = 124$	Compare and test reading with phonological awareness instruction vs. reading alone vs. phonological awareness alone vs. control training effects on phonological awareness and reading.

(Continued)

117

TABLE 4.1
CONTINUED

Hurford et al. (1993)	Phoneme discrimination and segmentation	Normal achievement, $N = 187$ Low achievement, $N = 10$ Learning disabilities, $N = 12$ Grade 1	Examine PA development by group ability. Examine predictability of ability group membership by reading, IQ, and PA.
Hurford, Johnstone, et al. (1994)	Phoneme discrimination, phoneme segmentation	Normal achievement, low achievement, and reading disabilities, Grade 1, $N = 486$	Evaluate a screening tool and effects of training.
Hurford, Schauf, et al. (1994)	Phoneme discrimination, phoneme segmentation	All levels of ability, Grades 1–3, $N = 171$	Examine development of PA and reading skills, prediction, comparison of ability groups, and assessment of reliability of ability classification.
Hurford et al. (1993)	Phoneme discrimination	Normal achievement and reading disabilities, Grades 2, 3, 4; $N = 64$, Exp. 2 only second graders, $N = 10$	Investigate relation between discrimination and memory in children with reading disabilities.
Iverson & Tunmer (1993)	Phoneme segmentation, phoneme deletion	Poor reading ability, Grade 1, $N = 96$	Determine if Reading Recovery with systematic instruction in PA and link to letters would be more effective than regular Reading Recovery.
Korhonen (1995)	No PA, rapid serial naming	Reading and rapid serial naming disabilities, from ages 9–18, Finnish, $N = 9$	Assess persistence of reading, spelling, and rapid serial naming deficits from childhood to adulthood.
Leather & Henry (1994)	Deletion, blending, phoneme tapping	Grade 2, $N = 71$	Examine relations among complex memory span, simple memory span, phonological awareness, and beginning reading.
Lenchner et al. (190)	Phonemic segmentation, blending, and manipulation	Male, normal achievement and reading disabilities, Grade 4, $N = 38$	Examine relation among measures of PA and phonetic decoding with older students.

Study	PA task	Sample	Purpose
Lie (1991)	Segmentation	Total first graders, $N = 208$ Subgroups High intelligence, $N = 18$ Normal intelligence, $N = 18$ Low intelligence, $N = 18$ Norwegian	Examine effects of Grade 1 PA-instruction on Grade 1 reading and spelling, Grade 2 reading and spelling? Compare positional vs. sequential segmentation instruction. Examine effects per ability groups.
Lovett et al. (1994)	Blending and segmenting at phoneme level	Reading disabilities, mean age of 9.6 yrs., $N = 62$	Examine whether children with severe reading disability can acquire and apply systematic spelling-sound knowledge and demonstrate transfer of learning. Compare direct instruction PA and reading to word-identification strategies method.
Lundberg et al. (1988)	Rhyme, segmentation of all phonological units, initial phoneme identification	Normal achievement, kindergarten, Danish, $N = 390$	Examine whether PA be taught before reading instruction, what is learned during PA instruction, maintenance of effects, effect on reading and spelling, and specificity of effects.
Majsterek & Ellenwood (1995)	Blending, rhyme detection	Normal achievement preschool, kindergarten–Grade 2, $N = 76$	Evaluate a school-based screening procedure.
Mann (1993)	Phoneme segmentation	Normal achievement, kindergarten, $N = 100$	Examine relation between PA and future reading ability.
Manis et al. (1993)	Phoneme deletion	Dyslexia, ages 9-15, $N = 21$	Examine development of word recognition and spelling. Examine relations among phonological, orthographic, reading, and spelling skills. Identify primary deficit.
Mauer & Kamhi (1996)	Sound categorization, deletion	Normal achievement matched on mental and reading age, reading disabilities, $N = 40$	Examine the effect of phonological, short-term memory, rapid-naming, and visual effects on learning phoneme–grapheme correspondences by ability group.

(Continued)

TABLE 4.1
CONTINUED

McBride-Chang (1995)	Segmentation, deletion, phoneme identity by position	Normal achievement Grades 3 an 4, $N = 136$	Examine components of PA construct. Examine item difficulty factors.
McCutchen & Crain-Thorson (1994)	Alliteration in reading sentences, digit span	Skilled and less skilled reading ability, Grades 2 and 4, $N = 56$	Examine link between phonemic processes and comprehension via tongue-twister effect and short-term memory.
McDougall et al. (1994)	Rhyme discrimination, phoneme deletion	Good, average, poor reading ability, ages 7.6–9.6, $N = 69$	Examine relations among reading, short-term memory, and phonological skills. Investigate relation between short-term memory and ability.
McGuinness et al. (1995)	Segmenting, blending, addition, substitution, shifting, deletion of syllables and phonemes	Experiment 1: Wide range of ability, ages 5.11–7.9, $N = 95$ Experiment 2: Whole class, 5.11–7.9, $N = 45$	Develop and evaluate a predicative reading battery. Compare ADD reading method to a whole language method.
Naglieri & Reardon (1993)	No PA. short-term memory tasks.	Normal achievement and reading disabilities, ages 7.7–15.3, $N = 60$	Examine the relation between reading disabilities and the cognitive processes of planning, simultaneous, and successive processing.
O'Connor et al. (1993)	Rhyme, blend, segment	Developmental delays, ages 4, 5, 6; $N = 47$	Investigate benefits of teaching PA to children with developmental delays. Examine degree of generalization within tasks and across tasks.
O'Connor et al. (1995)	Segmentation and blending, broad array of PA skills	Low phonological skills, $N = 66$ Comparison group of high skilled nonreaders, $N = 25$	Examine intervention benefits for low-skilled with blending and segmenting w/letter-sounds vs. broad array of PA skills w/letter-sound vs. letter-sound instruction only. Examine transfer to reading and spelling.
Rack et al. (1994)	Phoneme identity	Poor decoders, age 5, $N = 18, 24, 15$	Examination of the direct-mapping hypothesis of reading acquisition.

Study	PA Tasks	Sample	Purpose
Seymour & Evans (1994)	Rhyme production, blending, segmenting, alliteration production by size of unit	Preschool, Grades 1 and 2, $N = 80$	Examine relation between levels of phonological unit per task (i.e., size) and learning to read. Examine development of PA and theories of PA as per level or size of unit.
Slocum et al. (1993)	Onset-rime blending, onset-rime segmentation, word manipulations	Less developed language skills, Head Start, $N = 35$	Examine effect of training in one task on transfer to learning a second task. Examine effect of training on generalization within task.
Stahl & Murray (1994)	Blending, segmentation, phoneme isolation, deletion at onset rime, cluster, and phoneme levels	Normal achievement, kindergarten and Grade 1, $N = 113$	Extend Yopp's work (1988). Separate task difficulty from linguistic complexity. Correlate PA measures with literacy measures.
Swank & Catts (1994)	Deletion, blending, segmenting, categorization	Normal achievement, Grade 1, $N = 54$	Assess effectiveness and reliability of four PA tasks as predictors of reading achievement.
Swanson & Ramalgia (1992)	Phoneme matching, rhyme	Normal reading achievement, reading disabilities, ages 8.83–13.75, $N = 59$	Compare reliance on phonological information in memory and spelling by ability group. Examine relation between phonological information and spelling.
Torgesen & Davis (1996)	Blending, segmenting, phoneme identity	Primarily low SES and racial minority, kindergarten, $N = 100$	Analyze individual differences in response to instruction. Identify predictors.
Torgesen et al. (1992)	Rhyme, blending, segmenting, phoneme identity	Middle to low phonological awareness, kindergarten, $N = 143$	Compare training in blending and segmenting to training in blending only. Extend Fox and Routh's work.
Treiman et al. (1994)	Phonemes	Kindergarten, Grades 1 and 2, $N = 61$	Examine effects of letter-name (phonemes in the names) on learning letter-sound correspondences and interaction with age or experience to print.
Truch (1994)	Segmenting, blending, addition, deletion, substitution, shifting at syllable and phoneme levels	Reading disabilities, ages 6–adult, $N = 281$	Analyze pre-post data after 80+ hours of training with the Auditory Discrimination in Depth Program (ADD) on PA, letter-sound correspondences, word identification, spelling, decoding in context.

(Continued)

TABLE 4.1
CONTINUED

Vandervelden & Siegel (1995)	Phoneme identity, phoneme location, sequential segmentation, deletion, and substitution	Normal achievement, ages 5–8, N = 120	Examine development and role of decoding pseudowords and PA in early literacy. In Experiment 2, examine changing interrelations among PA tasks and task difficulty during development of PA and decoding.
Vellutino & Scanlon (1987b)	Phoneme segmentation	Total Grades 2 and 6, N = 300, Subgroup High-skilled, N = 75, Low-skilled, N = 75	Examine evidence to support causal relation between phonological deficit and reading disabilities.
Vellutino et al. (1995)	No PA, rapid naming of objects, colors, letters	Poor and normal reading ability, Grades 2 and 6, N = 60	Investigate whether semantic deficits cause or are a consequence of reading disability. Investigate the relation between rapid naming, semantic deficits, and reading disabilities.
Wagner et al. (1993)	Segmentation, deletion, sound isolation, categorization, blending	Normal achievement, kindergarten and Grade 2, N = 184	Compare alternative models of phonological processing.
Wagner et al. (1994)	Phoneme deletion, sound categorization, first sound comparison, phoneme segmentation, blending at phoneme and onset-rime levels	Randomly sampled, kindergarten, N = 244	Discuss results of a longitudinal correlational study from kindergarten–Grade 2, development of reading-related phonological processing abilities and causal directions of latent variables.
Weiner (1994)	Blending, segmenting, deleting, substituting at phoneme level	Middle and low reading achievement, Grade 1, N = 79	Compare PA skill training vs. PA + decoding vs. PA = decoding + reading vs. control training effects on PA, standardized and informal tests of reading by ability group.
Yopp (1988)	All dimensions	Normal achievement, kindergarten, N = 96	Determine reliability, validity, and relative difficulty of PA tests.

REFERENCES

Ackerman, P. T., & Dykman, R. A. (1993). Phonological processing, confrontational naming, and immediate memory in dyslexia. *Journal of Learning Disabilities, 26,* 597–609.

Adams, M. (1990). *Beginning to read: Thinking and learning about print.* Cambridge, MA: MIT Press.

Adams, A.-M., & Gathercole, S. E. (1995). Phonological working memory and speech production in preschool children. *Journal of Speech and Hearing Research, 38,* 403–414.

Badian, N. A. (1993a). Phonemic awareness, naming, visual symbol processing, and reading. *Reading and Writing: An Interdisciplinary Journal, 5,* 87–100.

Badian, N. A. (1993b). Predicting reading progress in children receiving help. *Annals of Dyslexia, 43,* 90–109.

Badian, N. A. (1994a). Do dyslexic and other poor readers differ in reading-related cognitive skills? *Reading and Writing: An Interdisciplinary Journal, 6,* 45–63.

Badian, N. A. (1994b). Preschool predictions: Orthographic and phonological skills, and reading. *Annals of Dyslexia, 44,* 3–25.

Ball, E. W., & Blachman, B. A. (1991). Does phoneme awareness training in kindergarten make a difference in early word recognition and developmental spelling? *Reading Research Quarterly, 24*(1), 49–66.

Barinaga, M. (1996). Giving language skills a boost. *Science, 271,* 27–28.

Berninger, V. W., Cartwright, A. C., Yates, C. M., Swanson, H. L., & Abbott, R. D. (1994). Developmental skills related to writing and reading acquisition in the intermediate grades. *Reading and Writing: An Interdisciplinary Journal, 6,* 161–196.

Blachman, B. A. (1994). What we have learned from longitudinal studies of phonological processing and reading, and some answered questions: A response to Torgesen, Wagner, & Rashotte. *Journal of Learning Disabilities, 27,* 287–291.

Blachman, B. A., Ball, E. W., Black, R. S., & Tangel, D. M. (1994). Kindergarten teachers develop phoneme awareness in low-income, inner-city classrooms. *Reading and Writing: An Interdisciplinary Journal, 6,* 1–18.

Bowers, P. G. (1993). Text reading and rereading: Determinants of fluency beyond word recognition. *Journal of Reading Behavior, 25,* 133–153.

Bowers, P. G., & Wolf, M. (1993). Theoretical links among naming speed, precise timing mechanisms and orthographic skill in dyslexia. *Reading and Writing: An Interdisciplinary Journal, 5,* 69–85.

Bowey, J. A. (1994). Phonological sensitivity in novice readers and nonreaders. *Journal Experimental Child Psychology, 58,* 134–159.

Brady, S., Fowler, A., Stone, B., & Winbury, N. (1994). Training phonological awareness: A study with inner-city kindergarten children. *Annals of Dyslexia, 44,* 26–51.

Byrne, B., & Fielding-Barnsley, R. (1989). Phonemic awareness and letter knowledge in the child's acquisition of the alphabetic principle. *Journal of Educational Psychology, 81,* 313–321.

Byrne, B., & Fielding-Barnsley, R. (1993) Evaluation of a program to teach phonemic awareness to young children: A 1-year follow-up. *Journal of Educational Psychology, 85,* 104–111.

Byrne, B., & Fielding-Barnsley, R. (1993). Recognition of phoneme invariance by beginning readers. *Reading and Writing: An Interdisciplinary Journal, 5,* 315–324.

Carlisle, J. F., & Nomanbhoy, D. M. (1993). Phonological and morphological awareness in first graders. *Applied Psycholinguistics, 14,* 177–195.

Cary, L., & Verhaeghe, A. (1994). Promoting phonemic analysis ability among kindergartners. *Reading and Writing, 6,* 251–278.

Castle, J. M., Riach, R., & Nicholson, T. (1994). Getting to a better start in reading and spelling: The effects of phonemic awareness instruction within a whole language program. *Journal of Educational Psychology, 86,* 350–359.

Catts, H. W. (1993). The relationship between speech-language impairments and reading disabilities. *Journal of Speech and Hearing Research, 36,* 948–958.

Cornwall, A. (1992). The relationship of phonological awareness, rapid naming and verbal memory to severe reading and spelling disability. *Journal of Learning Disabilities, 25*(8), 532–538.

Cunningham, A. (1990). Explicit vs. implicit instruction in phonemic awareness. *Journal of Experimental Child Psychology, 50,* 429–444.

Cunningham, A. E., & Stanovich, K. E. (1993). Children's literacy environments and early word recognition subskills. *Reading and Writing: An Interdisciplinary Journal, 5,* 193–204.

Das, J. P., Mishra, R. K., & Kirby, J. R. (1994). Cognitive patterns of children with dyslexia: A comparison between groups of high and average nonverbal intelligence. *Journal of Learning Disabilities, 27,* 235–242, 253.

Davidson, M., & Jenkins, J. R. (1994). Effects of phonemic process on word reading and spelling. *Journal of Educational Research, 87,* 148–157.

Defior, S., & Tudela, P. (1994). Effect of phonological training on reading and writing acquisition. *Reading and Writing, 6,* 299–320.

Eden, G. F., Stein, J. F., Wood, M. H., & Wood, F. B. (1995). Verbal and visual problems in reading disability. *Journal of Learning Disabilities, 28,* 272–290.

Fawcett, A. J., & Nicolson, R. I. (1994). Naming speed in children with dyslexia. *Journal of Learning Disabilities, 27,* 641–646.

Felton, R. H. (1993). Effects of instruction on the decoding skills of children with phonological-processing problems. *Journal of Learning Disabilities, 26,* 583–589.

Felton, R. H., & Pepper, P. P. (1995). Early Identification and intervention of phonological deficits in kindergarten and early elementary children at risk for reading disability. *School Psychology Review, 24,* 405–414.

Fletcher, J. M., Shaywitz, S. E., Shankweiler, D. P. , Katz, L., Liberman, I. Y., Stuebing, K. K., Francis, D. J., Fowler, A. E., & Shaywitz, B. A. (1994). Cognitive profiles of reading disability: Comparisons of discrepancy and low achievement definitions. *Journal of Educational Psychology 86,* 6–23.

Foster, K. C., Erickson, G. C., Foster, D. F., Brinkman, D. & Torgesen, J. K. (1994). Computer assisted instruction in phonological awareness: Evaluation of the DaisyQuest program. *Journal of Research and Development in Education, 27,* 126–137.

Fox, B., & Routh, D. K. (1984). Phonemic analysis and synthesis as word attack skills: Revisited. *Journal of Educational Psychology, 76,* 1059–1064.

Hatcher, P. J., Hulme, C., & Ellis, A. W. (1994). Ameliorating early reading failure by integrating the teaching of reading and phonological skills: The phonological linkage hypothesis. *Child Development 65,* 41–57.

Hurford, D. P., Darrow, L. J., Edwards, T. L., Howerton, C. J., Mote, C. R., Schauf, J. D., & Coffey, P. (1993). An examination of phonemic processing abilities in children during their first-grade year. *Journal of Learning Disabilities, 26*(3), 167–177.

Hurford, D. P., Johnston, M., Nepote, P., Hampton, S., Moore, S., Neal, J., Mueller, A., McGeorge, K., Huff, L., Awad, A., Tatro, C., Juliano, C., & Huffman, D. (1994). Early identification and remediation of phonological-processing deficits in first-grade children at risk for reading disabilities. *Journal of Learning Disabilities, 27,* 647–659.

Hurford, D. P., Schauf, J. D., Bunce, L., Blaich, T., & Moore, K. (1994a). Early identification of children at risk for reading disabilities. *Journal of Learning Disabilities, 27,* 371–382.

Hurford, D. P., & Shedelbower, A. (1993a). The relationship between discrimination and memory ability in children with reading disabilities. *Contemporary Educational Psychology, 18,* 101–113.

Iverson, S., & Tunmer, W. E. (1993). Phonological processing skills and the Reading Recovery program. *Journal of Educational Psychology, 85,* 112–126.

van Ijzendoorn, M. H., & Bus, A. G. (1994). Meta-analytic confirmation of the nonword

reading deficit in developmental dyslexia. *Reading Research Quarterly, 29*, 267–275.
Korhonen, T. T. (1995). The persistence of rapid naming problems in children with reading disabilities: A nine-year follow-up. *Journal of Learning Disabilities, 28*, 232–239
Leather, C. V., & Henry, L. A. (1994). Working memory span and phonological awareness tasks as predictors of early reading ability. *Journal of Experimental Child Psychology, 58*, 88–111.
Lenchner, O., Gerber, M. M., & Routh, D. K. (1990). Phonological awareness tasks as predictors of decoding ability: Beyond segmentation. *Journal of Learning Disabilities, 23*(4), 240–247.
Liberman, I. Y., & Shankweiler, D. (1985). Phonology and the problems of learning to read and write. *Remedial and Special Education, 6*(6), 8–17.
Lie, A. (1991). Effects of a training program for stimulating skills in word analysis in first-grade children. *Reading Research Quarterly, 26*(3), 234–250.
Lovett, M. H., Borden, S. H., De Luca, T., Lacerenza, L., Benson, N. J., & Brackstone, D. (1994). Treating the core deficits of developmental dyslexia: Evidence of transfer of learning after phonologically- and strategy-based reading training programs. *Developmental Psychology, 30*, 805–822.
Lundberg, I. (1995). The computer as a tool of remediation in the education of students with reading disabilities-A theory-based approach. *Learning Disabilities Quarterly, 18*, 89–98.
Lundberg, I., Frost, J., & Petersen, O.-P. (1988). Effects of an extensive program for stimulating phonological awareness in preschool children. *Reading Research Quarterly, 23*(3), 263–284.
Lyon, G. R. (1995, May). *Representing Human Learning and Behavior Branch Center for Mothers and Children*. Paper presented to Committee on Labor and Human Resources Subcommittee on Disability Policy United States Senate. National Institute of Child Health and Human Development, and National Institutes of Health.
Lyon, G. R., & Chhabra, V. (1996). The current state of science and the future of specific reading disability. *Mental Retardation and Developmental Disabilities Research Reviews, 2*, 2–9.
Majsterek, D. J., & Ellenwood, A. E. (1995). Phonological awareness and beginning reading: Evaluation of a school-based screening procedure. *Journal of Learning Disabilities, 28*, 449–456.
Mann, V. (1993). Phoneme awareness and future reading ability. *Journal of Learning Disabilities, 26*, 259–269.
Mann, V. A., & Brady, S. (1988). Reading disability: The role of language deficiencies. *Journal of Consulting and Clinical Psychology, 56*, 811–816.
Manis, F. R., Custodio, R., & Szeszulski, P. A. (1993). Development of phonological and orthographic skill: A 2-year longitudinal study of dyslexic children. *Journal of Experimental Child Psychology, 56*, 64–86.
Mauer, D., & Kamhi, A. G. (1996). Factors that influence phoneme-grapheme correspondence learning. *Journal of Learning Disabilities, 29*, 259–270.
McBride-Chang, C. (1995). What is phonological awareness? *Journal of Educational Psychology, 87*, 179–192.
McCutchen, D., & Crain-Thoreson, C. (1994). Phonemic processes in children's reading comprehension. *Journal of Experimental Child Psychology, 58*, 69–87.
McDougall, S., Hulme, C., Ellis, A., & Monk, A. (1994). Learning to read: The role of short-term memory and phonological skills. *Journal of Experimental Child Psychology, 58*, 112–133.
McGuinness, D., McGuinness, C., & Donohue, J. (1995). Phonological training and the alphabet principle: Evidence for reciprocal causality. *Reading Research Quarterly, 30*, 830–852.
Naglieri, J. A., & Reardon, S. M. (1993). Traditional IQ is irrelevant to learning disabilities—Intelligence is not. *Journal of Learning Disabilities, 26*, 127–133.
O'Connor, R. E., Jenkins, J. R., Leicester, N., & Slocum, T., A. (1993). Teaching phonological awareness to young children with learning disabilities. *Exceptional Children, 59*, 532–546.

O'Connor, R. E., Jenkins, J. R., & Slocum, T. A. (1995). Transfer among phonological tasks in kindergarten: Essential instructional content. *Journal of Educational Psychology, 87,* 202–217.

Rack, J. P., Hulme, C., & Snowling, M. J. (1994). The role of phonology in young children learning to read words: The direct-mapping hypothesis. *Journal of Experimental Child Psychology, 57,* 42–71.

Rack, J. P., Snowling, M. J., & Olson, R. K. (1992). The nonword reading deficit in developmental dyslexia: A review. *Reading Research Quarterly, 27*(1), 29–52.

Seymour, P. K., & Evans, H. M. (1994). Levels of phonological awareness and learning to read. *Reading and Writing, 6,* 221–250.

Slocum, T. A., O'Connor, R. E., & Jenkins, J. R. (1993). Transfer among phonological manipulation skills. *Journal of Educational Psychology, 85,* 618–630.

Snider, V. E. (1995). A primer on phonological awareness: What it is, why it's important, and how to teach it. *School Psychology Review, 24,* 443–455.

Snowling, M. J. (1991). Developmental reading disorders. *Journal of Child Psychology and Psychiatry and Allied Disciplines, 32*(1), 49–77.

Spector, J. (1995). Phonemic awareness training: Application of principles of direct instruction. *Reading & Writing Quarterly, 11,* 37–51.

Stahl, S. A., & Murray, B. A. (1994). Defining phonological awareness and its relationship to early reading. *Journal of Educational Psychology, 86,* 221–234.

Stanovich, K. E. (1985). Explaining the variance in reading ability in terms of psychological processes: What have we learned? *Annals of Dyslexia, 35,* 67–96.

Stanovich, K. E. (1986). Matthew effects in reading: Some consequences of individual differences in the acquisition of literacy. *Reading Research Quarterly, 21,* 360–407.

Stanovich, K. E. (1988a). Explaining the differences between the dyslexic and the garden-variety poor reader: The phonological-core variable-difference model. *Journal of Learning Disabilities, 21,* 590–612.

Stanovich, K. E. (1988b). The right and wrong places to look for the cognitive locus of reading disability. *Annals of Dyslexia, 38,* 154–177.

Stanovich, K. E. (1994). Constructivism in reading education. *The Journal of Special Education, 28,* 259–274.

Swank, L. K. (1994). Phonological coding abilities: Identification of impairments related to phonologically based reading problems. *Topics in Language Disorders, 14,* 56–71.

Swank, L. K., & Catts, H. W. (1994). Phonological awareness and written word decoding. *Language, Speech, and Hearing Services in Schools, 25,* 9–14.

Swanson, H. L., & Ramalgia, J. M. (1992). The relationship between phonological codes on memory and spelling tasks for students with and without learning disabilities. *Journal of Learning Disabilities, 25,* 396–407.

Torgesen, J. K. (1985). Memory processes in reading disabled children. *Journal of Learning Disabilities, 18,* 350–357.

Torgesen, J. K., & Barker, T. A. (1995). Computers as aids in the prevention and remediation of reading disabilities. *Learning Disabilities Quarterly, 18,* 76–87.

Torgesen, J. K., & Davis, C. (1996). Individual difference variables that predict response to training in phonological awareness. *Journal of Experimental Child Psychology, 63,* 1–21.

Torgesen, J. K., & Hecht, S. A. (1996). Preventing and remediating reading disabilities: Instructional variables that make a difference. In M. F. Graves, P. van den Broek, & B. M. Taylor (Eds.), *The first R: Every child's right to read* (pp. 133–158). New York: Teachers College Press.

Torgesen, J. K., Morgan, S. T., & Davis, C. (1992). Effects of two types of phonological awareness training on word learning in kindergarten children. *Journal of Educational Psychology, 84,* 364–370.

Torgesen, J. K., Wagner, R. K., & Rashotte, C. A. (1994). Longitudinal studies of phonological processing and reading. *Journal of Learning Disabilities, 27,* 276–286.

Torgesen, J. K., Wagner, R. K., Simmons, K., & Laughon, P. (1990). Identifying phonological coding problems in disabled readers: Naming, counting, or span measures? *Learning Disability Quarterly,13,* 236–243.

Treiman, R., Weatherston, S., & Berch, D. (1994). The role of letter names in children's learning of phoneme-grapheme relations. *Applied Psycholinguistics, 15,* 97-122.

Truch, S. (1994). Stimulating basic reading processes using auditory discrimination in depth. *Annals of Dyslexia, 44,* 60-80.

Vandervelden, M. C., & Siegel, L. S. (1995). Phonological recoding and phoneme awareness in early literacy: A developmental approach. *Reading Research Quarterly, 30,* 854-873.

Vellutino, F. R. (1991). Introduction to three studies on reading acquisition: Convergent findings on theoretical foundations of code-oriented versus whole-language approaches to reading instruction. *Journal of Educational Psychology, 83,* 437–443.

Vellutino, F. R., & Scanlon, D. M. (1987). Phonological coding, phonological awareness and reading ability: Evidence from a longitudinal and experimental study. *Merrill-Palmer Quarterly, 33,* 321–363.

Vellutino, F. R., & Scanlon, D. M. (1987a). Linguistic coding and reading ability. In S. Rosenberg (Ed.), *Advances in applied psycholinguistics* (Vol. 2, pp. 1–69). New York: Cambridge University Press.

Vellutino, F. R., Scanlon, D. M., & Spearing, D. (1995). Semantic and phonological coding in poor and normal readers. *Journal of Experimental Child Psychology, 59,* 76–123.

Wagner, R. K. (1986). Phonological processing abilities and reading: Implications for disabled readers. *Journal of Learning Disabilities, 19,* 623–630.

Wagner, R. K. (1988). Causal relations between the development of phonological processing abilities and the acquisition of reading skills: A meta-analysis. *Merrill-Palmer Quarterly, 34,* 261–279.

Wagner, R. K., & Torgesen, J. K. (1987). The nature of phonological processing and its causal role in the acquisition of reading skills. *Psychological Bulletin, 101,* 192–212.

Wagner, R. K., Torgesen, J. K., Laughon, P, Simmons, K, & Rashotte, C. A. (1993). Development of young readers' phonological processing abilities. *Journal of Educational Psychology, 85,* 83–103.

Wagner, R. K., Torgesen, J. K., & Rashotte, C. A. (1994). Development of reading-related phonological processing abilities: New evidence of bi-directional causality from a latent variable longitudinal study. *Developmental Psychology, 30,* 73–87.

Weiner, S. (1994). Effects of phonemic awareness training on low- and middle-achieving first grader's phonemic awareness and reading ability. *Journal of Reading Behavior, 26,* 277–300.

Yopp, H. K. (1988). The validity and reliability of phonemic awareness tests. *Reading Research Quarterly, 23,* 159–177.

5

Phonological Awareness: Instructional and Curricular Basics and Implications

Sylvia B. Smith
Deborah C. Simmons
Edward J. Kameenui
University of Oregon

REVIEW OF CONVERGING EVIDENCE

Research of more than two decades has affirmed the importance of phonological awareness and its relation to reading acquisition. Recent reviews of the literature (Hurford et al., 1993; Mann, 1993) have indicated that the presence of phonological awareness is a hallmark of good readers while its absence is a consistent characteristic of poor readers. In considering the relation between phonological awareness and reading, we identified six areas of converging evidence in the research (Smith, Simmons, & Kameenui, 1995):

1. The phonological processing ability explains significant differences between good and poor readers. (Phonological awareness is a component of phonological processing.)
2. Phonological awareness may be a group of highly related, independent abilities or a general ability with multiple dimensions.
3. Phonological awareness has a reciprocal relation to reading acquisition.
4. Phonological awareness is necessary but not sufficient for reading acquisition.
5. Phonological awareness deficits and delays can be reliably identified in young children.
6. Phonological awareness is teachable and promoted by attending to instructional variables.

In this chapter, we describe the instructional implications of these areas of converging evidence for students with diverse learning needs. We attempt to connect research and practice by responding to two focal questions: (a) What are the research-based instructional priorities or big ideas? and (b) For the instructional priority of phonological awareness, what is the existing research evidence regarding curriculum design?

RESEARCH-BASED INSTRUCTIONAL PRIORITIES IN PHONOLOGICAL AWARENESS: BIG IDEAS

Our research synthesis in chapter 4 revealed moderate support for the notion that phonological awareness is either a general ability which has multiple dimensions of varying complexity or a group of independent, but strongly related abilities. A commonly recognized definition of phonological awareness is sensitivity to the sound structure of language and a conscious ability to detect, combine, and manipulate different sizes of sound units. Although research has not definitively concluded which dimensions are obligatory for beginning reading, the converging evidence suggests the preeminent lasting effects of a delay in phonological awareness. Thus, the research convergence points to a priority of early identification of students with low phonological awareness.

Further underscoring the research convergence, none of the primary or secondary sources reviewed disputed the hypothesis that phonological awareness plays a central role in reading acquisition. Because phonological awareness has been established as one of the prerequisites for reading acquisition, phonological awareness instruction, therefore, is obligatory, not optional. In this respect, the training studies reviewed in the research synthesis converged to provide strong support for the importance of phonological awareness instruction prior to reading instruction across abilities and emerging evidence for the importance of concurrent or integrated phonological awareness and remedial reading instruction. Moreover, for diverse learners, strong effects of phonological awareness training on subsequent reading and spelling achievement underscored the critical importance of early identification and intervention for phonological awareness development.

In the following section, we discuss the big idea of phonological awareness in relation to a framework of curriculum design principles. Specifically, we use the principles of *conspicuous strategies, mediated scaffolding, strategic integration, primed background knowledge,* and *judicious review* to render the implications more explicit and employable. When applied to phonological awareness, these procedural principles illustrate how to translate research into practice.

In our review, we did not find similar level of procedural details for each design principle despite strong support for the underlying big idea of phonological awareness. For example, research indicated many procedural details for scaffolding, but few for judicious review. The following section should not be viewed as a prescription, but rather as an application of principles that can be used to make tangible the details of instruction required for students with diverse learning needs.

EVIDENCE OF CURRICULUM DESIGN
IN PHONOLOGICAL AWARENESS

In this section, we focus on five curriculum design principles: conspicuous strategies; mediated scaffolding; strategic integration; primed background knowledge; and judicious review, while addressing the question: For the instructional priorities of phonological awareness, what is the existing research evidence regarding curriculum design?

Conspicuous Strategies

Conspicuous strategies are sequences of teaching events and teacher actions that make explicit the steps required to hear and manipulate sounds (Dixon, Carnine, & Kameenui, 1992). Research findings recommend that phonological awareness instruction be explicit, not left to either natural development in the absence of instruction or inference by the learner during instruction. A characteristic feature of explicit instruction is the use of conspicuous strategies that offer a plan of action, in this context, for learning new phonological awareness skills. Phonological awareness strategies need to be obvious and salient to the learner for two reasons.

First, phonemes are not easy to isolate because we seldom hear pure phonemes. Rather, phonemes are coarticulated (i.e., merged and not pronounced as discrete sounds) and subject to distortion (addition of vowels; e.g., /duh/ instead of /d/) when produced orally (Ball & Blachman, 1991; Spector, 1995). Therefore, researchers suggest that identification of phonemes requires an artificial analysis rather than discrimination of a naturally perceived acoustical unit (Ball & Blachman, 1991). Similarly, developmental work in phonological awareness suggests that identification of phonemes is neither natural nor acquired in the absence of instruction for many children (Liberman & Shankweiler, 1985).

Second, in normal speech development, infants articulate single phonemes and small groups of phonemes (e.g., eee, eee, eee; ba, ba, ba). Over time, children learn to pay attention to meaning, not individual sounds. In contrast, reading acquisition involves moving from translating letters to sounds and combing those sounds to form words that, in turn, lead to word meanings in the child's listening vocabulary. In short, acoustical properties and hierarchical development in language obscure perception of individual phonemes. Thus, conspicuous strategies are necessary to make phonemes prominent in children's attention and perception.

Features of conspicuous strategies common across studies in which students consistently achieved positive and durable improvement in phonological awareness, reading, and spelling included direct teaching of phonological detection and manipulation, which involves: teacher modeling of specific sounds, and student producing specific sounds.

Direct teaching of phoneme identification and manipulation may include using concrete representation of sounds to make the mental manipulations of phonemes overt for the learner and teacher. (See Fig. 5.1 for an illustration of a template used with concrete representations; e.g., blank tiles.) *Concrete representation* involves using a neutral object to stand for a sound. For example, in a segmentation strategy, students hear the teacher model a sound, then say the phoneme while simultaneously moving a blank tile that represents the phoneme (Ball & Blachman, 1991; O'Connor, Jenkins, & Slocum, 1993). In contrast, a strategy for identifying phonemes that does not include concrete representation might ask students to pull the first sound away from the rest of the word in their mind and then say the sound pulled away.

Three blank tiles for each square in template (example of degree of high scaffolding)

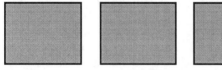

(O'Connor et al., 1993)

Tiles with letters added after sound-symbol relations instruction (examples of scaffolding a more difficult task, i.e., using sound-symbol relations).

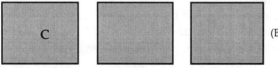

(Ball & Blachman, 1991)

FIG. 5.1. Template for concrete representation instruction. Example for three-phoneme word.

Letter-sound correspondences are a type of concrete representation of sound. That is, letters represent sounds via visual symbols. Several studies incorporated letter-sound correspondence and phonological awareness activities. Findings suggested that this combination facilitated students' understanding of the relation between sounds and written symbols. Research has not established the optimal sequence of instruction for all learners. For example, it is unclear whether all learners would benefit more from auditory instruction (i.e., phonological awareness without letter-sound correspondences) followed by the addition of letter-sound correspondence, or from simply beginning instruction by combining the teaching of letter-sound correspondence and phonological awareness.

The following sequence summarizes a typical research-based strategy for teaching segmenting: (a) teacher models segmentation (word often prompted with a picture), (b) children touch or move a concrete representation of a sound and vocally produce segmented phonemes, (c) children repeat the word. In addition, after letter-sound correspondences are learned, letter tiles are used as concrete representations.

Mediated Scaffolding

Mediated scaffolding is external support provided by the teacher, tasks, and materials during initial learning of sounds and strategies for consciously hearing and manipulating sounds. The amount and type of mediated scaffolding used is determined by the needs of individual students in relation to the task. Therefore, scaffolding is variable, determined by the interaction between the materials and the learners. Such variation refers not only to the teacher support provided during initial learning, but also the gradual reduction of support as children become more fluent in phonological awareness skills. As illustrated next, the support can take the form of instructional sequence of dimensions, task adjustment, materials variations, or teacher support.

Instructional Sequence of Dimensions. Phonological awareness dimensions fall on a continuum of difficulty. (See Fig. 4.3, Range of difficulty for phonological awareness dimensions, p. 77.) For example, the following instructional sequence would represent scaffolding the difficulty of phonological dimensions. First, provide instruction in rhyme followed by blending, segmentation, and deletion. Whereas, an instructional sequence that provided instruction in deletion prior to blending would not represent scaffolding the sequence of instruction.

Task Adjustment. Phonological awareness tasks can be adjusted by focusing on factors that contribute to difficulty. This is done by attending to a continuum of difficulty for each factor. In phonological awareness, these factors include number of phonemes in a word (e.g., *cat* is easier than *sand*); size of a phonological unit (e.g., compound words are easier than phonemes); phoneme position in words (e.g., initial sounds are easiest and medial sounds are most difficult); and phonological properties of words (e.g., continuants, such as /m/, are easier than stop sounds, such as /t/ (see Table 5.1).

Our research synthesis indicated that a common characteristic of effective phonological interventions was attention to a continuum of difficulty for each of the factors that contribute to the difficulty of a phonological task (i.e., number of phonemes; size of the phonological unit manipulated in the task; phoneme position in the word; phonological properties of words; and the specific dimension that the task represents such as blending). Of the five factors, the phonological properties of words have received the most significant empirical attention. For example, across studies continuant sounds were typically introduced before stop sounds, because stop sounds are more difficult to elongate and, therefore, more difficult to isolate, detect, and manipulate. Stop sounds were often introduced later because of the articulatory distortion that often occurs when a stop sound is produced in isolation. For example, it is difficult for many children to detach the vowel sound /u/ when voicing the /t/. Similarly,

TABLE 5.1
Dimensions That Contribute to Phonological Difficulty

Dimension	Easy	Example	Difficult	Example
Word length	1-3 phonemes. Length reduces memory load.	At, sat	More than 3. Length increases memory load.	Class, swing, pumpkin
Size of phonological unit	Compound words, syllables, onset-rimes	Carwash kit-ty am, Sam, pan	Phonemes	Individual sounds of letters. Example: /m/
Position of phonemes in words	First then last	First and last sound in sit, kit, mit	Middle	Identify middle phoneme in "school."
Phonological properties of phonemes and clusters in words	Continuants (sounds that can be extended)	Say mmmmman.	Consonant clusters, later developing phonemes	What are the first sounds in "school"?

Similarly, consonant clusters often are more difficult than continuants (e.g., /f/ in *fish* can become /*fffish*/ in contrast to /st/ in *star* which is impossible to elongate and difficult to analyze because /t/ is a stop sound).

The importance of attending to factors and their continua of difficulty supports the theory that perception and coding of linguistic material explains many differences in children's ease of reading acquisition. Moreover, attention to the relative difficulty of factors aligns with empirical evidence. Thus, research consistently documents that the problematic aspect of language for many children is the phonological component. When instruction is scaffolded (e.g., graduating difficulty of task), the problematic aspect of reading (i.e., phonological features of language) is mediated and systematically lessened. Empirical evidence strongly indicates that scaffolding phonological complexity meets the needs of all learners and the specific needs of diverse learners.

Table 5.1 presents an overview of phonological dimensions and the continuum of difficulty for each. However, Table 5.1 does not show the complex interrelations that can occur among the dimensions. For example, a short word (few phonemes), *trip*, which contains an initial consonant cluster, /tr,/ (difficult phonologically because initial sound cannot be elongated—the /r/ is difficult for some young children to pronounce, and clusters are more difficult than single phonemes) can be used for segmenting, which is a more difficult task. In beginning instruction, the teacher should present the simplest features of instructional examples to ensure that diverse learners are successful initially with beginning reading tasks.

Last, task difficulty can be mediated by (a) attending to the continuum of difficulty for phonological awareness dimensions in designing the scope and sequence of instruction, and (b) providing sufficient instruction and practice for the more difficult dimensions that are directly related to reading acquisition. See Table 5.1 for the continuum of difficulty. Examples of these types of task mediation could include teaching blending (easier dimension) before deletion (more difficult dimension) and providing instruction for segmenting as a phonological awareness task in contrast to providing instruction for segmenting only in the context of print.

Materials Scaffolding. Materials used in phonological awareness activities include puppets, stories, pictures, blank tiles or markers, alphabet letter tiles, and template cards with boxes for the sounds in words. Studies with young children frequently employed puppets who spoke in "broken up" ways (segmentation) to illustrate strategies. In addition, materials, such as concrete representations and picture cue cards, are used to help focus children's attention. An example of a high degree of material scaffolding is the number of markers and squares in a template to equal the number of phonemes in a word to be segmented (see Fig. 5.1).

Use of the template in research typically progressed according to the following sequence (e.g., Ball & Blachman, 1991; O'Connor et al., 1993). First, children moved blank tiles to a square for each sound during segmentation activities. After the children had mastered some letter-sound correspondences, one of the blank tiles was replaced by a letter tile. Typically, when letter tiles were introduced, the letter tile would represent the initial phoneme because it was the easiest. In addition, only one letter tile would be used initially to lessen the difficulty of the task.

Teacher Scaffolding. Multiple studies included scaffolds in which teachers modeled phoneme sound production; explicitly drew attention to how the sound feels when it is produced (Lie, 1991); modeled strategies for detecting, saying, and moving phonemes; and verbally stressed the target phoneme. An example of a low degree of teacher scaffolding involves prompting during application and practice of recently learned skills.

The following research-based sequence summarizes mediated scaffolding (Ball & Blachman, 1991; Byrne & Fielding-Barnsley, 1989; Cunningham, 1990; Lie, 1991; O'Connor et al., 1993):

1. The teacher models the sound / strategy.
2. Children use the strategy to produce the sound.
3. Steps 1 and 2 are repeated across multiple examples for each dimen-sion and level of difficulty across phonological dimensions.
4. Children are prompted to use the strategy during guided practice.
5. More difficult examples across continua of difficulty for each dimen-sion and for each feature of each dimension are introduced and Steps 1–5 are followed.

Strategic Integration

Strategic integration refers to the planful consideration and sequencing of phonologic and alphabetic tasks to promote reading acquisition or remediation of reading disabilities. It occurs when previously learned phonological skills are integrated with new skills, such as letter-sound correspondences and decoding. Though phonological awareness plays a causal role in reading acquisition, our review of the research indicated that phonological awareness is necessary but insufficient for successful reading acquisition. Alphabetic understanding is also a prerequisite to learning to read new words independently. Consequently, strategic integration of letter-sound correspondence instruction with phonological awareness is necessary in beginning reading instruction. Such a combination helps children acquire alphabetic understanding and improves their phonological awareness better than phonological awareness instruction alone. In addition, researchers have found that the effectiveness of phonological awareness/letter-sound correspondence instruction is strengthened by integrating direct instruction in reading (Cunningham, 1990; Hatcher, Hulme, & Ellis, 1994; Snowling, 1991). Moreover, strategic integration of phonological awareness instruction with remedial reading instruction at the level of deficit (i.e., the phoneme) is beneficial (Lovett, Borden, De Luca, Lacerenza, & Brackstone, 1994).

The following sequence, derived from the research, characterizes the strategic integration of phonological awareness, alphabetic understanding and reading instruction (Ball & Blachman, 1991; O'Connor et al., 1993; Blachman, 1994; Byrne & Fielding-Barnsley, 1989; Cunningham, 1990).

1. Begin with phonological awareness activities (e.g., teach detection and segmenting).
2. Use simple phonological units (e.g., 1 to 2 phonemes, continuants) and focus on initial sounds.
3. After student mastery of simple phonological awareness skills, introduce letter-sound correspondences for phonemes used in phonological awareness activities.
4. Increase the complexity of phonological units over time (e.g., 3 to 4 phonemes, stop sounds, final and medial sounds).
5. Apply knowledge and strategies gained in Steps 1 to 4 to decode words. When students know sufficient numbers of letter-sound correspondences, begin reading instruction (i.e., blending and segmenting) concurrently with phonological awareness instruction. Design instruction by attending to interactions among continua of difficulty for each dimension and for each characteristic of each dimension. Continue with additional letter-sound correspondences.

Primed Background Knowledge

Primed background knowledge includes relevant and essential language skills and strategies with sounds that optimize new learning of phonological awareness. An analysis of the previous integration sequence suggests that progress in the sequence depends on facile retrieval and application of previously learned phonological awareness skills and letter-sound correspondences. For diverse learners, acquiring such facility may require that the teacher primes background knowledge, including letter-sound correspondences and dimensions of phonological awareness. For example, the ability to detect individual phonemes is relevant to segmenting. Therefore, a system for activating and linking previously learned skills to advanced application (e.g., from detection to segmentation) is critical for diverse learners.

Priming background knowledge was not an obvious or common feature of the training studies reviewed in the research synthesis, because of a relatively narrow focus and length of time for most of these studies. In a yearlong phonological awareness intervention however, Lundberg, Frost, and Petersen, (1988) noted that the progression through the tasks was designed to be slow to ensure mastery, even for children who were low in phonological awareness ability. Nevertheless, Lundberg et al. (1988) did not report any methods used to prime background knowledge as students moved through the yearlong sequence of phonological skills acquisition.

Judicious Review

Judicious review refers to the sequence and schedule of opportunities provided children to apply and develop facility with sounds. Although much of the phonological awareness research did not systematically investigate judicious review for diverse learners, the importance of such review is implied. For example, the systematic progression from easy to more difficult features across the continua of phonological difficulty, which characterized all training studies, implied practice and review (see Table 5.1). Moreover, computer-aided instruction provides the potential to increase the amount of individualized, judicious review (Foster, Erickson, Foster, Brinkman, & Torgesen, 1994; Lundberg, 1995; Torgesen & Barker, 1995). Two types of review found in phonological awareness instruction research are guided practice and daily review (Cunningham, 1990).

Guided practice is a type of scaffolding that includes varying amounts of assistance. For example, students may be told when to use a specific strategy that had been previously taught, followed by the teacher modeling the strategy, and concluding with students using the strategy with immediate teacher feedback. This amount of assistance in the same lesson could be reduced to a verbal prompt of the strategy (e.g., the metacognitive strategy to "cut up" unfamiliar words in their minds (Cunningham, 1990).

Daily review links previous to current lessons, thereby helping to prime background knowledge and skills. Thus, a carefully planned system of review interwoven with the presentation of new material enhances the development of automaticity, or fluency, that enables short-term memory to process increasing amounts of information. To get beyond the starting point in reading acquisition, attention to the design principle of judicious review is pivotal.

CONCLUSION

The purpose of this discussion was to relate research and practice by responding to two focal questions: (a) What are the research-based instructional priorities, or big ideas? and (b) For the instructional priority of phonological awareness, what is the existing research evidence regarding curriculum design?

An overwhelming convergence of multiple lines of research has firmly established the importance of phonological awareness in reading acquisition. The existence of both causal and reciprocal relations between phonological awareness and reading acquisition fixes phonological awareness as an instructional priority. Moreover, research indicates that deficits in processing the phonological features of language explain a significant proportion of beginning reading problems and correlated difficulties in reading comprehension, background knowledge, memory, and vocabulary differences. Thus, for diverse learners, early identification of phonological awareness deficits combined with early intervention is pivotal in ensuring success in learning to read.

From the research, we concluded that the use of the design principles (i.e., conspicuous strategies, mediated scaffolding, strategic integration, primed background knowledge, and judicious review) facilitates perception of, quality of representation and, therefore, retrieval of phonologically coded material. This conclusion is particularly significant for beginning readers, especially diverse learners, who have difficulty becoming aware of the abstract, phonological features of words to which we do not consciously attend (Adams, 1990).

In our review, we did not find similar levels of procedural details for each design principle, despite strong support for the underlying big idea of phonological awareness. For example, more procedural details were found for conspicuous strategies, scaffolding, and strategic integration than for primed background knowledge and judicious review. The purpose of conspicuous strategy instruction is to make explicit the phonological dimensions, particularly phonemes, to which we do not typically attend (Adams, 1990). Moreover, mastery of one strategy does not guarantee mastery of a subsequent strategy without instruction. Results from the research suggested that the curriculum design principle, scaffolding, makes a significant difference in learner outcomes, particularly for diverse learners. It follows then that, if all materials and tasks are scaffolded, all strategies necessary for reading acquisition are strategically integrated and, given sufficient judicious review, diverse learners would learn to read with greater likelihood of success.

REFERENCES

Adams, M. (1990). *Beginning to read: Thinking and learning about print.* Cambridge, MA: MIT Press.

Ball, E. W., & Blachman, B. A. (1991). Does phoneme awareness training in kindergarten make a difference in early word recognition and developmental spelling? *Reading Research Quarterly, 24,* 49–66.

Byrne, B., & Fielding-Barnsley, R. (1989). Phonemic awareness and letter knowledge in the child's acquisition of the alphabetic principle. *Journal of Educational Psychology, 81,* 313–321.

Cunningham, A. (1990). Explicit vs. implicit instruction in phonemic awareness. *Journal of Experimental Child Psychology, 50,* 429–444.

Dixon, R., Carnine, D. W., & Kameenui, E. J. (1992). *Curriculum guidelines for diverse learners* (Monograph for National Center to Improve the Tools of Educators). Eugene, University of Oregon.

Foster, K. C., Erickson, G. C., Foster, D. F., Brinkman, D. & Torgesen, J. K. (1994). Computer assisted instruction in phonological awareness: Evaluation of the DaisyQuest program. *Journal of Research and Development in Education, 27,* 126–137.

Hatcher, P. J., Hulme, C., & Ellis, A. W. (1994). Ameliorating early reading failure by integrating the teaching of reading and phonological skills: The phonological linkage hypothesis. *Child Development 65,* 41–57.

Hurford, D. P., Darrow, L. J., Edwards, T. L., Howerton, C. J., Mote, C. R., Schauf, J. D., & Coffey, P. (1993). An examination of phonemic processing abilities in children during their first-grade year. *Journal of Learning Disabilities, 26,* 167–177.

Liberman, I. Y., & Shankweiler, D. (1985). Phonology and the problems of learning to read and write. *Remedial and Special Education, 6*(6), 8–17.

Lie, A. (1991). Effects of a training program for stimulating skills in word analysis in first-grade children. *Reading Research Quarterly, 26,* 234–250.

Lovett, M. H., Borden, S. H., De Luca, T., Lacerenza, L., Benson, N. J., & Brackstone, D. (1994). Treating the core deficits of developmental dyslexia: Evidence of transfer of learning after phonologically- and strategy-based reading training programs. *Developmental Psychology, 30,* 805–822.

Lundberg, I. (1995). The computer as a tool of remediation in the education of students with reading disabilities—A theory-based approach. *Learning Disabilities Quarterly, 18,* 89–98.

Lundberg, I., Frost, J., & Petersen, O. -P. (1988). Effects of an extensive program for stimulating phonological awareness in preschool children. *Reading Research Quarterly, 23,* 263–284.

Mann, V. (1993). Phoneme awareness and future reading ability. *Journal of Learning Disabilities, 26,* 259–269.

O'Connor, R. E., Jenkins, J. R., & Slocum, T. A. (1993). *Unpacking phonological awareness: Two treatments for low-skilled kindergarten children.* Unpublished manuscript, University of Washington.

Smith, S. B., Simmons, D. C., & Kameenui, E. J. (1995). *Synthesis of research on phonological awareness: Principles and implications for reading acquisition* (Tech. Rep. No. 21). Eugene: University of Oregon, National Center to Improve the Tools of Educators.

Snowling, M. J. (1991). Developmental reading disorders. *Journal of Child Psychology and Psychiatry and Allied Disciplines, 32*(1), 49–77.

Spector, J. (1995). Phonemic awareness training: Application of principles of direct instruction. *Reading & Writing Quarterly, 11,* 37–51.

Torgesen, J. K., & Barker, T. A. (1995). Computers as aids in the prevention and remediation of reading disabilities. *Learning Disabilities Quarterly, 18,* 76–87.

6

Word Recognition:
Research Bases

David J. Chard
The University of Texas at Austin

Deborah C. Simmons
Edward J. Kameenui
University of Oregon

Despite popular perception that reading is acquired as naturally as spoken language, there is overwhelming evidence that growing numbers of Americans fail to become functionally literate. In addition to the unfortunate trend of increasing illiteracy, links between illiteracy and other societal difficulties are clear. For example, the Orton Dyslexia Society (cited in Adams, 1990) reported that adults without basic literacy skills accounted for 75% of the unemployed, one third of mothers receiving Aid to Families with Dependent Children, and 60% of prison inmates. Meanwhile, illiterate youth represent 85% of juveniles appearing in court. Together, these correlates suggest that the cost of illiteracy is tragic and long lasting both in human and economic terms.

Juel (1991) asserted that the urgency created by adult illiteracy may have contributed to our lack of knowledge of the reading process. That is, poor performances by older students on national assessments of higher order reading and writing shifted the focus of research from beginning reading to more higher order reading processes such as comprehension strategies. In concentrating on reading and writing at higher levels, research and practice have largely ignored individual differences in reading acquisition (Juel, 1991). Yet, converging evidence (Daneman, 1991; Juel, 1991; Stanovich, 1991, 1993/1994) indicates that individual differences in early reading are most responsible for the variation in performance between mature readers and beginning readers. In short, the overriding difference between readers and prereaders is their ability to read words.

Word recognition refers to linking the printed representation of a word with its meaning (Stanovich, 1991). Understanding the particulars of word recognition is important for two reasons. First, higher order reading skills such as comprehension, vocabulary development, and purposeful, enjoyable reading and writing are dependent on accurate word recognition (Stanovich, 1991). Second, word recognition is central to reading acquisition (Daneman, 1991; Juel, 1991; Stanovich, 1991). Consider the following analogy. The reading process can be likened to the sport of mountain climbing. The trip up a mountain is difficult and strenuous for some climbers, whereas others are less challenged. These differences may be a result of the climbers' conditioning and experience in climbing, their familiarity with the mountain, and/or their starting point, and the tools with which they are equipped. Regardless of these differences, every climber experiences the location on the mountain that becomes the "crux" of the climb, the critical place on the mountain where passage assures a successful climb. For some climbers, the crux cannot be negotiated on the first attempt, but experience and practice on the terrain result in eventual success. For other climbers, the crux may be negotiated on the first pass. Yet other climbers may experience failure in attempting the crux and reject climbing altogether. Despite the challenge posed by a particular section of the climb, the goal is not to negotiate the crux, but to arrive at the summit and enjoy the view.

Likewise, learning to read is a complex activity. As with mountain climbing, some readers find the task more complex than others. Learning to read is mediated by a variety of skills related to language development (e.g., print awareness, phonological awareness). Beginning readers approach learning to read with differential levels of these mediating skills or "tools" necessary for reading acquisition. For example, some children may have the necessary tools to begin reading as a result of being raised in literature-rich environments. Still others may be unfamiliar with the tools and may struggle without support or direct guidance. For all readers, the "summit" of reading acquisition is independent reading resulting in clear communication, strong reading comprehension, articulate writing, critical analysis skills, and more. Before reaching the reading summit, however, every reader must recognize words; that is, the reader must identify (encode) the word, translate the printed word into its corresponding sound (phonologically recoding), and access the word's meaning (lexical access). Quite simply, word recognition is the "crux" of reading (Daneman, 1991; Stanovich, 1991).

METHODOLOGY

Sources

Our review of research included 15 secondary sources (Adams, 1990; Daneman, 1991; Ehri, 1991; Foorman, 1995; Juel, 1991; Liberman & Liberman, 1990; Liberman, Shankweiler, & Liberman, 1991; Spector, 1995;

Stahl & Miller, 1989; Stanovich, 1991, 1993/1994; Sulzby & Teale, 1991; Torgesen, 1985; Wagner, 1986; Wagner & Torgesen, 1987) and 12 primary studies (Byrne & Fielding-Barnsley, 1989; Haskell, Foorman, & Swank, 1992; Levy, Nicholls, & Kohen, 1993; Lovett, Borden, De Luca, Lacerenza, Benson, & Brackstone, 1994; Lovett, Warren-Chaplin, Ransby, & Borden, 1990; Lundberg, Frost, & Petersen, 1988; Sawyer, 1992; Sindelar, Monda, & O'Shea, 1990; Spector, 1992; Vellutino & Scanlon, 1987; Weinstein & Cooke, 1992; Weir, 1989). The 15 secondary sources included 11 descriptive narratives, 3 descriptive analyses, and 1 quantitative research synthesis. The descriptive secondary sources included 5 book chapters and 1 book. More detailed information about each source is provided in Table 6.1 at the end of this chapter.

Participant Characteristics

Participants in the research reviewed included students identified as general low performers, students with learning or reading disabilities, remedial readers not considered to have learning disabilities, high achievers, and culturally disadvantaged, language delayed, and linguistically diverse students. In terms of age, subjects ranged from preschoolers to eighth graders; however, the majority of studies focused on kindergarten and first grade. With the exception of two primary studies (Ehrlich, Kurtz-Costess, & Loridant, 1993; Lundberg et al., 1988), studies targeted English-speaking subjects.

Summarization of Methodology

Two independent reviews of each source were conducted. Responses were grouped under three categories: general conclusions, learner characteristics, and instructional implications. Convergence within the categories was achieved through a multiple-step process. Reliability was achieved through a process that combined independent reviews, intercoder comparisons of data categorization, coding clarification, and refinement with reliability checks on all sources. The primary author of this chapter used the convergent responses from the review and the coding process in concert with a second examination of each source to derive general areas of convergence.

Definitions

Word recognition, the central focus of this chapter, refers to the process of seeing a word and accessing its meaning. Several definitions will facilitate the detailed discussion of word recognition that follows. *Phonological awareness*, a critical prerequisite to word recognition, is the understanding that words are composed of sounds. Another prerequisite to word recognition, *alphabetic understanding*, is the understanding that words are composed of individual letters and that these letters correspond to sounds. Phonological awareness and alphabetic understanding combine to form a broader construct, the *alphabetic principle* or *alphabetic insight*. Automatic word recognition begins with *phonological recoding*, the process of translating words into their phonological counterparts using letter-sound rules. For example, the word "man" would be converted into its component letters (*m, a, n*), then into its corresponding sounds (/m/, /a/, /n/) and blended into its phonological referent to the word "man." Finally, this phonological referent can be used for *lexical access* of the word's meaning. That is, it can be matched with a definition held in the reader's mental dictionary. Throughout our discussion we repeat these definitions for clarity.

Chapter Overview

The intent of this chapter is to identify and discuss areas of converging evidence regarding the centrality of word recognition to the reading process. The characteristics, contexts, and conditions of learners and learning are discussed based on data and conclusions from the research on beginning reading. Research on beginning reading is very technical and focuses on models that explain the process of word recognition. We have attempted to distill evidence that cuts across a variety of models and frames of reference in beginning reading research including cognitive, instructional, and educational psychology, linguistics, and special education. Each general area of convergence regarding the reading process and word recognition proceeds from a discussion of the general development of skilled readers to the unique experiences of students with diverse learning needs. Available research on interventions are also reviewed. Some general areas of convergence do not contain subsections on diverse learners or interventions because of a lack of relevant research. Figure 6.1 represents a graphic depiction of the chapter's structure.

GENERAL AREAS OF CONVERGENCE

Our review of the beginning reading literature provided evidence on the development of word recognition skills and the importance of word recognition to reading acquisition and higher order reading activities. The four general areas of convergence from the studies reviewed for this chapter are:

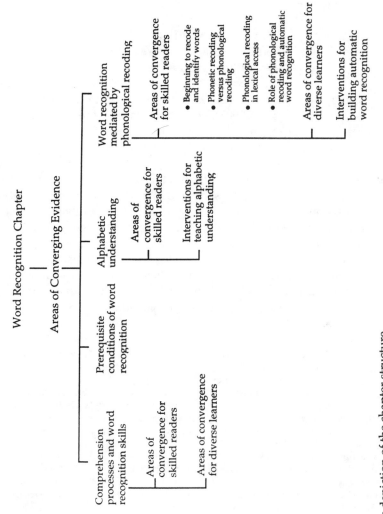

FIG. 6.1. Graphic depiction of the chapter structure.

1. Comprehension processes and word recognition skills.
2. Prerequisite conditions of word recognition.
3. Alphabetic understanding.
4. Word recognition mediated by phonological recoding.

AREA OF CONVERGENCE 1:
Comprehension Processes and
Word Recognition Skills

Readers appear to differ in the ease with which they achieve deeper levels of understanding (Daneman, 1991). These differences in the comprehension of meaning are important; however, the dependence of reading comprehension on fluent word recognition cannot be ignored. Comprehension of subtle language concepts and relationships are not dependent on word recognition skill until the reader tries to comprehend those concepts and relationships as they are communicated in print. Indeed, word recognition skills lead to improved reading comprehension ability rather than the reverse (Daneman, 1991; Juel, 1991; Stanovich, 1991). According to Stanovich (1991), if fluent word recognition does not produce a clearly identified word in working memory, "comprehension processes do not have the raw materials to operate efficiently and understanding of text will be impaired" (p. 443). Consider the following altered passage suggested by M. Sprick (personal communication, May 5, 1994) which simulates reading at 80% accuracy:

He had never seen dogs fight as these w__ish c___ f____t, and his first ex_____ t____t him an unf_____able l_____n. It is true, it was a vi_____ ex_____, else he would not have lived to pr_____it by it. Curly was the v_____. They were camped near the log store, where she, in her friend__ way, made ad_____ to a husky dog the size of a full-_____ wolf, th____ not half so large as _he. __ere was no w_____ing, only a leap in like a flash, a met_____ clip of teeth, a leap out equal__ swift, and Curly's face was ripped open from eye to jaw.
It was the wolf manner of fight__, to st___ and leap away; but there was more to it than this. Th__ or forty huskies ran _o the spot and not com_____d that s____t circle. Buck did not com_____d that s____t in_____, not the e___ way with which they were licking their chops. Curly rushed her ant_____, who struck again and leaped aside. He met her next rush with his chest, in a p_____ fash___ that tum___ed her off her feet. She never re_____ed them. This was __at the on_____ing huskies had w_____ for. (London, 1981, p. 55)

Fluency is a combination of accuracy and reading rate. As illustrated by the effort required to read the above passage, even a small percentage of words, if not read accurately, will slow the reader and create gaps in understanding. Although much of the story can be gleaned from this passage, as it stands, clearly, more recognized words would produce a stronger image and, perhaps, a greater chance of it being understood and remembered. Thus, word recognition fluency, while not the goal of reading instruction, is necessary for good comprehension.

Areas of Convergence for Skilled Readers

A description of the complex process of reading comprehension development is beyond the scope of this chapter. However, converging evidence suggests that the extent to which reading comprehension is dependent on word recognition varies with the level of reading development. Specifically, normal achievers' comprehension at approximately the end of first grade appears to be strongly affected by word recognition. Sawyer (1992) argued that comprehension's early dependence on word recognition may indicate that facility with the orthographic code (i.e., the printed symbols that represent the letters of the alphabet) is the "principal barrier" to comprehension in the first grade. This barrier posed by orthography is probably a function of early readers' focus on graphic cues, letter-phoneme or sound correspondences, and smooth sound blending to encode words that may or may not be a part of their limited vocabularies (Ehri, 1991).

In contrast, once readers achieve a degree of familiarity with the code (generally, sometime after first grade), comprehension seems to have a large direct effect on their word recognition (Sawyer, 1992). For example, readers who have learned the correspondence between letters and sounds may begin to associate certain letter patterns and whole words with their meanings. As their decoding ability becomes more fluent and letter patterns and words more familiar, skilled readers get better and better at changing clauses or whole sentences into their language equivalents and then holding them in their original form (Adams, 1990). That is, they are able to change the coded (written) words into their corresponding language. Even after skilled readers access a word's meaning, they continue to recode the word from its written to its phonological form. Reportedly, this action helps the reader maintain the word's meaning in short-term memory and facilitates reading comprehension (Baddeley, reported in Adams, 1990). Thus, it seems that good word decoders comprehend more; and as expected, stronger comprehension enhances a reader's ability to decode and hold clauses or whole sentences in working memory.

Areas of Convergence for Diverse Learners

Not surprisingly, less skilled readers' comprehension continues to be highly dependent on word recognition skills (Stanovich, 1991). In part, this is due to the relation between the translation of written words into their spoken (phonological) representations, word recognition, and the subsequent storage of the meaning of sentences or clauses in short-term memory. The amount of assistance readers receive from their ability to translate written words to phonological representations varies directly with the speed with which items to be remembered are encoded (Baddeley, Thomson, & Buchanan; Case, Kurland, & Goldberg; Dempster; cited in Adams, 1990). Poor and young readers who are not yet facile at processing letters and sounding out words fail to recode words in meaningful groups and, therefore, are less likely to maintain the meaning of a clause or sentence in short-term memory (Adams, 1990). In effect, readers who are less able to generate high-quality phonological representations as a part of word recognition are at a disadvantage and at risk for memory loss (Daneman, 1991). Thus, poor word recognition appears to limit storage of and access to word meanings, and ability to access or remember sequences of words.

Once again, our emphasis on reading comprehension's dependence on word recognition is not intended to minimize the significance of reading comprehension. Any comprehensive review of the reading process must address differences in readers' ability to comprehend and understand the message in the print, as well as their ability to recognize words from print.

AREA OF CONVERGENCE 2:
Prerequisite Conditions of Word Recognition

Having investigated the relation between word recognition and the goal of reading, we step back to consider factors that appear to facilitate beginning word recognition. Juel (1991) noted that children who are nearly ready to begin reading words have developed four prerequisite skills. Specifically, they understand that words can be "spoken" or "written"; print corresponds to speech; words are composed of phonemes (sounds); and words are composed of letters that correspond to phonemes. Although these conditions are not necessary for children to begin formal reading instruction, abundant evidence suggests they facilitate learning to recognize words. In the following section, we discuss briefly children's understanding of the communicative function of print and phonological awareness.

The first two conditions necessary for word recognition, recognizing the existence of words in print and in speech and understanding that print is encoded speech, are most likely nurtured as children are read to or observe others reading. Informal interactions between children and their parents during story reading help familiarize children with print and its conventions such as left-to-right directionality, punctuation, and page formats (Stahl & Miller, 1989). Sulzby and Teale (1991) referred to these conditions as understanding the communicative function of print. In a review of early literacy research, Weir (1989) found that children as young as 3 years show understanding of the social uses of written language, print conventions, and an ability to interact with print (see Gunn et al., this volume).

The third condition necessary for word recognition, phonological awareness (i.e., understanding that words are composed of sounds), is discussed in detail in the chapter on phonological awareness (this volume). Therefore, we do not discuss areas of convergence for skilled readers and diverse learners or phonological awareness interventions. However, a brief discussion is provided to reinforce the relation between phonological awareness and word recognition.

Phonological awareness has been defined in a number of ways. Spector (1992) referred to it as the ability to perceive spoken words as a sequence of sounds. Alternatively, Wagner and Torgesen (1987) defined phonological awareness as the awareness of and access to the sounds of language. Although a single definition is elusive, it is clear that phonological awareness is inextricably coupled with beginning reading. Thus, research since the early 1990s has validated repeatedly the importance of phonological awareness to reading acquisition (see reviews by Adams, 1990; Ehri, 1991; Juel, 1991; Spector, 1995; Stanovich, 1993/1994; Wagner & Torgesen, 1987). Yet it remains debatable whether phonological awareness is prerequisite to word recognition, or whether it is interactive and, therefore, is augmented by word recognition.

A child with phonological awareness is aware of the internal phonological structure of words (Liberman, Shankweiler, & Liberman, 1991). Practically speaking, this means the child is aware that spoken words are made up of individual sounds; sounds can be blended into words; and the same sounds may be found in different words (e.g., *m* in *m*an and *m* in ri*m*). Emergent readers enter formal reading instruction with differential awareness of words' phonological structure. However, as Juel (1991) pointed out, "some form of phonological awareness is necessary for successfully learning to read alphabetic languages" (p. 778). In fact, Juel, Griffith, and Gough (cited in Juel, 1991) reportedly found that most children who could not decode well in first grade had entered school with little phonological awareness.

Our description of phonological awareness is simplified for purposes of clarity and should not be interpreted as diminishing its importance. Phonological awareness is not a self-contained skill that is mastered in isolation. To the contrary, we discuss phonological awareness as preceding word recognition because its phonological basis makes it well suited for development during early language learning.

Researchers have attempted to distinguish phonological awareness from one of its more specified components, phonemic awareness. Whereas phonological awareness implies a broader understanding of the connection between words and sounds, phonemic awareness is "the ability to deal explicitly and segmentally with sound units smaller than the syllable" (Stanovich, 1993/1994, p. 283). Therefore, phonemic awareness differs from phonological awareness in its degree of specificity. A detailed description of phonemic awareness, its relation to phonological awareness, and its role in word recognition are beyond the scope of this chapter but are discussed by Smith et al. (this volume). In the next section, we describe how the awareness of sounds in words is linked to print and ultimately to understanding our alphabetic language.

AREA OF CONVERGENCE 3:
Alphabetic Understanding

Converging evidence about the fourth prerequisite to word recognition, alphabetic understanding, warrants its own discussion. Alphabetic understanding refers to a child's understanding that words are composed of individual letters (graphemes) and "the use of grapheme–phoneme relations to read words" (Ehri, 1991, p. 387).

Alphabetic understanding is concerned with the "mapping of print to speech" and establishing a clear link between a letter and a sound. It is not enough that a child knows each letter and can point to or print each one, but as Adams (1990) stated,

> Very early in the course of instruction, one wants the students to understand that all twenty-six of those strange little symbols that comprise the alphabet are worth learning and discriminating one from the other because each stands for one of the sounds that occur in spoken words. (p. 245)

Liberman and Liberman (1990) concluded that preliterate children are not very aware that words are formed by letters of the alphabet, but those who have alphabetic understanding perform predictably superior to those who have less. Foorman's (1995) review of studies focused on alphabetic understanding revealed that learners receiving more rather than less explicit letter-sound correspondence instruction appeared to grow more quickly in their phonemic segmentation skills.

Areas of Convergence for Skilled Readers

Children's responses to words differ qualitatively before and after they master letter-sound correspondence. Gough, Juel, and Roper-Schneider (cited in Juel, 1991) found that first graders without letter-sound knowledge made more errors than their peers who had mastered letter-sound correspondence. Moreover, errors made by the children with letter-sound knowledge were most often caused by improper "sounding-out" of the word. In contrast, children without letter-sound knowledge tended to substitute words that they saw often in their book. In short, students who had not learned the correspondence between letters and sounds guessed at words based on first sounds, physical features of the words, or context.

Interventions for Teaching Alphabetic Understanding

Is alphabetic understanding critical enough to warrant explicit teaching of letter-sound correspondence to beginning readers? Juel (1991) cited eight studies that provide considerable evidence of the importance of alphabetic understanding in accounting for differences between good and poor readers. Similarly, in a recent investigation, Haskell et al. (1992) found that students who received explicit training in letter-sound correspondence either at the onset-rime (e.g., /b/ - /at/ is "bat" a la *Sesame Street*) or at the phoneme level (e.g., /b/ - /a/ - /t/ is "bat") were more accurate on a word recognition test consisting of regular and irregular words than students who received whole-word training or no training.

Lovett et al. (1990) compared the effects of explicit training of letter-sound correspondence in word recognition with whole-word training in word recognition with readers with disabilities. Children with severe reading disabilities more than doubled the number of regular and irregular words they could identify on instructed word lists after receiving either letter-sound or whole-word training. While the results of this study were positive, the investigators reported that neither treatment group showed posttest advantage on uninstructed words, untaught rhymes, or pseudoword (i.e., words that conform to rules of phonics, but have no meaning) recognition. Lovett et al. (1990) suggested the subjects might have lacked the ability to segment syllables in words and, therefore, were unable to acquire or apply rules or analogies to reading.

Other studies have investigated the effects of letter-sound correspondence as part of an intervention on language and reading skills. In a series of experiments studying the relation between phonological awareness, letter-sound correspondence, and word recognition, Byrne and Fielding-Barnsley (1989) found that young children can read by analogy or onset-rime "naturally occurring units for learning how print matches to speech" (i.e., processing new words by recognizing the same word parts found in familiar words, e.g., tap, lap, map) if they know that phonemes are separate segments in words; that the same phonemes can occur in different words; and letter-sound correspondences. Because these researchers identified reading by analogy as an indication of alphabetic understanding, their findings suggested that neither phonological awareness nor letter-sound correspondence was sufficient for acquisition of the alphabetic principle (i.e., phonological awareness, knowledge of the segmental structure of words, and letter-sound correspondence). What is important here is that these experiments were designed to show that not knowing any one part of the alphabetic principle can hinder acquisition of reading. As Byrne and Fielding-Barnsley (1989) stated:

> The major hurdle for young learners in understanding the basic principle of alphabetic writing is the realization that the speech stream is composed of a small stock of interchangeable units, the phonemes. It is not sufficient to achieve this insight in order to discover the alphabetic principle as the child learns to read his or her first words. But explicit instruction in letter–phoneme relations, added to phonemic awareness, makes it likely that the child can compute the representational functions of those letters, whatever their position in otherwise unknown words . . . (p. 320)

Juel (1991) asserted logically that the "principal advantage" to an alphabetic language is the predictable correspondence between its graphemes and phonemes. This advantage is supported by mounting evidence that mastering these correspondences facilitates the transition from contextual guessing to efficient word recognition.

AREA OF CONVERGENCE 4:
Word Recognition Mediated
by Phonological Recoding

Torgesen (1985) described word recognition as a process involving the following steps:

> The phonological constituents of words must be obtained from their graphic representations, stored in sequence, and then blended together while the child searches memory for a real word that roughly matches the string of phonemes produced by the blending operations. (p. 354)

The prerequisites for word recognition may be enough for some children to make the link with very little guidance between the written word and its meaning (Ehri & Wilce, cited in Juel, 1991). For many children, however, more explicit instruction is necessary. Designing explicit instruction for word recognition requires deeper understanding of the reading process. In the following section, we review research on the nature of phonological recoding and its role in word recognition.

Areas of Convergence for Skilled Readers

Beginning to Recode and Identify Words. Early in reading acquisition, before children have mastered letter-sound correspondence, they focus primarily on context while attending to print only minimally (Juel, 1991). For example, if beginning readers read *Goldilocks and the Three Bears*, they may utilize beginning sounds, pictures, sight words, and story context to figure out unknown words such as "porridge" or "soft." This represents initial attempts at phonological recoding, the process of translating a printed word into its phonological counterpart via letter/sound rules (Daneman, 1991; Wagner & Torgesen, 1987). While for most readers this is just an initial attempt at phonological recoding, poor readers continue to use this inefficient and ineffective strategy when the task is to read independently.

As Ehri (1991) suggested, initial phonological recoding, which involves recoding letter strings into their corresponding sounds and blending the stored sounds into words, begins very overtly and slowly. As children learn to distinguish each sound, they begin, sometimes laboriously, to decode written words by attending to every letter. Chall (cited in Juel, 1991) agreed,

> [B]eginners . . . have to engage, at least temporarily, in what appears to be less mature reading behavior—becoming glued to print—in order to reach the real maturity later. They have to know about the print in order to leave the print. (p. 771)

Juel (1991) cited five studies suggesting that children begin to slowly and overtly decode words independent of formal reading instruction. While the "glued to print" approach is not a desirable way to read, it seems to occur naturally as children transition from letter-sound correspondence to word recognition.

Phonetic Recoding Versus Phonological Recoding. Some researchers interested in reading and memory have termed the first two steps of phonological recoding, namely, recoding the letters into sounds and storing them in short-term memory, "phonetic recoding." They hypothesize that efficient phonetic recoding is critical if beginning readers are to use minimal cognitive resources on the storage of letter sounds and maximum cognitive resources on actually blending the sounds to form words (e.g., Torgesen, 1985; Vellutino & Scanlon, 1987; Wagner, 1986).

Several longitudinal correlational studies examined the effect of efficient phonetic recoding on reading acquisition (Mann & Liberman, Mann cited in Wagner, 1986; Wagner & Torgesen, 1987). According to Wagner and Torgesen (1987), these results support their hypothesis that phonetic recoding plays a causal role in reading acquisition. Perhaps, as phonetic recoding becomes more efficient, beginning readers become better at blending the phonemes together to make words. Wagner and Torgesen (1987) cautioned, however, that no studies have measured reading skill while simultaneously tracking phonetic recoding skill. Thus, we do not know if the relation between reading acquisition and efficient phonetic recoding is unidirectional or reciprocal.

Phonological Recoding in Lexical Access. The manner in which skilled readers link the orthographic representation of a word with its meaning has generated a considerable amount of research and debate in recent years. In particular, the role of phonological recoding in mediating word recognition has been highly contentious. Phonological recoding can be illustrated with the following example: the word "sun" can be converted into its component graphemes (letters: s, u, n), which in turn can be translated into corresponding phonemes (/s/-/u/-/n/) and blended to create the phonological referent to "sun." Once the word has been recoded into its phonological representation (i.e., language equivalent), it can be matched with a similar string of sounds in the reader's lexicon (stored vocabulary; Torgesen, 1985; Wagner, 1986; Wagner & Torgesen, 1987).

While evidence of the importance of phonological recoding in initial reading acquisition is vast (see Stanovich, 1991), the exact nature of the role phonological recoding plays in word recognition is not so clear. Daneman (1991) described the differing theories about the role of phonological recoding as follows:

> Some theories propose that fluent readers access word meanings directly from the visual representation (Smith, 1971; Thibadeau, Just, & Carpenter, 1982); others argue for phonological recoding (Massaro, 1975; van Orden, 1987); and others for a dual route, with the visual route being faster and used for familiar words while the phonological route is slower and used for unfamiliar words (Coltheart, Davelaar, Jonasson, & Besner, 1977; McCusker, Hillinger, & Bias, 1981). (p. 514)

Stanovich (1991) dismissed the idea of a dual route for a more interactive model of word recognition:

The older question was phrased in a very discrete manner. Phonological information was activated either before lexical access or subsequent to it. Such a conceptualization fails to capture the continuous and distributed nature of phonological processing within the word recognition module. Activation of phonological codes by visual letter codes appears to take place almost immediately after stimulus onset, and these phonological codes immediately begin activating word codes, thus contributing to the ongoing word recognition process. (p. 438)

Citing 16 independent studies, Stanovich (1991) noted that despite the controversy and varying theories, there is substantial evidence that phonological recoding is important for early reading acquisition. Therefore, the issue seems to be not whether beginning readers utilize phonological recoding to access word meanings, but to what degree phonological recoding mediates word recognition.

Role of Phonological Recoding and Automatic Word Recognition. Presumably, if a particular word is in a child's spoken vocabulary and then is encountered in text, the child can recode the orthographic representation into its phonological representation and subsequently access the word in the lexicon. Some reading theorists believe that once children begin to decode unknown words independently, the orthographic representation of words becomes closely associated with their semantic representation (e.g., Ehri & Wilce, cited in Juel, 1991). Others hypothesize that decoding becomes very rapid so as to appear automatic (e.g., Gough & Hillinger, cited in Juel, 1991). This disagreement on how word recognition becomes more automatic also has spawned models of dual access to word recognition; that is, some words can be recognized directly from their orthographic (printed) representation, while others can be accessed through rapid decoding.

Stanovich's (1991) research synthesis on word recognition attempted to clarify the dual-access dilemma by reporting a hypothesized model of word recognition (Perfetti, cited in Stanovich, 1991) that accommodates phonological recoding in lexical access, as well as more expeditious approaches to word recognition. When a reader encounters visual letter codes, phonological recoding appears to be immediately activated and, in turn, immediately activates word codes in the reader's vocabulary or lexicon. When word recognition is slow, as in the case of low-frequency words, phonological recoding is allowed to proceed to facilitate word recognition. In the case of high-frequency words, on the other hand, word recognition may occur before phonological recoding has even been fully activated.

Using an interactive model, Adams (1990) described word recognition as an interaction between orthographic, meaning, and phonological processors. Adams' model supports findings that phonological recoding is activated immediately upon presentation of a word (Perfetti, Bell, & Delaney; Tannenhaus, Flanigan, & Seidenberg; Van Order, Johnston, & Hale; cited in Adams, 1990). Complete phonological recoding of a word may occur, however, either before or after the meaning of the word has been accessed. Adams (1990) explained that phonological recoding has an inverse relationship with the frequency of the words to be recognized in reading.

> When readers encounter a meaningful word that they have read many times before . . . the word's meaning and phonological image will also be evoked with near instantaneity. For texts consisting entirely of such highly familiar words, it follows that phonological translation might indeed be somewhat superfluous. (p. 160)

Because texts composed entirely of familiar words are uncommon, it is in the presence of less familiar words that phonological recoding becomes important. In sum, when orthographic activation is slow (i.e., the word or its parts are unfamiliar), the phonemes are activated and, thus, word recognition is mediated by phonological recoding. If the orthographic representation is familiar (i.e., high-frequency, familiar words), word meanings may be accessed before the phonological representations are fully activated. Therefore, the phonological access of the word may follow lexical access. Regardless of the model used to depict the word recognition process, the interaction of word frequency and phonological recoding speed appears to determine the automaticity of word recognition. Unlike the causal relation between phonological awareness and reading ability, difficulties in developing a measure that taps just phonological recoding makes it difficult to establish a similar relation (Wagner & Torgesen, 1987).

Questions persist regarding what unit becomes automatically recognized and by what process such automaticity occurs (i.e., recognition of the whole word, word parts, or individual letters). However, increased speed in word recognition has obvious benefits. As Juel (1991) noted,

> Whatever the processing reason behind the increased speed with which words can be identified, the freedom from deliberate attention to word identification allows the child to attend more to meaning, to use contextual information to facilitate the construction of meaning, and to reflect more broadly upon the content that is read. (p. 767)

Juel (1991) cited eight studies on the automaticity of word recognition, concluding that "by second or third grade, children can recognize many words while their attention is focused on another task—a sign that word recognition is automatic" (p. 770).

The effect of orthographic sensitivity to word parts on word recognition speed has prompted considerable, yet somewhat divergent, research findings. Ehri's (1991) review of 16 studies revealed that orthographic sensitivity follows automatic phonological recoding skill and repeated reading of phonologically regular and irregular words sharing the same patterns. Other studies showed that skilled readers become sensitive to rule-governed word parts as opposed to word parts that occur frequently but do not adhere to alphabetic rules. Many researchers have reported that during the development of orthographic sensitivity, readers begin to read words by analogy (Marsh, Friedman, Welch, & Desberg, cited in Ehri, 1991). These findings have been refuted by other researchers who suggest that children can be trained to read by analogy even before they learn to decode words (Goswami; cited in Ehri, 1991). Both lines of research regarding word recognition by analogy have been criticized for their methodology.

Foorman (1995) reviewed studies focused on teaching children to read applying onset-rimes. In general, findings suggested that onset-rime instruction facilitates beginning reading acquisition. Haskell, Foorman, and Swank (1992) found that children receiving phoneme or onset-rime instruction outperformed those receiving whole-word or whole language instruction. Moreover, children receiving phoneme instruction outperformed other groups on regular words while those receiving onset-rime instruction outperformed other groups on exception words. Finally, Haskell et al. (1992) found that better readers receiving phoneme instruction began to induce an onset-rime strategy in spelling new words. Foorman (1995) suggested that the phoneme group's application of an onset-rime strategy corroborates earlier findings that onset-rime based reading may be a result of rather than an alternative to good phoneme-based decoding skills. Further research in this area will help clarify the relation between onset-rime and phoneme-based instruction in word recognition.

Although the results of research on reading by analogy remain equivocal, numerous studies have established that children become orthographically sensitive around the second grade (e.g., Leslie & Thimke, cited in Ehri, 1991). Juel (cited in Stanovich, 1991), for example, found that fifth graders' word recognition speed benefited from their sensitivity to orthographic patterns, while second graders were constrained more by the decodability of words. Ehri (1991) postulated that Juel's findings may show that frequency of exposure to words is not as critical as a reader's more advanced lexical knowledge of different words for increasing the speed of word recognition.

Areas of Convergence
for Diverse Learners

What is it about word recognition that poses problems for diverse learners? Daneman (1991) commented that differences between good and poor readers are not perceptual, but involve accessing name or meaning codes for words. Likewise, correlations between reading ability and retrieval of word meanings are consistently low, as if to suggest that speed of lexical access does not contribute largely to reading ability (Daneman, 1991). However, phonological recoding does appear to account for individual differences in reading ability both in young readers as well as adults (Jorm & Share, cited in Daneman, 1991; Stanovich, 1986).

Typically, pseudowords are used to measure readers' phonological recoding speed because they isolate the application of letter-sound correspondence and blending from word meaning. Indeed, the reading task on which good and poor readers differ the most is the pseudoword recognition task (Hogaboam & Perfetti; Perfetti & Hogaboam; Stanovich; cited in Wagner & Torgesen, 1987). Poor readers exhibit differential sensitivity to the structural and meaning attributes of printed words. Poor readers are more sensitive to word meanings than to word structures and are especially insensitive to the phonological attributes of words (Vellutino & Scanlon, 1987). The results of studies examining phonological recoding and reading ability strongly suggest that access to and manipulation of phonological codes prior to lexical access play important roles in word recognition. As for alphabetic understanding, recent primary research in the area of automatic word recognition is limited. In the next section, we review four recent studies that investigated increasing automaticity in word recognition.

Interventions for Building
Automatic Word Recognition

Facility with phonological recoding is necessary for automatic word recognition and fluent reading. Primary research investigating methods for improving reading fluency has focused on various repeated reading techniques. In a study of the effects of a combination of repeated readings and explicit memory instruction on reading fluency and reading comprehension, Sindelar, Monda, and O'Shea (1990) found that readers at all skill levels improved their fluency and recall from an instructional level to a mastery level after three readings of the same text and explicit instructions to remember as much of the story as possible. Sindelar et al. (1990) noted that the effects were positive and comparable for students both with and without learning disabilities. To explain the effects of the repeated readings intervention, the researchers intimated that by increasing their fluency, students' attention previously allocated to word recognition was directed or redirected to understanding the meaning of the text. These findings suggest that multiple readings of stories would benefit all students in the classroom.

Similarly, Weinstein and Cooke (1992) studied the effects of repeated readings on 100-word reading passages for students with learning disabilities, comparing a fixed-rate criterion (i.e., 90 correct words per minute) with a criterion based on a set number of fluency improvements (i.e., three improvements). All four subjects in their study experienced an average of 60% fluency gain. The fixed-rate criterion produced slightly higher gains but required an average of 17.5 rereadings, while the criterion of three improvements required an average of 8.2 rereadings. Thus, while both methods are effective, using a fixed-rate criterion is less efficient. Weinstein and Cooke concluded that setting the criterion at three fluency improvements also offered students the opportunity to move more quickly through a wider range of materials, perhaps explaining the greater generalization of fluency to new material exhibited by students in the three fluency improvement group compared to students in the fixed-criterion group.

Levy et al. (1993) extended fluency intervention research by studying the combined effect of repeated readings with error detection for 24 good and 24 poor readers in Grades 3, 4, and 5. Readers read the same passage four times while crossing out misspelled words. Misspellings changed for each reading. Levy and her colleagues reported that both good and poor readers decreased their reading times for each reading while increasing their accuracy in recognizing misspelled words. Levy et al. concluded that repeated reading with error detection leads to more efficient and stronger word recognition skills for good and poor readers.

SUMMARY

Our review of the research literature suggested that learning to read words is anything but natural. On the contrary, learning to read words requires integration of numerous complex processes. Successful acquisition of these complex processes appears to be incidental for some children, but for others it must be systematically and planfully taught.

Four main areas of convergence bear implications for word recognition:

- Reading comprehension and other higher order reading activities are dependent on strong word recognition.
- Strong word recognition requires learner understanding that words can be "spoken" or "written"; print corresponds to speech; and words are composed of phonemes.
- Alphabetic understanding (i.e., a reader's understanding that words are composed of graphemes and letter-sound correspondence) facilitates word recognition.
- Phonological recoding (i.e., translating a word into its phonological counterpart) combined with word frequency mediates word recognition.

The graphic depiction in Fig. 6.2 likens aspects of beginning reading to the strands of a strong rope. That is, the strength of reading, like a rope, is dependent on a number of factors: the strength of the individual strands; strategic integration of the strands; and effective binding or connecting of the strands.

First, it is critical that the strands contributing to the rope, namely, prerequisites to word recognition (i.e., understanding the function of print and phonological awareness), alphabetic understanding, phonological recoding, and automaticity are robust, stable, and reliable. Next, the strength of the reading rope depends on strategic integration of the strands. Throughout the process of learning to read, storyreading and demonstrations of the role of reading for enjoyment as well as more functional purposes should be integrated with learning to read independently. Once early readers are taught some letter-sound correspondences, they can learn to blend those sounds into simple words. Similarly, as children begin to blend sounds into words, the words can be put into sentences so children can read connected texts. This type of careful

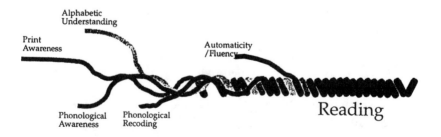

FIG. 6.2. Integration of word recognition components in reading.

integration contributes to strong reading abilities. Finally, systematic, carefully monitored, and planfully sequenced instruction binds the individual strands together to facilitate fluent reading.

Many students do not require the same level of instruction as many diverse learners do. Failing to ensure effective instruction in the prerequisites of reading, phonological recoding, automaticity, and fluency may put diverse learners at great pedagogical risk. For example, if efforts are not taken to train phonological recoding explicitly, many readers may not be able to read newly encountered words. Similarly, if fluency building is not emphasized, students may remain disfluent readers indefinitely. Ultimately, if we provide diverse learners with the tools and strategies for achieving automatic and fluent word recognition, we increase their chances for successful reading experiences.

TABLE 6.1
Secondary and Primary Sources

Secondary Sources

Authors	Dimension of Beginning Reading	Subjects	Purpose
Adams (1990)	General		Review of relevant research on developing reading and reading readiness capacities in young children
Daneman (1991)	General	Prereaders through adult readers; low- and normally achieving and reading disabled	Isolates the cognitive components of reading and considers which cognitive components contribute to individual differences
Ehri (1991)	General	Primary and elementary; normally achieving	Develops an explanation for reading success and describes three-phase course of reading development
Foorman (1995)	General	Primary and elementary; normally achieving	Reviews research relevant to the debate over phonics and whole language as approaches to reading instruction
Juel (1991)	General	Preschool to Grade 1; normally achieving	Summarizes theoretical models of reading acquisition and enumerates factors that move a child from prereading to reading
Liberman & Liberman (1990)	General	Preschool and kindergartners; low- and normally achieving	Explores two predominant views of reading instruction and their implications for reading problems
Liberman, Shankweiler, & Liberman (1991)	Alphabetic principle		Describes the alphabetic principle, its role in reading acquisition, and instructional implications

Spector (in press)	Phonemic awareness	Preschool and primary; low-achieving readers	Summarizes research on how instructional practices influence phonemic awareness and provides instructional recommendations for developing phonological abilities
Stahl & Miller (1989)	Whole language; language experience	Kindergarten through Grade 3	Examines effects of whole language and language experience approaches on beginning reading achievement; qualitative research synthesis
Stanovich (1991)	Word recognition		Reviews literature on word recognition and explores the central role of word recognition in the reading process
Stanovich (1993)	General		Reviews author's career in beginning reading research including phonological awareness and the debate between phonics and whole language
Sulzby & Teale (1991)	Emergent literacy	1–7 years old	Reviews recent studies on the nature and course of young children's literacy learning and their implications
Torgesen (1985)	Memory processes	Reading disables	Reviews research on (a) the complexity and diversity of memory processes, (b) the relation between memory and general intelligence, and (c) the causal relation between memory disabilities and reading failure
Wagner (1986)	Phonological processing	4–10 years old; prereaders and learning disabled	Examines (a) the nature of phonological processing, (b) the causal relation between the development of phonological processing and reading acquisition, and (c) the effects of phonological training on children with reading disabilities

(Continued)

TABLE 6.1
CONTINUED

			Purpose; Experimental Design
Wagner & Torgesen (1987)	Phonological processing	3–7 years old; prereaders	Investigates the reciprocal and causal roles between three types of phonological processing (i.e., awareness, recoding in lexical access, and recoding in working memory) and reading acquisition

Primary Sources

Authors	Dimension of Beginning Reading	Subjects	Purpose; Experimental Design
Byrne & Fielding-Barnsley (1989)	Phonemic awareness/Alphabetic principle	Preschool; prereaders	Determines what conditions will lead to acquisition of the alphabetic principle; multiple method
Haskell, Foorman, & Swank (1992)	Onset-rime training	First grade; normally achieving	Compares the effects of onset-rime, phoneme, and whole-word-level training on word reading accuracy; pre–post group design
Levy, Nicholls, & kohen (1993)	Fluency	Grades 3, 4, and 5; good and poor readers	Examines changes in students' error detection upon multiple reading of the same text; multiple method
Lovett et al. (1994)	Word identification	Elementary grades (7–11 years old); dyslexic	Compares the effects of two training programs, one using phonological analysis and blending with letter-sound correspondence instruction and the other using a metacognitive strategy approach to decoding, on measures of transfer to real words; pre–post group design

Study	Focus	Sample	Description
Lovett, Warren-Chaplin, Ransby, & Borden (1990)	Word recognition	Multiple ages (7–13 years old); learning disabled	Examines the effects of letter-sound instruction on the word recognition skills of disabled readers; pre–post group design
Lundberg, Frost, & Peterson (1988)	Phonological awareness	Preschool through Grade 2; normally achieving	Evaluates a phonological awareness training program focusing on (a) the effects of training before reading instruction, (b) the transfer of phonological awareness to new metalinguistic tasks, (c) the long-term effects of training on reading and spelling acquisition, and (d) the effects of training on general language competence; pre–post design
Sawyer (1992)	Word recognition; segmentation of words and sentences	Grades 1–3; normally achieving	Investigates the relationship between language variables and measures of reading along the K–3 continuum; longitudinal design, path analysis
Sindelar, Monda, & O'Shea (1990)	Fluency	Primary and elementary (K–5); normally achieving and learning disabled	Examines the effects of repeated readings on fluency and recall for instructional and mastery-level readers; factorial design
Spector (1992)	Phonemic awareness; dynamic assessment	Kindergarten	Investigates the ability of dynamic assessment of phonemic awareness to predict progress in beginning reading; multiple regression
Vellutino & Scanlon (1987)	Phonological coding/ Phonological awareness	Primary (K and Grade 2) and intermediate (Grade 6); normally achieving and learning disabled	Examines the causal relation between phonological coding deficits and reading disorders; correlational and pre–post group designs
Weinstein & Cooke (1992)	Fluency	Primary and elementary (ages 7–10); learning disabled	Compares the effectiveness of two repeated reading procedures on fluency; multitreatment, single-subject design (ABACA)
Weir (1989)	Preschool literacy	Preschool (ages 3–4); normally achieving	Examines current opinion on the most appropriate means of enhancing understanding about print

REFERENCES

Adams, M. (1990). *Beginning to read: Thinking and print.* Cambridge, MA: MIT Press.

Byrne, B., & Fielding-Barnsley, R. (1989). Phonemic awareness and letter knowledge in the child's acquisition of the alphabetic principle. *Journal of Educational Psychology, 81,* 313–321.

Daneman, M. (1991). Individual differences in reading skills. In R. Barr, M. L. Kamil, P. B. Mosenthal, & P. D. Pearson (Eds.), *Handbook of reading research* (Vol. 2, pp. 512–538). New York: Longman.

Ehri, L. C. (1991). Development of the ability to read words. In R. Barr, M. L. Kamil, P. B. Mosenthal, & P. D. Pearson (Eds.), *Handbook of reading research* (Vol. 2, pp. 383–417). New York: Longman.

Ehrlich, M. -F., Kurtz-Costess, B., & Loridant, C. (1993). Cognitive and motivational determinants of reading comprehension in good and poor readers. *Journal of Reading Behavior, 25*(4), 365–381.

Foorman, B. (1995). Research on "The Great Debate": Code-oriented versus whole language approaches to reading instruction. *School Psychology Review, 24,* 376–392.

Haskell, D. W., Foorman, B. R., & Swank, P. R. (1992). Effects of three orthographic/phonological units on first-grade reading. *Remedial and Special Education, 13,* 40–49.

Juel, C. (1991). Beginning reading. In R. Barr, M. L. Kamil, P. B. Mosenthal, & P. D. Pearson (Eds.), *Handbook of reading research* (Vol. 2, pp. 759–788). New York: Longman.

Levy, B. A., Nicholls, A., & Kohen, D. (1993). Repeated readings: Process benefits for good and poor readers. *Journal of Experimental Child Psychology, 56,* 303–327.

Liberman, I. Y., & Liberman, A. M. (1990). Whole language vs. code emphasis: Underlying assumptions and their implications for reading instruction. *Annals of Dyslexia, 40,* 51–76.

Liberman, I. Y., Shankweiler, D., & Liberman. A. M. (1991). The alphabetic principle and learning to read. In D. Shankweiler & I. Y. Liberman (Eds.), *Phonology and reading disability: Solving the reading puzzle* (pp. 1–33). Ann Arbor: University of Michigan Press.

London, J. (1981). The call of the wild. In A. Sinclair (Ed.), *The call of the wild, White Fang, and other stories.* New York: Penguin Classics. (Original work published by MacMillan Co. in 1903)

Lovett, M., Borden, S., De Luca, T., Lacerenza, L., Benson, N. J., & Brackstone, D. (1994). Treating the core deficits of developmental dyslexia: Evidence of transfer of learning after phonologically- and strategy-based reading training programs. *Developmental Psychology, 30,* 805–822.

Lovett, M., Warren-Chaplin, P. M., Ransby, M. J., & Borden, S. (1990). Training the word recognition skills of reading disabled children: Treatment and transfer effects. *Journal of Educational Psychology, 82,* 769–780.

Lundberg, I., Frost, J., & Petersen, O. P. (1988). Effects of an extensive program for stimulating phonological awareness in preschool children. *Reading Research Quarterly, 23,* 263–284.

Sawyer, D. J. (1992). Language abilities, reading acquisition, and developmental dyslexia: A discussion of hypothetical and observed relationships. *Journal of Learning Disabilities, 25,* 82–95.

Sindelar, P. T., Monda, L., & O'Shea, L. (1990). Effects of repeated readings on instructional- and mastery-level readers. *Journal of Educational Research, 83,* 220–226.

Spector, J. E. (1992). Predicting progress in beginning reading: Dynamic assessment of phonemic awareness. *Journal of Educational Psychology, 84,* 353–363.

Spector, J. E. (1995). Phonemic awareness training: Application of principles of direct instruction. *Reading & Writing Quarterly, 11,* 37–51.

Stahl, S. A., & Miller, P. D. (1989). Whole language and language experience approaches for beginning reading: A quantitative research synthesis. *Review of Educational Research, 59,* 87–116.

Stanovich, K. E. (1986). Matthew effects in reading: Some consequences of individual differences in the acquisition of literacy. *Reading Research Quarterly, 21,* 360–407.

Stanovich, K. E. (1991). Word recognition: Changing perspectives. In R. Barr, M. L. Kamil, P. B. Mosenthal, & P. D. Pearson (Eds.), *Handbook of reading research* (Vol. 2, pp. 418–452). New york: Longman.

Stanovich, K. E. (1986). Matthew effects in reading: Some consequences of individual differences in the acquisition of literacy. *Reading Research Quarterly, 21,* 360–407.

Stanovich, K. E. (1993/1994). Romance and reality. *The Reading Teacher, 47,* 280–290.

Sulzby, E., & Teale, W. (1991). Emergent literacy. In R. Barr, M. L. Kamil, P. B. Mosenthal, & P. D. Pearson (Eds.), *Handbook of reading research* (Vol. 2, pp. 727–757). New York: Longman.

Torgesen, J. K. (1985). Memory processes in reading disabled children. *Journal of Learning Disabilities, 18,* 350–357.

Vellutino, F. R., & Scanlon, D. M. (1987). Phonological coding, phonological awareness, and reading ability: Evidence from a longitudinal and experimental study. *Merrill-Palmer Quarterly, 33,* 321–363.

Wagner, R. K. (1986). Phonological processing abilities and reading: Implications for disabled readers. *Journal of Learning Disabilities, 19,* 623–630.

Wagner, R., & Torgesen, J. (1987). The nature of phonological processing and its causal role in the acquisition of reading skills. *Psychological Bulletin, 101,* 192–212.

Weinstein, G., & Cooke, N. L. (1992). The effects of two repeated reading interventions on generalization of fluency. *Learning Disability Quarterly, 15,* 21–28.

Weir, B. (1989). A research base for prekindergarten literacy programs. *The Reading Teacher, 42,* 456–460.

CHAPTER

7

Word Recognition: Instructional and Curricular Basics and Implications

David J. Chard
The University of Texas at Austin

Deborah C. Simmons
Edward J. Kameenui
University of Oregon

Learning to read words is anything but natural. On the contrary, it requires integration of numerous complex processes. Although successful acquisition and application of these processes is incidental for many children, others require systematic and planful teaching. From our synthesis of beginning reading research, four areas of convergence bear implications for word recognition for children with diverse learning needs.

- Reading comprehension and other higher order reading activities depend on strong word recognition skills.
- Strong word recognition requires prerequisite learner understanding that words can be "spoken" or "written," print corresponds to speech, and words are composed of phonemes.
- Alphabetic understanding (i.e., a reader's understanding that words are composed of graphemes and letter-sound correspondences) facilitates word recognition.
- Phonological recoding (i.e., translating a word into its phonological counterpart, remembering the correct sequence of sounds, blending the sounds together, and searching memory for a real word that matches that string of sounds) combined with word frequency mediates word recognition.

It is important to note that our focus on learning to read words independently does not pre-empt or preclude simultaneous attention to other reading processes. Rather, throughout the process of learning to read, story reading and demonstrations of the role of reading for information should be integrated with learning to master the code. Once early readers learn some letter-sound correspondences, they can learn to blend those sounds into simple words. Similarly, as children begin to blend sounds into words, the words can be put into sentences to form connected texts.

In the next section, we describe big ideas from our review that are instructionally important and empirically validated. We attempt to connect research and practice by responding to two focal questions: What are the research-based instructional priorities, or "big ideas," in word recognition? For the instructional priorities of word recognition, what is the existing research evidence regarding curriculum design?

RESEARCH-BASED INSTRUCTIONAL PRIORITIES
IN WORD RECOGNITION: BIG IDEAS

The four main areas of convergence identified from the review of reading research by Chard, Simmons, and Kameenui (1995) are captured by three big ideas that serve as a framework for designing instruction in word recognition for diverse learners:

1. Teach prerequisite skills in combination with word recognition instruction.
2. Teach alphabetic understanding (i.e., letter-sound correspondence) in combination with word recognition.
3. Teach blending of words and encourage readers to make sense of the words they blend.

The prerequisites to word recognition of print awareness and phonological awareness are addressed in detail in two other syntheses (see chaps. by Gunn, Simmons, & Kameenui; Smith, Simmons, & Kameenui) and, therefore, are not addressed in this discussion. In the following section, we discuss Big Ideas 2 and 3 in relation to a framework of curriculum design principles that include *conspicuous strategies, strategic integration, mediated scaffolding, primed background knowledge,* and *judicious review* to render the implications more explicit and employable.

In the final section, we discuss these procedural curriculum design principles in combination with the big ideas of teaching (a) word recognition in combination with prerequisite skills, (b) alphabetic understanding, and (c) phonological recoding to illustrate how to translate research into practice. Because recent research has not focused on reading acquisition, but rather on reading and writing at higher levels (Juel, 1991; Pearson, 1993), we found conceptual convergence that students need the big ideas of word recognition, but procedural paucity on how to teach the big ideas. In other words, the procedural details were often scant despite strong support for the underlying concepts (i.e., phonological recoding). The following sections should not be viewed as a prescription, but rather as reasonable extensions of areas of convergence.

EVIDENCE OF CURRICULUM DESIGN
IN WORD RECOGNITION

Conspicuous Strategies

Conspicuous strategies are sequences of teaching events and teacher actions that make explicit the steps to enable a learner to read words automatically and fluently. To apply the big idea of alphabetic understanding, for example, a teacher must develop a plan of action for how to teach students letter-sound correspondences and how to apply those correspondences to word recognition. The plan of action would involve a series of teacher actions and salient steps for the learner to apply letter-sound correspondences independently. For diverse learners, such steps must be explicit and unambiguous.

Alphabetic Understanding. The first step in a conspicuous strategy for alphabetic understanding is to teach individual letter-sound correspondences. However, before offering an example of a conspicuous strategy, it may be helpful to describe instruction of letter-sound correspondences that is not conspicuous. For example, it would not be conspicuous to teach letter-sound correspondence within the context of words. Approaches such as this place extraordinary responsibility on the learner to isolate the letter-sound correspondence being taught from other letters in proximity. Some commercial reading programs attempt to teach letter-sound correspondences within words to avoid decontextualized language as when one pronounces phonemes in isolation (see Adams, 1990, for discussion on this topic). Still other programs avoid a conspicuous approach to teaching letter-sound correspondences by not addressing letter-sound correspondences at all (Adams, 1990). Evidence suggests that neither approach leads students efficiently to the instructional goal—alphabetic understanding.

In contrast to inconspicuous strategies, an explicit and unambiguous approach to teaching letter-sound correspondences would begin when the teacher presents a letter symbol and models the corresponding sound. For example, the teacher points to the letter m on the board or in a book and says "mmmmmmm." Next, the teacher tests student acquisition of the correspondence by having the group produce the sound corresponding to the letter *m*. Finally, once the teacher is certain that students know the correspondence, individuals can be tested.

This strategy is simple and conspicuous. Each letter-sound pair is presented in isolation without the distractions of other correspondences. The approach benefits the reader by ensuring that the connection between letter and corresponding sound is salient, and with frequent exposure the connection becomes automatic for students. Such automaticity is critical for poor readers to begin to sound out and blend words. Despite converging evidence implying the importance of a conspicuous strategy for alphabetic understanding, no primary studies in this review were identified that tested this principle explicitly.

Phonological Recoding. Across models of word recognition, researchers agreed on the importance of *phonological recoding*, which refers to the process of identifying the sounds in a word, blending the sounds together, and searching for the meaning of the word in memory. Although phonological recoding need only occur a few times for typical readers to be able to read with ease and speed, diverse learners must be encouraged to look carefully at spellings and sounds and to repeatedly sound out and blend words (Reitsma, cited in Adams, 1990). Phonological recoding can be taught as an explicit strategy once students master a few letter-sound correspondences. The next step is to sound out the letters of words and blend them together. Blending the sounds in words is familiar to students who have practiced auditory blending tasks as part of phonemic awareness.

A conspicuous strategy for sounding out and blending words could be taught with the teacher first pointing to each letter of a word and then saying its sound without stopping between the sounds. Second, the teacher could sound out the word again with the students. Careful monitoring of the children's sounding out informs the teacher whether the children are automatic with the letter-sound correspondences. Next, the students can sound out the word as the teacher points to the sounds. Finally, students should be encouraged to blend the word at a normal speed. The teacher should take care to test individual students.

The foregoing strategy is required as it represents the first step in teaching phonological recoding. As learners master letter-sound correspondences and become more facile with sounding out and blending, similar strategies can be taught that emphasize frequent sounding out and blending of word parts (e.g., "an" or "it") and common spelling patterns (e.g., "-th" or "-ing") that can be preceded by a host of beginning sounds. Research evidence strongly supports that for skilled readers word recognition is effortless and automatic because they repeatedly sound out and blend familiar words (see Adams, 1990, for detailed discussion). Therefore, frequent opportunities to sound out and blend words is particularly critical for diverse learners. Practice at blending common word parts and letter patterns promotes automaticity as students no longer approach each word as a new string of letters.

Strategic Integration

Teaching conspicuous strategies in isolation compromises the utility of the strategies. Repeatedly, research reported the relation between print awareness, phonemic awareness, alphabetic understanding, phonological recoding, and comprehension. Therefore, it is imperative that word recognition instruction reflect the strategic integration of these processes. *Strategic integration* refers to the planful consideration and sequencing of phonologic and alphabetic tasks to promote reading acquisition. Numerous studies have determined that the most efficacious approach to early reading includes a combination of instruction in phonemic awareness and letter-sound correspondence. Similarly, phonological recoding is a combination of letter-sound correspondences, blending, and comprehension strategies. In the following section, we describe considerations for integrating the components of word recognition in early reading instruction.

Alphabetic Understanding. The simplicity of teaching letter-sound correspondences belies the complexity of integrating such correspondences with other correspondences and within words. The first point of integration is to *provide students the opportunity to discriminate new letter-sound correspondences from previously learned correspondences.* Being able to discriminate letter-sound correspondences is important for beginning readers to understand the nature of our alphabetic language (Adams, 1990). Toward that goal, teachers could present newly introduced letters in the proximity of earlier introduced and mastered letters, with new letters appearing more often than previously learned letters.

Because the goal of word recognition instruction is to teach learners to read connected text as quickly as possible, it is necessary to choose strategically the order in which to teach letter sound correspondences. The following guidelines may help:

1. Teach most common letter-sound correspondences (e.g., a, m, t, s, i, f, d, r) before less common ones (e.g., p, y, x, q, z).

2. Expedite learners' movement from sounding out and blending words to reading connected text by teaching those correspondences in which the same sound is represented by multiple patterns (e.g., /e/ as in me, sea, see, neat, and green).

These instructional strategies will enable learners to generalize sounds across a number of new words and will make meaningful texts more accessible.

Phonological Recoding. It is imperative that learners begin reading words before they learn all letter-sound correspondences. Therefore, as soon as learners have mastered a few letters, they should be used to construct decodable words. Thus, a second point of integration: *Learners should be taught how to blend the sounds to form words.* Initially, students may struggle with the sounding-out and blending process. With planfully integrated instruction, however, the number of mastered letter-sound correspondences will increase gradually, the process of sounding out and blending will become more automatic, and the numbers of words being recoded will expand.

A third point of strategic integration is *the use of words in context.* As students learn the strategy for sounding out and blending words, it is crucial that they read these decodable words in stories. Although it is extremely difficult to create interesting stories with highly stipulated decodable vocabularies, there are a number of ways to move learners from reading only isolated words to reading words in context. For example, although the list of decodable words is short, teachers can systematically point out decodable words and have learners read them in the story. This requires careful selection of stories containing words that learners are able to read.

The following steps should be considered in the strategic integration of phonological recoding:

1. Select as examples words that utilize the most common sounds of letters.
2. Select words to be taught that include only letters that students have mastered in letter-sound correspondences.
3. Teach the connection between strategies explicitly (e.g., "We have been learning the sounds of some letters. Today those letters are going to be put into words. We are going to say those sounds and blend them together to make the words.").
4. Integrate phonological recoding of words into classroom story reading as quickly as possible (i.e., If instruction focuses on sounding out and blending the word "and," have learners find the word "and" in the day's story and have them read it at each occasion).
5. Initially, create or find stories that contain only words students can read independently.

Mediated Scaffolding

Diverse learners may not benefit fully from traditional reading curricula. Although reading research has consistently supported systematic phonics for helping diverse learners read successfully, most reading curricula do not contain a systematic phonics component. Diverse learners' need for systematic instruction can be accommodated by using mediated scaffolds.

Mediated scaffolds are external supports provided by the teacher, tasks, and materials during initial learning of word recognition. As such, mediated scaffolds provide learners with guidance and support toward independence. Beginning readers' acquisition of letter-sound correspondences can be mediated in a number of ways, so that students move successfully and efficiently from unknowing to knowing. Mediated scaffolding can come in the form of teacher assistance, peer assistance, and task sequence and selection. The scaffolds should meet the needs of the beginning reader and should be diminished as the reader grows more facile with the prerequisites of reading, letter-sound correspondences, and phonological recoding.

Alphabetic Understanding. For diverse learners, teacher-mediated scaffolding must take the form of prompt, direct error correction and teacher modeling of newly introduced letter-sound correspondences. Knowledge of letter-sound correspondences must be automatic. Therefore, student errors must be identified and corrected before students have opportunities to practice incorrect responses. In addition, new letter-sound correspondences must be modeled explicitly for beginning readers. Unfortunately, many commercial reading programs replace modeling new information with testing. For example, instead of modeling /m/ while pointing to the letter, directions are common in which the teacher "asks students what sound the letter *m* makes" before any initial instruction on the correspondence. Omitting the modeling step in teaching letter-sound correspondences is similar to missing the first rung on the ladder of alphabetic understanding. Without modeling, the burden is placed on the learner to intuit the corresponding sound, reducing the probability that the learner will learn the correspondence successfully.

Choosing which letter-sound correspondences to teach and which order to teach them in serves as another form of mediated scaffolding. Although there are no explicit empirically validated guidelines for ordering the introduction of letter-sound correspondences, some logical principles may be considered.

1. Teach the most common sound for each new letter. For example, when introducing the letter *g*, it would be appropriate to teach the sound of *g* in "get" instead of the sound of *g* in "gem." Limiting the number of sounds associated with each letter enables the beginning reader to reach automaticity on the most commonly used sounds.
2. Introduce the most common letters before less common letters. Very simply, it makes more sense to teach the letter-sound correspondence for *m* before *x* because more words contain the letter *m* than the letter *x*.
3. Separate letters and sounds that are either visually or auditorily similar to reduce the beginning reader's chance of confusion. For example it is important to separate /a/, /e/, and /i/ because it is difficult to discriminate these three sounds. It is equally important to separate the introduction of the letters *d* and *b* or *n* and *h*.
4. Introduce lower-case letters prior to upper-case letters. For example, instead of teaching that /b/ corresponds with *b* and *B*, limiting the correspondence to the lower-case *b* allows students to master that connection before learning the upper-case correspondence.

In sum, mediated scaffolding systematically structures the load and distribution of print and sound stimuli that the beginning reader has to consider, while providing ample time to acquire and practice newly learned letter-sound correspondences.

Phonological Recoding. When students begin to sound out and blend words, teacher scaffolding is crucial. Teacher demonstration must illustrate that sounds should be connected without stops between individual sounds. The difficulty of teaching children to connect sounds during phonological recoding should not be underestimated. For example, students must coordinate saying one sound while identifying the corresponding sound of the next letter. Once the process has been modeled, a second scaffold involves the teacher sounding out with students before expecting them to recode independently. In a third form of scaffolding, the teacher points to each sound as students sound out words. This focuses attention on the importance of each individual sound (Adams, 1990).

Task scaffolds differ from teacher scaffolds by being embedded in the tasks and designed to promote reading by reducing the information students must generate independently. For example, in initial attempts to sound out and blend words children should focus on only two or three words. A reduced number of words allows students to focus on the goal of the initial task, namely, sounding out and blending words. Similarly, tasks can be sequenced such that only firm letter-sound correspondences are included in the phonological recoding tasks. Also, new letter-sound correspondences should be reviewed and mastered before appearing in the sounding out and blending tasks.

Initially, phonological recoding tasks are difficult due to the awkwardness of the process. As students learn the strategy, they should be encouraged to sound out and blend the words "in their head" and read the word as a whole. This progression of tasks approximates the end goal of word reading.

Primed Background Knowledge

Alphabetic Understanding. Teaching letter-sound correspondences as the key to alphabetic understanding without connection to words and text may seem like teaching in a vacuum. However, if carefully linked to the beginning reader's background knowledge, letter-sound instruction provides students with information about familiar sounds and symbols that they know are important to the message in text.

To be more specific, connecting letters to sounds first seems to be a clear extension of learning the names and shapes of letters. Adams (1990) discussed in detail the importance of teaching letter names and shapes as a precursor to letter-sound correspondence. Adams argued that most children have a firm grasp of letter names before entering school because their parents teach them the "Alphabet Song" (to the tune of "Twinkle, Twinkle Little Star") without showing them the letters. After that, many children are introduced to the letter shapes and the opportunity to trace or write the letters. This progression provides a strong platform from which to leap into letter-sounds.

As a result, consideration should be given to what children know about letters and sounds before letter-sound correspondences are taught. Indeed, some researchers suggest that children who are not facile at identifying the names of letters when presented the letter symbol should be pretaught the letters and their names. It is argued that primed background knowledge of letter names will serve as an anchor for the more complex letter-sound correspondences to follow. Additionally, phonological awareness exercises that introduce children to a wide range of phonemes are a critical precursor to linking letters to sounds. Logically, it makes more sense to link the letter *s* with /s/ if students have already learned and practiced /s/ in phonological exercises such as segmenting the word *sam* into *s - a - m*.

Phonological Recoding. Prerequisite knowledge for sounding out and blending words (i.e., print awareness, phonological awareness, letter-sound correspondences) must be primed prior to engaging students in tasks involving phonological recoding. This means sequencing the prerequisites in such a manner that learners are not expected to perform tasks for which they are not adequately prepared. For example, before students are taught to sound out and blend words, it is important that they have learned how to segment and blend words auditorily (i.e., in the absence of print). Background knowledge of segmenting and blending facilitates a smooth transition to sounding out and blending words in print.

Similarly, care should be taken to teach letter-sound correspondences to mastery before they appear in words to be sounded out and blended. Carefully sequenced instruction prevents students and teachers from becoming frustrated with tasks that involve phonological recoding. Very simply, providing a foundation of background knowledge builds strong word recognition skills.

Judicious Review

Judicious review refers to the sequence and schedule of opportunities readers have to apply and develop facility with sounds and the alphabet. Successful word recognition depends on an intricate review process to reinforce component skills. Although the basic notion of review is simple, the requisite characteristics of *effective* and *judicious* review are demanding and, therefore, often not realized. We have identified four critical dimensions of judicious review. Specifically, judicious review should be sufficient to enable students to perform tasks without hesitation, distributed over time, cumulative with information integrated into more complex tasks, and varied to illustrate the wide application of students' understanding of the information. Beyond these characteristics, teachers must determine what to review, when to review, and how to design effective review activities.

What to Review. Review activities must focus on content that is essential for improving word recognition. Thus, review should include letter-sound correspondences, spelling patterns, and exercises that occur frequently in oral and written language; are essential to a majority of words; and are of high quality. That is, time should be spent on activities that generalize across most words that students will encounter. Because the content of review will differ from student to student, informal progress monitoring helps discriminate what students have yet to master and what can be reviewed less frequently.

When to Review. Research on review has shown that repeated, shorter review distributed over time is more effective than review that is presented all at once (e.g., Dempster, 1991). Word recognition activities are particularly well suited for distributed review. For example, letter-sound correspondences can be introduced and later reviewed in groups. Newly learned information should be reviewed frequently, but as the information is mastered, greater amounts of time can be interjected between review sessions. It is not advisable to remove information from review activities based on initial success, however. If students are expected to maintain mastery of items, as is the case with many components of word recognition, teachers must ensure that high-utility information and skills are reviewed cumulatively.

Scheduling review the way we have proposed here seems logistically complex. Indeed, the complexity is real. This is primarily because the skills and information learned in beginning reading are likely to affect students' long-term academic success. Care should be taken at this early stage to assist students in maintaining the critical components of word recognition. Fortunately, many studies have documented the effectiveness of repeated reading of favorite books and passages as a system of review once readers become facile with phonological recoding (e.g., Sindelar, Monda, & O'Shea, 1990; Weinstein & Cooke, 1992).

Designing Review Activities. Contrary to popular belief, review activities need not be rote rehearsal or what many people refer to as "drill and kill." Rather, it is incumbent on teachers to develop flexible and creative methods of helping students maintain knowledge. The only requirement is that review activities include important knowledge and provide opportunities to assess students' understanding.

The following guidelines should be considered in designing review activities for developing strong word recognition skills:

1. Examine students' reading to detect error patterns that have implications for further instruction.
2. Create "review sets" that target specific word recognition activities. For example, for alphabetic understanding, include review sets of letters that were newly introduced, particularly difficult (e.g., /e/ and /i/), as well as correspondences that have not been reviewed recently.
3. Schedule review activities that can be used on multiple occasions within a lesson or across a day. For example, students might read the same short passages (5–10 sentences) three times during a reading lesson. Each reading can be timed to determine fluency gains.
4. Designate more review for new rather than familiar reading tasks.

CONCLUSION

We would be remiss if we were to leave the reader with the impression that teaching word recognition should sacrifice attention to building comprehension skills. Indeed, this is not the case. Research suggests that comprehension and word recognition have a reciprocal effect on one another. That is, comprehension is dependent on word recognition, and strong word recognition, while not dependent on comprehension, is enhanced by readers' interest in the content of text.

Keeping in mind the importance of integrating word recognition and beginning comprehension instruction, we must focus on the needs of diverse learners. Diverse learners are at risk of failure in reading. Based on our review of word recognition research, it appears that many diverse learners require a qualitatively different form of instruction; one that is more systematic and planful. Primary emphasis must be placed on helping diverse learners acquire the "deep and thorough knowledge of letters, spelling patterns, and words, and of the phonological translations of all three" (Adams, 1990, p. 416) that are critical to later reading success. Towards this end, we have proposed three big ideas for word recognition instruction:

1. Teach prerequisite skills in combination with word recognition instruction.
2. Teach alphabetic understanding (i.e., letter-sound correspondence) in combination with word recognition.
3. Teach blending of words and encourage readers to make sense of the words they blend.

These big ideas are supported by the proposed framework of instructional design principles including conspicuous strategies, mediated scaffolding, strategic integration, primed background knowledge, and judicious review. Primary emphasis on this framework and planful integration with other literacy activities may reduce the risk faced by diverse learners in beginning reading as it is commonly taught.

REFERENCES

Adams, M. (1990). *Beginning to read: Thinking and learning about print.* Cambridge, MA: MIT Press.
Chard, D. J., Simmons, D. C., & Kameenui, E. J. (1995). *Understanding the primary role of word recognition in the reading process: Synthesis of research on beginning reading* (Tech. Rep. No. 15). Eugene, OR: National Center to Improve the Tools of Educators.
Dempster, F. N. (1991). Synthesis of research on reviews and tests. *Educational Leadership*, 71–76.

Juel, C. (1991). Beginning reading. In R. Barr, M. L. Kamil, P. B. Mosenthal, & P. D. Pearson (Eds.), *Handbook of reading research* (Vol. 2, pp. 759–788). New York: Longman.

Pearson, P. D. (1993). Reading. In *The encyclopedia of educational research* (Vol. 3, pp. 1075–1085). New York: Macmillan.

Sindelar, P. T., Monda, L., & O'Shea, L. (1990). Effects of repeated readings on instructional- and mastery-level readers. *Journal of Educational Research, 83,* 220–226.

Weinstein, G., & Cooke, N. L. (1992). The effects of two repeated reading interventions on generalization of fluency. *Learning Disability Quarterly, 15,* 21–28.

8

Vocabulary Acquisition: Research Bases

Scott K. Baker
Deborah C. Simmons
Edward J. Kameenui
University of Oregon

We can directly access the meanings of only the words we already know. The referents of new words can be verbally explained only in terms of old words. This can be done either explicitly, by presenting their definitions, or implicitly, by setting them in a context of old words that effectively constrains their meanings.

—Adams (1990, p. 205)

The enduring effects of the vocabulary limitations of students with diverse learning needs is becoming increasingly apparent. Nothing less than learning itself depends on language. Certainly, as Adams (1990) suggested, most of our formal education is acquired through language. Learning something new does not occur in a vacuum. Rather, new learning always builds on what the learner already knows. Adams suggested that new learning is the process of forming novel combinations of familiar concepts. Learning, as a language-based activity, is fundamentally and profoundly dependent on vocabulary knowledge. Learners must have access to the meaning of words that teachers, or their surrogates (e.g., other adults, books, films, etc.), use to guide them into contemplating known concepts in novel ways (i.e., to learn something new). With inadequate vocabulary knowledge, learners are being asked to develop novel combinations of known concepts with insufficient tools.

Becker (1977) was among the first to highlight the importance of vocabulary development by linking vocabulary size to the academic achievement of disadvantaged students (Baumann & Kameenui, 1991). Thus, he asserted that vocabulary deficiencies were the primary cause of

academic failure of disadvantaged students in Grades 3 through 12. Almost
a decade later, Stanovich (1986) proposed a model of school failure that
emphasized the interrelated development of phonological awareness,
reading acquisition, and vocabulary growth.

Research suggests that many students can be taught the phonological
awareness skills they need to become proficient readers (Liberman &
Liberman, 1990; Stanovich, 1986). In addition, there is empirical support
that students who begin school behind typical peers in important areas
such as vocabulary and language development can master basic reading
skills as quickly and as well as typical peers under optimal instructional
conditions (Carnine, Silbert, & Kameenui, 1990).

However, as Becker (1977) observed, the primary difficulty with
sustaining early gains in reading is the lack of adequate vocabulary to
meet the broad academic demands that begin in the upper elementary
grades and continue throughout schooling. In contrast to phonological
awareness and early reading achievement, no research evidence supports
the contention that specific vocabulary development method or program
can bridge the vocabulary gap that exists at the onset of schooling between
groups of students with poor versus rich vocabularies, and that continues
to widen throughout school and beyond.

A flurry of vocabulary research has been conducted since Becker's
(1977) observations about the relation between vocabulary knowledge and
academic achievement. Beyond Becker's findings, three additional reasons
may account for this renewed interest in vocabulary development. First,
because vocabulary and reading are closely related, the highly publicized
concern about declining literacy levels, has affected vocabulary research
(Adams, 1990). Second, as Beck and McKeown (1991) observed, "the shift
to an information-processing orientation in psychology . . . provided rich
theory from which to draw in conceiving the relationship between words
and ideas" (p. 790). Research in vocabulary and literacy demonstrates that
building knowledge requires more than accumulating facts about specific
elements such as word definitions. Third, related to Beck and McKeown's
(1991) comments about building knowledge, is a shift in education from
emphasizing basic skills to problem-solving and higher order thinking
skills. This shift has resulted in additional research directed toward
understanding language and vocabulary acquisition within the context of
prior knowledge and constructivist pedagogy.

Defining Success in Vocabulary Development

It is necessary to distinguish between two contrasting ways of gauging
the success of curricular and instructional programs designed to increase

vocabulary development. On one hand, successful programs can be defined in an absolute sense by determining whether they lead to increases in vocabulary beyond what occurs during incidental learning opportunities, or as a result of other explicit attempts to increase word knowledge. Alternatively, successful programs can be defined in a relative sense by the extent to which they reduce the well-documented vocabulary gap between students with poor versus rich vocabularies (Stanovich, 1986; White, Graves, & Slater, 1990).

The difference between these gauges of success is significant. For example, extensive research evidence supports the use of a number of methods of increasing vocabulary development in an absolute sense (Graves, 1986). However, there is no evidence that any single method or comprehensive program seriously decreases the vocabulary gap that exists between students with poor vocabularies and those with rich vocabularies. The crucial issue, then, is whether implementation of a program designed to enhance vocabulary development significantly reduces the vocabulary gap between groups of students without restricting the vocabulary development of average- and high-achieving students.

Organization of the Chapter

Our goal in this chapter is to identify and discuss areas of recent research on vocabulary development, especially as it relates to diverse learners. In the first section, we describe the methodology of the research review. In the second section, we present five areas of convergence in the research literature on vocabulary acquisition, highlighting issues related to diverse learners.

METHODOLOGY

Sources

Our review of vocabulary research included 7 secondary sources, and 18 primary sources. A brief description of the primary sources is listed in Table 8.1 at the end of this chapter. The principal secondary sources included four book chapters (Anderson & Nagy, 1991; Baumann & Kameenui, 1991; Beck & McKeown, 1991; Kameenui, Dixon, & Carnine, 1987) and three review articles (Graves, 1986; McKeown & Beck, 1988; Paul & O'Rourke, 1988). A brief description of these secondary sources is also presented in Table 8.1.

In addition to these seven principal secondary sources, eight sources (Adams, 1990; Becker, 1977; Biemiller, 1977–1978; Carey, 1978; Juel, 1988;

Liberman & Liberman, 1990; Nagy & Anderson, 1984; Stanovich, 1986) were used to support important points or provide information not already covered in the secondary sources devoted specifically to vocabulary development.

Participant Characteristics

The studies reviewed included students identified as general low performers, students with learning or reading disabilities, remedial readers not considered to have learning disabilities, high achievers, as well as culturally disadvantaged, language delayed, and linguistically diverse students. Research sources were utilized only if they addressed diverse learners in some way. Diverse learners were defined as those students who by virtue of their instructional, experiential, cognitive, socioeconomic, linguistic, and physiological backgrounds bring different and often additional requirements to traditional instruction and curriculum.

Summarization of Methodology

Two independent reviewers read and coded each primary and secondary source, except the Graves (1986) and Kameenui et al. (1987) chapters, and the Oetting, Rice, and Swank (1995) article, which were read and coded by one reviewer because they were not included in the initial vocabulary search.

All references were coded on three dimensions: general conclusions, learner characteristics, and instructional implications. Convergence within the dimensions was achieved through a multiple-step process. Reliability was attained by combining independent reviews, intercoder comparisons of data categorization, coding clarification, and refinement with reliability checks on all sources. To derive general areas of convergence, the primary author of this chapter used the convergent responses from the review and coding process in concert with a second examination of each source.

Other chapters in this volume have included separate sections on findings and implications for skilled and diverse learners. This pattern was difficult to follow with the research on vocabulary acquisition. Our understanding of the outcomes of vocabulary acquisition clearly surpasses our understanding of the process of vocabulary acquisition. However, the early indication is that the acquisition process is similar for all students regardless of vocabulary knowledge. Consequently, it may be more useful to discuss differences in word knowledge as differences on a continuum rather than as different processes that distinguish students with poor from students with rich vocabularies. In addition, studies that theorize about the process of vocabulary acquisition compare and contrast students with poor versus rich vocabularies in the same sections. Therefore, we follow this strategy as much as possible in this chapter.

AREAS OF CONVERGENCE

In examining the research evidence on vocabulary acquisition, five themes emerged and converged. These themes addressed (a) vocabulary size differences between students, (b) accounting for those differences theoretically, (c) successful methods to improve the vocabularies of students with diverse learning needs, and (d) the relation between vocabulary knowledge and reading achievement.

AREA OF CONVERGENCE 1:
The Vocabulary Gap Between Groups of Students

The first area of convergence is that vocabulary differences between students are extensive. In this section, we present evidence that the difference in the number of words known by students with poor vocabularies versus students with rich vocabularies is extensive, grows over time, and becomes apparent early.

Vocabulary Size

In their review of vocabulary acquisition, Beck and McKeown (1991) noted that estimating vocabulary size was probably the oldest type of vocabulary research. Thus, during the 20th century, scores of studies have focused exclusively on estimating vocabulary size. Given the complexity of defining word knowledge (Baumann & Kameenui, 1991), it is not surprising that such estimates have varied considerably. For example, Graves (1986) reported that studies of vocabulary size conducted prior to 1960 resulted in estimates ranging from 2,500 to 26,000 words for typical first-grade students, and from about 19,000 to 200,000 words for university graduate students. These discrepancies were due to lack of specificity regarding (a) differences between words and word families (e.g., is a student who knows the meaning of *run, ran,* and *running* credited with knowing one, two, or three words?); (b) definitions of word knowledge (e.g., recognizing the meaning of a word in a multiple-choice question versus producing a definition for the word); and (c) the source used to represent English vocabulary (e.g., dictionaries vs. word frequency lists; Beck & McKeown, 1991).

As researchers began to specify more precisely the parameters of vocabulary knowledge, more accurate and consistent estimates of vocabulary size were generated. For example, Nagy and Anderson (1984) attempted to determine the number of printed words used in English materials in Grades 3 through 9 by examining the textbooks, workbooks, novels, magazines, and encyclopedias used in the classroom. Their estimate of 88,533 word families is now widely used as the domain of words that students in Grades 3 through 9 can be expected to know.

Beck and McKeown (1991) provided another estimate of the number of words students know by examining recent studies that used more defined criteria following the tradition established by Nagy and Anderson (1984). Through more precise measures, for example, estimates of the vocabulary size for 5- to 6-year-olds dropped from a range of between 2,500 to 26,000 words to between 2,500 to 5,000 words.

In summary, estimates of vocabulary size have become more consistent during the last 10 years. Methodological procedures that have helped reduce past variances include defining more precisely the domain of words being drawn upon to assess knowledge, and considering the difference between words and word families when calculating estimates.

Vocabulary Growth

Closely related to vocabulary size is vocabulary growth, or the number of new words students learn each year. Not surprisingly, the methodological problems that have plagued estimates of vocabulary size have also plagued estimates of growth. Thus, estimates of vocabulary growth have varied widely. For instance, early research on vocabulary growth resulted in estimates that students learned as few as 1,000 words to as many as 7,300 new words per year (Beck & McKeown, 1991). As definitions of vocabulary knowledge have become more refined, estimates of growth have become more consistent. For example, three widely cited reviews of vocabulary research suggest that the number of new words students learn, especially in the primary grades, is about 3,000 new words per year (Baumann & Kameenui, 1991; Beck & McKeown, 1991; Graves, 1986).

Students who learn the meaning of 3,000 words per year must learn approximately 8 words per day. This incredible growth may be due in part to neurological makeup, in which children act as "spontaneous apprentices in the business of language, acquiring new words at such a phenomenal rate" (Miller, cited in Liberman & Liberman, 1990, p. 58). In addition, such high growth rates can be accomplished only if flexible definitions of word knowledge and learning are used. In discussing vocabulary knowledge, Carey (1978) distinguished between "fast mapping" and "extended mapping." In fast mapping, an individual is able to learn a very cursory meaning of a word quickly, sometimes after just one exposure. It is not until extended mapping occurs, however, that an individual gains full understanding of a word's meaning. To attain extended mapping sometimes takes years and multiple exposures to a word. Carey hypothesized that school-aged children may be working on as many as 1,600 word mappings simultaneously. That is, at any point in time as many as 1,600 words are at various stages of mapping. So, if a student learns the meaning of eight new vocabulary words per day, the majority of those words are learned at only a very basic level of understanding.

Vocabulary Differences Between Students

Even as methodological improvements in vocabulary research have occurred, one unequivocal finding has remained: Students with poor vocabularies know alarmingly fewer words than students with rich vocabularies. For example, Beck and McKeown (1991) discussed a study conducted by Smith in 1941, who reported that high-achieving high school seniors knew four times as many words as their low-achieving peers. Smith also reported that high-achieving third graders had vocabularies that were about equal to those of low-achieving twelfth graders.

In 1982, Graves, Brunetti, and Slater (cited in Graves, 1986) reported a study on differences in the reading vocabularies of middle-class and disadvantaged first graders. In a domain of 5,044 words, disadvantaged first graders knew approximately 1,800 words, whereas the middle-class students knew approximately 2,700 words. Using a larger domain of words (19,050), Graves and Slater (cited in Graves, 1986) reported that disadvantaged first graders knew about 2,900 words and middle-class first graders approximately 5,800 words.

One of the most alarming patterns in terms of vocabulary-growth differences between students is that important differences are apparent regardless of how early vocabulary is measured, sometimes as early as when students begin school. Because reading-achievement differences between students also develop as early as first grade (Biemiller, 1977–1978; Juel, 1988), the vocabulary gap widens rapidly. As Beck and McKeown (1991) pointed out, "Even if some students are learning as many as seven new words a day, many others may be learning only one or two" (p. 795).

Recent studies have extended our understanding of vocabulary differences between students. In an important study, White et al. (1990) investigated reading vocabulary size and growth differences between students in Grades 1 through 4 in two low socioeconomic status (SES) schools and one middle SES school. Reading vocabulary was defined as the number of printed words that were both decoded and understood. White et al. (1990) found that even in Grade 1, there were important differences in the size of the reading vocabularies of students in the middle SES school (about 4,800 words out of 19,050) compared to students in the two low SES schools (about 3,500 and 2,500 words, respectively). Also, the differences between the number of words known by students at each grade level indicated that vocabulary increases may exceed the 3,000 words per year commonly referenced (e.g., Baumann & Kameenui, 1991; Beck & McKeown, 1991; Graves, 1986). A prevailing finding was that vocabulary growth appeared to differ on the basis of SES. The vocabulary size of the students in the middle SES school increased by about 5,200 words per year while that of the students in the two low SES schools increased by about 3,500 words per year.

Although White et al. (1990) investigated reading vocabulary (i.e., words students could decode and understand), the overall vocabulary differences between students in three schools were not attributable exclusively to decoding skills. For example, word meanings of at least 96% of the *frequently used* words were known by students in all three schools, but only 85% and 82% of the *moderately used* words decoded by students in the two low SES schools were known, compared to 91% for students in the middle SES school. For *infrequently used* words, students in the two low SES schools knew the meanings of 61% and 64% of the words they decoded, whereas students in the middle SES school knew the meaning of 79% of the words they decoded.

The White et al. (1990) findings illustrate how the vocabulary problems of students who begin school with poor vocabularies worsen over time. At Grade 1, the vocabulary difference between students in the middle SES school and students in the two low SES schools were about 1,300 and 2,300 words, respectively. At Grade 3, vocabulary differences of approximately 5,000 words were found between students in the middle SES school and students in the two low SES schools.

Simmons and Kameenui (1990) attempted to identify important developmental changes in the relation between reading comprehension and vocabulary knowledge. They found that 10- and 12-year-old students with learning disabilities had less extensive vocabularies than matched-aged peers without disabilities. Their most interesting finding was that for 10-year-olds, differences in vocabulary knowledge between students with and without learning disabilities prevailed even after statistical adjustments were made for differences in reading achievement. For the group of 12-year-olds, however, the effect of learner classification was no longer significant following adjustments for level of reading comprehension. Simmons and Kameenui (1990) attributed this finding to the increased interdependence between reading achievement and vocabulary knowledge as students advance in grade. In other words, vocabulary knowledge can be more easily identified as an isolated skill early in the primary grades versus later. This finding has implications not only for the timing of vocabulary interventions, but also for how the general focus of interventions might change depending on the students' age and skill.

In summary, estimates of vocabulary size have become more consistent in recent years. In general, students learn an impressive number of words per year, perhaps 3,000 or more. However, vocabulary growth varies tremendously between students, and many diverse learners acquire vocabulary knowledge at much lower rates than other students. One of the most alarming findings is that vocabulary differences between students appear early and the vocabulary gap grows increasingly large over time.

AREA OF CONVERGENCE 2:
Individual Differences in Vocabulary Development

The second area of convergence in the vocabulary literature is that researchers have attempted to identify critical factors that contribute to individual differences in vocabulary development. Although investigators have pursued very different lines of inquiry, they are united by a search for student characteristics that impede adequate growth. It is unlikely that a search for a specific cause of poor vocabulary development will prove fruitful. Instead, causal explanations are likely to be a complex combination of multiple factors. The purpose of this section is to describe recent research investigating individual differences in vocabulary development, which can be grouped into three general categories: generalized linguistic deficiencies, memory deficits, and poor word learning strategies.

Generalized Linguistic Differences

Stahl and Erickson (1986) argued that the vocabulary problems of some students are part of a well-established empirical trail of "language performance differences between reading disabled and normally achieving children at nearly all levels of linguistic performance and school ages" (p. 285). They compared four models to account for these linguistic differences: a general language deficit model, a speed of verbal information processing model, a word decoding model, and a rule abstraction model (i.e., difficulties inducing rules that govern language use).

To test these models, Stahl and Erickson (1986) had third-grade students with and without disabilities and first-grade students without disabilities perform numerous tasks designed to measure language performance at syntactic, semantic, orthographic, and discourse levels. Their findings indicated that third-grade students without disabilities consistently performed better than third-grade students with disabilities on multiple measures of language proficiency. However, comparisons between third-grade students with disabilities and first-grade students without disabilities revealed no significant differences. Results of regression analyses indicated that the rule abstraction model accounted for the measures of language performance better than the other two models. The implications suggest that some students' poor vocabulary development is the result of faulty or incomplete use of rule-governed structures of language. Stahl and Erickson concluded that for children who are "deficient in the ability to abstract or induce rules, the instruction should be explicit, limiting the requirement that the child figure out rules by him or herself" (p. 289). Thus, rather than having students try to use context clues to derive the meaning of important, unknown words they encounter in written text, a better strategy might be to provide students with a short definition of difficult words prior to reading the text, upon which they can build deeper contextualized understanding of the words during reading.

A study by Boucher (1986), however, contradicted the notion that students with disabilities suffer in all areas of linguistic performance. Boucher (1986) found great similarities in the meaning of the words used in natural speech by groups of sixth graders with and without disabilities. Both of these student groups also showed the same degree of consistency in word meaning across situations, and the same general lack of language adaptation in response to changes in the age of the listener.

These results suggest that the same words used by students with poor vocabularies and students with rich vocabularies are used with the same intended meaning. The problem for students with poor vocabularies may be that they do not acquire the meaning of new words as rapidly as students with rich vocabularies. The results of Boucher's (1986) study imply that students with poor vocabularies use the words they are taught as appropriately as students with rich vocabularies. Therefore, it appears that key to increasing vocabulary development is ensuring that students with poor vocabularies not only learn the meaning of words, but have the opportunity to use them frequently.

It may be that receptive language tasks more clearly illustrate differences between students with and without disabilities than expressive language tasks. Highnam and Morris (1987) found that students with disabilities performed significantly poorer than students without disabilities on a series of semantic interpretation tasks in which they judged the appropriateness of responses to simple "wh" questions. For example, to the question "Whose coat is that?" an appropriate response would be "That is John's coat," and an inappropriate response would be "That is a red coat."

This finding supports Stahl and Erickson's (1986) hypothesis that students with disabilities have difficulty with rule-governed structures of language.

In one of the few studies to look at vocabulary learning via verbal exchange, Oetting et al. (1995) found that 6-, 7-, and 8-year-old children with language disabilities learned significantly fewer words than normally achieving children in the course of watching two, 6-minute videotaped stories. The authors suggested the findings were consistent with a processing deficit account of vocabulary difficulty because working memory is critical for learning new words in ongoing narrative contexts. However, the authors also speculated that an additional problem contributed to vocabulary learning difficulties of diverse learners. Because students with language disabilities in their study learned *object* words (e.g., vessels, artisan) much easier than they did *attribute* words (radiant, nurturant), *action* words (e.g., surge, sever), or *affective* words (e.g., smug, dejection), they suggested that the vocabulary problems of children with language disabilities may also involve processing (storage and retrieval) difficulties of the grammatical content of new words. In other words, some of the vocabulary learning problems of diverse learners may be tied to deficits in their ability to exploit and hold in memory the abstract grammatical properties of words.

Memory Deficits

Many recent studies have investigated whether memory deficits account for individual differences in vocabulary development. In one of the most comprehensive studies in this area, Swanson (1986) argued that semantic memory deficiencies may underlie the difficulties some students experience when learning the meaning of words. Swanson tested three assumptions: (a) students' paucity of word knowledge is the result of weak associative connections between words, including connections at semantic, phonemic, and orthographic levels; (b) students' deficient organization of information in semantic memory; and (c) students' inefficient use of procedures to activate semantic, phonemic, and orthographic features of words.

To test these assumptions, Swanson (1986) had groups of students with and without learning disabilities listen to lists of word pairs that were related semantically (e.g., red, black; table, chair); phonemically (e.g., sit, pit); and structurally (e.g., sun, small [words that began with the same letter]). Prior to hearing the words, students were given either orienting instructions to listen for words from one of the three categories (e.g., "Listen for words that rhyme with 'sit'") or no specific instructions for remembering the words. Consistent with many other studies investigating the recall of linguistic items, Swanson (1986) found that students with learning disabilities recalled fewer words than students without disabilities. In addition, both groups of students recalled more words when orienting instructions were given for one of the word categories.

Among Swanson's (1986) most important findings was that students with disabilities clustered words by categorical membership (i.e., semantically, phonemically, and structurally) less well than students without disabilities. Also, students with disabilities did less well than students without disabilities in activating word features from semantic memory to match the demands of a task. Specifically, students without disabilities recalled a higher percentage of correct words when they were given orienting instructions to remember specific categories of words. This finding was true for all three orienting conditions. The author interpreted this finding as implying that students with disabilities manifest qualitatively different selective attention patterns in recalling word features compared to students without disabilities.

Swanson (1986) concluded that students with disabilities are more diffuse in their attention to target word features than other students. In addition, he stated that these students "fail to activate a critical number of word features [e.g., semantic phonemic, orthographic] in semantic memory and, therefore, may resort to an alternative means of processing information" (p. 483). Importantly, Swanson (1986) noted that the semantic organizational difficulties of students with disabilities are "due to inadequately built-up word knowledge" (p. 485). Students with disabilities do not have an "adequately developed hierarchical class of word knowledge, but instead have something like a small collection of word features linked in some way" (p. 485). In contrast, students without disabilities possess a high level of "knowledge or accumulation of facts about words which become increasingly accessible by means of well-trodden information processing routes" (p. 485).

In a similar study, Lorsbach and Gray (1985) investigated developmental differences in processing the semantic features of words. Showing 70 slides that paired a verbally presented word label with a visual referent of the word, they instructed groups of second- and sixth-grade students with and without learning disabilities to remember as many of the paired items as possible. On a subsequent recognition test in which paired items were again presented, students were to identify which of the items were the same as those presented in the initial trial and which were different. Items that were not exact replications were related to the original items in one of three ways: Acoustic distractors were items with labels that were homophonous (i.e., same sounding) with one of the target items; visual distractors consisted of a line drawing identical to that used for one of the targets but with a new label that gave it a completely different referent; semantic distractors were composed of a label synonymous with that of a target, but presented with a new line drawing that was clearly different from the original.

For both groups of second-grade students, and for sixth-grade students with learning disabilities, visual distractors produced significantly greater numbers of false recognitions than acoustic or semantic distractors. This indicates that for these students visual attributes were dominant, whereas acoustic and semantic features assumed a less prominent role in memory recognition. Sixth-grade students without learning disabilities, however, committed more false recognitions faced with semantic distractors than with acoustic or visual distractors. In other words, the older students without disabilities seemed to process the semantic meaning of the target items more thoroughly than their visual features. Lorsbach and Gray (1985) attributed their findings to the possibility that students with learning disabilities "do not spontaneously incorporate semantically related information in their rehearsal activities" (p. 226).

Walker and Poteet (1989) investigated whether depth of word processing and the match between learning and assessment conditions interacted with student vocabulary skills in later recall tasks. They tested fourth and fifth graders with and without learning disabilities on their ability to recall words presented in one of two conditions. In a shallow-processing condition, stimulus word pairs either rhymed or did not rhyme; in a deeper-processing condition, the stimulus word was embedded in a sentence that either did or did not make sense semantically. On the recall test, retrieval cues either matched the processing condition in the initial learning situation (e.g., initial learning: *fan/man*; retrieval cue: *fan/___*) or were different (e.g., initial learning: *fan/man*; retrieval cue: *On a hot day the ___ feels good*).

Overall, students without learning disabilities recalled more target words than students with learning disabilities. With both groups, more target words were recalled when the deeper-level cues were used (i.e., target word embedded in a sentence versus rhyming pair), especially when the target word made sense semantically. Finally, all groups recalled more words when the type of retrieval cue (i.e., rhyme or sentence) matched the learning cue. The authors concluded that word learning can be enhanced by "adding as much semantic context to new information as possible" (i.e., deeper-level processing) and suggested that "new information should be tied to previous learning to assist students in creating naturally occurring semantic relationships that will aid in later recall" (p. 31).

Differences in Strategies
for Learning Word Meanings

Other researchers have investigated whether students with poor vocabularies use different strategies to learn the meaning of words than students with rich vocabularies. Griswold, Gelzheiser, and Shepherd (1987) tested groups of eighth graders with and without learning disabilities on a sentence completion task after they had studied a list of words. Although students with learning disabilities learned a smaller percentage of unknown words than students without disabilities (36.7% vs. 67.4%), the two groups did not differ in the strategies used to learn the words, or in the amount of time spent studying the words.

Griswold et al. (1987) also found that strategy use did not account for the percentage of unknown words that students learned. The vocabulary learning score was accounted for primarily by the reading and vocabulary skills students had *prior to the study*, as measured by performance on standardized reading vocabulary and comprehension tests. Thus, students who knew more word meanings prior to studying unknown words learned the meanings of more new words after studying. The authors suggested that "prior knowledge contributes more to vocabulary learning than memorization strategies as they are typically defined" (p. 625). The results of this study have implications for the timing of vocabulary interventions, and the importance of explicitly highlighting the semantic associations between words as one way to help students build background knowledge.

Another explanation of individual differences in vocabulary development may be that students with poor vocabularies have ineffective strategies for retaining the meaning of words they have learned. Fawcett and Nicolson (1991) taught 24 difficult words to a group of adolescents with reading disabilities and poor vocabularies and a group of adolescents with reading disabilities and rich vocabularies. Once again, students with rich vocabularies learned more word meanings than students with poor vocabularies. The authors attributed this finding to semantic richness— that is, the density of meaning and linkages among words. Fawcett and Nicolson's (1991) main finding was that the adolescents with poor vocabularies appeared to forget more over a 6-month posttraining period. Although they offered no explanation for this finding, the authors recommended that vocabulary development programs for students with poor vocabularies seriously address increasing the conceptual linkages among vocabulary items. In addition, for long-term retention to occur, it may be necessary for students to be taught strategies for using the words they learn. This effect can be understood in terms of Carey's (1978) notion of extended mapping. That is, the more frequently students use words they have learned, the faster the words will become part of their active and usable vocabulary.

Reminiscent of Carey's (1978) notion of "fast mapping" and "extended mapping," Van Daalen-Kapteijns and Elshout-Mohr (cited by Beck & McKeown, 1991) hypothesized that acquiring the meaning of words begins with a rough formulation of word meaning followed by empty slots reserved for additional information. These researchers found that college students did form initial rough notions of word meanings and that the integration of additional information differed between students with poor and rich vocabularies. Essentially, Van Daalen-Kapteijns and Elshout-Mohr noted that students with poor vocabularies had difficulty adjusting their model of word meaning when they acquired new information about the meaning of a word. For example, students who initially learn that *set* means to "put in a specified position; place: *set a book on a table*" might have difficulty adjusting their model of the meaning of *set* to accommodate other meanings such as "to prescribe or establish: *set a precedent*" (examples from the *American Heritage Dictionary*, 1992). This finding is consistent with current learning disability theories, in which students with disabilities are thought to show less flexible use of learning strategies in response to changes in task demands than students without disabilities.

In summary, findings regarding the causes of individual differences in vocabulary acquisition are far from conclusive. In general, more effort has been spent on identifying within-child factors that contribute to insufficient growth than environmental factors. Within-child factors have included biological factors such as language and memory impairments, and potential instructional factors such as strategy differences.

AREA OF CONVERGENCE 3:
Different Instructional Procedures
for Different Goals

In accounting for individual differences in vocabulary knowledge it also is important to consider how complete an individual's understanding of a word's meaning is (Shore & Durso, 1990). Depth of understanding varies considerably from person to person. For example, a person's understanding of the word "bachelor" may occur at one of many levels. At the most basic level, bachelor may be understood strictly in its dictionary sense as "an unmarried man" (*American Heritage Dictionary*, 1992). At a much deeper level, the word "bachelor" may constitute information about age, gender, independence, functional living, organizational tendencies, and a host of other metaphoric and literal interpretations (Anderson & Nagy, 1991). The third area of convergence, therefore, is that instructional procedures to teach word knowledge must match the goals for depth of word knowledge. To understand this issue, it is important to first address the strongest criticism leveled against a direct instructional approach to facilitate student vocabulary development.

An Argument Against Direct Instructional
Approaches of Word Meanings

Anderson and Nagy's (1991) chapter, "Word Meanings," presents a comprehensive treatment of depth of word knowledge and a provocative analysis of vocabulary development with clear implications for decreasing the absolute gap between students with poor and rich vocabularies. Anderson and Nagy's criticism of direct instructional approaches to vocabulary development begins with an analysis of what they refer to as the *standard theory* of word knowledge, according to which word meanings "can be characterized in terms of *criterial features*—that is, necessary and sufficient conditions for inclusion in the [definition] of a word" (p. 693). Anderson and Nagy suggested that the standard theory grew out of efforts to align a theory of vocabulary acquisition with the general scientific principle of parsimony: in other words, to equate word meaning with the "necessary and sufficient conditions" for knowledge. However, they suggested that "there is no convincing, a priori reason to assume that, in representing word meanings, the human mind avoids redundancy and strives for parsimony of representation" (p. 695). In essence, Anderson and Nagy believe that the meaning of words can be fully appreciated and understood only to the extent that they are analyzed in the context of connected oral speech or written text. Furthermore, the variety of contexts in which words can appropriately be used is so extensive, and the crucial nuances in meaning so constrained by context, that teaching word meanings in an abstract and decontextualized manner is essentially futile and potentially misleading.

Words are such "slippery customers" argued Anderson and Nagy (1991), that even when the standard theory attempts to provide for the contextual understanding of word meanings, it would be a monumental task to include a full range of contexts to define adequately the way words are used. For example, Anderson and Nagy (1991) described the countless problems that arise when attempting to arrive at a standard meaning of the verb *give*. According to Webster's *New Third International Dictionary* (1964), the first standard meaning of *give* is "to confer ownership of something without receiving a return." As Anderson and Nagy (1991) pointed out, this definition works fine in the context of "John gave Mary a present," but in the context of "John gave Mary a kiss," or "Mary gave an excellent performance," the standard meaning of "conferred ownership" is crude at best.

When the standard meaning of *give* is supplemented by attempts to provide adequate contextual examples, not only does its meaning begin to lose the important element of parsimony (the *Third International Dictionary* contains 56 related contexts for *give* subsumed under 14 major groupings), but it still only partially accounts for the range of adequate contextual examples. For instance, some of the contextual entries for *give* include: (a) administer a medicine (e.g., *give* a shot of penicillin); (b) perform the action necessary or appropriate for a public performance (e.g., *give* a concert); (c) yield or furnish as a product, consequence, or effect (e.g., the candle *gave* its final flicker); (d) deliver or deal by some bodily action (e.g., *give* him a shove); and (e) deliver verbally (e.g., *give* a valid argument; examples from Anderson & Nagy, 1991). Because these uses of *give* are related, support for the standard theory would be provided if it were possible to substitute the same synonym in each expression and preserve its meaning. This clearly is not the case, however, as Anderson and Nagy (1991) stated, "you can say *set forth* a valid argument, but you cannot, in any normal situation say *set forth* a warm greeting; you can say *grant* him permission, but you cannot say *grant* him a shove" (p. 698).

In an earlier paper, Nagy and Anderson (1984) argued that:

> any program of direct vocabulary instruction ought to be conceived in full recognition that it can cover only a small fraction of the words that children need to know. Trying to expand children's vocabularies by teaching them words one by one, ten by ten, or even hundred by hundred would appear to be an exercise in futility. *Vocabulary instruction ought, instead to teach skills and strategies that would help children become independent word learners.* The challenge to those who would advocate spending valuable instructional time with individual words is to demonstrate that such instruction will give the child an advantage in dealing with the ocean of words not instructed. (p. 328; italics added)

Nagy and Anderson's (1984) argument concerning the futility of implementing *only* a system of direct instruction to significantly increase the word knowledge of students with poor vocabularies is most likely correct, but the argument needs clarification. *Any* one-dimensional approach will be inadequate for seriously reducing the vocabulary gap between students with poor and rich vocabularies. Thus, Anderson and Nagy (1991) correctly suggested that teaching students that words mean precisely what is specified in standard definitions is a poor technique.

However, it also seems unwise to avoid helping students establish, as quickly as is possible and reasonable, a foundation of vocabulary knowledge upon which they can build intricate structures of contextualized understanding (Paul & O'Rourke, 1988).

Researchers who advocate a more explicit approach to teaching word meanings recognize the limitations of teaching words in isolation as this quote from Kameenui et al. (1987) illustrates:

> Vocabulary instruction must move beyond the teaching of words directly as a primary activity. Because students derive the meanings of many words incidentally, without instruction, another possible role of instruction is to enhance the strategies readers use when they do in fact learn words incidentally. Directly teaching such strategies holds the promise of helping students become better independent word learners. (p. 140)

Anderson and Nagy (1991) suggested that the primary instructional procedure for facilitating strong vocabulary development is to ensure that students develop independent strategies for learning the meaning of words as they occur in context. Although student independence in learning word meanings from context should be the ultimate goal of a comprehensive vocabulary development program, there are two problems with relying too heavily on this approach.

First, the students with the greatest vocabulary needs are the same students whom Stanovich (1986) described as actively selecting, shaping, and evoking environments that are not conducive to rapid growth in reading or vocabulary. In essence, students who are not successful in developing early reading skills tend to become frustrated by reading activities, and thus do not engage in the volume of reading necessary to significantly influence their vocabulary development. Although it may be difficult for advocates of direct vocabulary instruction to demonstrate that instruction with individual words gives the child an advantage in dealing with the "ocean of words not instructed" (Anderson & Nagy, 1991, p. 328), it is equally difficult to demonstrate how systematic increases in the amount of reading by poor readers can approximate (even surpass if the vocabulary gap is to be reduced) the amount of reading by good readers.

The second problem with overrelying on independent word learning strategies is that it is unclear how this would address the needs of students in kindergarten and first grade (i.e., before most students are reading). Already at this early age, many students have serious vocabulary limitations compared to their peers (White et al., 1990), but they do not have adequate reading skills to engage in the amount of reading necessary to reduce the gap. Therefore, reconciling the differences between advocates of direct vocabulary instruction in word meanings and those who advocate for the development of independent word learning strategies can be done most easily through flexible and integrated approaches to vocabulary development.

Depth of Word Knowledge

Recent secondary sources in vocabulary research (e.g., Baumann & Kameenui, 1991; Beck & McKeown, 1991; Graves, 1986) discussed the importance of considering levels of word knowledge in determining vocabulary development. As Beck and McKeown (1991) stated, "knowing a word is not an all-or-nothing proposition; it is not the case that one either knows or does not know a word. Rather, knowledge of a word should be viewed in terms of the extent or degree of knowledge that people can possess" (p. 791). A comprehensive vocabulary development program that addresses levels of word knowledge in its instructional and assessment strategies has the potential to emphasize a range of approaches from independent word learning strategies to teacher-directed strategies that focus on the meanings of individual words. For example, a comprehensive instructional sequence might entail explicitly teaching the meaning of words for which students have no knowledge (e.g., *bachelor*—unmarried man). By arranging specific learning opportunities, the student might develop a deeper understanding of the word *bachelor* through independent strategies. The primary strategy might involve multiple exposures to the word *bachelor* in connected written text (McKeown & Beck, 1988).

Thus, considering levels of word knowledge may help determine the type of strategy to be used to facilitate improvement in vocabulary knowledge. Baumann and Kameenui (1991) discussed three levels of word knowledge that can be used to consider depth of understanding and related instructional procedures: *association, comprehension,* and *generation*.

A student with *associative* knowledge is able to link a new word with a specific definition or a single context. To possess *comprehension* knowledge, a child must either demonstrate a broad understanding of a word in a sentence or be able to use definitional information to find a antonym, classify words into categories, and so forth. Finally, *generative* knowledge is characterized by the ability to produce a novel response to a word, such as an original sentence, or a restatement of the definition in the child's own words.

Thus, whether a student needs to have associative, comprehension, or generative knowledge of a word's meaning has ramifications for the type of instructional procedures that should be used (McKeown & Beck, 1988). For example, very different instructional strategies might be used with a student who needs to have a very general sense of a word's meaning to understand part of a story (e.g., the word *Occurrence* in *The Occurrence at Owl Creek Bridge* can be understood as *What Happened*) versus a student who needs to know the meaning of a word in sufficient depth to use the word in discourse (e.g., a person would have to understand the word *Powers* in *The Rise and Fall of the Great Powers* at a deep level to understand the book).

AREA OF CONVERGENCE 4:
Multiple Methods of Enhancing
Individual Word Knowledge

The fourth area of convergence in vocabulary research is that many different instructional methods have yielded positive results in increasing vocabulary knowledge. The majority of vocabulary intervention research has examined the effectiveness of increasing students' knowledge of individual, specific words.

Many methods to increase vocabulary knowledge have resulted in more words learned than otherwise occurred during normal incidental learning opportunities. However, Beck and McKeown (1991) concluded that a single best method of vocabulary instruction has not been identified. Recent studies, combined with the information in many secondary sources, provide a clear picture of the strengths and weaknesses of efforts to increase understanding of individual words.

In considering vocabulary growth, we need to distinguish between *intentional* and *incidental* learning. The majority of word meanings are learned through incidental word learning opportunities (Baumann & Kameenui, 1991). That is, through normal everyday experiences with oral and written language, students learn most of the approximately seven words they acquire each day. In some cases, students learn word meanings intentionally, however. For example, the classroom teacher may request that students be able to generate original sentences for 10 new vocabulary words per week. Such intentional word learning opportunities can be either teacher- or student-directed. Intentional vocabulary learning interventions are labor-intensive, however, because they require that direct efforts be expended on word learning activities. Techniques that utilize high amounts of teacher time are particularly labor-intensive.

Recent Studies on Teaching Specific Words

Baumann and Kameenui (1991) noted that even studies employing definition or synonym instruction, which have come under increasingly strong criticism, report that the number of words learned exceeds the number acquired during incidental learning opportunities. Recent studies have examined the benefit of using alternative vocabulary-learning techniques, such as semantic mapping/features analysis, and keyword and computer-assisted methods, versus more traditional techniques.

Semantic Mapping/Features Analysis. Bos and Anders (1990) compared the effects of three knowledge-based interactive vocabulary instructional techniques with a traditional definition approach to vocabulary instruction. Participants were 61 junior high students with learning disabilities who were learning from science text. In knowledge-based instruction, students were assigned to one of three groups. Students in the semantic mapping group constructed a hierarchical relationship map from a vocabulary list. Students in the semantic-feature analysis group predicted the relationships among concepts using a relationship matrix. Students in the semantic/ syntactic feature analysis group predicted the relationships among concepts and the answers for cloze-type sentences using a relationship matrix as a guide. Finally, students in the (access/instrumental [definition] instruction group) were directly taught the definitions of the vocabulary terms, emphasizing oral recitation, correct and automatic pronunciation of each vocabulary word or phrase, and memorization of concise context-related definitions.

Students read a passage from their science text and then met as a group to discuss the text in a postreading activity. Then, they were instructed to write all they could recall about the topic. Their performance was evaluated on the basis of vocabulary learning, reading comprehension, and the quality of written recalls. Bos and Anders (1990) found that on the reading test overall (vocabulary and comprehension items), and specifically on the reading comprehension items, students in the three interactive interventions scored higher than students engaged in definition learning.

In addition to vocabulary growth, the use of semantic maps may result in consistent improvements in reading comprehension. Sinatra, Berg, and Dunn (1985) found that the use of two types of semantic maps, one with class, property, and example connections, and one modeled after typical story grammar elements, resulted in improved reading comprehension scores for three students with learning disabilities on 11 of 15 comparisons. Despite the small sample size, the authors suggested their findings supported the theory that students with learning disabilities have difficulty organizing and recalling verbal information.

In an investigation with a similar focus to the study by Bos and Anders (1990), Fawcett and Nicolson (1991) taught five students with reading disabilities and rich vocabularies and eight students with reading disabilities and poor vocabularies 24 vocabulary words and 24 matched untrained words. The students, ages 11 to 14, were trained for an average of either 10 minutes per word or 3.3 minutes per word in an enriched training condition (i.e., generating sentences and contexts, cross-linking words, and identifying affective reactions, stressing semantic links with related concepts); or a traditional training condition (i.e., worksheets, crosswords, word bingo, and missing letters in order to link words with definitions).

Students were tested on word knowledge using a multiple-choice format and lexical decision speed and accuracy (i.e., deciding if an item was a word or nonword as quickly as possible). All students scored higher on word knowledge at posttest than pretest. Neither the enriched training nor greater amount of training (10 minutes per word vs. 3.3 minutes per word) led to significantly better word knowledge. This finding indicates that if the goal is word knowledge at a rudimentary level (i.e., associative level; Baumann & Kameenui, 1991), then modest amounts of instruction may suffice. Some evidence in this study suggests that amount of training but not type of training may have influenced another level of word understanding, speed of lexical access. Thus, students trained on words for 10 minutes were able to recognize items as words or nonwords faster than students trained for 3.3 minutes.

Keyword Method. The keyword method has received considerable support as a technique for teaching word meanings to students (Baumann & Kameenui, 1991). In the keyword method, the student is taught to construct a visual image that connects the target word and a familiar, concrete word (similar auditorially) that shares some common feature. For example, in the word *carlin,* which means *old woman,* the keyword *car* might be used to have the student generate the image of an old woman driving a car. When asked to recall the meaning of *carlin,* the student retrieves *car* because of its acoustic similarity to *carlin,* and then recalls the visual image and the meaning of carlin (example from Pressley, Levin, & McDaniel, 1987, cited in Baumann & Kameenui, 1991).

Critics have argued that the keyword method works better for concrete words (e.g., carlin) than abstract words (e.g., festive). To examine this contention, Mastropieri, Scruggs, and Fulk (1990) compared the keyword method to a more traditional rehearsal method. They taught 25 students with learning disabilities eight abstract and eight concrete words using either a keyword method or a rehearsal method. In the rehearsal method, students were instructed on word meanings using experimenter-led drill and practice, rapid-paced questioning, and corrective feedback. The keyword method was more successful than the rehearsal method on a production test in which students provided an oral definition of the word, and a generalization measure in which students provided the appropriate word given a novel instance of the word. In addition, Mastropieri et al. (1990) found that the keyword method was just as successful for teaching the meanings of abstract as concrete word meanings (4.96 vs. 5.71 words).

Condus, Marshall, and Miller (1986) examined the effectiveness of four vocabulary intervention techniques with 64 students with learning disabilties. The instructional interventions were the keyword method, picture context, and sentence-experience context. In addition, students in the control group could choose any method they wanted to learn the vocabulary word meanings. Students were taught 50 words in 10- to 20-minute training periods conducted three times per week over 5 weeks. Vocabulary performance was measured with a multiple-choice test. Immediately following the intervention, students in the keyword group and in the two context groups outperformed control students on the vocabulary test. Students in the keyword group outperformed students in all the other groups. At an 8-week follow-up, the keyword group mean was nearly twice the mean of the lowest experimental group (sentence–experience; 28 words vs. 15 words) and more than three times greater than the control group mean (9 words correct).

Computer-Assisted Methods. Two recent studies have examined the effectiveness of computer-assisted interventions for increasing knowledge of individual words. Three features in particular, seem to make computer-assisted interventions attractive. First, such interventions require less direct teacher time than teacher-led instruction. Second, they have the potential to individualize instruction and facilitate the alignment of instructional techniques and vocabulary goals. Third, they have the potential to systematically imbed important instructional design features within the intervention framework, including systematic review, instructional scaffolding, and integration across academic areas.

Johnson, Gersten, and Carnine (1987) used two computer-assisted instructional vocabulary programs to teach the meaning of 50 words to 25 high school students with learning disabilities. Students were matched on vocabulary pretest scores and randomly assigned to one of two computer-assisted instructional groups. The differences between the groups were the size of the teaching sets and the procedures for cumulative review. One program provided teaching and practice exercises on small sets of words (i.e., 10) and cumulative review exercises on all words learned in the program, whereas the other presented exercises on two sets of 25 words and no cumulative review. Students received computer-assisted vocabulary instruction for a maximum of eleven 20-minute sessions.

The major finding was that significantly more students in the small teaching set reached mastery within 11 sessions than students in the large teaching set group. Learning was measured using a criterion-referenced test. Students in both groups learned approximately the same number of words (17.3 vs. 18.95) and retained the information over time, as measured by the maintenance test (15.8 vs. 17.25). Students in the small teaching set with cumulative review seemed to learn the material more efficiently.

A second study on computer-assisted instruction was conducted by Reinking and Rickman (1990). Computer-mediated texts provided students immediate access to the definitions of difficult words in a passage on a computer screen. That is, students either selected to view the definitions of words at their discretion, or the definitions of the target words were automatically presented. In two noncomputer-assisted conditions, students could look words up at their discretion in a dictionary or a glossary. Results showed that students in the two computer-assisted groups scored significantly higher on the multiple-choice vocabulary test and the passage comprehension test than students in the dictionary or glossary groups. The means between the groups on the multiple-choice vocabulary test, however, indicated that the effects were not particularly strong and may have been attenuated by a ceiling effect. Mean scores for students in the dictionary and glossary groups (26.4 and 26.5 correct, respectively, out of 32) were only two or three items lower than students in the self-select and computer-select groups (28.7 and 29.4, respectively). In addition, test performance seemed to be only marginally affected by the number of definitions provided to students. Students in the glossary group, for example, looked up an average of 2.1 words, whereas students in the self-select computer group looked up an average of 9.6 words. Thus, students either had some understanding of the majority of words considered difficult prior to the study, or they learned enough about the meaning of the words during passage reading to answer the items correctly on the vocabulary test.

In summary, vocabulary interventions typically include procedures to enhance student understanding of individual words. In general, innovative vocabulary interventions are superior to traditional instructional procedures that focus on transmitting a single definition of a target word. These more effective procedures include semantic/syntactic features analysis, the keyword method, and computer-assisted methods.

AREA OF CONVERGENCE 5:
Reading Achievement and
Vocabulary Acquisition

The fifth and final area of convergence in research on vocabulary development is that students need to develop strong beginning reading skills to be able to engage successfully in the volume of reading necessary for them to learn large numbers of word meanings through reading connected text (Anderson & Nagy, 1991). The only realistic chance students with poor vocabularies have to catch up to their peers with rich vocabularies requires that they engage in extraordinary amounts of independent reading. Furthermore, research finding are increasingly clear that opportunities for developing adequate reading skills are limited. In fact, the status quo in beginning reading instruction may be entirely insufficient to meet the reading and vocabulary needs of many diverse learners (Adams, 1990; Liberman & Liberman, 1990). For example, according to Juel's (1988) longitudinal study, there was an 88% chance that a poor reader at the end of first grade would remain a poor reader at the end of fourth grade. Stanovich (1986) explained how the development of strong beginning reading skills facilitated vocabulary growth, which in turn facilitated the further increases in reading. This reciprocal, causal relation between reading and vocabulary seems to continue unabated throughout development.

The amount of independent reading that diverse learners need to engage in to reduce the vocabulary gap that separates them from normal achieving peers is extensive. Researchers generally agree that students do learn word meanings in the course of reading connected text, but the process appears to be very time consuming (Baumann & Kameenui, 1991; Beck & McKeown, 1991). That is, students have to engage in considerable amounts of reading to be exposed to unknown words a sufficient number of times for them to be learned.

Beck and McKeown (1991) asserted that "research spanning several decades has failed to uncover strong evidence that word meanings are routinely acquired from context" (p. 799). Their conclusion was that some learning from context does occur, but that the effect is not very powerful. A number of other studies have examined the effects of learning words through normal reading activities (incidental learning). For example, Jenkins, Stein, and Wysocki (cited in Beck & McKeown, 1991) studied the effects of learning words in context with fifth-grade students. The contexts were created so that a word's meaning was either strongly implied or a synonym was provided. Jenkins et al. found that students learned the meaning of words that had been encountered 6 or 10 times, unless exposure to meaning occurred prior to passage reading, in which case two encounters were sufficient to produce positive effects. Nagy, Herman, and Anderson (cited in Beck & McKeown, 1991) calculated that the probability of learning a word from a single contextual encounter was between .05 and .11, depending on the learning criterion used.

Oetting et al. (1995) investigated incidental word learning in the context of verbal stimuli. They investigated the likelihood that 6-, 7-, and 8-year-old children with and without disabilities would learn the meanings of 20 experimental words, each presented five times in the course of two, 6-minute videotaped stories. Assessing students' receptive vocabulary knowledge using a format similar to the Peabody Picture Vocabulary Test, they found that students increased from correctly identifying an average of 5.33 words to 10 (out of 20) from pretest to posttest. Students with disabilities increased from 5.32 to 7.60. A group of normally achieving control students who watched a different videotape stayed about the same. Oetting et al. concluded that the actual word learning that occurred in the context of a relatively short 12-minute period was quite impressive for both students with and students without disabilities in the experimental conditions. It is alarming however, that in such a short period of time, students without disabilities learned about twice as many words as students with disabilities (4.67 vs. 2.28). When these different rates of learning are extended across days, years, and literally hundreds of stories and other verbal interactions, the growth in the magnitude of the vocabulary gap between diverse learners and normal achieving students becomes apparent.

By the time students are in the upper elementary grades, reading accounts for much of the vocabulary learning that occurs. Even though independent reading may not be an efficient way to learn word meanings, the procedure does not have to be efficient to be effective, and thus, to ultimately result in powerful overall effects (Anderson & Nagy, 1991). Given that students in the primary and middle grades read anywhere from 100,000 to more than 10 million words of connected text per year (Nagy & Anderson, 1984), it is unnecessary for students to be efficient in deriving the meaning of words from text for the procedure to result in considerable vocabulary learning.

Relatedly, the connection between reading comprehension and vocabulary knowledge is strong and unequivocal (Baumann & Kameenui, 1991; Paul & O'Rourke, 1988; Stanovich, 1986), although the precise nature of the causal relation between the two constructs is still under investigation. As Stanovich (1986) stated:

> The correlation between reading ability and vocabulary knowledge is sizable throughout development. Although, as in most areas of reading research, correlational evidence is much more plentiful that experimental evidence, there is a growing body of data indicating that variation in vocabulary knowledge is a causal determinant of differences in reading comprehension ability. It seems probable that like phonological awareness, vocabulary knowledge is involved in a reciprocal relationship with reading ability, but that—unlike the case of phonological

awareness—the relationship is one that continues throughout reading development and remains in force for even the most fluent adult readers. (p. 379)

Arguing that reading instruction should be an integral component of a comprehensive vocabulary building program we return to Becker's (1977) observation that vocabulary knowledge was the primary factor limiting the reading and academic success beyond Grade 3 of students from impoverished backgrounds. We can use a similar rationale to argue that if the spiraling negative effects of reading problems are to be avoided, comprehensive vocabulary development programs should be implemented with students prior to Grade 3.

SUMMARY

Vocabulary acquisition is crucial to academic development. Not only do students need a rich body of word knowledge to succeed in basic skill areas, they also need a specialized vocabulary to learn content area material. A foundation of vocabulary knowledge must be in place early if children are going to perform successfully in school. The following points capsulize our findings of recent research on vocabulary acquisition.

- Students learn an amazing number of words during their early school years, as many as approximately 3,000 per year on the average, or 8 words per day. However, the number of words students learn varies greatly. As some students are learning eight or more words per day, other students are learning only one or two.
- Even as early as kindergarten, sizable differences are found between students in the number of words known. This vocabulary gap tends to increase significantly throughout school. Thus, early differences in vocabulary knowledge have strong implications for students' long-term educational success.
- Multiple factors may contribute to differential rates of vocabulary growth. Biological factors that may partially account for differential rates of vocabulary growth include general language deficits and memory problems. Also, a strong relation has been found between environmental indicators such as socioeconomic status and vocabulary knowledge, indicating that home factors may contribute substantially to students' vocabulary knowledge.
- Nearly all strategies of increasing vocabulary knowledge result in greater learning than occurs during typical opportunities. These methods have included semantic mapping and semantic features analysis procedures, the keyword method, and computer-assisted instruction.

- Words can be known at different levels of understanding. Therefore, choice of vocabulary intervention procedure should be based on the procedure's efficiency with respect to teacher and student time, and its usefulness in helping students learn the meaning of other words independently.
- Directly teaching word meanings does not adequately reduce the gap between students with poor versus rich vocabularies because of the size of the gap. It is crucial, therefore, that students also learn strategies for learning word meanings independently.
- The relation between reading comprehension and vocabulary knowledge is strong and unequivocal. Although the precise causal direction of the relation is not understood clearly, there is evidence that the relation is largely reciprocal.
- The development of strong reading skills is the most effective independent word learning strategy available. However, those students who are in the greatest need of vocabulary acquisition interventions tend to be the same students who read poorly and fail to engage in the amount of reading necessary to learn large numbers of words.
- The meaning of words is learned during independent reading activities, but the effects do not appear to be very powerful. Words need to be encountered in text multiple times before their meaning becomes part of a student's vocabulary. However, although independent reading is not an efficient way to learn word meanings, the tremendous number of words typical students in the primary and middle grades encounter in written text nevertheless result in considerable vocabulary learning.
- Improvements in beginning reading instruction are crucial if students are to develop the skills necessary to engage in significant amounts of independent reading and hence acquire a sufficiently large vocabulary.

TABLE 8.1
Description of Vocabulary Studies

Author	Vocabulary Dimension	Participants	Purpose
Anderson & Nagy (1991)	Theoretical models of word knowledge	All age groups. Primary focus on normal achievers	To discuss the nature of people's knowledge about word meaning and how word meaning is acquired and used in reading comprehension
Baumann & Kameenui (1991)	Vocabulary instruction	Studies involved varying populations including normal to high achieving, disadvantaged, and students with learning disabilities. Students ranged in grade from third through college level (a few studies included kindergarten and first graders)	To discuss (a) the theoretical and pedagogical issues that haunt research on vocabulary instruction, (b) ways by which we can best teach vocabulary, and (c) what we know and do not know about teaching vocabulary
Beck & McKeown (1991)	Vocabulary acquisition	Studies reflect varied populations	To discuss (a) what the role of instruction is in vocabulary acquisition, (b) what it means to know the meaning of a word, (c) what we know about vocabulary size and growth, and (d) how word knowledge is measured
Kameenui, Dixon, & Carnine (1987)	Vocabulary instruction	Primary focus on students who have at least minimal levels of reading skill.	To discuss the link between vocabulary learning and reading comprehension within the context of reading instruction, and to propose a comprehensive instructional program for increasing vocabulary development and reading comprehension

(Continued)

TABLE 8.1
CONTINUED

Graves (1986)	Vocabulary learning and instruction	School-age students	To explore vocabulary size, depth of word knowledge, and how to assess word knowledge. The study also discusses the effects of vocabulary on reading comprehension, teaching individual words, and the instruction that currently takes place in schools
McKeown & Beck (1988)	Matching vocabulary goals to vocabulary instruction	School-age students	To (a) discuss the design features of effective vocabulary instruction, (b) explore issues that affect vocabulary instruction design, and (c) promote an instructional model for vocabulary acquisition
Paul & O'Rourke (1988)	Relationship between multimeaning words and reading comprehension	Primary focus on low-performing students	To (a) present general findings regarding prevalence of polysemic words in reading materials, (b) discuss the relationship between vocabulary instruction and reading comprehension, and (c) give examples of teacher-directed, theory-based instructional techniques.

Primary Studies

Bos & Anders (1990)	Increasing student knowledge of individual words and reading comprehension skills	Junior high students with learning disabilities. $N = 61$	To compare effectiveness of three knowledge-based interactive vocabulary strategies
Boucher (1986)	Semantics and pragmatics-- being competent in interpersonal communication	Grade 5 and 6 students with and without learning disabilities. $N = 10$	To determine if there are differences in the verbal language of students with and without learning disabilities and identify any changes between these groups on the basis of listener age
Condus, Marshall, & Miller (1986)	Increasing student knowledge of individual words	12-year-old students with learning disabilities. $N = 64$	To investigate the effectiveness of an imposed keyword mnemonic strategy and two other instructional procedures on vocabulary acquisition and maintenance
Fawcett & Nicolson (1991)	Using parents to enhance student knowledge of individual words	Adolescents with dyslexia, ages 11 to 14. $N = 13$	To investigate whether children with dyslexia show similar training effects to those reported in other studies
Griswold, Gelzheiser, & Shepherd (1987)	The strategies students use to learn word meanings	Grade 8 students with and without learning disabilities. $N = 76$	To investigate whether the failure to spontaneously produce appropriate strategies for memorizing word definitions accounts for vocabulary differences between students
Highnam & Morris (1987)	Appropriateness of linguistic stress and semantic interpretation in discourse	9-year-old students with and without learning disabilities. $N = 20$	To examine differences between students in the ability to recognize the appropriate use of linguistic stress and semantic interpretation in discourse

(Continued)

213

TABLE 8.1
CONTINUED

Johnson, Gersten, & Carnine (1987)	Increasing student knowledge of individual words	Students with learning disabilities in Grades 9 through 12. $N = 25$	To compare the effects of two methods of computer-assisted vocabulary instruction on the acquisition and maintenance of word meaning
Lorsbach & Gray (1985)	The process by which stimulus attributes are selected for storage in long-term memory	Students with and without learning disabilities in Grades 2 and 6. $N = 72$	To compare the encoding preferences of students with and without learning disabilities
Mastropieri, Scruggs, & Fulk (1990)	Increasing student knowledge of individual words	Students in Grades 6 through 8 with learning disabilities. $N = 25$	To investigate if students with learning disabilities learn the meanings of concrete and abstract words equally well using the keyword method; and whether they adapt their acquired vocabulary to semantically novel instances
Oetting, Rice, & Swank (1995)	Incidental learning of novel vocabulary via videotaped stories	6-, 7-, and 8-year-old students with and without specific language disabilities. $N = 66$	To compare rates of incidental vocabulary learning for different word types: object words, attribute words, action words, and affective words
Reinking & Rickman (1990)	Computer-assisted strategies to increase student knowledge of individual words	Normally achieving students in Grade 6. $N = 60$	To determine if intermediate-grade readers' vocabulary learning and comprehension would be affected by two types of computer-assisted strategies
Shore & Durso (1990)	Partial knowledge in vocabulary acquisition	Volunteers from psychology introduction class. $N = 132$	To assess levels of word knowledge by filtering words through a series of questions that required increasingly less understanding of the target word

Simmons & Kameenui (1990)	The effects of task form on vocabulary knowledge	10- and 12-year-old students with and without learning disabilities. $N = 48$	To examine the effect of task demands on vocabulary learning with different students
Sinatra, Berg, & Dunn (1985)	Recall and organization of information within written texts	Primary and elementary students with learning disabilities. $N = 3$	To show how the semantic mapping approach can improve the reading comprehension of students with learning disabilities
Stahl & Erickson (1986)	Causes of language problems in students with disabilities	Students in Grades 1 and 3 with and without learning disabilities. $N = 38$	To compare the performance of students on a variety of language and reading tasks to explicate the causes of language problems in students with disabilities
Swanson (1986)	Semantic memory	Students with and without disabilities. $N = 32$	To determine if semantic memory deficiencies underlie the encoding processes of students with learning disabilities
Walker & Poteet (1989)	Memory performance--deep encoding and efficient recall	Students in Grades 4 and 5 with and without learning disabilities. $N = 60$	To investigate differences between students on their performance on a cued recall memory test, and to examine the interaction between processing level and retrieval cues
White, Graves, & Slater (1990)	Reading vocabulary and socioeconomic status	Students in Grades 1 to 4 in three schools with different cultures and socioeconomic status levels. $N = 47$ to 91 in each grade at each school	To estimate the vocabulary size and growth of students in Grades 1 through 4

REFERENCES

Adams, M. J. (1990). *Beginning to read: Thinking and learning about print.* Cambridge, MA: MIT Press.

American Heritage Dictionary of the English language. (1992). (3rd ed.). Boston: Houghton Mifflin.

Anderson, R. C., & Nagy, W. E. (1991). Word meanings. In R. Barr, M. L. Kamil, P. B. Mosenthal, & P. D. Pearson (Eds.), *Handbook of reading research* (Vol. 2, pp. 690–724). New York: Longman.

Baumann, J. F., & Kameenui, E. J. (1991). Research on vocabulary instruction: Ode to Voltaire. In J. Flood, J. J. D. Lapp, & J. R. Squire (Eds.), *Handbook of research on teaching the English language arts* (pp. 604–632). New York: Macmillan.

Beck, I., & McKeown, M. (1991). Conditions of vocabulary acquisition. In R. Barr, M. Kamil, P. Mosenthal, & P. D. Pearson (Eds.), *Handbook of reading research* (Vol. 2, pp. 789–814). New York: Longman.

Becker, W. C. (1977). Teaching reading and language to the disadvantaged—What we have learned from field research. *Harvard Educational Review, 47,* 518–543.

Biemiller, A. (1977/1978). Relationships between oral reading rates for letters, words, and simple text in the development of reading achievement. *Reading Research Quarterly, 13,* 223-253.

Bos, C. S., & Anders, P. L. (1990). Effects of interactive vocabulary instruction on the vocabulary learning and reading comprehension of junior-high learning disabled students. *Learning Disability Quarterly, 13,* 31–42.

Boucher, C. R. (1986). Pragmatics: The meaning of verbal language in learning disabled and non-disabled boys. *Learning Disability Quarterly, 9,* 285–294.

Carey, S. (1978). The child as word learner. In M. Halle, J. Bresman, & G. Miller (Eds.), *Linguistic theory and psychological reality* (pp. 265–293). Cambridge, MA: MIT Press.

Carnine, D., Silbert, J., & Kameenui, E. J. (1990). *Direct instruction reading.* Columbus, OH: Merrill.

Condus, M. M., Marshall, K. J., & Miller, S. R. (1986). Effects of the keyword mnemonic strategy on vocabulary acquisition and maintenance by learning disabled children. *Journal of Learning Disabilities, 19,* 609–613.

Fawcett, A. J., & Nicolson, R. I. (1991). Vocabulary training for children with dyslexia. *Journal of Learning Disabilities, 24,* 379–383.

Graves, M. F. (1986). Vocabulary learning and instruction. In E. Z. Rothkopf (Ed.), *Review of research in education, 13,* 49–89.

Griswold, P. C., Gelzheiser, L. M., & Shepherd, M. J. (1987). Does a production deficiency hypothesis account for vocabulary learning among adolescents with learning disabilities? *Journal of Learning Disabilities, 20,* 620–626.

Highnam, C., & Morris, V. (1987). Linguistic stress judgments of language learning disabled students. *Journal of Communication Disorders, 20,* 93–103.

Johnson, G., Gersten, R., & Carnine, D. (1987). Effects of instructional design variables on vocabulary acquisition of LD students: A study of computer-assisted instruction. *Journal of Learning Disabilities, 20,* 206–212.

Juel, C. (1988). Learning to read and write: A longitudinal study of 54 children from first through fourth grades. *Journal of Educational Psychology, 80,* 837–847.

Kameenui, E. J., Dixon, D. W., & Carnine, D. (1987). Issues in the design of vocabulary instruction. In M. G. McKeown & M. E. Curtis (Eds.), *The nature of vocabulary acquisition* (pp. 129–145). Hillsdale, NJ: Lawrence Erlbaum Associates.

Liberman, I., & Liberman, A. (1990). Whole language vs. code emphasis: Underlying assumptions and their implications for reading instruction. *Annals of Dyslexia, 40,* 51–76.

Lorsbach, T. C., & Gray, J. (1985). The development of encoding processes in learning disabled children. *Journal of Learning Disabilities, 18*, 222–227.

Mastropieri, M. A., Scruggs, T. E., & Fulk, B. J. (1990). Teaching abstract vocabulary with the keyword method: Effects on recall and comprehension. *Journal of Learning Disabilities, 23*, 92–107.

McKeown, M. G., & Beck, I. L. (1988). Learning vocabulary: Different ways for different goals. *Remedial and Special Education, 9*(1), 42–46.

Nagy, W., & Anderson, R. C. (1984). How many words are there in printed school English? *Reading Research Quarterly, 19*, 304–330.

Oetting, J. B., Rice, M. L., & Swank, L. K. (1995). Quick incidental learning (QUIL) of words by school-age children with and without specific language impairment. *Journal of Speech and Hearing Research, 38*, 434–445.

Paul, P. V., & O'Rourke, J. P. (1988). Multimeaning words and reading comprehension: Implications for special education students. *Remedial and Special Education, 9*(3), 42–52.

Reinking, D., & Rickman, S. S. (1990). The effects of computer-mediated texts on the vocabulary learning and comprehension of intermediate-grade readers. *Journal of Reading Behavior, 22*, 395–411.

Shore, W. J., & Durso, F. T. (1990). Partial knowledge in vocabulary acquisition: General constraints and specific detail. *Journal of Educational Psychology, 82*, 315–318.

Simmons, D. C., & Kameenui, E. J. (1990). The effect of task alternatives on vocabulary knowledge: A comparison of students with learning disabilities and students of normal achievement. *Journal of Learning Disabilities, 23*, 291–297.

Sinatra, R. C., Berg, D., & Dunn, R. (1985). Semantic mapping improves reading comprehension of learning disabled students. *Teaching Exceptional Children, 17*, 310-314.

Stahl, S. A., & Erickson, L. G. (1986). The performance of third grade learning disabled boys on tasks at different levels of language: A model-based exploration. *Journal of Learning Disabilities, 9*, 285–290.

Stanovich, K. E. (1986). Matthew effects in reading: Some consequences of individual differences in the acquisition of literacy. *Reading Research Quarterly, 21*, 360–406.

Swanson, H. L. (1986). Do semantic memory deficiencies underlie learning readers' encoding processes? *Journal of Experimental Child Psychology, 41*, 461–488.

Walker, S. C., & Poteet, J. A. (1989). Influencing memory performance in learning disabled students through semantic processing. *Learning Disabilities Research, 5*, 25–32.

White, T. G., Graves, M. F., & Slater, W. H. (1990). Growth of reading vocabulary in diverse elementary schools: Decoding and word meaning. *Journal of Educational Psychology, 82*, 281–290.

CHAPTER

9

Vocabulary Acquisition: Instructional and Curricular Basics and Implications

Scott K. Baker
Deborah C. Simmons
Edward J. Kameenui
University of Oregon

REVIEW OF CONVERGING EVIDENCE

Early literacy acquisition is fundamental to school success and long-term social, vocational, and economic adjustment. Many students, including a growing percentage of diverse learners, depend largely on the quality of instruction in the early primary grades to develop the literacy skills needed for school success. The importance of early reading and writing instruction has been heavily publicized. In contrast, vocabulary development, although clearly recognized, has not received the same degree of instructional attention as other literacy skills. After all, "vocabulary development" is not an academic subject like reading, mathematics, and science. However, although vocabulary development pervades every subject from reading to mathematics to physical education, it is difficult to isolate for instructional purposes. Still, a lucid argument can be made for a much more active and vigorous educational commitment to increasing the vocabulary growth of diverse learners who often experience vocabulary problems and delays.

Based on our review of the research on vocabulary acquisition (Baker, Simmons, & Kameenui, this volume), five areas of convergence were identified that have implications for vocabulary development in daily instructional routines:

- Vocabulary differences between students are extensive. Differences arise early, and the vocabulary gap between students grows larger over time.

- Researchers have attempted to identify critical factors that contribute to individual differences in vocabulary growth. Most explanations center on student characteristics that can be grouped into three categories: generalized linguistic deficiencies, memory deficits, and poor word learning strategies.
- Instructional procedures to teach word meanings should be consonant with goals for depth of word knowledge.
- Various instructional methods have led to increases in students' knowledge of individual words, beyond gains that could be expected from typical incidental learning opportunities. However, a single best method of vocabulary instruction has not been identified.
- Students need strong beginning reading skills to engage successfully in the volume of reading necessary to gain exposure to and possibly learn large numbers of word meanings from independent reading of connected text.

In this chapter, we discuss the implications of these areas of convergence in relation to a framework of curriculum design principles that has received empirical support for enhancing the academic achievement of diverse learners. Referring to the major guidelines of the vocabulary framework as *big ideas*, we use the validated instructional principles of *conspicuous strategies, strategic integration, mediated scaffolding, primed background knowledge,* and *judicious review* to render these big ideas more explicit and employable.

In considering the research support for vocabulary development, it is necessary to reiterate an important point made in our review of the research on vocabulary acquisition (Baker, Simmons, & Kameenui, this volume): Successful vocabulary interventions can be judged by whether they result in increased word learning above what might otherwise occur during typical incidental and explicit learning opportunities; or they can be judged more broadly, to the extent that they meaningfully reduce the gap between students with poor versus rich vocabularies. The instructional framework we present is designed to address both of these criteria for success. Most persuasive, however, is evidence that the more comprehensive goal of reducing the vocabulary gap between students has been attained.

In the next section, we describe big ideas from our review of research on vocabulary acquisition that are instructionally important and empirically validated. We attempt to connect research and practice by responding to two focus questions: (a) What are the research-based instructional priorities or "big ideas" in vocabulary development? and (b) For the instructional priorities of vocabulary development, what is the existing research evidence regarding curriculum design?

Although there is research support for each of the vocabulary intervention techniques we discuss, the framework we propose to comprehensively address the vocabulary delays of diverse learners is based more on a logical analysis of the problem than clear and warranted research evidence. Comprehensive vocabulary programs have been discussed in numerous secondary sources (e.g., Baumann & Kameenui, 1991; Beck & McKeown, 1991; Graves, 1986; Kameenui, Dixon, & Carnine, 1987; McKeown & Beck, 1988), but the effectiveness of comprehensive vocabulary development programs that address the needs of diverse learners has not been investigated. The following section should not be viewed as a prescription, but rather as an application of principles that can be used to make tangible the details and relations of instruction for students with diverse learning needs.

RESEARCH-BASED INSTRUCTION PRIORITIES IN VOCABULARY ACQUISITION: BIG IDEAS

From the five areas of convergence, we have derived two big ideas that we believe successfully frame the major guideposts of comprehensive vocabulary instructional programs for diverse learners.

1. Interventions to address the vocabulary delays of diverse learners should align goals for depth of word knowledge with instructional techniques.

Goals for word knowledge correspond to the "depth of knowledge" an individual has about a word's meaning. This depth includes knowledge of the different contexts in which a word is used (e.g., the 26 contextual uses of the word set as a verb, 6 uses of *set* as a adjective, and 9 uses of *set* as a noun; *American Heritage Dictionary*, 1992), and familiarity with critical features that define a word's meaning (e.g., *parka* is a garment, is used in cold weather, has a hood, and is frequently used in the rain; Anderson & Nagy, 1991). Depth of word knowledge covaries with the requirements of the task used to assess knowledge, and an individual does not need to know *all* definitions of a word and *all* its contextual meanings to use a word successfully. What is important is that instruction parallels the expectation of word usage.

"Depth of word knowledge" can most accurately be represented on a continuous scale ranging from *little or no understanding of a word's meaning to full understanding*. Numerous authors have used terms corresponding to minimal, partial, and full knowledge to describe qualitatively different levels of word knowledge (e.g., Baumann & Kameenui, 1991; Beck & McKeown, 1991; Graves, 1986; Kameenui et al., 1987). We use Baumann

DEPTH OF UNDERSTANDING   INSTRUCTIONAL STRATEGIES

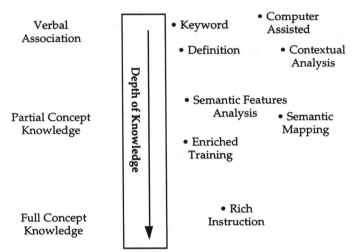

FIG. 9.1. Evaluating the alignment between goals for depth of word knowledge and instructional technique.

and Kameenui's (1991) descriptors, *verbal association knowledge, partial concept knowledge,* and *full concept knowledge,* to discuss depth of word knowledge and its relation to instruction.

The minimum level of knowledge is *verbal association knowledge,* which enables a person to link a new word with a specific definition or a single context. In *full concept knowledge,* an individual understands and can use a word in novel instances, knows the varied meanings of multiple-meaning words, and is able to discriminate a word's meaning from the meanings of other similar words. *Partial concept knowledge* falls between verbal association knowledge and full concept knowledge. Specifically, an individual may be able to use a word in a limited number of ways, understand some of the meanings of multiple-meaning words, and have difficulty discriminating a word's meaning from the meanings of other similar words.

We interpret the vocabulary research as suggesting that the goals for vocabulary knowledge should guide instructional technique. In Fig. 9.1, we present a guideline for evaluating the "fit" between goals for depth of knowledge and instructional techniques that have been supported empirically. Obviously, in something as fluid and dynamic as vocabulary knowledge, a comfortable "fit" between goals and instructional techniques requires considerable flexibility. However, the guideline should be useful when considering the value and efficiency of instructional choices.

For example, the *keyword method* is more likely to result in *verbal association knowledge* than *full concept knowledge.* This is true because, by definition, the *keyword method* teaches the association between a target word and its predominant definition. At the other end of the continuum, a procedure such as McKeown and Beck's (1988) *rich instruction* includes a variety of procedures to facilitate *partial* and *full concept knowledge*, including generating definitions and sentences, classification tasks, oral and written production tasks, game-like tasks, and tasks that stress the relations between target words and previously acquired vocabulary. *In rich instruction*, the goal is for students to learn word meanings at a deep level of understanding. Each method, whether keyword, semantic maps, rich instruction, and so on, has empirical support, yet its value must be evaluated in light of the task and textual expectations.

2.   Interventions to increase the vocabulary knowledge of diverse learners should move systematically toward ensuring that students become independent word learners.

Students learn approximately 3,000 words per year during the early grades. Obviously, it is educationally impossible for students to learn even a sizable portion of these new words through direct instructional approaches. Instead, students must and do learn word meanings independently. However, the vocabulary gap between students with poor versus rich vocabularies expands yearly throughout students' academic careers, clearly indicating that some students are better word learners than others. Thus, the second big idea in a comprehensive vocabulary development program is that *students with poor vocabularies, including diverse learners, need strong and systematic educational support to become successful independent word learners.* For many students, the critical framework that helps pave the way to successful independent word learning skills is established early through exposure to written text and development of strong skills in reading and writing. With diverse learners, however, the foundation for vocabulary learning independence requires systematic instruction that occurs early and is applied intensely for a long period of time.

Students develop an extensive lexicon prior to learning a print system (Beck & McKeown, 1991). However, reading is probably the most important mechanism for vocabulary growth throughout a student's school-age years and beyond (Anderson & Nagy, 1991; Baumann & Kameenui, 1991). Around kindergarten and first grade, typical students know between 2,500 and 5,000 root words (Beck & McKeown, 1991), the vast majority of which are high-frequency, utilitarian words. An increasingly large percentage of the approximately 3,000 words students learn per year in the early primary grades are more complex, infrequently used words reserved primarily for specialized academic activities. Reading allows students to "reflect" on the meaning of these types of words in a way that speech cannot.

Thus, a comprehensive vocabulary development program that meets the needs of diverse learners should (a) teach words that are strategic to academic success and not typically acquired independently, and (b) include systematic procedures to make students independent word learners, primarily by helping them become voracious readers (Anderson & Nagy, 1991).

EVIDENCE OF CURRICULUM DESIGN IN VOCABULARY ACQUISITION

Conspicuous Strategies

Strategies are sequences of teaching events and teacher actions that make explicit the steps that enable a learner to achieve an outcome. In vocabulary development, for example, strategies represent procedures to facilitate word learning at a desired level of understanding, and independence in the implementation of word learning strategies. Many students develop efficient vocabulary learning strategies on their own. Research indicates, however, that diverse learners are likely to develop the same strategies as their normal achieving peers, but tend to use them less efficiently (Griswold, Gelzheiser, & Shepherd, 1987). By making strategies conspicuous, teachers can better understand where, why, and how strategy use succeeds and fails.

Matching Vocabulary Goals With Instruction. For diverse learners, a comprehensive vocabulary development program should include goals for learning *many* words at the level of *verbal association* and *fewer* words at the level of *partial* and *full concept* knowledge (McKeown & Beck, 1988). Goals incorporating multiple levels of understanding are important in order for students (a) to learn the words necessary to decrease the gap between themselves and their normally achieving peers, and (b) to develop a larger lexicon of words at sufficient depth to be part of students' expressive, everyday vocabulary.

Determining which words to teach at the level of *verbal association, partial concept knowledge,* and *full concept knowledge* is critical. Factors influencing this decision include the general importance of the word in everyday use; the importance of the word in more specialized, academic use; the student's current knowledge of the target word and semantically related words; and characteristics of the word that are more conducive to certain kinds of instructional techniques, such as the *keyword method* or *semantic mapping.* The overriding principle in these four considerations is the need to balance the importance of word knowledge with the purpose, effectiveness, and efficiency of instructional techniques.

For example, teachers might use the story *The Polar Express* (Van Allsburg, 1985) in the early primary grades to teach students word meanings using multiple conspicuous strategies. This might occur during shared story reading. At the *verbal association level,* teachers may increase the meaningfulness of the story for students, including diverse learners, by teaching numerous words as they occur in the context of the story. For instance, the words *rustle* ("I did not *rustle* the sheets") and *hissing* ("From outside came the sounds of *hissing* steam and squeaking metal") appear early in the story and might be difficult for some students to understand. The meaning of these words can be clarified for students by simple explanations that *rustle* means *move* and *hissing* is a *sharp sound like that made by a train.* Rustle and hissing do not appear again in the story and are not integral to the story's meaning, yet they are interesting and can be taught efficiently, meaningfully, and conspicuously at the *verbal association level.*

Many teachers may believe that reading a story in this manner interrupts the flow of the story and, therefore, makes it more difficult for students to understand and appreciate. Two points are critical regarding this issue. First, teaching word meanings during story reading may come after the story has been read through once without interruption. Second, vocabulary-building activities can be conducted in the context of *interactive reading,* which most educators agree is an important component of shared story reading. Interactive reading allows students to be active participants in the story and enables teachers to model and gauge reading comprehension and vocabulary understanding. Teaching word meanings at the verbal association level first and foremost reinforces the basic importance of knowing the meaning of words; however, it also provides an opportunity for teachers to model how word meanings depend to a great extent on the context in which the word is used. At a more abstract level, students may begin to develop an awareness that a word's meaning is determined by a combination of its relatively permanent standard "definition," as well as the less definitive contextual restriction in which it is used.

At the other end of the continuum, *The Polar Express* contains important words that teachers might want to teach at a deeper level of understanding. Two examples are *sleigh* and *conductor,* which are used repeatedly and are integral to the story's meaning. Sleigh and conductor are words the students may have some knowledge of already, which should facilitate their being learned at a deeper level of understanding. A technique such as *semantic mapping* might help students learn these words at a level of understanding beyond verbal association. Sinatra, Berg, and Dunn (1985) presented one way to use semantic maps that classroom teachers may find useful. For the word *conductor* from *The Polar Express*, the semantic map might focus on comparing train conductors and other individuals responsible for operating passenger transportation systems, such as airplane pilots, ship captains, and bus drivers.

Similarly, a semantic map for *sleigh* might be constructed in which sleigh is presented as one vehicle in a class of vehicles (e.g., cars, horses, bikes, boats) and also, perhaps, as one toy in a class of toys (e.g., bike skates, skis, surf boards). More specific knowledge goals might restrict the semantic map to vehicles and toys used in the snow. The conspicuousness of these strategies is demonstrated in the way teachers help students make the connection between words and concepts, as dictated by student responses and the extensiveness of their answers. In addition, the extensiveness of instruction would dictate the depth of knowledge children were likely to attain for particular target words. For example, deeper levels of knowledge might be attained if (a) students wrote stories with *conductor* or *sleigh* as important themes, (b) learned the parts of a sleigh, (c) learned different meanings of *conductor*, or (d) learned about the root word, *conduct*.

Enhancing Independent Vocabulary Growth. For good reason, few things give educators as much satisfaction as watching a young skilled reader "devour" books. Early reading success is the clearest path to academic achievement and life-long learning. Also for good reason, few things are as painful to educators as students who struggle and ultimately fail to learn to read proficiently. Reading failure is a clear path to academic difficulty and is related to numerous debilitating long-term consequences including school dropout, teenage pregnancy, crime, unemployment, and economic hardship.

In relation to vocabulary development, the single most important contribution to independent word learning is ensuring that students develop strong word-recognition skills in first and second grade. By the end of second grade, students' word-recognition skills should be sufficiently automatic so that they are focusing on the primary purpose of reading: to derive meaning from text (Adams, 1990). When students are focusing primarily on reading comprehension, attention can turn from vocabulary learning techniques that are primarily teacher driven to techniques that are primarily student driven.

In many ways, the critical aspect of a smooth transfer from teacher-driven, conspicuous strategies to independent student activities is the extent to which students learn to effectively use the vocabulary learning strategies that teachers modeled during shared story reading: noting the importance of word meanings, analyzing word meanings in the context of surrounding contextual information, using tools such as dictionaries and glossaries, creating semantic maps to understand the relations between words and concepts, and recognizing that some words require a deeper understanding than others for greater story appreciation.

Students can begin to learn word meanings independently by reading connected text, either on their own or with a teacher. During early reading instruction it may be valuable if teachers monitor how students incorporate vocabulary learning strategies so they can reinforce students for engaging in these activities correctly. A second, and potentially very useful, approach is to have students engage in vocabulary-growth activities with the assistance of computer programs. Two recent studies demonstrated the effectiveness of using computers to build vocabulary knowledge (Johnson, Gersten, & Carnine, 1987; Reinking & Rickman, 1990). The Reinking and Rickman study addressed building vocabulary knowledge in the context of story reading. Students read stories displayed on a computer screen. Difficult words were highlighted and their contextual meanings were automatically presented when students scrolled to the relevant sections of the passage.

A number of validated benefits and potential benefits are associated with the use of computers to build vocabulary knowledge during reading. First, students can easily access the meaning of words they do not know, typically at the level of verbal association knowledge. Computer applications also have the potential to increase student depth of word knowledge. For example, helping students understand the relation between words through semantic maps seems especially suited to computer software.

Many students develop effective word learning strategies independently. Not only do some students develop the effective use of multiple strategies, such as analyzing a word in context and developing overt or covert semantic maps highlighting the relations between words, but they also develop an awareness of how much knowledge is required to understand and use word meanings according to learning demands. For diverse learners, however, the strategies that students with strong vocabulary skills use to learn word meanings need to be made conspicuous. The steps need to be sequenced efficiently and effectively, and the relevance of the vocabulary tasks must be clearly tied to important learning outcomes.

Strategic Integration

Strategic integration refers to the planning, consideration, and sequencing of vocabulary tasks to promote vocabulary development. New information that is integrated strategically with previously learned information and across learning settings has the greatest likelihood of being retained over time. In vocabulary development, this occurs (a) by having students practice words whose meanings they have learned in multiple subject areas or learning contexts, and (b) by systematically building new word knowledge on previous word knowledge. The research support is clear that to incorporate new words into their receptive or expressive lexicons, students need multiple exposures to words and multiple opportunities to practice using words.

Matching Vocabulary Goals With Instruction. A simple rule of thumb, based on research evidence and logical analysis, is that the greater the depth of knowledge of a word's meaning that is sought, the more important it is to use that word in multiple contexts. For example, Ms. Reyes, a middle-school teacher, wants her students to understand the term *economics* at a deep level. Ms. Reyes first teaches the definition of *economics* at the beginning of the year as the "study of things having to do with earning and spending money." Slowly, deeper understanding of *economics* is achieved by integrating the term into the history curriculum through a problem–solution–effect model of instruction, in which the problems peoples have had historically are represented as stemming from two fundamental causes: *economic problems* and *human rights problems* (Carnine, Crawford, Harniss, & Hollenbeck, 1995). Examples from history and current events that highlight how problems can be tied to an economic component (e.g., the American Revolution, Germany's aggression in World War II, Iraq's invasion of Kuwait) set the stage for a deeper understanding of *economics.* Further integration can occur by having students consider (a) the ways their lives are affected by *economic* forces, (b) an upcoming election from an *economics* perspective, (c) how parsimony in science and math can be conceptualized as economical, and (d) the politics of capitalist, socialist, and communist countries in terms of classic *economics* theory.

In an example more applicable to the primary grades, *strategic integration* of word knowledge at the level of verbal association might occur through an activity in which teachers identify two or three daily target words to which they will expose their students throughout the day during typical classroom routines and interactions. For example, three target words on one day might be *certain, compromise,* and *twilight.* These words could be used by the teacher during daily classroom conversation (e.g., "Be *certain* to clean your work areas before you leave for recess"), planned activities (e.g., presenting a potential problem in which students have to discuss how *compromise* can be achieved), or spontaneous informal assessment ("Jeremy, at one time of day is it *twilight*?").

In developing knowledge at the verbal association and partial concept levels, it is important to systematically and strategically integrate the vocabulary teachers use throughout typical classroom activities. This strategy may significantly increase the opportunities students have to learn the meanings of important words. Unfortunately, although recommended (Baumann & Kameenui, 1991; Graves, 1986), the empirical base for the vocabulary effects of oral exposure to language has not been investigated in recent vocabulary research. We consider this a key research area to enhance the vocabulary development of diverse learners in the early primary grades.

Enhancing Independent Vocabulary Growth. One of the best ways to facilitate greater independence in vocabulary growth is through the strategic integration of vocabulary learning opportunities in multiple curricular areas. In many ways, the concept of an integrated curriculum corresponds closely to what is known about vocabulary learning in general. That is, to develop more extensive vocabularies, students need multiple opportunities to practice using new words. Such opportunities might be a likely consequence of a curriculum that is more thematically than subject-based, which is a likely result of an integrated curriculum.

For example, much has been written about the positive benefits of integrating reading and writing opportunities to facilitate early literacy acquisition. In fact, it is common in whole-language classrooms for students to develop beginning reading skills by reading their own compositions. Writing facilitates student independence in vocabulary acquisition, because it is fundamentally an individual experience, and through its deliberate pace and ease of modification and change, a writer can choose words carefully and reflectively. Teachers who are able to challenge students to use opportunities to write as the context for extending their vocabulary development are likely to facilitate broad and deep vocabulary growth.

Little research has been conducted on general vocabulary growth resulting from student writing opportunities. Reading research does show, however, a positive relation between the number of times an individual is exposed to a word and the likelihood that the individual learns the meaning of the word. In the context of challenging writing opportunities, it seems that not only might students be exposed to words multiple times, but the context in which such exposure occurs may facilitate deeper reflection on word meanings than occurs typically during speech or reading opportunities.

The integration of reading and writing to promote independent vocabulary growth may apply to content area subjects. In this case, the strategic integration of reading, writing, and content area knowledge should enhance both general and content-specific vocabulary growth. For example, asking students to read about current models of government and then to write about the similarities and differences between them by comparing and contrasting democratic republics, socialist republics, and communist republics might result in students learning and using important vocabulary terms such as *capitalism, market-oriented, laissez-faire, distribution, welfare, state controlled, congress, legislation,* and *economics.*

Mediated Scaffolding

Mediated scaffolds are external supports provided by the teacher, tasks, and materials during initial learning. In vocabulary development, for example, there is a close relationship between mediated scaffolding and conspicuous strategies. The main idea behind mediated scaffolding is to provide as many strategic steps as necessary for the student to learn a word's meaning, and to systematically remove the support or scaffolding as the student's knowledge develops. Greater teacher support is generally associated with more conspicuous teacher demonstrations of strategy use.

Matching Vocabulary Goals With Instruction. In vocabulary development, the type of scaffolding provided depends on two things—the strategy used and the depth of knowledge desired. For example, when the keyword method is used, verbal association knowledge is typically desired; therefore, this method is most appropriate for words that are not known or only partially known. The instruction includes providing a definition of the target word, the keyword, and the image that connects the target word with the keyword. The image has to be chosen carefully because unless students clearly associate the keyword with the image, and the image with the definition, students are unlikely to recall the meaning of the target word.

Pressley, Levin, and McDaniel (1987; cited in Baumann & Kameenui, 1991) presented an example in which the word *carlin,* which means old woman, was taught using the keyword method. The keyword for *carlin* was *car,* and the image for accessing the definition was *an old woman driving a car.* This type of support represents a strong degree of scaffolding. To date, research with the *keyword method* has not determined whether students can generate the necessary components of keyword instruction to learn word meanings successfully. If possible, this would reduce the amount of scaffolding required. Current findings indicate that the keyword method works with a great deal of teacher scaffolding and, consequently, may need to be reserved for critical words that are not typically or effectively acquired through other methods requiring verbal association knowledge. For instance, in a study by Mastropieri, Scruggs, and Fulk

(1990), the words chosen were not high-frequency words (e.g., *oxalis, carnelian, soutache, vituperation, octroi, nescience*) and, thus, might be learned satisfactorily at a level of *verbal association knowledge*.

Other strategies at the verbal association level, such as definition, contextual analysis, and computer-assisted instruction, may require a great deal of early scaffolding, which is reduced as students develop the skills to use the methods independently. In these cases, procedures to reduce the amount of scaffolding are straightforward. The text itself frequently incorporates naturally occurring scaffolding that teachers can capitalize on to help reinforce words through contextual analysis. For example, the following sentences from *Charlotte's Web* (White, 1952) and *The Polar Express* (Van Allsburg, 1985) provide a "rich" amount of information to determine the meaning of the target words:

- "Everybody lined up at the fence and stood for a moment *admiring* Wilbur and the beautiful green crate" (White, 1952, p. 125; from this sentence *admiring* can be taken to mean liking what one is looking at).
- "We sang Christmas *carols* and ate candies with nougat centers as white as snow" (Van Allsburg, 1985, p. 7; from this sentence *carols* can be taken to refer to a type of song that has something to do with Christmas).

To suggest that these sentences include a *rich* amount of information means that the sentence itself provides useful support in determining the meaning of the target word. In contrast, many sentences provide "lean" information for determining the meaning of a target word. For example, the following sentences provide less scaffolding than the previous two:

- "It is not easy to look *radiant*, but Wilbur threw himself into it with a will" (White, 1952, p. 114).
- "Fern's sneakers were *sopping* by the time she caught up with her father" (White, p. 2).

These sentences provide a *lean* amount of information to indicate the meaning of the target word. Obviously, information in previous or later sentences may provide useful clues, but in general, the more removed the information is from the target word, the greater the contextual analysis skills required of the learner.

For diverse learners, teachers might begin by utilizing rich contexts as a means of scaffolding instruction. As students develop contextual analysis skills, contexts can become systematically more lean.

In cases where deeper levels of word knowledge are desired,

scaffolding might be used to help students establish relations between words. For example, in creating semantic maps, relevant categories might be determined initially by the teacher, such as modes of transportation and winter sports activities for developing greater understanding of *conductor* and *sleigh*. To remove a layer of scaffolding, students as a group might generate categories to teacher-supplied words. In a less scaffolded condition, students might generate the semantic map categories independently. Eventually, students might assume responsibility for identifying the target words they believe are most important in understanding the text, as well as the categories that will help facilitate deeper vocabulary understanding.

Enhancing Independent Vocabulary Growth. To achieve independent word-learning strategies, the goal is to provide enough scaffolding so that students develop independence, but not so much that they become reliant on external support. In most instructional activities, it should be clear that students are assuming greater independence in vocabulary development. For example, written compositions should reflect increasingly diverse and rich vocabulary. Students also should be able to demonstrate the reading strategies they use to determine the contextual meaning of a word, how to construct a semantic map indicating the relation between words, and verbally define and explain the meaning of important words. If students are unable to demonstrate these types of skills when requested, it may be an indication that they need more support and guidance in learning the meanings of new vocabulary words.

As with the match between vocabulary goals and instructional methods, scaffolding can be provided to help students achieve greater learning independence in two ways: through direct teacher intervention, or through modifying or changing curriculum materials. For example, teachers might directly increase the amount of scaffolding provided to students by specifying the vocabulary words they want them to know from a particular story, rather than having students identify and learn the most important words independently.

Similarly, if computers are being used to facilitate reading and vocabulary acquisition, scaffolding might be provided by having the computer software rather than the student determine which word meanings are defined on screen. In the Reinking and Rickman (1990) study, middle-school teachers identified words in reading passages they believed would give typical sixth-grade students difficulty. The authors found that the diverse learners who were required to view the meaning of these vocabulary words on screen as they read the passage learned more word meanings than diverse learners who determined the words themselves.

Priming Background Knowledge

Priming background knowledge helps students draw on their personal experiences as a means to understand new information. In many cases, teachers may help students acquire the necessary background knowledge to learn critical information or skills. In facilitating vocabulary growth, it is helpful to activate student background knowledge when considering the match between vocabulary goals and instructional strategies, and when promoting word-learning independence.

Matching Vocabulary Goals With Instruction. Priming background knowledge is essential when considering the match between vocabulary goals and instructional techniques. As Adams (1990) noted, learning *anything* only occurs in the context of what the learner already knows. At the level of verbal association, for example, telling students that *elated* means *happy* assumes that they know the meaning of *happy*. Teaching the meaning of the word *atom* at a deeper level of understanding than a verbal association level (i.e., "a tiny particle") requires background knowledge of the term *atom*. If the goal is for students to understand the role of atoms in how atom bombs are made, how nuclear energy works, what *fission* means, or how atoms are configured and arranged structurally, then students must know something about electrons, protons, and neutrons. In other words, students need background knowledge about the structure of atoms to learn about them at a deeper level of understanding.

In general, the deeper the understanding desired about the meaning of a word, the more background knowledge a student needs. If sufficient background knowledge does not exist, it may be necessary to teach it directly or to arrange for students to acquire it through reading or other independent activities.

It is reasonable, and perhaps sometimes desirable, to provide students with instruction and other learning opportunities that enable them to acquire background knowledge and a deep understanding of a word's meaning nearly simultaneously. This is most true in subjects such as science, where much of the content and related vocabulary tends to be restricted to subject-specific discussions. For example, instruction related to the meaning of the word *atom* might begin at the verbal association level and proceed directly toward full concept knowledge. The overriding concept on which the instruction is based might be *elements of matter*, which requires an understanding of the terms *elements* and *matter*. The definition of *atom* might then proceed quickly to schemata of its structure with examples of various atom types. Finally, practical applications of the behavior of subatomic particles might be explored. For more literary, abstract, or widely used words such as *democracy* and *perseverance*, it may be more difficult to achieve a deep understanding because their meanings are closely tied to students' experiences and background knowledge, which varies widely from student to student.

Enhancing Independent Vocabulary Growth. One of the great challenges for educators in the early primary grades is helping students become independent learners. Independent learning in general cannot be separated from student independence in learning new vocabulary. Like learning in general, the amount of independence students assume for learning word meanings is integrally tied to mediated scaffolding. To a large extent, classroom teachers in the primary grades should provide strong scaffolding to help students develop the knowledge they need to become independent academic learners. This may be done by arranging early instructional opportunities that capitalize on students' natural curiosity to learn. Considerable scaffolding may be needed as learning requirements assume a more academic focus. For example, as students begin to develop academic background knowledge, they can become increasingly independent for learning more complex skills such as reading comprehension and vocabulary learning strategies.

For example, as a precursor to writing their own stories, first-grade students might discuss a particular story based on the pictures in an illustrated book. Then, as the teacher reads the story, the students and the teacher can discuss these initial predictions in relation to actual content. This type of activity helps students develop the background knowledge they need to write the story they just read and discussed, and begin writing stories they develop on their own. Considerable scaffolding may be required for students to "write" about stories that have been read to them or that they make up on their own, but most students steadily improve in the degree of independence they assume in this activity as well. Thus, discussing the possible story content from pictures and comparing such predictions to actual content helps students develop some of the background knowledge they need to be able to write independently. In turn, independent story writing provides some of the background knowledge students need to begin using their writing opportunities to expand their vocabulary use.

Judicious Review

Judicious review refers to the review and application of previously learned information that is carefully distributed, cumulative, and varied. One of the advantages of vocabulary development is that incorporating new words in an active lexicon allows for a natural "review" of previously learned vocabulary. In other words, because speaking is an activity that most individuals engage in frequently and consistently throughout typical everyday experiences, if new vocabulary words are to become part of a student's everyday lexicon, then periodic opportunities to use new words should occur. With infrequently used words, review activities must be planned to avoid that word meanings are forgotten.

Two issues in relation to diverse learners are important in this regard. First, diverse learners may be less likely than normal achievers to make new vocabulary words part of their active lexicons unless they are taught explicitly to do so. Second, there is evidence that diverse learners do forget new word meanings more quickly than normal achievers (Fawcett & Nicolson, 1991).

Matching Vocabulary Goals With Instruction. In matching goals with instruction, judicious review offers two primary benefits. First, reviewing previously learned vocabulary words ensures that students continue to understand target words at intended levels of meaning. This is true, however, only to the extent that the review techniques match the desired depth of understanding. For example, if the word *coup* was learned at a deep level of understanding, in which its standard definition (i.e., a sudden successful stroke or act) as well as its relation to military takeovers and 20th-century politics was explained, then review activities should reflect the richness of this understanding. If, on the other hand, review activities only address the standard definition of *coup*, then many students may forget the deeper meaning of the word.

The second and perhaps more significant benefit of reviewing previously learned vocabulary is that it sets the stage for learning words at a deeper level of understanding. For example, a student might initially learn that a *bank* is a place to safely keep money. In reviewing the meaning of *bank* over time, however, students might learn more about banks as lending institutions (e.g., services provided, titles of the individuals who work in a bank, the names of common banks), as well as different meanings of *bank*, including piled-up cloud mass, inclination of an airplane, type of shot in pool or basketball, and the rising ground bordering a lake, river, or sea.

Enhancing Independent Vocabulary Growth. If textbooks and classroom assignments continue to challenge students to expand their vocabulary knowledge, an important component of maintaining and enhancing student independent word learning skills is achieved. However, if students are not continually challenged to expand their vocabularies, the degree to which they learn word meanings independently may begin to be reduced. This reduction in student independent learning is more of an issue for diverse learners than normal achievers. Diverse learners are less likely to have been exposed to the rich language environments that characterize the experiences of many normal achievers. This rich experience with language may provide the necessary context needed for word learning that characterizes many life-long word learners. Teachers can play a critical role in helping diverse learners develop into life-long word learners by consistently reviewing the importance of vocabulary development by verbally reinforcing their students for independent word-learning efforts and by assigning classroom activities that require a range of independent word-learning strategies.

Students also may reduce the extent to which they investigate word meanings independently if they begin to view the vocabulary demands as too difficult. In cases such as these, teachers can respond in at least a couple of ways. First, they can provide more scaffolding and reduce the amount of vocabulary learning students need to do independently. Second, they can reduce the number of new vocabulary words to which students are exposed. For example, teachers might shift from teaching more words at less depth (i.e., verbal association knowledge) to achieving greater depth of word knowledge (i.e., full concept knowledge).

The point is that until students have developed a sustaining drive to understand the meaning of words, judicious review activities must be incorporated to ensure that students understand the importance of learning word meanings, use effective strategies to learn word meanings, and make consistent progress in using the words they are learning.

CONCLUSION

The need for comprehensive programs to increase the vocabulary skills of diverse learners is clear. For instance, many diverse learners have sizable vocabulary delays compared to normal achievers even before kindergarten. Moreover, the vocabulary gap between students tends to increase significantly over time and exacts profound consequences on reading achievement and success in content-area subjects.

Most vocabulary research has been conducted with students in the late primary- and middle-school grades, focusing primarily on evaluating the effectiveness of interventions to increase student learning of individual words. The evidence indicates that nearly all intervention methods are successful to some degree, especially when compared to gains that occur during typical incidental learning opportunities. To date, however, no single method has been demonstrated as meaningfully reducing the vocabulary gap between students with poor vocabularies and students with rich vocabularies. With few exceptions, comprehensive vocabulary programs with the potential to reduce the vocabulary gap between students have been proposed in various forms but have not been investigated empirically.

In this section, we described a framework for (a) increasing the vocabulary skills of diverse learners and (b) reducing the vocabulary gap between students. In reviewing the recent literature on vocabulary learning and diverse learners, we identified five areas of convergence. From these areas of convergence, two *big ideas* were derived that provide the framework for discussing a comprehensive vocabulary development program. These big ideas were:

- Interventions to address the vocabulary delays of diverse learners should align goals for depth of word knowledge with instructional techniques.
- Interventions to increase the vocabulary knowledge of diverse learners should move systematically toward ensuring that students become independent word learners.

From these big ideas, five principles of instructional design were used to structure the comprehensive intervention framework: *conspicuous strategies, strategic integration, mediated scaffolding, primed background knowledge,* and *judicious review.* Each of these principles has received empirical support as increasing the academic achievement of diverse learners. Although many of these principles have been validated for increasing the vocabulary skills of diverse learners in isolation, they have not been used in a comprehensive way to increase vocabulary growth and decrease the vocabulary gap between students. Thus, it is imperative that the effectiveness of comprehensive vocabulary programs is monitored carefully and that programmatic changes are made when student growth is not adequate.

REFERENCES

Adams, M. J. (1990). *Beginning to read: Thinking and learning about print.* Cambridge, MA: MIT Press.

American Heritage Dictionary of the English Language. (1992). (3rd ed.). Boston: Houghton Mifflin.

Anderson, R. C., & Nagy, W. E. (1991). Word meanings. In R. Barr, M. L. Kamil, P. B. Mosenthal, & P. D. Pearson (Eds.), *Handbook of reading research* (pp. 690–724). New York: Longman.

Baumann, J. F., & Kameenui, E. J. (1991). Research on vocabulary instruction: Ode to Voltaire. In J. Flood, J. Jensen, D. Lapp, & J. R. Squire (Eds.), *Handbook of research on teaching the English language arts* (pp. 604–632). New York: Macmillan.

Beck, I., & McKeown, M. (1991). Conditions of vocabulary acquisition. In R. Barr, M. Kamil, P. Mosenthal, & P. D. Pearson (Eds.), *Handbook of reading research* (pp. 789–814). New York: Longman.

Carnine, D., Crawford, D., Harniss, M., & Hollenbeck, K. (1995). *Understanding U.S. history: Through the Civil War.* Eugene, OR: Considerate Publishing.

Fawcett, A. J., & Nicolson, R. I. (1991). Vocabulary training for children with dyslexia. *Journal of Learning Disabilities, 24,* 379–383.

Graves, M. F. (1986). Vocabulary learning and instruction. In E. Z. Rothkopf (Ed.), *Review of research in education, 13,* 49–89.

Griswold, P. C. , Gelzheiser, L. M., & Shepherd, M. J. (1987). Does a production deficiency hypothesis account for vocabulary learning among adolescents with learning disabilities? *Journal of Learning Disabilities, 20,* 620–626.

Johnson, G., Gersten, R., & Carnine, D. (1987). Effects of instructional design variables on vocabulary acquisition of LD students: A study of computer-assisted instruction. *Journal of Learning Disabilities, 20,* 206–213.

Kameenui, E. J., Dixon, D. W., & Carnine, D. (1987). Issues in the design of vocabulary instruction. In M. G. McKeown & M. E. Curtis (Eds.), *The nature of vocabulary acquisition* (pp. 129–145). Hillsdale, NJ: Lawrence Erlbaum Associates.

Mastropieri, M. A., Scruggs, T. E., & Fulk, B. J. (1990). Teaching abstract vocabulary with the keyword method: Effects on recall and comprehension. *Journal of Learning Disabilities, 23,* 92–107.

McKeown, M. G., & Beck, I. L. (1988). Learning vocabulary: different ways for different goals. *Remedial and Special Education, 9*(1), 42–52.

Reinking, D., & Rickman, S. S. (1990). The effects of computer-mediated texts on the vocabulary learning and comprehension of intermediate-grade readers. *Journal of Reading Behavior, 22,* 395–411.

Sinatra, R. C., Berg, D., & Dunn, R. (1985). Semantic mapping improves reading comprehension of learning disabled students. *Teaching Exceptional Children, 17,* 310–314.

Van Allsburg, C. (1985). *The polar express.* Boston: Houghton Mifflin.

White, E. B. (1952). *Charlotte's web.* New York: Harper & Row.

CHAPTER 10

Text Organization:
Research Bases

Shirley V. Dickson
Northern Illinois University

Deborah C. Simmons
Edward J. Kameenui
University of Oregon

Reading comprehension is a multifaceted process, with performance indicators ranging from simple recall to interpretations of Shakespearean plays, analyses of concepts, and applications in new contexts. Factors such as IQ, instructional approach, task dimensions, motivation, and time on task affect comprehension. Within the broad area of reading comprehension, this synthesis focuses on the relation between the organization of text and reading comprehension.

The choice of this focus and its subsequent limitations is deliberate. Textbooks may be the most predominant instructional tool in America (Esler & Esler, cited in Scruggs & Mastropieri, 1993; Goodlad, cited in Kinder & Bursuck, 1991), with educators depending largely upon them as the basis for their instruction (Kinder & Bursuck). Although research suggests that textbook organization affects reading comprehension, evaluations of textbooks have found many to be poorly written. Poorly written textbooks may play a part in the comprehension difficulties of poor readers, especially those who have difficulty recalling content, organizing information, identifying main ideas, and discriminating between relevant and nonrelevant information.

In a descriptive narrative of social studies textbooks and instructional approaches, Kinder and Bursuck (1991) reported on critiques of social studies textbooks by six different groups of evaluators. For example, Kinder and Bursuck stated that Armbruster and colleagues found many poorly written, incoherent textbooks that often failed to use precise language or make clear the relations among concepts, ideas, and sentences. Further, American history textbooks frequently (a) did not make obvious the major concepts of history (White, cited in Kinder & Bursuck); (b) provided a brief mention of everything with little, if any, analysis (Tyson & Woodward, cited in Kinder & Bursuck; Zakariya, cited in Kinder & Bursuck); (c) tended to trivialize history content (Crabtree, cited in Kinder & Bursuck); and (d) did not present information in a way that would help students organize facts into a coherent whole (Beck, McKeown, & Gromoll, cited in Kinder & Bursuck).

Scruggs and Mastropieri (1993) found similar difficulties with science textbooks. In their descriptive narrative on instructional approaches in science, these authors reported that science textbooks provided extensive coverage of content but little opportunity for in-depth practice of important concepts (Mastropieri & Scruggs, cited in Scruggs & Mastropieri, 1993).

Although textbooks frequently are poorly written, incoherent, and fail to show relations between information, students are expected to use them as a primary source of information. Meanwhile, many students have demonstrated difficulties with skills that are central to reading comprehension (i.e., identifying main topics, significant supporting information, and relations between a text's main topics; Seidenberg, 1989). These reading comprehension difficulties parallel the criticisms that textbooks often do not clarify the main idea (Baumann & Serra, cited in Seidenberg, 1989) or make clear the relations between concepts, ideas, and sentences (Armbruster & Anderson, cited in Kinder & Bursuck, 1991).

With increasing frequency, students with diverse learning needs, including students with disabilities, are in mainstream classrooms (Leo, 1994; U.S. Department of Education, 1992). In these contexts, students have demonstrated varying reading comprehension difficulties, whether the text was a story, social studies chapter, science experiment, or mathematics word problem. For example, when retelling stories, diverse learners appeared to recall less information than their normally achieving counterparts (Montague, Maddux, & Dereshiwsky, 1990). They displayed difficulty understanding characters in stories (e.g., interactions, intentions) and making inferences (Montague et al., 1990). Further, when reading content area texts such as social studies or science, diverse learners exhibited difficulty distinguishing between relevant and irrelevant information (Seidenberg, 1989), identifying and recognizing the interrelations between main ideas (Seidenberg, 1989), organizing information, and memorizing and retaining isolated facts (e.g., the acts leading to the Revolutionary War in isolation from the concept that Britain wanted to benefit economically from the colonies; Lovitt, cited in Kinder & Bursuck, 1991; Smith, cited in Kinder & Bursuck, 1991). Although special instructional techniques can enhance the achievement of students with disabilities, success in general education classrooms is defined by, and largely dependent upon, performance in the mainstream curriculum materials and instructional approaches (Scruggs & Mastropieri, 1993).

This chapter focuses on the effects and implications of text organization, both physical presentation and text structure, and on reading comprehension, with special emphasis on the comprehension of diverse learners.

METHODOLOGY

Sources

This review of research examining the relation between text organization and comprehension included 7 secondary and 10 primary sources. Table 10.1 at the end of the chapter presents a short description of each source. Of the secondary sources, 3 (i.e., Graesser, Golding, & Long, 1991; Pearson & Fielding, 1991; Weaver & Kintsch, 1991) were book chapters in the *Handbook of Reading Research: Volume II* (Barr, Kamil, Mosenthal, & Pearson, 1991). Four secondary sources were articles (i.e., Kinder & Bursuck, 1991; Scruggs & Mastropieri, 1993; Seidenberg, 1989; Talbott, Lloyd, & Tankersley, 1994). One secondary source was a quantitative synthesis using meta-analysis (i.e., Talbott et al., 1994); 1 was a descriptive analysis with a database (i.e., Weaver & Kintsch); and 5 were descriptive narratives with research references (i.e., Graesser et al.; Kinder & Bursuck; Pearson & Fielding; Scruggs & Mastropieri; Seidenberg). Of the primary sources, 3 were descriptive studies (Englert & Thomas, 1987; Montague et al., 1990; Zabrucky & Ratner, 1992) and 7 involved interventions (i.e., Boyle, 1996; Casteel, 1990; Dole, Brown, & Trathen, 1996; Gurney, Gersten, Dimino, & Carnine, 1990; Horton, Lovitt, & Bergerud, 1990; Newby, Caldwell, & Recht, 1989; Williams, Brown, Silverstein, & deCani, 1994).

Participant Characteristics

In this review, attention is focused on students with diverse learning needs. Diverse learners are defined here as students who, because of their instructional, experiential, socioeconomic, linguistic, physiological, or cognitive backgrounds, differ in their instructional and curricular requirements. The three book chapters included in this review provided context and information primarily about learners in general education ranging in ages from kindergarten through college. The secondary and primary research articles were selected because they included students with diverse learning needs. Descriptive terms of students with diverse learning needs included low readers, achievers, or performers; poor comprehenders; remedial readers; at-risk students; Chapter I students; and students with learning disabilities, dyslexia, behavior disorders, or mild mental retardation. In the reviewed studies, terms describing normal achievers included good comprehenders, general education students, and normal achievers. High-performing students were described as high readers or achievers.

Summary of Methodology

Two independent reviews of each source were conducted. Each source was reviewed and coded for (a) general conclusions, (b) learner characteristics, and (c) instructional implications, and a multiple-step process was used for convergence of evidence. Following the independent reviews, findings were discussed and clarified by the original reviewers at weekly group meetings. Next, the data for each category were checked by two additional reviewers for reliability, coding clarification, and refinement. Finally, the data were entered into a database. The primary author of this chapter further examined the database for converging areas in text organization and carefully reread and examined the secondary and primary sources for supporting information for each area of convergence.

Definitions

Text organization includes the physical presentation of text and text structures. *Physical presentation* of text includes visual textual cues such as headings and subheadings, signal words, and location of main idea sentences. *Text structures* are more abstract, less visual presentations of text that involve organizational patterns of text written to convey a purpose (e.g., persuade, describe, compare/contrast, or entertain with a story). Terms used in this chapter are defined next. For clarity, we repeat these definitions throughout the chapter.

- *Global comprehension:* Comprehension measured by questions about the topics and main ideas of text (Weaver & Kintsch, 1991). Related terms: macroprocesses, macropropositions.
- *Local comprehension:* Comprehension measured by questions about details (Weaver & Kintsch, 1991). Related terms: microprocesses, micropropositions.
- *Macropropositions:* The top-level "gist" information or meaning of a passage; macropropositions are critically important for understanding and long-term recall of text (Weaver & Kintsch, 1991). Related terms: global meaning, macroprocesses.

• *Micropropositions:* The smallest definable units of meaning in text (Weaver & Kintsch, 1991). Related terms: local comprehension, microprocesses.

• *Physical features:* A term used here to include headings, subheadings, signal words, location of topic or main idea sentences, and spacing between "chunks" or idea units within sentences.

• *Semantic cues:* Indicators of a text structure (Meyer, Brandt, & Bluth, 1980; Seidenberg, 1989). One example of a semantic cue is a topic sentence that uses words to indicate the text structure of the upcoming passage. For example, "The production of woolen yarn is a long and difficult process," signals sequence text structure (Seidenberg).

• *Signal words:* Words such as "first," "finally," "as a consequence of," and "as a result of" that emphasize the structure or organization of a passage, but do not add content information (Meyer et al., 1980; Seidenberg, 1989).

• *Syntactic cues:* Indicators of a text structure; key signal words such as "first" and "then" signal sequence text structure (Seidenberg, 1989), whereas "in contrast," "but," and "similarly" signal compare/contrast text structure (Englert & Thomas, 1987).

• *Text structure:* The logical connections among ideas in text and subordination of some ideas to others (Meyer et al., 1980); an overall organizing principle for viewing a topic in text (Meyer & Freedle, 1984); top-level organization patterns (Pearson & Fielding, 1991). Related terms: text type, rhetorical form, rhetorical schemata (Weaver & Kintsch, 1991); macrostructure (Pearson & Fielding; Weaver & Kintsch); genres of text, top-level structures (Pearson & Fielding); structural patterns (Seidenberg, 1989). Examples of text structures include narrative, persuasive, sequence, problem/solution, descriptive, and compare/contrast.

• *Textual cues:* Headings and subheadings, topic sentences, signal words, and author's direct statements of importance (Seidenberg, 1989). Textual cues include semantic and syntactic signals of differing text structures (Seidenberg).

Overview of Synthesis

In this review on the relation between the organization of text and reading comprehension, three converging areas of research evidence are presented. The first two areas support a relation between explicit physical presentation of text and text structure and reading comprehension. The discussion of these two areas of convergence includes (a) definitions, research evidence, and relations to comprehension; (b) student awareness; (c) strategic use; (d) relations to normally achieving and diverse learners; and (e) implications and interventions. The third area of convergence supports the relations between explicit instruction in the physical presentation of text and text structure and reading comprehension. The discussion of this

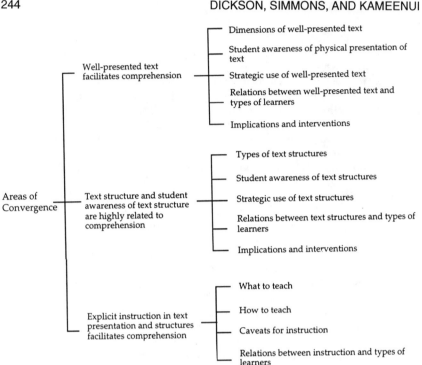

FIG. 10.1. Overview of a synthesis of the research on text organization and its relation to reading comprehension.

area of convergence includes: what to teach, how to teach, caveats, and relations to normally achieving and diverse learners (see Fig. 10.1).

GENERAL AREAS OF CONVERGENCE

The studies reviewed for this chapter provided evidence that the organization of text, students' awareness of that organization, and students' strategic use of text organization affect their comprehension. The organization of text includes the visual, physical organization (e.g., headings, subheadings, location of main idea, spacing) as well as less visible, more abstract text structures (e.g., narrative, sequence, or descriptive text structures; see Fig. 10.2). The three general areas of convergent evidence from this literature review are:

1. Well-presented physical text facilitates reading comprehension.
2. Text structure and student awareness of text structure are highly related to reading comprehension.

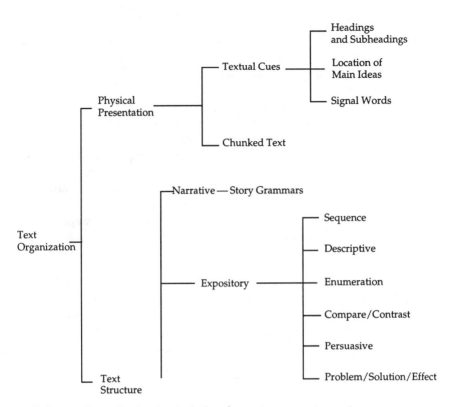

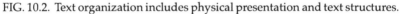

FIG. 10.2. Text organization includes physical presentation and text structures.

3. Explicit instruction in the physical presentation of text and text structure facilitates reading comprehension.

AREA OF CONVERGENCE 1:
Well-Presented Physical Text Facilitates Reading Comprehension

Well-presented physical text enables readers to identify the relevant information in text, including main ideas and relations between ideas, skills that are central to comprehension (Lorch & Lorch, cited in Seidenberg, 1989; Miller & Kintsch, cited in Seidenberg, 1989). The components of well-presented physical text are the visual cues that highlight or emphasize main ideas and relations between ideas. Visual cues include location of main idea sentences, author's direct statements of importance, signal words, headings and subheadings, and spacing that divides sentences into "chunks" or meaningful thought units (see Fig. 10.2).

This discussion includes: the dimensions of well-presented text and their relation to comprehension; student awareness of well-presented text; strategic use of well-presented text; relations to learners; and implications and interventions.

Dimensions of Well-Presented Text

The dimensions of well-presented text include those that clearly indicate the main idea, the relations between important information, and the thought units within a sentence. The ability to identify the main idea and relations between important information is important for reading comprehension. Indicators of main ideas and relations between important information focus readers' attention on the global, macrostructure of a text, while the indicators of thought units within sentences focus readers' attention on phrases rather than letters and words. While the indicators of main ideas and relations between information use location, semantic, and syntactic cues, the indicators of thought units within sentences rely upon spacing.

Clarity and Location of Main Idea Statements. The ability to identify main ideas is central to comprehension (Lorch & Lorch, cited in Seidenberg, 1989; Miller & Kintsch, cited in Seidenberg, 1989). Seidenberg cited empirical support showing that the ability to comprehend main ideas differentiates good and poor readers and is directly related to general comprehension ability (e.g., Baumann, cited in Seidenberg, 1989; Winograd, cited in Seidenberg, 1989; Wong, cited in Seidenberg, 1989), summarizing, and outlining (e.g., Rinehart et al., cited in Seidenberg;, 1989 Richgels et al., cited in Seidenberg, 1989). Yet, main idea statements often do not appear as the first sentence in a paragraph or are omitted from content area textbooks (Baumann & Serra, cited in Seidenberg, 1989). In a review of text-processing research, Seidenberg found that general education students ranging from elementary school through college-age demonstrated difficulties analyzing the main ideas of textbooks, especially if the main ideas were implied in the text rather than clearly stated.

The importance of a clearly stated main idea is supported by several studies cited by Seidenberg (1989). For example, when the main idea was not explicitly stated in text (a) elementary-age and college-age students had difficulty inventing topic sentences (Brown & Day, cited in Seidenberg, 1989); (b) college-age students had difficulty integrating and summarizing information from different paragraphs of a reading passage (Brown & Day, cited in Seidenberg, 1989); and (c) summarization training was not sufficient to improve sixth-grade students' comprehension (Rinehart, Stahl, & Erickson, cited in Seidenberg, 1989).

The clarity and coherence with which main ideas are presented in text have been found to facilitate their identification (Kieras, cited in Seidenberg, 1989; Lorch & Lorch, cited in Seidenberg, 1989). In her review of text-processing research, Seidenberg described clear and coherent presentation as including (a) ordering topics systematically (Kieras, cited in Seidenberg, 1989; Lorch & Lorch, cited in Seidenberg, 1989); (b) stating a good topic organization in the opening paragraph (Kieras, cited in Seidenberg, 1989; Lorch & Lorch, cited in Seidenberg, 1989); (c) placing the topic sentence of a paragraph at the beginning of a paragraph rather than embedding or inferring it (Kieras, cited in Seidenberg, 1989; Lorch & Lorch, cited in Seidenberg, 1989); and (d) arranging supporting details in recognizable patterns that exemplify superordinate–subordinate relations (Hare & Mulligan, cited in Seidenberg, 1989; Memory, cited in Seidenberg, 1989; Meyer et al., cited in Seidenberg, 1989; Pearson & Johnson, cited in Seidenberg, 1989; Slater, Graves, & Piche, cited in Seidenberg, 1989).

Cues to the Relations Between Important Ideas. Another skill that is important for comprehension is the ability to form relations between important information in text. Textbooks make interrelations between information clear by using semantic and syntactic cues. Semantic cues include topic sentences to signal text organization. For example, "The production of woolen yarn is a long and difficult process," signals sequence text structure (Seidenberg, 1989). Syntactic cues include noncontent signal words such as "first," "second," and "finally" to indicate sequential organization (Seidenberg) and "in contrast," "but," and "similarly" to indicate compare/contrast text structure (Englert & Thomas, 1987). Headings and subheadings are additional cues to interrelations between important ideas in a text (Seidenberg).

Despite the importance of interrelations between important ideas, Armbruster and colleagues (cited in Seidenberg, 1989) found many poorly written, incoherent textbooks that failed to use precise language or make clear the relations between concepts, ideas, and sentences. Both normally achieving students and students with diverse learning needs have demonstrated difficulty identifying relations between important ideas. Seidenberg reported that elementary students made minimal use of superordination of information and demonstrated difficulty integrating information.

An example of students' difficulties in identifying relations between ideas is found in three studies by Horton et al. (1990). Although the purpose of their study was to examine the effects of graphic organizers on student ability to organize information, the performance of students who studied without graphic organizer instruction serves as an example of student ability to form relations between important ideas in text. Horton et al. found that the normally achieving students who read and reread a passage from their textbooks and studied for 20 minutes in any way they chose scored 50% to 64% correct on a dependent measure (i.e., a graphic organizer) that required them to identify and show how concepts and supporting facts were related. In the same study, remedial readers scored an average of 39% to 44% correct, while students with learning disabilities scored an average of 10% to 30% correct when required to identify and show how concepts and supporting facts were related on a graphic organizer.

Spaces Between Meaningful Thought Units. Casteel (1990) took a different approach to the physical presentation of text. Rather than examining the effect of location of topic sentences, semantic cues, or headings, he examined the effect of *chunking,* or using spaces to divide information in sentences into meaningful thought units or phrases (e.g., noun phrases, verb phrases). Chunking information allows "perception and recall of idea units rather than letters or single words" (Gillet & Temple, cited in Casteel, 1990, p. 269).

In the Casteel (1990) study, thought units were separated from each other by four spaces rather than the traditional one space between words. When compared with using traditionally spaced text, chunking, or placing extra spaces between meaningful thought units, resulted in significantly higher reading comprehension scores on a multiple-choice measure for 26 eighth-grade low-ability readers (i.e., at or below the fourth stanine on vocabulary or comprehension subtests of the *California Achievement Test*). By comparison, the chunked passages did not significantly affect the comprehension scores of 24 high-ability readers (above the fourth stanine on vocabulary or comprehension subtests of the *California Achievement Test*), though their comprehension scores for chunked text were relatively higher than their scores for traditionally spaced text. Casteel concluded that chunked text benefited low performers and was not a detriment for high performers. While it may be difficult for teachers to chunk material in textbooks, Casteel suggested having students chunk verb, noun, and object phrases by placing vertical lines between the chunks or underlining chunks prior to reading.

Student Awareness of the
Physical Presentation of Text

Student awareness of the physical presentation of text facilitated their ability to identify main ideas and interrelations between important information. Students better identified main ideas and their supporting details if they were aware that main ideas and their supporting details occurred in recognizable patterns that exemplified superordinate–subordinate relations (Hare & Mulligan, cited in Seidenberg, 1989; Memory, cited in Seidenberg, 1989; Meyer, Brandt, & Bluth, cited in Seidenberg, 1989; Pearson & Johnson, cited in Seidenberg, 1989; Slater, Graves, & Piche, cited in Seidenberg, 1989). Additionally, student recognition and use of visual textual cues (e.g., headings, signal words, location of main ideas) contributed to their ability to identify the important ideas in text and their interrelations (Garner & McCaleb, cited in Seidenberg, 1989; Winograd, cited in Seidenberg, 1989).

While chunking (i.e., using spaces to separate thought units in sentences) has support as another method for physically presenting text to facilitate comprehension, Casteel (1990) did not discuss student awareness of chunked text. It may be that chunked text makes meaningful thought units visual to low ability readers, whereas high-ability readers are aware of and use textual cues (i.e., headings, signal words, location of main ideas) to identify meaningful thought units.

Strategic Use of Well-Presented Text

"Strategies" refer to an organized set of actions designed to accomplish a task. Readers use the physical structure of passages as the basis for strategies to identify main ideas or summarize. The reviewed studies examined the use of (a) organizational patterns and (b) headings, subheadings, and topic sentences as the bases of strategies but not the use of chunking or spacing text to separate thought units in sentences.

One strategy based on the physical presentation of text is the use of the organizational structure of passages to identify main ideas. For example, the reader tests the first sentence to see if it expresses a reasonable main idea. The reader then evaluates each succeeding sentence based on whether is relevant or irrelevant to the proposed main idea. If the sentences do not align with main idea, they may revise the main idea (Kieras, cited in Seidenberg, 1989). A second strategy based on the physical presentation of text involves the use of headings, subheadings, and paragraph topics to summarize text. Students who were taught this strategy recalled text information better than students who answered questions about the text or studied longer (Taylor & Beach, cited in Pearson & Fielding, 1991).

**Relations Between Well-Presented
Text and Types of Learners**

Normally Achieving Learners. Summarizing, integrating information, and forming relations between important information are important reading comprehension skills. Fluent readers use textual cues to identify important information to include in summaries (Winograd, cited in Seidenberg, 1989). However, when the main idea is implicit rather than clearly presented, normally achieving students have demonstrated difficulty identifying main ideas and integrating information (Seidenberg, 1989). Normally achieving students have also demonstrated difficulty showing the relations between concepts or important pieces of information (e.g., Horton et al., 1990).

Chunking text (i.e., using spaces to separate thought units in sentences) is another form of the physical presentation of text. Chunked text appears to neither benefit nor hinder high-ability readers (Casteel, 1990). Although high-achieving readers demonstrated some improvement in comprehension while reading chunked text, the improvement was not significant.

Diverse Learners. Students with learning disabilities have demonstrated difficulty following main ideas, recognizing main topics and their interrelations, and recognizing that main topics are supported by superordinate and subordinate ideas or examples (Seidenberg, 1989). Seidenberg proposed that when students with learning disabilities have comprehension difficulties, teachers need to consider whether the students are able to identify the important information in a reading passage. Therefore, they may need explicit training to increase sensitivity to important text information. Winograd (cited in Seidenberg, 1989) found that poor readers often chose important information based on what was of high personal interest to them and made decisions about what to include in their summaries on a sentence-by-sentence basis, rather than using textual cues to identify important information. Additionally, poor readers demonstrated difficulty integrating separate idea units into larger units (Winograd, cited in Seidenberg, 1989) and organizing their reading input in a meaningful way (Casteel, 1990).

Implications and Interventions

Text that clearly signals main ideas and relations between ideas facilitates comprehension. Techniques for clearly presenting text include (a) ordering topics systematically; (b) stating topic organization in the opening paragraph; (c) placing topic sentences at the beginning of paragraphs; (d) arranging supporting details in recognizable patterns that exemplify superordinate–subordinate relations; (e) using precise language to make clear the relations between concepts, ideas, and sentences; (f) using signal words such as "first," "second," and "finally;" and (g) using headings, subheadings, and topic sentences to cue the interrelations between important ideas.

Additionally, one study in this review (i.e., Casteel, 1990) indicated that additional spacing between idea units facilitated reading comprehension for low readers and did not interfere with the reading comprehension of high-ability readers. As a result of these findings, publishers may want to place extra spaces between idea units in sentences, or teachers may want to teach low-performing students to draw vertical lines between or underline the idea units in the sentences in their textbooks.

AREA OF CONVERGENCE 2:
Text Structure and Student Awareness of Text Structure are Highly Related to Reading Comprehension

In general, "text structure" refers to the organizational features of text that serve as a frame or pattern (Englert & Thomas, 1987) to guide and help readers identify important information (Seidenberg, 1989) and logical connections between ideas (Meyer et al., 1980; Seidenberg, 1989). Text structure appears to play an important role in reading comprehension. Moreover, there is strong empirical evidence that readers' awareness of text structure is highly related to reading comprehension.

Text structure usually refers to two types of text: narrative and expository. *Narrative* is more common than expository text and is usually a story written to entertain the reader (Weaver & Kintsch, 1991). By comparison, common *expository* texts include persuasion, explanation, comparison/contrast, enumeration or collection, problem–solution, and description, designed primarily to inform the reader (Weaver & Kintsch; see Fig. 10.2). The distinction between narrative and expository text is not a simple dichotomy, however. For example, novelists may write stories to persuade or inform, just as writers of expository text may write to entertain (Pearson & Fielding, 1991). Following is a discussion of narrative and expository text structures and their differing effects upon readers, student awareness of text structures, strategic use of text structures, relation of text structures to learners, and implications and interventions.

Types of Text Structures

Narrative Text Structure. The most familiar and most studied (Graesser et al., 1991) text structure is narrative text or stories. Although there is no prevailing consensus on the definition of narrative text and some debate over the features of a story, narrative text depicts events, actions, emotions, or situations that people in a culture experience (Graesser et al., 1991). A story is written to inform, excite, or entertain readers (Pearson & Fielding,

1991) and may report actual or fictitious experiences (Graesser et al., 1991). Although there are no clear boundaries between categories, narratives include myths, epics, fables, folktales, short stories, novels, tragedy, and comedy. The depictions of events are organized so that the audience can eventually anticipate them. That is, readers must be able to infer motives of characters and the causal relations among events.

Narratives normally involve (a) animate beings as characters with goals and motives; (b) temporal and spatial placements usually presented at the beginning of the story; (c) a problem or goal faced by the main character that imitates a major goal; (d) plots or a series of episodes that eventually resolve the complication; (e) impacts upon the reader's emotions and arousal levels; and (f) points (e.g., justice, honesty, loyalty), morals, or themes.

Just as there is no consensus on the definition of narrative text, there is no consensus on how stories are constructed. There are various theories about the components, levels, dimensions, and perspectives of narrative text, but each theory falls short of capturing all of the potential intricacies of stories or the ways in which stories involve the reader's emotions. Each theory includes (a) recommendations for what makes stories interesting, (b) the reader's knowledge of the world, (c) inferences, (d) memory of the story, and (e) reading comprehension. Theories also contain logic, principles, concepts, or constraints to determine how a story is constructed. Names for these various theories included causal network (Trabasso & associates, cited in Graesser et al., 1991); conceptual graph structures (Graesser & associates, cited in Graesser et al., 1991); scripts (Schank & Abelson, cited in Graesser et al., 1991); story points (Wilensky, cited in Graesser et al., 1991); plot unit (Lehnert, cited in Graesser et al., 1991); and analysis of thematic affect units (Dyer & associates, cited in Graesser et al., 1991). They are described in greater detail in Graesser et al., 1991.

One theory, story grammar, is the oldest theory of narrative structure and the one most used in research during the last 10 years. Just as there are many theories of narrative text structure, there are many story grammars.

A story grammar refers to "abstract linguistic representation of the idea, events, and personal motivations that comprise the flow of a story" (Pearson & Fielding, 1991, p. 821). A story grammar captures the important properties of a story and guides comprehension of stories that have "(a) a single main protagonist who encounters a problem-solving situation, (b) a goal that the protagonist attempts to achieve, (c) a plot that unravels how the protagonist attempts to achieve the goal, and (d) an outcome regarding whether the goal was achieved" (Graesser et al., 1991, p. 179). Further, story grammars specify the (a) major components of a story (e.g., Thorndyke's setting, theme, plot, resolution; Stein and Glenn's episode, initiating event, internal response, attempt, consequence, reaction; cited in Graesser et al., 1991); (b) hierarchical relations between story grammar components; and (c) rules that govern what information is included or deleted within the story, order of information, relations between story components, and embedding of episodes within story components such as the beginning, outcome, or ending. More complex stories normally have multiple episodes and follow rules that allow changes and deletions of story grammar components (Graesser et al., 1991).

The assumption behind story grammar theory is that story grammar components and their hierarchical relations represent frames or patterns that readers can use to store information in long-term memory. Pearson and Fielding (1991) cited five references that support the validity of story grammars as models of comprehension by providing evidence that adults' and children's story retellings matched the sequential order of story grammar components and that the frequency of recalled information correlated with the hierarchical position of the information in the story grammar framework. Story grammars generate predictions about patterns of passage recall, passage summarization, importance ratings of statement, passage statement clusters, and reading time, but there has been controversy over whether story grammars or other representations of knowledge (e.g., knowledge about planning, social action, motives) can explain these predictions (Graesser et al., 1991). Despite these controversies, Graesser et al. concluded that story grammars unite dozens of empirical trends into one theory of story construction.

Expository Text Structures. While narrative text structure primarily entertains, expository text primarily communicates information (Weaver & Kintsch, 1991). Textbooks, essays, and most magazine articles are examples of expository text (Pearson & Fielding, 1991). Seidenberg (1989) posited that the ability to comprehend and formulate expository prose is essential for achievement in school. When learners read content area material such as social studies or science, they must attend to a variety of text structures (Englert & Hiebert, 1984). While narrative text structure has largely focused on story grammars, research on expository text has spanned a much broader range of organizational patterns. Common expository text structures include compare/contrast, classification, illustration, procedural description (Weaver & Kintsch, 1991), sequence, enumer-ation or collection, problem-solution, and description (Meyer & Rice, 1984). Each type of expository text structure is represented by an organizational pattern that includes differing types of relations between important information in the text. Kintsch (cited in Weaver & Kintsch, 1991) described three types of relationships between ideas in expository text: (a) general-to-particular, as in identification, definition, classification, or illustration; (b) object-to-object, as in comparison/contrast; and (c) object-to-part, as in structural analysis to tell how to put something together, functional analysis to tell how something works, or causal analysis to tell a cause or consequence.

Research evidence suggests that well-structured expository text facilitates comprehension of main ideas or topics, rather than facts. For example, Kintsch and Yarbrough (cited in Weaver & Kintsch, 1991) found that students who read well-structured essays that showed clear relations between ideas, performed better on a measure of global comprehension (macroprocesses; e.g., topic and main-point questions) than did students who read essays on the same content in which the order of paragraphs did not follow principles of organization and in which cues to text structure were deleted. Performance was equal on a measure of local comprehension (microprocesses), measured using cloze procedures (i.e., a measure in which students fill in the missing words deleted from a passage they have read).

Differing Effects of Narrative and Expository Text Structures. Narrative and expository texts have been found to have differential effects on readers, with narrative appearing easier to comprehend and monitor than expository text. Zabrucky and Ratner (1992) examined the effects of eight narrative and eight expository passages on the comprehension monitoring and recall of 16 good and 16 poor sixth-grade readers. Some passages contained a sentence that was inconsistent with the rest of the passage, while other passages did not. Text was presented on a computer screen, one sentence at a time. Reading times and students' verbal reports were used to examine students' evaluation of their comprehension and look-backs to inconsistencies during reading.

For both good and poor readers, text type affected recall and comprehension monitoring. Students recalled significantly more idea units from narrative than expository passages. When comparing texts with inconsistencies to texts without inconsistencies, students looked back more frequently for inconsistent narrative than inconsistent expository text, suggesting that inconsistencies were more apparent in narrative than in expository text. Students were also better able to verbally report on passage consistency after reading narrative than expository passages. Students reread expository passages more frequently than narrative passages when the passages did not contain inconsistent information, indicating that students found expository text more problematic than narrative text. Additionally, students reread more frequently when inconsistent text was adjacent to the correct sentence than when it was far from the correct sentence.

Student Awareness of Text Structures

Although well-organized text structure appears important to reading comprehension, it may not be sufficient to facilitate comprehension. Often "awareness" of text structures adds an important dimension. In the text structure literature, various terms are used to describe the reader's awareness of text structure: familiarity (Graesser et al., 1991; Gurney et al., 1990; Weaver & Kintsch, 1991); knowledge (Englert & Thomas, 1987; Graesser et al.; Gurney et al., 1990; Montague et al., 1990; Seidenberg, 1989); awareness (Englert & Thomas, 1987; Seidenberg, 1989); sensitivity (Seidenberg); and recognition (Seidenberg, 1989). In this chapter, we use the authors' original terms as much as possible. If the findings or conclusions of two or more authors are summarized, a term that captures the spirit of both studies is used.

In their reviews of text-processing and expository text structure research, Seidenberg (1989), Weaver and Kintsch (1991), and Pearson and Fielding (1991) discussed the importance of the reader's awareness (Seidenberg), familiarity (Weaver & Kintsch), or knowledge (Pearson & Fielding) of text structure. Weaver and Kintsch reported that learners "familiar" with text structure who read well-structured, clearly cued text performed better on measures of global comprehension (e.g., main topics) than students who did not demonstrate familiarity with test structure.

Student awareness of structural patterns in expository writing (e.g., sequence, causation, comparison/contrast) facilitated recall of not only more text information, but more theses or main ideas (Seidenberg, 1989). Pearson and Fielding (1991) reported two consistent findings: "First, students who are knowledgeable about and/or follow the author's structure in their attempts to recall a text remember more than those who do not. Second, more good than poor readers follow the author's structure in their attempt to recall a text" (p. 827). Both Weaver and Kintsch (1991) and Seidenberg noted that "awareness" of text structure benefits reading comprehension of global ideas or main theses.

Research evidence suggests that students vary in their awareness of different text structures. For example, there is strong research support that students have a greater awareness of narrative than expository text structures (Graesser et al., 1991) and that students remember and comprehend narrative text structure easier than they do expository text structure (Zabrucky & Ratner, 1992). Indeed, in a primary study comparing the differences between students with learning disabilities and normally achieving students in processing narrative text, Montague et al. (1990) concluded that most school-aged children have acquired knowledge of a story schema (awareness of narrative prose) and use that knowledge during story comprehension and production tasks.

Graesser et al. (1991) posed three reasons for the "privileged status" of narrative text structure. First, narrative content is more familiar to students than expository content. Graesser et al. referred to the more familiar content as mutual knowledge, with narrative text structure having a higher density of "mutual knowledge" (e.g., shared experiences, world knowledge structures) than expository text structure. Second, this familiar content of narrative includes *event sequences* (e.g., intentional acts in pursuit of goals; events that occur in the material world). Event sequences are the core content of children's and adults' experience in everyday life. According to Nelson (cited in Graesser et al., 1991), everyday event sequences are the primary form of world knowledge for children. Third, narrative structure is prevalent in oral language. Contrary to narrative text structure's familiar content, expository prose is written primarily to convey new knowledge.

Just as students are more aware of narrative text structure than expository text structure, their awareness of the many expository text structures varies. In a primary study of expository text structure, Englert and Thomas (1987) examined student awareness of four types of expository text structures: description, enumeration, sequence, and comparison/contrast texts. The study included 36 students reading at grade-level or above, 36 low-achieving students, and 36 students with learning disabilities, evenly divided between Grades 3 and 4 (younger group) and Grades 6 and 7 (older group). Students' sensitivity to the text structures was measured using a 12-item task requiring students to discriminate between sentences that presented details (a) related to the paragraph topic and text structure and (b) distracted or presented intrusive information. Englert and Thomas found that sequence text structure was significantly easier than enumeration and description text structures, and enumeration and sequence text structures were significantly easier than compare/contrast text structure.

While examining students' sensitivity to the four different text structures, Englert and Thomas (1987) also concluded that awareness of text structure may be developmental. Of the participants in their study, 54 were younger (Grades 3 and 4) and 54 were older students (Grades 6 and 7). The older students (including students with learning disabilities) exhibited significantly more awareness of expository text structure than the younger students.

Strategic Use of Text Structures

In her narrative review of text-processing research, Seidenberg (1989) reported that a number of studies (e.g., Hiebert, Englert, & Brennan, cited in Seidenberg; Kintsch & Yarbrough, cited in Seidenberg, 1989) have provided evidence that effective readers use strategies linked to text structure awareness to effectively identify and recall main ideas and supporting information and to summarize (Winograd, cited in Seidenberg, 1989). Students with learning disabilities, on the other hand, although they may have acquired a repertoire of strategies for processing information, do not spontaneously apply them when engaged in activities that require goal-directed or planning activity (Torgesen, cited in Montague et al., 1990; Wong, cited in Montague et al., 1990).

Relations Between Text Structures and Types of Learners

Normally Achieving Learners. Normally achieving students appear more facile with both narrative and expository text structures than diverse learners. One indicator of facility with text is the number of times readers look back at text to correct comprehension failures. Good readers had significantly more look-backs than poor readers for difficult (i.e., expository) text and significantly more look-backs for expository than narrative passages. Good readers also had more look-backs for inconsistent text than poor readers, though the differences were not significant. Good readers correctly reported significantly more inconsistencies than poor readers (Zabrucky & Ratner, 1992).

In a comparative study of students' narrative text-structure processing, Montague et al. (1990) concluded that students without learning disabilities recalled more information than students with learning disabilities and included more information in their story retells. Similarly, Zabrucky and Ratner (1992) found that good readers had significantly more recall than poor readers for both narrative and expository text.

The ability to identify main topics, significant supporting information, and interrelations among a text's main ideas are processes that appear central to comprehension (Lorch & Lorch, cited in Seidenberg, 1989; Miller & Kintsch, cited in Seidenberg, 1989). Effective readers appear to use strategies linked to expository text structure awareness to process text information (Hiebert, Englert, & Brennan, cited in Seidenberg, 1989; Kintsch & Yarbrough, cited in Seidenberg, 1989; McGee, cited in Seidenberg, 1989). Additionally, effective readers used textual cues and the meaning of the whole text to identify important information to include in summaries (Winograd, cited in Seidenberg, 1989).

Not all normally achieving readers appeared to be aware of text structure, however. In a study that included ninth-grade, eleventh-grade, and college-age students, Garner (cited in Seidenberg, 1989) found that, across age levels, students were deficient in their awareness of and ability to integrate information.

Diverse Learners. Zabrucky and Ratner (1992) found that poor readers did not differ in the number of times they monitored their comprehension by looking back at sentences for narrative and expository text. Because narrative is easier to comprehend than expository text, Zabrucky and Ratner concluded that poor readers did not regulate their understanding when reading difficult text. In addition, there was no difference in poor readers' and good readers' detection of inconsistencies during reading. However, poor readers were less able than good readers to comment accurately on passage consistency after reading. Poor readers were no different than good readers in reading problematic or inconsistent text. However, poor readers demonstrated significantly less recall than good readers (Zabrucky & Ratner).

Many comprehension difficulties of diverse learners have been attributed to their deficits in text structure awareness (Englert & Thomas, 1987). For example, one hypothesis for why students with learning disabilities appear to recall less narrative text than normally achieving students (Montague et al., 1990) is that they have an incomplete "schema" or awareness of narrative prose. In a primary study of narrative text structure and students with learning disabilities, Montague et al. concluded that the incomplete development of a story grammar by students with learning disabilities, as demonstrated in their significantly shorter story recalls, may be due to these students' lack of expertise in interpreting or expressing the affective information about the characters in the story (e.g., human intentions, social interactions, problem solving). Students with learning disabilities may also be deficient in their discrimination of various levels of meaning in stories and less aware of subtle differences in the importance of story propositions compared to students without learning disabilities. Additionally, students with learning disabilities had difficulty recalling fine details, using connective words that signal temporal and causal relations, and identifying text-based inferences in stories.

One facet of text structure awareness that differentiated between poor and good readers was the ability to recognize inconsistencies in expository content. Examining text structure awareness of normally and low-achieving students and students with learning disabilities, Englert and Thomas (1987) found that normally achieving students identified significantly more inconsistencies in text than low-achieving students, who, in turn, identified significantly more inconsistencies in text than students with learning disabilities. This difference existed even when students with learning disabilities were matched by reading ability and IQ with younger, normally achieving students.

The inconsistencies task consisted of paragraphs written in description, enumeration, sequence, and comparison/contrast text structures. Each paragraph contained three sentences, one that indicated the topic of the paragraph, one that signaled the specific type of text structure, and one that provided an exemplar detail sentence that met topic and text structure requirements. For the decision task, four sentences were presented. Two extended the ideas introduced in the first two sentences and were consistent with the established topic sentence. Two were distracters. Students were required to decide the degree to which each sentence fit the topic and text structure of the paragraph stems.

Englert and Thomas (1987) concluded that the deficit in text structure awareness in students with learning disabilities affected their ability to use the interrelationships in text to predict forthcoming relevant details based on the text structure, to extract essential from nonessential information, and to be sensitive to their own comprehension failures. Thus, students with learning disabilities did not look back to the original stimulus sentences to confirm the relationship between the main idea and supporting details. This study also indicated that, similarly to normally achieving students, students with learning disabilities and low achievers appeared to acquire text structure knowledge developmentally (Englert & Thomas).

Another area affected by poor readers' lack of sensitivity to text structure is summarization. Seidenberg (1989) reported that eighth-grade poor readers did not appear to use text structure awareness to summarize text. Although they appeared aware of the need to include important ideas in a summary, they had difficulty identifying important ideas in a reading passage and constructing an internal topic structure representation of the text information. Rather than use the strategic skills required to produce an adequate summary or the meaning of the whole text, they made sentence-by-sentence decisions determined by the position of information and by what was important to them (Winograd, cited in Seidenberg, 1989).

Implications and Interventions

The evidence is clear that text structure and students' awareness of text structure are positively related to reading comprehension. Student sensitivity to text structure may be developmental and varies according to text structure type. Generally, narrative is easier than expository text for students and some types of expository text are easier than others (e.g., sequence was found to be easier than enumeration and description, which in turn was found to be easier than compare/contrast; Englert & Thomas, 1987).

Teachers should be aware of these variations and may want to attend more carefully to text structure as students move to reading more expository text in the upper-elementary school grades. Zabrucky and Ratner (1992) posed that teachers be concerned with increasing students' awareness of different text structures and informing students of the impact of these structures on evaluation, regulation, and memory. Students should be taught to adjust their reading and rereading skills and to assess their readiness for recall when text information varies in difficulty. This instruction may be more effective if it occurs for narrative before expository text.

Additionally, among many models of narrative text, story grammars are the most studied (Graesser et al., 1991) and have been linked to improved comprehension (Pearson & Fielding, 1991). As a result, story grammars are valid and useful to teach.

Kinder and Bursuck (1991) argued for a unified social studies curriculum that "integrated facts and concepts into a network of knowledge" (p. 319). Research evidence suggests that well-structured expository text facilitates comprehension of main ideas or topics, rather than facts (Weaver & Kintsch, 1991). Consequently, clearly written and organized expository text structures in textbooks would facilitate students' reading comprehension of a "network of knowledge."

Students tend to receive limited sustained practice in reading and writing expository prose (Applebee, cited in Englert & Thomas, 1987). One reason students with learning disabilities may differ significantly from low-achieving peers in discriminating between relevant and inconsistent information in text passages may be that they lack experience with expository text. Consequently, students with learning disabilities must be exposed to good models of expository text structure (Englert & Thomas).

Diverse learners appear deficient in text structure awareness, which indicates a need for specific instruction in text structure (Seidenberg, 1989). As noted by Englert and Thomas (1987), "Unfortunately, since students gain knowledge via expository prose, teachers who do not direct attention to the text structures that underlie expository discourse may be depriving students with learning disabilities of important opportunities to develop self-sufficiency in communication skills essential to their independence as adults" (p. 103).

AREA OF CONVERGENCE 3:
Explicit Instruction in Text Organization
Facilitates Comprehension

Research in both the physical presentation of text and text structures supported the benefits of explicit instruction in these areas. Seidenberg (1989) concluded that instruction in the physical presentation of text facilitates the reading comprehension of students with learning disabilities. Instruction in text structures had strong empirical support for benefiting reading comprehension. For example, primary studies provided evidence of the effectiveness of instruction in narrative text structure for students with learning disabilities (e.g., Dole et al., 1996, Gurney et al., 1990; Newby et al., 1989; Williams et al., 1994). Finally, Pearson and Fielding (1991) provided strong evidence of the benefit of "just about any" (p. 832) type of instruction in expository text structure.

In this section, we discuss what to teach, how to teach, caveats, and relations between instruction and learners. The discussion of what to teach includes physical presentation of text, narrative text structure, expository text structures, visual representations of text, and strategies. The discussion of visual representations of text is lengthy and could have been a convergent area of its own. However, it is one of several ways to teach text structure and, therefore, more properly belongs within the converging evidence that supports instruction in text organization. Note that the discussion of strategies is subsumed under what to teach, rather than being treated separately as it was in the two previous areas of convergence. The discussion of "how to teach" highlights information that is presented in more detail in this book in a subsequent chapter on text organization and curricular and instructional implications for diverse learners.

What to Teach

Physical Presentation of Text. In her review of information-processing studies, Seidenberg (1989) concluded that students with learning disabilities benefited from explicit, task-specific instruction on (a) how to recognize the physical presentation of important information in text, including topic sentences and where these usually occur in well-organized paragraphs and (b) headings and subheadings and their purposes. In the same review, Seidenberg identified two additional structural cues to teach students: the patterns that exemplify subordinate and superordinate relations, and signal words (e.g., "first," "finally").

Taylor and colleagues (cited in Pearson & Fielding, 1991) found that teaching students a summarizing strategy using the headings, subheadings, and paragraph topics of textbooks resulted in more recalled text information than answering questions or studying.

Narrative Text Structure. Even though narrative text structure may be taught using any number of models (e.g., story grammars, causal networks, conceptual graph structures, scripts and plans), story grammars are the oldest and most studied (Graesser et al., 1991). Moreover, they have been validated as benefiting reading comprehension (e.g., Dole et al., 1996; Gurney et al., 1990; Newby et al., 1989; Pearson & Fielding, 1991; Williams et al. 1994) and predicting readers' performance (Graesser et al.). Additionally, they have been viewed as unifying several research trends in narrative text structure into one theory (Graesser et al.).

Story grammar instruction usually includes a simplified version of story grammar components as well as practice in identifying category-relevant information (Pearson & Fielding, 1991). Pearson and Fielding found strong support that instruction in a story grammar resulted in improved reading comprehension of stories beyond those used in the studies' interventions and "real" stories (i.e., stories not adapted to fit narrative text structure).

The primary studies included in this chapter provide specific examples of the effectiveness of story grammar instruction for diverse learners. Gurney et al. (1990), Newby et al. (1989), Williams et al. (1994), and Dole et al. (1996) provided support for teaching a story grammar to students (a) with dyslexia in high school (Gurney et al.), (b) with learning disabilities between 8 and 10 years of age (Newby et al.) and in Grades 5 through 8 (Williams et al.), and (c) scoring in the lower quartile of the reading portion of the Stanford Achievement Test at pretest in Grades 5 and 6 (Dole et al.).

In each primary study, students were taught story grammar elements, although each study varied in the number of specific elements. Specifically, Newby et al. (1989) included the largest number of elements: main character, problem encountered by the main character, setting, events or attempts by main character to solve the problem, and solution or resolution of the problem. Gurney et al. (1990) taught four story grammar components: main character and main problem/conflict; character clues (e.g., characters' actions, dialogue, thoughts, physical attributes, and reactions to other characters and events); resolution; and theme. Dole et al. (1996) included the fewest story grammar elements: main characters, problem, and resolution. Williams et al. (1994) focused on theme, teaching students to derive a theme by identifying the main character, central event, and outcome, and judging whether the outcome was good or bad.

The effects of story grammar instruction were students' improved ability to comprehend qualitatively important ideas from stories. "Qualitatively important" was defined as the most important or central ideas in a story (Newby et al., 1989), the story grammar elements (Gurney et al., 1990; Williams et al., 1994), or vocabulary, literal, and inferential information based on the story grammar elements main character, problem, and resolution (Dole et al., 1996).

Instruction in how to derive the theme of a story resulted in improved ability to identify familiar themes (themes that had been specifically taught) in unfamiliar stories for fifth- and sixth-grade normally achieving students and students with learning disabilities (Williams et al., 1994). It is difficult to draw conclusions about the generalization of theme instruction to identifying unfamiliar themes (themes not specifically taught) in stories. Williams et al. conducted two studies to examine the effects of theme instruction. In the first study, conducted in general education classrooms, normally achieving students and students with learning disabilities generalized theme instruction. The second study included only students with learning disabilities who were considered too "low functioning" by their school district to receive instruction in general education classrooms. These "low functioning" students with learning disabilities did not generalize theme instruction. Not enough information is available to conclude that differences in generalization were due to ability or placement in general education classrooms. Williams et al. concluded that students with learning disabilities benefit from instruction in theme identification even when there is no generalization.

Although students' comprehension of qualitatively important information improved, results for story details were mixed. Williams et al. (1994) found that instruction in main character, central event, outcome, and deriving a theme facilitated recall of story details for students with learning disabilities but not for nondisabled students. Two studies failed to find effectiveness for students' recall of detail (Newby et al., 1989) or answers to typical basal literature questions that focused on literal or minor details (Gurney et al., 1990).

Gurney et al. (1990) and Williams et al. (1994) noted that a story grammar provided students with learning disabilities a framework that helped them comprehend stories at a more sophisticated level. However, Williams et al. concluded that story grammar instruction aids retention of lower-level story details, whereas Gurney et al. posited that story grammar instruction guided students away from minor details toward identification and articulation of important ideas. Students receiving typical basal instruction (define vocabulary words, set purpose for reading or activate background knowledge, read, answer questions), on the other hand, demonstrated no improvements in answering traditional basal questions (Gurney et al.) or recalling ideas (Newby et al., 1990; Williams et al., 1994).

Montague et al. (1990) concluded that instruction should focus on the goals, motives, thoughts, and feelings of the characters in the stories. This focus increased the amount of information students wrote about the characters and, consequently, the length of the stories they generated.

In summary, instruction in story grammar elements provided a framework that facilitated students' comprehension of the important ideas of a story, but not necessarily the details. Students with learning disabilities may require additional focus on the goals, motives, thoughts, and feelings of the characters in stories.

Expository Text Structures. In their review of research on comprehension instruction, Pearson and Fielding (1991) found "incredibly positive support for just about any approach to text structure instruction for expository text" (p. 832) for facilitating comprehension and short- and long-term memory for text. Approaches to text structure instruction included both systematic attention to clues that signal how authors relate ideas to one another and systematic attempts to impose structure upon text. Their review included five studies that taught students top-level structures (e.g., cause-effect, problem-solution) and how to use these structures for reading and studying, that resulted in enhanced recall and comprehension, and 13 series of studies that taught students to study or create visual representations of key ideas in text including networking, flowcharting, Con Struct, mapping, conceptual frames, graphic organizers, conceptual mapping, and other visual organization devices that resulted in facilitation of comprehension.

Seidenberg (1989) found similar empirical support for teaching text structure. Three of the studies she reviewed included instruction in text structure or awareness of top-level information (e.g., main ideas), resulting in improved recall of content, comprehension of unfamiliar content, and expository writing compared to students who did not receive similar instruction. Seidenberg added that instruction should include how to recognize and use the various text structures.

Although the ability to comprehend expository text has been called essential for school success (Seidenberg, 1989), many researchers have found textbooks, particularly social studies textbooks, to be lacking in explicit text structure or organization (e.g., Armbruster & colleagues, cited in Kinder & Bursuck, 1991; White, cited in Kinder & Bursuck).

Kinder and Bursuck (1991) reported on one preliminary examination in which history content instruction was organized through a problem–solution–effect text structure. Three junior high school special education classrooms of 4 to 10 students identified as having behavior disorders participated in a multiple-baseline study. During baseline, "traditional" instruction in American history consisted of (a) read, (b) discuss, (c) answer textbook and workbook questions, and (d) test. Students' test scores at this stage ranged from 45% to 57%. A problem–solution–effect text structure was then introduced. Instruction consisted of (a) read; (b) analyze the problem, solution, and effect with teacher help; (c) write problem–solution–effect text structure notes; (d) develop timelines; and (e) write definitions of text-identified vocabulary words. Average scores on tests ranged from 78% to 85%. Students demonstrated the most difficulty developing problem and solution statements, a skill that requires comprehension skills. Only toward the end of the intervention were students able to begin to state the problem and solution in their own words. More research is needed to determine whether students could independently apply the strategy to published textbooks or other texts (Kinder & Bursuck).

Zabrucky and Ratner (1992) suggested that teachers be concerned not only with increasing students' awareness of different text structures, but also with informing students of the impact text structures have on evaluation, regulation, and memory. They suggested generalizing metacognitive skills to more difficult expository passages after training with narrative passages.

Visual Representations of Text. Pearson and Fielding (1991) reported that 13 series of studies teaching students to study or create visual representations of key ideas in text (e.g., networking, flowcharting, Con Struct, mapping, conceptual frames, graphic organizers, conceptual mapping) benefited reading comprehension. Armbruster, Anderson, and colleagues (cited in Pearson & Fielding, 1991) reasoned that instruction should also include opportunities to use and construct graphic organizers. Two types of visual representations of text, networking (Dansereau & colleagues, cited in Pearson & Fielding, 1991) and flowcharting (Geva, cited in Pearson & Fielding, 1991) have frequently been found to be more effective for low-performing students than for high-performing students (Pearson & Fielding). It may be that high-performing students develop their own strategies, whereas low-performing students require careful instruction in strategies (Pearson & Fielding).

A series of three primary studies provided additional support for the benefit of instruction in visual representations of text for students with a range of abilities. Horton et al. (1990) conducted these studies in 7th- and 10th-grade general education classrooms (i.e., social studies, science, and health) containing students with heterogeneous abilities ranging from students with learning disabilities ($n = 1 - 5$), remedial students ($n = 0 - 9$), and students without identified disabilities ($n = 36 - 175$). The study compared four types of instruction in graphic organizers with student-selected self-study.

Self-study consisted of reading and rereading an assigned textbook passage for 15 minutes, and studying or taking notes for 20 minutes in a manner of the students' own choosing (e.g., diagram, outline, write short statements of main ideas, formulate and answer questions, or define key terms).

Graphic organizer instruction consisted of reading and rereading for 15 minutes, and completing and studying graphic organizers for 20 minutes. On a blank graphic organizer designed by the researcher, teachers directed student attention to general relations between the categories shown on a diagram. In Study 1, teachers led students in either filling in the graphic organizer or using a prefilled graphic organizer. In Study 2, students were allowed 15 minutes to independently complete a graphic organizer using a cover sheet that contained page and paragraph numbers for locating answers in the textbook, with a teacher providing assistance when required. In Study 3, students completed a graphic organizer using a list of phrases that fit appropriate places on the graphic organizer. Students in the experimental groups studied their completed graphic organizers for 5 minutes before taking the test that consisted of filling in a blank 15-item graphic organizer.

Instruction in using graphic organizers to visually represent text had consistent effects regardless of content area (i.e., social studies, science, and health) or grade level (i.e., middle and high school). Specifically, in 10 minutes, students who received instruction in graphic organizers filled in significantly more correct responses on the test graphic organizer than did students in the self-study groups. The results for each type of learner in the study were as follows: (a) Students with learning disabilities in the graphic organizer groups averaged 70% correct compared to 20% correct for self-study students with learning disabilities, (b) remedial students in the graphic organizer groups averaged 74% correct compared to 42% for remedial students in the self-study groups, and (c) general education students in the graphic organizer groups averaged 86% compared to 56% for those in the self-study groups.

Each type of graphic organizer instruction offered instructional benefits. In teacher-directed instruction (Study 1), the teacher determined the pace of activity, kept students on task, drew a range of students into the discussion, and embellished facts and ideas. In student-directed graphic organizers with references to page and paragraph numbers (Study 2), students extracted information from text independently and practiced using referential cues. The teachers were free to provide individual help. In the clue or phrases condition (Study 3), the clues provided a structure similar to a teacher-directed lesson, but students had to interact independently with the text.

Horton et al. (1990) concluded that graphic organizers helped make mainstreaming a valid instructional delivery system for all students. However, the studies had two limitations. First, researchers rather than teachers constructed and filled in the original graphic organizers. In a replication of Study 2, researchers taught teachers to make their own graphic organizers. It took teachers about 60 minutes to prepare one organizer for a 1,500-word passage. Horton et al. suggested that teachers who teach the same content area classes collaborate or share graphic organizers, making the procedure more efficient.

The second limitation was the dependent measure used—a graphic organizer that matched what students in the graphic organizer groups studied before taking the test. Students filled in the dependent measure from memory. The graphic organizer dependent measure was selected to maximize students' retrieval of information by matching as closely as possible the form in which the information was taught. However, this study did not indicate whether instruction using graphic organizers would facilitate reading comprehension measured using more traditional measures (e.g., multiple choice, free response, oral response).

Boyle (1996) directly addressed the limitations of the studies by Horton et al. (1990). Students with learning disabilities and educable mental retardation in middle school ($n = 15$) received six 50-minute sessions of instruction and practice in constructing a visual organizer of content on a blank sheet of paper. The steps included: recording and circling the topic of a passage; recording the main idea and three details of each paragraph; circling the recorded main idea and linking its details; and linking all circles. Students performed significantly better than those not receiving instruction ($n = 15$) on curriculum-based measures of literal and inferential comprehension of below-grade and grade-level passages, and the silent reading portion of a formal reading inventory but not on the Stanford Diagnostic Reading Test, a standardized timed measure. Boyle suggested that, even though generic visual representations of text appear effective for improving reading comprehension for students with learning disabilities, research is required to determine whether instruction in visual representations based on specific text structures would be more useful to students with learning disabilities than generic visual representations.

In summary, instruction in some type of visual representation of text facilitates comprehension for students with differing abilities. Many models exist for effectively teaching students how to impose structure on text. Further study is needed to determine which models are more efficient for a wide range of abilities in a classroom.

Strategies. A major contribution of research has been to transform reading skills (e.g., summarize, identify main ideas, identify relations between main ideas) into explicit strategies that students can be taught directly (Seidenberg, 1989). This includes teaching students how to use (a) the physical presentation of text (e.g., location of topic sentences, headings, subheadings, signal words) as a strategy to identify main ideas and form interrelations between concepts, main ideas, and supporting details (Seidenberg); (b) a story grammar to identify the important ideas in narrative text (Dole et al., 1996; Gurney et al., 1990; Newby et al., 1989) or themes (Williams et al., 1994); and (c) expository text structures to identify concepts and interrelations or to impose interrelations upon poorly written text. Examples of imposing text structure include visual representations of text (Horton et al., 1990; Pearson & Fielding, 1991) and note sheets organized around text structure (Englert & Thomas, 1987). Strategy instruction holds particular promise for students with learning disabilities as they seem to lack the ability to engage in strategic activities and do not spontaneously access and use cognitive strategies when these are needed (Seidenberg).

Strategies to identify the main idea in text appear particularly important. Because the ability to comprehend main ideas differentiates good and poor readers and seems directly related to general comprehension abilities, Seidenberg (1989) emphasized teaching students strategies to identify main ideas using topic sentences, headings, and subheadings. She noted, however, that main idea statements are often omitted from texts and that students demonstrated difficulties in using or comprehending text (e.g., summarizing, integrating important information) when there was no explicit main idea. When main idea statements are not explicitly stated or located in the beginning of the paragraph, students with learning disabilities who have not learned to generate main idea statements are unable to use a main idea strategy to derive or recall information from content area textbooks. Consequently, Seidenberg concluded that students with learning disabilities require instruction in how to invent main idea statements.

How to Teach

The secondary and primary studies reviewed for this chapter provided strong support for explicit and direct instruction in text presentation and text structure. In addition, Seidenberg (1989) argued for explicit instruction in how to recognize or produce different text structure types. Pearson and Fielding (1991) cited studies that used either a model-lead-test or model-guided practice-independent practice format. This discussion of how to teach is brief. Relevant details and examples are presented by Dickson, Simmons, and Kameenui in the following chapter.

Generally, instructional planning began with targeting the skills to be taught (Seidenberg, 1989) and subsequently developing lessons to teach the components of the skill or strategy. Instruction in the primary and secondary studies followed a general pattern of (a) explaining the skill or component of text structure; (b) telling the importance; (c) modeling how, when, and where to use the skill and how to evaluate the effectiveness of the skill; (d) providing guided and independent practice; (e) teaching for transfer; and (f) evaluating. Seidenberg suggested including activities in which students actively participate in the learning process and apply and generalize the given skill.

Additionally, the studies reviewed provided evidence for the effectiveness of sequencing instruction from less to more complex text structures, models, and tasks. Examples and details for sequencing instruction are presented in a subsequent chapter of this book on instruction in text structure, in a discussion of mediated scaffolding.

Caveats for Instruction

Englert and Thomas (1987) cautioned that intervention studies are essential to determine whether development of text structure knowledge results in long-lasting improvements in comprehension. Although not pertaining to text structure per se, another caveat comes from the results of a review by Talbott et al. (1994) that specifically addressed reading comprehension interventions for students with learning disabilities. These authors reviewed 48 studies examining the effects of interventions designed to improve the comprehension of students identified with learning disabilities and that included a control group. Because few studies reported details about students (e.g., ethnicity, gender, socioeconomic status), Talbott et al. concluded that generalization of results is limited. "We don't know whether reading comprehension interventions are effective for diverse groups of learners; for girls and boys, or for students with diverse ethnic and economic backgrounds, and at all economic levels" (p. 26). Though researchers have developed effective methods to teach reading comprehension to students with learning disabilities, much research remains to be done.

First, various interventions need to be compared with each other to discern the "best" (p. 27) among them. In their review, Talbott et al. found no significant differences among reading comprehension studies that employed six major types of interventions: cognitive, cognitive-behavioral, vocabulary, pre- and mid-reading, direct instruction, and computer-assisted. Second, studies need to employ rigorous methods (e.g., random assignment, detailed subject description). Third, more teachers rather than researchers need to conduct the actual interventions. Finally, researchers need to develop techniques to enable students to reach high levels of comprehension. Studies also need to address effects of intervention on students' higher order reading comprehension skills. In the majority of studies, researchers assessed recall of factual information from text rather than higher order skills (e.g., inferential, evaluative, and appreciative).

Relations Between Instruction in Text
Organization and Types of Learners

Normally Achieving Learners. It appears that normally achieving students benefit from explicit, direct instruction in text structure. Much of the research in text structure instruction used a model-lead-test or model-guided practice-independent practice format for normally achieving students (Pearson & Fielding, 1991). Almost any instruction in expository text structure resulted in improved comprehension, as well as short- and long-term memory (Pearson & Fielding). For narrative text, instruction in story grammar facilitates the comprehension of story grammar components and identification of a theme of a story but may not help normally achieving students recall details (e.g., Williams et al., 1994).

Transfer of skills from materials in which instruction occurred to new materials is an important consideration in instruction. Instruction in narrative text structure transferred to improved comprehension of story grammar elements in "actual," unadapted stories not used in the intervention (Pearson & Fielding, 1991). Additionally, students taught to identify a particular theme (e.g., perseverance) in a story transferred the skill to identifying novel or untaught themes in new stories (Williams et al., 1994).

The results of research in graphic organizers for normally achieving students are equivocal. Some studies demonstrated benefit for low-, but not high-performing students (Pearson & Fielding, 1991); others supported benefit for both high and low performers (e.g., Horton et al., 1990).

Diverse Learners. Diverse learners have benefited from explicit, task-specific instruction on how to recognize and use the physical structure (e.g., topic sentences, headings, signal words; Seidenberg, 1989), as well as narrative (Gurney et al., 1990; Newby et al., 1989) and expository text structures (Seidenberg). Instruction in narrative text structure appeared to provide students with a framework for recalling the important ideas in stories. Because the benefits for identifying details were mixed, further study is required. Additionally, students with learning disabilities may require instructional focus on the goals, motives, thoughts, and feelings of characters in stories (Montague et al., 1991).

Diverse learners may benefit from instruction in strategies, and when and how to apply them (Seidenberg, 1989). In particular, instruction in strategies for identifying story grammar components and main ideas in expository text may be useful for these learners.

For students with dyslexia, studies have examined whether to teach using their strengths or remediating their weaknesses (Newby et al., 1989).

Newby et al. examined teaching story grammar to five 8- to 10-year-old students using instruction based on their strengths. Two students were identified as having difficulties with the sequential phonetic processes of written text (i.e., dysphonetic or auditory–linguistic dyslexia). Three students were identified as having difficulties processing words as wholes (i.e., dyseidetic or visual–spatial dyslexia).

The students displaying sequential phonetic difficulties were taught story grammar components using pictographs with no regard for sequential order. The students drew or briefly noted story components on index cards. The three students who were identified as having difficulties with processing words as wholes were taught story grammar components using sequentially based instruction. They were taught to identify first the main character, then the setting, continuing through the story grammar components in a prescribed manner. Instruction resulted in recall of a greater percentage of important ideas than in baseline. One of the two dysphonetic students and all of the three dyseidetic students showed clear increases. While this study pointed to the effectiveness of intervention by subtype, more research is required to draw clear conclusions. Newby et al. (1989) suggested that the study did not provide enough information to indicate if instruction based on the strengths of dyslexic subtypes was effective, or if training in story grammar in general was just as effective.

SUMMARY

This review of the literature examining the relation between text organization and comprehension resulted in three areas of convergence:

- Well-presented physical text facilitates reading comprehension.
- Text structure and student awareness of text structure are highly related to reading comprehension.
- Explicit instruction in the physical presentation of text and text structure facilitates reading comprehension.

The first two areas are three-pronged, involving presentation and structure of text, students' awareness of text presentation and structure, and students' strategic use of text presentation and structure. Text presentation facilitates reading comprehension if (a) main ideas are clearly stated and located at the beginnings of paragraphs and (b) the relations between important information are clearly indicated by headings, subheadings, signal words, and sentences or paragraphs signaling text organization placed at the beginning of the passage. Extra spacing between thought units in sentences facilitates attention to ideas within sentences. Text structure facilitates reading comprehension, with narrative text structure being generally easier for students to recall and monitor than expository text structures.

However, it may be that simply presenting text in a clear, well-organized manner is not sufficient. Research suggests that students' awareness of that presentation and strategic use of text are also needed to enable students to identify relevant and nonrelevant information, main ideas, and relations between ideas. Normally achieving students appear to strategically use text organization to identify main ideas and relations between ideas. However, if main ideas are not clearly stated, even normally achieving students have demonstrated difficulty identifying important information, summarizing, and integrating information.

Unlike normally achieving students, diverse learners appear less aware of text organization and its use as a strategy. Many comprehension difficulties of diverse learners have been attributed to their deficits in text structure awareness. For example, they have demonstrated difficulty identifying main ideas and discriminating between relevant and nonrelevant information. While demonstrating a knowledge of strategies, they fail to demonstrate a use of strategies.

The first two convergent areas and the importance of students' awareness and strategic use of text presentation lead to the third convergent area—explicit instruction in text organization facilitates comprehension. Research supports instruction in the physical presentation of text, text structures, and strategic use of text organization to benefit reading comprehension. Research evidence also supports explicit instruction that follows a general pattern of (a) explain the skill or component of text structure; (b) tell the importance; (c) model how, when, and where to use the skill and how to evaluate the effectiveness of the skill; (d) provide guided and independent practice; (e) teach for transfer; and (f) evaluate.

The effect on reading comprehension of the presentation and structure of text is more global than local. Well-presented and structured text results in better comprehension of main ideas and relations between ideas than poorly presented or structured text. Likewise, students who are aware of or have had instruction in the physical presentation of text or text structure demonstrate more global comprehension than students who lack awareness or have not had instruction. Although students who are aware of text structure recall more than students who are not aware of text structure, there is often no difference between these students for local (i.e., details) comprehension.

TABLE 10.1
Secondary and Primary Sources

Authors	Text Organization	Participants	Purpose
Graesser, Golding, & Long (1991)	Narrative	Types of readers were not described	Review definitions of narrative text and theories of narrative representation and comprehension
Kinder & Bursuck (1991)	Expository (social studies)	Described one study; students with behavior disorders, LD, mild mental retardation; three junior high classrooms, 4–10 students each	Review social studies textbooks and instruction; propose an instructional approach for students with LD
Pearson & Fielding (1991)	Narrative & expository	High-ability, good readers, poor readers, heterogeneous groups including low achievers and students with LD; kindergarten, elementary, intermediate, junior high, high school, adults	Review of studies to improve reading comprehension
Scruggs & Mastropieri (1993)	Expository (science instruction)	Students with disabilities including language and literacy areas, mental retardation, behavior disorders, LD, hearing or visual impairments, etc.	Review content- vs. activities-based science instruction
Seidenberg (1989)	Physical presentation & expository	Students with LD	Review text-processing literature and propose instructional approaches for students with LD
Talbott, Lloyd, & Tankersley (1994)		Students with LD; 48 studies	Review comprehension interventions

(Continued)

273

TABLE 10.1
CONTINUED

Weaver & Kintsch (1991)	Expository	Types of readers were not described	Review models and studies of expository text comprehension
Primary Sources			
Boyle (1996)	Graphic organizer	Grades 6, 7, & 8; 20 LD & 10 EMR	Intervention; compared instruction in constructing graphic organizers with taking notes or making outlines as desired; matched pairs group design
Casteel (1990)	Physical, "chunks"	Grade 8; 25 high & 25 low readers	Intervention; compared chunked and traditional text and ability level; matched-pairs group design
Dole, Brown, & Trathen (1996)	Narrative	Grades 5 & 6; 51% below lowest quartile on the reading portion of Stanford Achievement Test	Intervention; compared instruction in how to identify main characters, central problem, and resolution with presenting the topic, key vocabulary, concepts, related ideas critical for comprehension, and main characters and central problem; group design
Englert & Thomas (1987)	Expository	Grades 3 & 4; Grades 6 & 7; 18 LD, 18 low achievers, 18 normal achievers in each	Descriptive; compared text structure knowledge of description, enumeration, sequence, and comparison/contrast for young and old readers; group design

Gurney, Gersten, Dimino, & Carnine (1990)	Narrative	High school; 7 LD	Intervention; traditional instruction followed by story grammar instruction; modified multiple baseline
Horton, Lovitt, & Bergerud (1990)	Graphic organizers	*Study 1 & 2:* Grade 7; 127 general, 0 remedial, 5 LD; Grade 10; 36 general, 9 remedial, 3 LD; *Study 3:* Grade 7; 151 general, 0 remedial, 3 LD; Grade 10; 175 general, 9 remedial, 1 LD	Intervention; compared graphic organizers and self-study; group design
Montague, Maddux, & Dereshiwsky (1990)	Narrative	Grades 4 & 5, 7 & 8; & high school; 12 with LD and 12 without LD in each combination	Descriptive; compared learner type for quantitative and qualitative differences in narrative; group design
Newby, Caldwell, & Recht (1989)	Narrative	Ages 8-10; two types of dyslexia; $n = 5$	Intervention; examined instruction based on learning strength; multiple baseline
Williams, Brown, Silverstein, & deCani (1994)	Narrative	*Study 1:* Grades 5 & 6; 31 with LD & 38 nondisabled *Study 2:* Grades 7 & 8; 93 LD in special education classrooms	Intervention; group design; *Study 1:* Compared instruction in deriving themes with whole-language, independent reading, interactive discussion *Study 2:* Compared instruction in deriving themes with instruction based on basal teacher's manual
Zabrucky & Ratner (1992)	Narrative & expository	Grade 6; poor & good comprehenders; $n = 16$ each	Descriptive; compared evaluation and regulation skills for good and poor readers using narrative and expository text; group design

REFERENCES

Barr, R., Kamil, M. L., Mosenthal, P., & Pearson, P. D. (Eds.). (1991). *Handbook of reading research* (Vol. 2). White Plains, NY: Longman.

Boyle, J. R. (1996). The effects of a cognitive mapping strategy on the literal and inferential comprehension of students with mild disabilities. *Learning Disability Quarterly, 19*, 86-93.

Casteel, C. A. (1990). Effects of chunked text material on reading comprehension of high and low ability readers. *Reading Improvement, 27*, 269–275.

Dole, J. A., Brown, K. J., & Trathen, W. (1996). The effects of strategy instruction on the comprehension performance of at-risk students. *Reading Research Quarterly, 31*, 62–88.

Englert, C. S., & Hiebert, E. H. (1984). Children's developing awareness of text structures in expository materials. *Journal of Educational Psychology, 76*, 65–75.

Englert, C. S., & Thomas, C. C. (1987). Sensitivity to text structure in reading and writing: A comparison between learning disabled and non-learning disabled students. *Learning Disability Quarterly, 10*, 93–105.

Graesser, A., Golding, J. M., & Long, D. L. (1991). Narrative representation and comprehension. In R. Barr, M. L. Kamil, P. Mosenthal, & P. D. Pearson (Eds.), *Handbook of reading research* (Vol. 2, pp. 171–204). White Plains, NY: Longman.

Gurney, D., Gersten, R., Dimino, J., & Carnine, D. (1990). Story grammar: Effective literature instruction for high school students with learning disabilities. *Journal of Learning Disabilities, 23*, 335–342, 348.

Horton, S. V., Lovitt, T. C., & Bergerud, D. (1990). The effectiveness of graphic organizers for three classifications of secondary students in content area classes. *Journal of Learning Disabilities, 23*, 12–22.

Kinder, D., & Bursuck, W. (1991). The search for a unified social studies curriculum: Does history really repeat itself? *Journal of Learning Disabilities, 24*, 270–275.

Leo, J. (1994). Mainstreaming's 'Jimmy problem.' *U.S. News and World Report,* June 27, p. 22.

Meyer, B. J. F., Brandt, D. M., & Bluth, G. J. (1980). Use of top-level structure in text: Key for reading comprehension of ninth-grade students. *Reading Research Quarterly, 16*, 72–103.

Meyer, B. J. F., & Freedle, R. O. (1984). Effects of discourse type on recall. *American Educational Research Journal, 21*, 121–143.

Meyer, B. J. F., & Rice, G. E. (1984). The structure of text. In P. D. Pearson, R. Barr, M. L. Kamil, & P. Mosenthal (Eds.), *Handbook of reading research* (Vol. 1, pp. 319–351). White Plains, NY: Longman.

Montague, M., Maddux, C. D., & Dereshiwsky, M. I. (1990). Story grammar and comprehension and production of narrative prose by students with learning disabilities. *Journal of Learning Disabilities, 23*, 190–197.

Newby, R. F., Caldwell, J., & Recht, D. R. (1989). Improving reading comprehension of children with dysphonetic and dyseidetic dyslexia using story grammar. *Journal of Learning Disabilities, 22*, 373–380.

Pearson, P. D., & Fielding, L. (1991). Comprehension instruction. In R. Barr, M. L. Kamil, P. Mosenthal, & P. D. Pearson (Eds.), *Handbook of reading research* (Vol. 2, pp. 815–860). White Plains, NY: Longman.

Scruggs, T. E., & Mastropieri, M. A. (1993). Current approaches to science education: Implications for mainstream education of students with disabilities. *Remedial and Special Education, 14*, 15–24.

Seidenberg, P. L. (1989). Relating text-processing research to reading and writing instruction for learning disabled students. *Learning Disabilities Focus, 5*(1), 4–12.

Talbott, E., Lloyd, J., & Tankersley, M. (1994). Effects of reading comprehension interventions for students with learning disabilities. *Learning Disability Quarterly, 17*, 223–232.

U.S. Department of Education. (1992). *To assure the free appropriate public education of all children with disabilities* (Fourteenth Annual Report to Congress on the Implementation of

The Individual with Disabilities Education Act). Washington, DC: Author.

Weaver, C. A., III, & Kintsch, W. (1991). Expository text. In R. Barr, M. L. Kamil, P. Mosenthal, & P. D. Pearson (Eds.), *Handbook of reading research* (Vol. 2, pp. 230–244). White Plains, NY: Longman.

Williams, J. P., Brown, L. G., Silverstein, A. K., & deCani, J. S. (1994). An instructional program in comprehension of narrative themes for adolescents with learning disabilities. *Learning Disability Quarterly, 17,* 205–221.

Zabrucky, K., & Ratner, H. H. (1992). Effects of passage type on comprehension monitoring and recall in good and poor readers. *Journal of Reading Behavior, 24,* 373–391.

CHAPTER

11

Text Organization: Instructional and Curricular Basics and Implications

Shirley V. Dickson
Northern Illinois University

Deborah C. Simmons
Edward J. Kameenui
University of Oregon

REVIEW OF CONVERGING EVIDENCE

In their review of the literature on reading comprehension, Pearson and Fielding (1991) concluded that "just about any approach to text structure instruction for expository text" (p. 832) facilitates reading comprehension. In a similar view, Englert and Thomas (1987) posited that "teachers who did not direct attention to" expository text structures may be "depriving LD students of important opportunities to develop self-sufficiency in communication skills essential to their independence as adults" (p. 103). However, any approach to instruction or attention directing is insufficient for benefiting diverse learners. Diverse learners typically lag behind their peers in reading comprehension and demonstrate difficulty recognizing patterns in text, discerning relevant information, and recalling information. As a result, they require instruction that enables them to independently access text for comprehension and narrow the gap between themselves and their normally achieving peers.

In the previous chapter on text organization and its relation to reading comprehension, Dickson, Simmons, and Kameenui reviewed secondary and primary research on text structure and the physical presentation of text and their relations to reading comprehension. Their review resulted in three convergent areas of evidence:

1. Well-presented physical text facilitates reading comprehension.
2. Text structure and student awareness of text structure are highly re-
    lated to reading comprehension.
3. Explicit instruction in the physical presentation of text and / or text
    structure facilitates reading comprehension.

Two instructional priorities or "big ideas" emerged from the three areas
of convergence. First, well-presented texts that explicitly reveal main ideas
and relations between main ideas facilitate reading comprehension.
Because teachers cannot control how texts are written, we address the
second instructional implication: Reading comprehension is facilitated by
explicit instruction in (a) the conventions of well-presented text and the
organizational patterns of text structures and (b) the uses of the conventions
of well-presented text and the organizational patterns of text structures to
identify main ideas and relations between relevant information.

Seidenberg (1989) proposed that the foundation for the design of more
effective instructional programs for students with learning disabilities can
be derived from research. With this in mind, the studies reviewed by
Dickson, Simmons, and Kameenui for the previous chapter on text
organization and its relation to reading comprehension were scrutinized
for convergence of teaching techniques. These techniques were then
reconceptualized according to six instructional principles developed by
Dixon, Carnine, and Kameenui (1992).

In the following section, we identify two instructional priorities, or
big ideas, for instruction. To make these big ideas more explicit and
employable, we discuss the principles of *conspicuous strategies, mediated
scaffolding, strategic integration, primed background knowledge,* and *judicious
review* and present examples of how they apply to instruction of text
presentation and text structure. The procedural principles, in combination
with the content of the big ideas, illustrate how to translate research into
practice. The following section should not be viewed as a prescription,
but rather as an application of principles that can be used to make tangible
the details of instruction for students with diverse learning needs. To
connect research and practice, we respond to two focal questions:

1. What are the research-based instructional priorities or big ideas in
    text organization?
2. For the instructional priorities or big ideas in text organization, what
    is the existing research evidence regarding curriculum design?

In the studies reviewed by Dickson, Simmons, and Kameenui in the
previous chapter on text organization, instruction was predominantly

explicit. That is, it consisted of the teacher (a) identifying concepts, skills, or strategies to teach; (b) demonstrating or modeling the concepts, skills, or strategies; (c) engaging students in guided practice; (d) providing students with independent practice; and (e) having students independently apply the new concept, skill, or strategy while reading their regular textbooks. The instructional principles presented in this chapter of instructional implications for diverse learners provide guidelines for an explicit instructional format.

RESEARCH-BASED INSTRUCTIONAL PRIORITIES IN TEXT ORGANIZATION: BIG IDEAS

Dixon et al. (1992) defined *big ideas* as concepts or principles within or across content areas that have the greatest potential for enabling students to apply what they learn in varied situations. Big ideas have also been addressed by Prawat (1989) and Brophy (cited in Kinder & Bursuck, 1991). For example, Prawat suggested that instruction in key concepts that are rich in relationships and applicable across a wide array of phenomena may facilitate students' access to knowledge. Brophy (cited in Kinder & Bursuck, 1991) posited that students be taught networks of information that stress relations between concepts and facts. Each of these authors stressed the importance of concepts and interrelations to knowledge acquisition.

In the area of text organization, two big ideas are the physical presentation of text and text structures. Although the physical presentation of text and text structures (e.g., narrative, persuasive, descriptive, compare/contrast) are not big ideas in the same sense as content area concepts (e.g., convection cells in science, supply and demand in economics), they are, nevertheless, concepts or *big ideas* that demonstrate great potential for application in varied situations. Thus, they enable readers to identify main ideas and relations between main ideas or concepts and independently access and comprehend the texts they read in a variety of content areas (e.g., history, science, health).

Physical Presentation of Text

Text that is well presented explicitly reveals the interrelations between concepts and facts. Moreover, well-presented text helps students identify main ideas (a skill central to comprehension), summarize, and outline (Seidenberg, 1989). In a review of text-processing research, Seidenberg concluded that instruction in how to recognize the physical textual presentation of important information and relations between important information benefits the reading comprehension of students with learning disabilities. Instruction should include headings and subheadings and an explanation of their purposes; signal words; and topic sentences and a description of where they usually occur in well-organized paragraphs.

Text Structure

Text structures (e.g., narrative, persuasive, descriptive, compare/contrast) establish the interrelations between ideas through well-organized patterns such as those associated with narrative, persuasive, explanatory, or compare/contrast text structures. Research generally indicates that awareness of text structure facilitates comprehension of concepts or main ideas, not of facts (e.g., Gurney, Gersten, Dimino, & Carnine, 1990; Newby, Caldwell, & Recht, 1989; Pearson & Fielding, 1991). Specifically, awareness of text structure enables readers to identify, summarize, and recall main ideas and supporting information (Seidenberg, 1989). In exception to the general findings, one primary study (Williams, Brown, Silverstein, & deCani, 1994) reported that instruction in a higher level of organization (specifically theme of a narrative) enhanced not only retention of major story components but also of lower level story details. This effect occurred for students with learning disabilities but not for students without learning disabilities.

A major benefit of big ideas is their application to varied situations. For text structure, this includes application to texts other than those used during instruction, varied comprehension skills, and composition. Although this chapter focuses on reading comprehension, ample evidence supports application of text structure to student generation of written compositions. Thus, text structure provides a framework for generating, organizing, and editing information in compositions (e.g., Englert & Thomas, 1987; Simmons et al., 1994). Knowledge of the general organizational patterns of text structure is important in both the reading comprehension and composition process (Scardamalia & Paris, cited in Seidenberg, 1989). Consequently, instruction in recognizing and using text structures is valid for improving both reading and writing performance (Slater, Graves, Scott, & Redd, cited in Seidenberg, 1989).

In summary, the physical presentation of text and text structure are *big ideas* that facilitate identifying and learning the key concepts and networks of information in textbooks and other materials students read. Furthermore, students can apply their knowledge or awareness of well-presented text and text structures to various content areas, reading comprehension tasks, and written composition.

The remaining five instructional principles (i.e., conspicuous strategies, mediated scaffolding, strategic integration, primed background knowledge, and judicious review) provide guidelines for instruction. The examples for each principle were taken from the procedures within the primary and secondary studies reviewed by Dickson, Simmons, and Kameenui in the chapter on text organization and its relation to reading comprehension. Although the instructional guidelines are presented separately here for clarity, in actual lesson plans they are thoughtfully interwoven to frame effective instruction for diverse learners.

EVIDENCE OF CURRICULUM DESIGN IN TEXT ORGANIZATION

Conspicuous Strategies

Strategies are an organized set of actions designed to accomplish a task. To be optimally effective, strategies must be neither too broad, nor too narrow and prescriptive (Dixon et al., 1992). Narrow, prescriptive strategies are more powerful in ensuring success but do not readily transfer to new situations. Broad, general strategies, on the other hand, are appropriate in many situations but are vague and difficult to teach (Prawat, 1989). Therefore, a middle-range strategy that is taught in a content-specific context may enable students to master the strategy, while seeing the strategy's purpose and effect (Prawat).

Use of the (a) conventions of physical presentation of text and (b) organizational patterns of text structures to identify main ideas and the relations between ideas has been translated into middle-range conspicuous strategies. Both are narrow enough to be teachable and useful in facilitating identification of main ideas and relations between relevant information, yet broad enough to be applied to new and varied texts and tasks. In order to make the strategic use of the conventions of text presentation and organizational patterns of text structures conspicuous to students, teachers must provide a great deal of specific information. Across the primary and secondary sources reviewed by Dickson, Simmons, and Kameenui for the chapter on text organization and its relation to reading comprehension, common instructional features for making strategies conspicuous included:

- Define and explain the strategy components;
- Inform students when and why the strategies are helpful;
- Inform students of the impact the strategies have on evaluation, regulation, and memory;
- Model use of the strategy;
- Teach the students to self-verbalize the strategy; and
- Provide feedback at key points in the learning process.

Physical Presentation of Text.   Seidenberg (1989) discussed instruction in the conventions of the physical presentation of text in her review of text-processing research and the reading instruction of students with learning disabilities. The conventions of text presentation become strategies for identifying main ideas and the relations between relevant information. Such strategies include specific attention to topic sentences and where they are usually located in well-organized paragraphs; headings and subheadings and their purposes; and signal words and their purposes. A strategy to create a hierarchical summary of passages, for example, includes using the passage's headings, subheadings, and paragraph topics.

Because many textbooks do not follow the conventions of well-presented physical text, frequently the main idea of a paragraph is stated late in the paragraph or is missing. Late or missing main ideas and the subsequent invention of main idea statements are problematic for both normally achieving and diverse learners (Seidenberg, 1989). Seidenberg concluded that a strategy to invent main idea statements facilitates identification of important information in reading passages. Although Seidenberg did not specifically identify the component steps of how to invent a main idea, she outlined the steps followed by most readers to identify a main idea (Kieras, cited in Seidenberg, 1989). The strategy steps apply when the main idea is explicitly stated in the first sentence of the paragraph; embedded in the paragraph, or missing. Kieras identified the following strategy steps:

1.   Test the first sentence as a main idea sentence.
2.   Test the sentences following the first sentence to see if they are relevant to the probable main idea.
3.   If the sentences do not fit the probable main idea, revise the main idea to one the sentences will fit.

Text Structure.   In addition to being useful for identifying main ideas and relations between relevant information, knowledge of text-structure types translates into middle-range comprehension strategies to (a) summarize passages, (b) adjust reading speed, (c) determine the need to reread, (d) assess readiness for recall, and (e) frame the appropriate organizational pattern for compositions. Middle-range strategies apply to narrative and expository texts.

To improve the reading comprehension of narrative text for diverse learners, Dole, Brown, and Trathen (1996), Gurney et al. (1990), Newby et al. (1989), and Williams et al. (1994) taught a story-grammar strategy. For example, Gurney et al. and Williams et al. taught students to use some components of story grammar (e.g., main character, problem, resolution, conclusion, character cues) to enhance students' identification of a more difficult story-grammar component, the theme of a story.

To make the strategy conspicuous, instruction in the four studies included (a) explicitly teaching the story-grammar elements (e.g., setting, main character, problem, character cues, attempts to solve the problem, and resolution); (b) telling how the story-grammar elements help understand and answer questions about stories; (c) modeling how to use the strategy to identify story parts (explained in the discussion of mediated scaffolding); and (d) providing written prompts to help the students use the strategy and recall information (e.g., pictographs, lists of story grammar elements, note sheets, explained in the discussion of mediated scaffolding).

Similar to narrative text structure, expository text structures form the basis of strategies for identifying important information and relations between important information (Seidenberg, 1989) and for summarizing and building macrostructures of passages (Pearson & Fielding, 1991). One strategy involves teaching a visual representation of six types of links or relations between information in texts:

> A is part of B,
> A is an example of B,
> A leads to B,
> A is like B,
> A has a feature of B, and
> A provides evidence or support of B
> (Holley et al., cited in Pearson & Fielding, 1991).

A second strategy involves teaching a generic rather than specific type of visual representation of text (Boyle, 1996; Dole et al., 1996). An example of a generic strategy is to teach students to: write the topic of the passage, write the main idea of a paragraph, write three details from the paragraph, circle the main idea and link the details to the main idea, continue for each paragraph, and link all of the circles (Dole et al.).

A third strategy base involves the repetitive top-level organization of text structures such as *problem–solution, description,* and *explanation.* Instruction includes (a) teaching visual frames designed around a text structure pattern (Armbruster & colleagues, cited in Pearson & Fielding, 1991), (b) identifying a particular text structure pattern and using it to organize reading and studying (Bartlett, cited in Pearson & Fielding), (c) teaching the components unique to the different text structure types (Raphael et al., cited in Seidenberg, 1989; Seidenberg, cited in Seidenberg, 1989), and (d) providing students with top-level information before they read (Samuels et al., cited in Pearson & Fielding, 1991).

A strategy for problem–solution–effect text structure involves asking four questions: What is the problem? Why is it a problem? What was the solution? and, What was the effect? Students divide their paper into three columns for note taking, one each for problems, solutions, and effects. This strategy transfers to social studies text not written explicitly in problem–solution–effect text structure (Kinder, cited in Kinder & Bursuck, 1991).

Mediated Scaffolding

Mediated scaffolding is the external support provided by teacher/peers, content, tasks, and materials during initial instruction in the conventions of text presentation and organizational patterns of text structures. Scaffolding occurs across and within lessons (Duffy & Roehler, 1989) as teachers weave together the various types of scaffolding to facilitate student learning and independent performance. Among the four types of mediated scaffolding discussed here, *personnel* or *teacher/peer scaffolding* occurs across a continuum, with more support occurring when new concepts, tasks, or strategies are introduced. Support is then faded as students gain fluency and assume more responsibility. *Content* and *task scaffolding* occur by proceeding from easier to more difficult content or tasks. However, at times, content and tasks are held constant as students learn and practice new strategies or procedures. Finally, *material scaffolding* guides students' thinking as they acquire new concepts, skills, or strategies. Students maintain access to scaffolded materials until they are able to apply the new knowledge independently.

Physical Presentation of Text.   Personnel or teacher/peer scaffolding occurs during instruction in the conventions of the physical presentation of text primarily through modeling. For example, when teaching how to build hierarchical summaries, the teacher first thinks out loud to show students how to apply the strategy using headings, subheadings, and paragraph topics. In the guided practice phase, peers and the teacher provide scaffolds by thinking aloud and sharing completed summaries with each other (Taylor et al., cited in Pearson & Fielding, 1991).

The literature reviewed by Dickson, Simmons, and Kameenui (see chap. 10, this volume) did not provide examples of *content, task, or material scaffolding* for instruction in the conventions of text presentation. However, examples from mediated scaffolding of instruction in text structures can be adapted. For example, instruction in identifying main ideas using the location of main idea statements in text can start by using paragraphs that begin with the main idea statement (content and task scaffolding). Next, students learn to identify main idea statements that are embedded in paragraphs by asking themselves if each sentence is relevant to the first sentence. If not, they revise the main idea statement. Finally, students practice the strategy using paragraphs that infer the main idea. Again, students ask themselves if each sentence is relevant to the first sentence. If not, they revise the main idea statement, continuing in this manner until they have generated a main idea statement that incorporates the sentences in the paragraph. Thus, content and tasks increase in difficulty as students gain proficiency in a preceding phase. Material scaffolding can consist of providing students with a list of the procedures to generate a main idea statement.

Text Structure.   One type of mediated scaffolding that occurs in the instruction of text structure is *personnel or teacher/peer scaffolding*. When teaching story grammar, the teacher models how to identify the story-grammar elements in a story. That is, the teacher thinks aloud (i.e., "I don't see a problem yet." "This is a problem, but I need to read on to see if this is the main problem in the story.") and models how to write the information on a notesheet (Gurney et al., 1990). As the instruction progresses, teachers gradually shift the responsibility for identification of story-grammar elements to the students (Dole et al., 1996; Gurney et al., 1990; Newby et al., 1989; Williams et al., 1994). One method for gradually transferring responsibility to students is for students to first model the strategy in small groups, then in pairs (Dole et al.), before students assume individual responsibility. If students experience difficulty identifying an element, the teacher can resume responsibility and model how to identify the element. For example, if students have difficulty making problem–solution statements, the teacher models identifying and making problem–solution statements until students demonstrate proficiency (Gurney et al.).

For expository text structures, the same procedure is followed. For example, for problem–solution text structure, the teacher models the procedure for identifying the problem, solution, and effect by asking and answering the following questions: (a) What is the problem? (b) Why was it a problem? (c) What was the solution? and (d) What was the effect? (Kinder, cited in Kinder & Bursuck, 1991).

Another form of teacher scaffolding is questioning. The teacher asks the students questions designed to help students organize the important story components or derive a theme (Williams et al., 1994). In another instance, teachers use questioning to determine how much support students require before working independently. For example, after teaching students to identify story-grammar elements in a story, the teacher asks specific story-grammar questions. If students answer incorrectly, the teacher models how to use story-grammar elements and the information in the story to answer the questions. If students' responses are partially correct, the teacher asks questions that guide students to more complete responses. As students gain proficiency, the teacher provides less guidance (Gurney et al., 1990). As students assume more responsibility for identifying the problem in expository text structure such as problem–solution, for example, the teacher asks probing questions and leads a discussion that facilitates identifying the problem (Kinder, cited in Kinder & Bursuck, 1991).

A second method for scaffolding, *content scaffolding*, occurs as teachers present easier content, concepts, or skills before introducing more difficult material. For example, in narrative text structure the easier story-grammar elements such as setting, main character, and problem are taught before the more difficult element "theme" (Gurney et al., 1990). New elements of story grammar are introduced using examples from stories students have previously read, allowing students to learn new story-grammar elements in content with which they are already familiar (Gurney et al.).

Another form of content scaffolding is the use of stories written at appropriate readability levels to assure that students can easily read and understand the stories while learning the new content—story grammar. For diverse learners, this is usually a reading level well below their grade level. As students gain proficiency with story grammar, the stories progress to grade level (e.g., Dole et al., 1996).

An additional example of content scaffolding involves instruction that proceeds from easier to more difficult text structures. For example, narrative text structure instruction occurs before the more difficult expository text structures. Of the expository text structures, sequence appears the easiest to teach, enumeration and description appear moderately difficult, and comparison/contrast appears to be more difficult (Englert & Thomas, 1987). When introducing an expository text structure that is new to students, the teacher uses a "pure" text structure model (i.e., contains easily identifiable components of an expository text structure type such as signal words "first" or "finally" to signal sequence text structure) for initial instruction and practice, before having students apply their new knowledge to more complex text or to their textbooks (Kinder, cited in Kinder & Bursuck, 1991; Seidenberg, 1989).

A third method for scaffolding instruction is to control tasks. One example of *task control* comes from research in story grammar. Tasks begin with simple recall and advance to identification and reading comprehension. When students first learn story grammar, they simply recall the names of the story-grammar elements. After students can fluently verbalize the elements, they apply story grammar by identifying the various elements in stories and answering comprehension questions based on story grammar (Gurney et al., 1990). Additionally, after identifying a theme for a story, the teacher can test students' understanding by having them generate a new story based on the identified theme (Williams et al., 1994). For expository text structures, students first learn to recognize different text structure types and then apply this knowledge to reading comprehension and writing tasks (Seidenberg, 1989).

Finally, a fourth form of scaffolded instruction, *material scaffolding,* occurs when students are provided with materials to guide their thinking. One example of scaffolded material for narrative text is a prompted notesheet that lists the story-grammar elements and a brief definition of each. Students use the notesheet to record story grammar and other pertinent information about a story (Gurney et al., 1990). Examples of material scaffolding for expository text structures include a (a) visual representation (e.g., network, graphic organizer, frame) patterned after one of the text structures (e.g., problem-solution, description, cause-effect; Pearson & Fielding, 1991), (b) cue card with the definitions of main idea and details (Boyle, 1996), and (c) mnemonic to remember the strategy (Boyle, 1996).

Strategic Integration

Strategic integration refers to integrating content, skills, or concepts that mutually support each other, communicate generalizations, or transfer to areas further and further removed from the original area of instruction (Dixon et al., 1992). Examples of strategic integration can be found in the investigations of instruction in physical text presentation and text structure involving diverse students reviewed by Dickson, Simmons, and Kameenui in chapter 10 in this book.

Physical Presentation of Text. Integrating instruction in summarization of passages with the use of textual clues (e.g., headings, subheadings, signal words, and location of main idea statements) to identify main ideas and relations between main ideas is an example of integration that uses the conventions of physical presentation of text. In a study by Taylor and colleagues (cited in Pearson & Fielding, 1991), the integration of summarization and the conventions of physical text presentation transferred to uninstructed texts on the same topics and facilitated recall better than answering questions on the passage or additional study.

Text Structure. Several studies provide evidence that instruction in text structure does not occur in isolation or with adapted text, but takes place integrated with the actual texts students use in school. For example, instruction in narrative text structure is integrated with reading stories from literature, basals, and high-school literature anthologies (Dole et al., 1996; Gurney et al., 1990; Pearson & Fielding, 1991; Williams et al., 1994). For expository text, after students learn a problem–solution–effect text structure, they apply this knowledge to identify problem–solution–effect information in poorly written passages from an eighth-grade American history textbook (Kinder, cited in Kinder & Bursuck, 1991).

Text structure skills that mutually support each other can also be integrated. For example, instruction in the story-grammar elements of main character and problem can be integrated because the story problem typically centers around the main character. Thus, identification of either the problem or the main character facilitates identification of the other (Gurney et al., 1990).

Instruction in text structure can be integrated with other comprehension skills. Instruction in a problem–solution–effect text structure can be integrated with writing cohesive notes based on the text structure, studying vocabulary, and creating a timeline, using an eighth-grade American history text (Kinder, cited in Kinder & Bursuck, 1991).

Finally, instruction in text structure can be transferred from reading to composing. Thus, knowledge of the organizational patterns of text structures provides diverse learners with a plan for generating, organizing, and editing expository text. Additionally, reading and writing are mutually supportive. Attention to text structure patterns and reading expository text helps students organize their writing. Further, writing about passages helps students improve their recall of content in passages (Seidenberg, 1989).

Primed Background Knowledge

In general, theorists agree on the importance of *primed background knowledge* to reading comprehension. The structure of a reader's preexisting knowledge affects how the new knowledge is remembered or understood (Weaver & Kintsch, 1991). Reading comprehension, particularly inferential comprehension, improves when relations are drawn between students' background knowledge and experiences and the content in the reading passage (Pearson & Fielding, 1991). Background knowledge is usually linked to knowledge of topics, themes, and concepts (Pearson & Fielding). However, the research reviewed for the previous chapter on text organization and its relation to reading comprehension supports the importance of priming or activating knowledge of the conventions of well-presented text and organizational patterns of text structures. When students lack pertinent background knowledge, it is important that teachers build that background knowledge for them. Any instruction in physical text presentation or text structures can be viewed as building background knowledge that will later form the frame for helping students organize and integrate new knowledge.

Physical Presentation of Text. Knowledge of the purpose of headings, subheadings, and signal words, and of the location of main ideas in paragraphs serves as background knowledge for reading and has been linked with identification of important ideas and their interrelations (Seidenberg, 1989). When students lack this knowledge, teachers can provide it by teaching students how the physical presentation of text indicates the main ideas and interrelations between them (Seidenberg).

Text Structure. Knowledge of text structure also serves as background knowledge to be primed in order to facilitate reading comprehension. Some ways teachers help students attend to text structure before reading include using graphic organizers, summarizing the macrostructure (i.e., hierarchical relations between main ideas), or focusing on story-grammar elements (Horton, Lovitt, & Bergerud, 1990; Pearson & Fielding, 1991).

For expository text structure, research evidence suggests that students who have preexisting awareness, knowledge, or sensitivity of text structure types demonstrate more recall of passages that they read than students who do not possess such background knowledge. When teachers or researchers prime or activate background knowledge, they need to consider background knowledge not only of concepts, but also of text structures. If students lack knowledge of text structures, the teacher needs to provide instruction in text structure to build background knowledge (Pearson & Fielding, 1991).

Judicious Review

Judicious review refers to the sequence and schedule of opportunities students receive to apply and develop facility with the conventions of well-presented text and the organizational patterns of text structures. Closely spaced, shorter reviews are more effective than single, longer reviews (Dempster, 1991). Effective review is also cumulative, that is, skills and strategies are integrated over longer periods of time (Dixon et al., 1992). Finally, review includes a "firming" cycle in which students practice newly taught skills and strategies (Kameenui & Simmons, 1990).

Physical Presentation of Text. The primary and secondary studies reviewed in the previous chapter on text organization and its relation to reading offered no specific examples for judicious review of instruction in the physical presentation of text. However, review of the physical presentation of text can flow from simple recall about where main ideas are located and the purpose of headings, subheadings, and signal words in text to application to well-organized and, finally, poorly organized texts. Students could also review by "repairing" poorly presented texts, writing summaries, and inventing main idea statements and inserting them at the beginning of poorly presented paragraphs.

Text Structure. Examples of sequenced, varying, and increasingly difficult review activities are found in story-grammar research (e.g., Williams et al., 1994). One method for sequencing review is to teach one new concept, teach new related concepts in subsequent lessons, then return to the original concept. For example, in lessons 2 and 3 the teacher introduces "perseverance" as a theme of a story. Students then identify the theme "perseverance" in lessons 5, 8, and 11 after learning other themes (e.g., "responsibility," "sincerity") in the lessons in between (Williams et al., Study 2). In one example of varied and increasingly difficult review activities, student first practice the story-grammar elements by verbalizing the names of the elements. Students then practice by identifying the story-grammar elements in stories that they have not previously read.

Although composition is not a focus of this chapter, a varied and more difficult review task for text structure consists of having students generate a composition in a recently learned text structure (Seidenberg, 1989; Simmons et al., 1994).

CONCLUSION

In summary, diverse learners have demonstrated difficulties identifying main ideas and their interrelations and therefore, may require explicit instruction to increase their sensitivity to important textual information and text-structure organizational patterns. Additionally, diverse learners select information of interest to themselves rather than relevant information to include in summaries and have difficulty integrating information and organizing what they read. To help narrow the gap between diverse learners and their normally achieving peers, diverse learners require well-designed instruction, based on instructional guidelines found in effective research procedures.

After our scrutiny of the primary and secondary studies in the previous chapter on text organization and its relation to reading comprehension, we identified examples of instruction that support six instructional design principles—*big idea, conspicuous strategies, mediated scaffolding, strategic integration, primed background knowledge,* and *judicious review.* These six principles can be interwoven and applied to explicit instruction in which teachers identify the concepts, skills, or strategies to be taught; model; and provide guided practice, independent practice, and practice in text materials. These steps enable diverse learners to experience success in their performance on mainstream curricular materials, which are predominantly textbooks.

The conventions of well-presented text and the repetitive organizational patterns of text structure are big ideas that enable diverse learners to better identify main ideas and the interrelations between relevant information in text. The ability to identify main ideas and inter-relations between relevant information is central to the comprehension process. Furthermore, being able to identify interrelations between relevant information helps students form the networks of information important to comprehension.

The research reviewed for the previous chapter on text organization and its relation to reading comprehension provided examples of how the conventions of well-presented text and the organizational patterns of text structures can be transformed into conspicuous strategies that can be taught to students. Additionally, these studies provided examples of how strategic use of the conventions of well-presented text and the organizational patterns of text structure can be taught using mediated scaffolding by teachers/peers, content, tasks, and materials. Teachers provide scaffolds by:

1. thinking aloud as they model use of the strategy;
2. presenting easier content before more difficult content;
3. assigning increasingly more difficult tasks—starting by asking students to recall components of well-presented text or a particular text structure, then asking students to identify components in well-written and then poorly written text, and finally by writing compositions or summaries in a particular text structure; and
4. making available graphic organizers or that remind students of strategic steps until they can perform tasks independently.

Instruction in the conventions of well-presented text and organizational patterns of text structures is integrated with reading processes such as summarizing texts, or with writing instruction. The conventions of well-presented texts and organizational patterns of text structures is taught, not in isolation, but with the actual textbooks students use in school. The conventions of well-presented texts and organizational patterns of text structures become background knowledge to be primed or activated, similar to the way teachers prime background knowledge of concepts, themes, and topics. Ways of priming background knowledge include advance frames or organizers of the reading text. Finally, it is important to use judicious review of the conventions of well-presented texts and organizational patterns of text structures through short, frequent reviews, varying tasks, and incorporating previously taught information.

REFERENCES

Boyle, J. R. (1996). The effects of a cognitive mapping strategy on the literal and inferential comprehension of students with mild disabilities. *Learning Disability Quarterly, 19,* 86–93.

Dempster, F. N. (1991). Synthesis of research on reviews and tests. *Educational Leadership, 71* 71–76.

Dixon, R., Carnine, D., & Kameenui, E. J. (1992). Curriculum guidelines for diverse learners. In *Monograph for the National Center to Improve the Tools of Educators.* Eugene: University of Oregon.

Dole, J. A., Brown, K. J., & Trathen, W. (1996.). The effects of strategy instruction on the comprehension performance of at-risk students. *Reading Research Quarterly, 31,* 62–88.

Duffy, G. G., & Roehler, L. R. (1989). Why strategy instruction is so difficult and what we need to do about it. In G. Miller, C. McCormick, & M. Pressley (Eds.), *Cognitive strategy research: From basic research to educational applications* (pp. 133–154). New York: Springer-Verlag.

Englert, C. S., & Thomas, C. C. (1987). Sensitivity to text structure in reading and writing: A comparison between learning disabled and non-learning disabled students. *Learning Disability Quarterly, 10,* 93-105.

Gurney, D., Gersten, R., Dimino, J., & Carnine, D. (1990). Story grammar: Effective literature instruction for high school students with learning disabilities. *Journal of Learning Disabilities, 23,* 335–342, 348.

Horton, S. V., Lovitt, T. C., & Bergerud, D. (1990). The effectiveness of graphic organizers for three classifications of secondary students in content area classes. *Journal of Learning Disabilities, 23,* 12–22.

Kameenui, E. J., & Simmons, D. C. (1990). *Designing instructional strategies: The prevention of academic learning problems.* Columbus, OH: Merrill.

Kinder, D., & Bursuck, W. (1991). The search for a unified social studies curriculum: Does history really repeat itself? *Journal of Learning Disabilities, 24,* 270–275.

Newby, R. F., Caldwell, J., & Recht, D. R. (1989). Improving reading comprehension of children with dysphonetic and dyseidetic dyslexia using story grammar. *Journal of Learning Disabilities, 22,* 373–380.

Pearson, P. D., & Fielding, L. (1991). Comprehension instruction. In R. Barr, M. L. Kamil, P. Mosenthal, & P. D. Pearson (Eds.), *Handbook of reading research* (Vol. 2, pp. 815–860). White Plains, NY: Longman.

Prawat, R. S. (1989). Promoting access to knowledge, strategy, and disposition in students: A research synthesis. *Review of Educational Research, 59,* 1–41.

Seidenberg, P. L. (1989). Relating text-processing research to reading and writing instruction for learning disabled students. *Learning Disabilities Focus, 5*(1), 4–12.

Simmons, D. C., Kameenui, E. J., Dickson, S., Chard, D., Gunn, B., & Baker, S. (1994). Integrating narrative reading comprehension and writing instruction for all learners. In C. K. Kinzer & D. J. Leu (Eds.), *Multidimensional aspects of literacy research, theory, and practice: Forty-third yearbook National Reading Conference* (pp. 572–582). Chicago: National Reading Conference.

Weaver, C. A., III, & Kintsch, W. (1991). Expository text. In R. Barr, M. L. Kamil, P. Mosenthal, & P. D. Pearson (Eds.), *Handbook of reading research* (Vol. 2, pp. 230–244). White Plains, NY: Longman.

Williams, J. P., Brown, L. G., Silverstein, A. K., & deCani, J. S. (1994). An instructional program in comprehension of narrative themes for adolescents with learning disabilities. *Learning Disability Quarterly, 17,* 205–221.

CHAPTER
12

Metacognitive Strategies: Research Bases

Shirley V. Dickson
Vicki L. Collins
Northern Illinois University

Deborah C. Simmons
Edward J. Kameenui
University of Oregon

Inattentive, passive, and disorganized are terms sometimes used to describe the learning characteristics of individuals with reading disabilities. Their inattentiveness, passivity, and disorganization have been attributed to their failure to use goal-oriented strategies effectively, efficiently, and flexibly (e.g., Meltzer, 1993; Winograd, cited in Johnston & Winograd, 1985; Wong, cited in Johnston & Winograd, 1985). In recent years, educators and psychologists describe this failure as a lack of metacognition or failure to think about thinking (e.g., Meltzer, 1993; Torgesen, 1994). In contrast, more successful readers are referred to as active learners who engage in metacognitive activities which include planning before reading, monitoring understanding during reading, and checking outcomes after reading (Brown & Palincsar, cited in Johnston & Winograd, 1985). It is generally agreed that, compared to their normally achieving peers, many poor comprehenders demonstrate metacognitive deficits.

The purpose of this research synthesis is to examine recent research on the relation between metacognition (i.e., reviews published since 1985 and primary research published since 1986) and reading comprehension, as it pertains to diverse learners. Through this review, we sought to identify areas of convergence useful for understanding characteristics of and instructional implications for diverse learners. In general, we found that reading metacognition is related to reading comprehension and that this relation may be affected by student motivation. Additionally, we identified dimensions of metacognition instruction that enhanced reading comprehension. Before describing convergent areas, we provide historical and contemporary contexts surrounding metacognition, discuss unresolved issues, and describe our synthesis methodology.

HISTORICAL AND CONTEMPORARY CONTEXTS

The notion of learners thinking about their own thinking dates back to at least Plato and Aristotle (Brown, 1987). Yet, metacognition, a term for the concept of thinking about or controlling one's own thinking and learning processes, was not introduced until 1976 by Flavell. Accordingly, the role of executive processes and their relation to reading did not receive substantial attention until the late 1970s. Since that time, theoretical and empirical interest in metacognition increased in the 1980s, and tended to diminish in the early 1990s (B. Wong, personal communication, September 25, 1995). A brief review of the evolution of metacognition in psychology and education is presented to provide a context for research and instructional implications addressed in this chapter.

In 1977, Flavell and Wellman proposed a theory of metamemory to explain young children's development and application of recall strategies (or lack thereof). Flavell and Wellman hypothesized that young children's failure to apply strategies for recalling information was because of their lack of awareness of "parameters that govern effective recall" (Wong, 1995, p. 1). Consequently, he concluded that their failure to recall resided in a deficiency in metamemory.

Soon after Flavell's introduction, interest in metacognition flourished. Brown (1980) applied metacognitive theory to reading and differentiated between cognitive and metacognitive processes. She identified metacognitive processes as reader-controlled strategies that included selecting and studying the most important part of text, selecting retrieval cues, and estimating readiness for tests.

In the late 1980s, formalized theories of metacognition were espoused. These theories varied as a function of researchers' understanding of metacognition components and the role of particular components (e.g., awareness, regulation, motivation). Borkowski, Johnston, and Reid (1987) emphasized motivation and the retraining of students' attributional beliefs about success from external control (e.g., luck, teacher, ease of task) to self (e.g., value of using a strategy). Paris, Wasik, and Turner (1991), recognizing the role of self-regulation and motivation in metacognition, emphasized self-awareness and self-efficacy. Zimmerman (1994), on the other hand, noting the importance of motivation and self-efficacy to self-regulation, posed that self-regulation differentiates between academic success and failure.

Research and practice in reading comprehension continue to reflect interest in metacognition (Tierney & Pearson, cited in Wong, 1992). Contemporary reforms in reading curricula (e.g., California English-Language Arts Framework) emphasize integrating metacognition, motivation, and strategies rather than teaching "decontextualized and disconnected" (Jensen & Rosner, cited in Paris et al., 1991) reading components (Paris et al.). One emphasis in reading curricula reform is to develop thoughtful readers who plan selectively, monitor comprehension while reading, and reflect on process and content after reading (Paris et al.). This current emphasis on thinking about reading reflects the prior endorsements of many researchers and practitioners who proposed that metacognition is an important dimension that enables readers to coordinate and regulate "deliberate efforts at efficient reading and effective studying" (Baker & Brown, cited in Wong & Wong, 1986, p. 102; Brown, cited in Wong & Wong, 1986, p. 102) and thereby enhances reading comprehension.

For diverse learners, there is empirical evidence to support the theory that metacognition is one explanatory factor of reading comprehension difficulties (e.g., Meltzer, 1993; Paris et al., 1991). However, lack of meta-cognition as an explanation of reading comprehension difficulties is relatively new (Torgesen, 1994) and in a formative stage of development.

POINTS OF DIFFERENCE AND UNRESOLVED ISSUES IN METACOGNITION

Metacognition is an emerging construct, influenced by the contributions of many disciplines (e.g., psychology, social sciences, education). An analysis of the pervasive issues in metacognition and empirical investigations examining its relation to reading comprehension reveals divergent, yet not incompatible, ways of understanding this relationship.

The following discussion focuses on three points of divergence: definition, theory, and measurement. Although discussed separately, definitional, theoretical, and measurement issues are not mutually exclusive. For example, measures to assess metacognition directly reflect a particular researcher's understanding of metacognition and its mediating role. Therefore, differences in the theoretical contribution and definition of metacognition are operationalized in instructional measures and methods. We attempt to clarify the significance of these multiple perspectives and operational definitions and their contribution to what we know about metacognition.

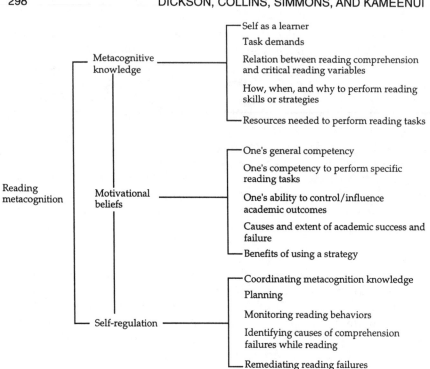

FIG. 12.1. Reading metacognition includes metacognitive knowledge, self-regulation and motivational belief components.

Definition

In general, metacognition is thinking about one's own thinking or controlling one's own learning. Most researchers agree that metacognition includes knowledge and self-regulation components; however, motivation is often added as a third component (e.g., Borkowski, 1992; Chan, 1994; Johnston & Winograd, 1985; Pintrich, Anderman, & Klobucar, 1994; Swanson, 1989; see Fig. 12.1). For reading metacognition, the knowledge component includes knowledge or awareness of (a) self as a learner; (b) task demands; and (c) relations between text, prior knowledge, and reading strategies and reading comprehension. Self-regulation includes: coordinating metacognitive knowledge such as self-knowledge and knowledge of text organization; planning; monitoring understanding; and identifying and remediating causes of comprehension failures. Although the metacognitive components of knowledge and self-regulation can be distinguished from each other, Brown (1987) suggested that attempts to separate components may lead to "oversimplification" of a complex process.

Because metacognition derives from various disciplines and is a fairly new construct, definitional vagaries abound. Vagaries arise because: (a) metacognition has been used as a "blanket term" (Brown, 1987) to denote a multifaceted range of interventions varying widely in scope, purpose, and dimension; (b) educators and psychologists disagree on the range of knowledge and activities classified as metacognitive (Billingsley & Wildman, 1990); and (c) it is difficult to distinguish "meta" from "cognitive" (Borkowski, 1992; Brown, 1987).

Difficulties distinguishing *meta* from *cognitive* arise for at least five reasons. First, it is difficult to distinguish metacognitive reading strategies from other reading processes such as thinking, reasoning, and perceiving. Second, reading strategies once considered cognitive are now considered metacognitive. These strategies include (a) establishing the purpose for reading; (b) modifying reading due to variations in purpose; (c) identifying important ideas; (d) activating prior knowledge; (e) evaluating text for clarity, completeness, and consistency; (f) compensating for failure to understand text; and (g) assessing one's level of comprehension (Baker & Brown, cited in Brown, 1987).

A third contributor to the difficulty of distinguishing *meta* from *cognitive* is the interchangeability in function of reading activities. For example, in the area of reading comprehension: "Asking yourself questions about the chapter might function either to improve your knowledge (a cognitive function) or to monitor it (a metacognitive function)" (Flavell, cited in Brown, 1987, p. 66).

Fourth, *meta* and *cognitive* may be difficult to distinguish because reading strategies are embedded in complex behavioral sequences and decision hierarchies, making the components problematic to demarcate (Paris et al., 1991). Finally, the difficult distinction between *meta* and *cognitive* may be the result of varying developmental influences on strategy application (Butterfield & Ferretti, cited in Torgesen, 1994). Metacognition develops slowly over time, well into the teen-age years.

In addition to definitional vagaries, research reveals theoretical and measurement issues that bear discussion and evaluation before interpreting research findings.

Theory

There is general consensus that metacognition derives from an information-processing paradigm. Research within the information-processing paradigm provides strong evidence that increased processing speed of basic processes frees capacity for higher order organizational and co-ordinating processes (Torgesen, 1994). Instruction within the information-processing paradigm emphasizes teaching cognitive and metacognitive processes in an academic context such as reading comprehension (Wong, 1992). Furthermore, research supports the benefit of such instruction for students with reading comprehension difficulties (e.g., Chan, Cole, & Barfett, 1987; Malone & Mastropieri, 1992; Paris et al., 1991; Schunk & Rice, 1992).

Within the information-processing paradigm, however, theoretical differences exist concerning human control of mental functions. These differences include: locus of executive control, automaticity, conscious access and control, and other- versus self-control in the learning process (Brown, 1987). Questions concerning locus of control and automaticity are important to the metacognitive construct but were not explicitly addressed in the reviewed studies. Therefore, we limit our discussion of theoretical differences to (a) conscious access and control and (b) other-control versus self-control in the learning process. For more information on theoretical differences, see Brown, 1987.

Conscious Access and Control. Whether or not humans have conscious access and control of their mental functions has important implications for teaching metacognition. One area of disagreement is whether access and control are tied to processes linked to specific situations or to processes used over a wide range of conditions (Brown, 1987). For example, if access and control are linked to specific situations, researchers and practitioners may be required to vary instruction according to whether the reading text is narrative or expository. If access and control are linked to processes used over a wide range of conditions, it may be sufficient to provide metacognitive instruction on narrative text and expect a transfer to expository text through varied types of practice rather than new instructional sequences.

Other- Versus Self-Control. The issue of other- versus self-control of learning directly affects the emphasis and sequence of metacognitive instruction. The theory of other-control is based on the Vygotskian notion that a great deal of learning is fostered by the activity of others such as parents, teachers, and peers. Through systematic support from others, social activity becomes personalized and internalized as a child develops. In contrast, self-regulation derives primarily from the work of Piaget and asserts that human learning takes place in the absence of external agents and that active learning involves continuous adjustments and "fine-tuning of action via self-regulating processes" (Brown, 1987, p. 88).

Related to the issue of other- versus self-control of learning is the question of whether effective, long-lasting benefits of metacognitive instruction are a result of direct instruction or instruction that induces metacognition indirectly. It is not difficult to envision how these theoretical differences translate into disparate methods of instruction all designed to promote metacognition. The difference in the role of control appears central to instructional interpretations. For example, in instruction designed to induce metacognition, the teacher may directly teach a cognitive strategy such as summarizing. Acquisition of the metacognitive dimension, however, would rely more on student control. In contrast, in direct meta-cognitive instruction, the teacher plays a strong initial role directly teaching knowledge or self-regulation. For example, the teacher might teach the importance of a strategy, where and when to use the strategy, or how to self-monitor strategy use, rather than leaving students to induce this information on their own.

Measurement

Like definitions and theories, variations exist in methods used to measure metacognition. The measures most commonly used to define and assess metacognition include self-talk, self-report, and questionnaires. However, these measures often lack reliability (Brown, 1987) and therefore complicate interpretation of findings.

Self-talk (i.e., explaining one's thinking processes and strategies) during problem solving is problematic because students, especially young children, may be incapable of simultaneously solving problems and commenting on the problem-solving process (e.g., Brown, 1987). In the case of retrospective self-reports (i.e., reporting one's thinking processes and strategies after-the-fact), adults, as well as young children, may have difficulty reporting their thinking processes therefore making self-report an inconsistent measure (Ericsson & Simon; Nisbet & Wilson; Smith & Miller; White; cited in Brown, 1987). Young children may reconstruct past events inaccurately and modify observations of their thought processes (e.g., Piaget, cited in Brown, 1987). Moreover, thought processes during problem solving may be transient (i.e., existing only during a particular task or context) and therefore more difficult to report than more stable metacognitive knowledge (i.e., knowledge of self as a learner, task demands, necessity to amend learning activities to match specific tasks). Additionally, self-talk and retrospective self-reports are problematic because skilled readers perform tasks automatically and are unlikely to think about underlying metacognitive processes. Furthermore, students with learning disabilities may not possess the language skills to report their metacognitive processes (Billingsley & Wildman, 1990).

Similar to self-talk and retrospective self-reports, questionnaires also have limitations. When answering questionnaires about hypothetical problem-solving situations, readers may describe a reading strategy but fail to demonstrate it in actual problem-solving situations relevant to the reported strategy (Whitehead, cited in Palincsar, David, Winn, & Stevens, 1991).

The questions used to elicit self-talk, self-reports, and questionnaire responses also contribute to measurement inconsistencies. General questions such as "How do you perform these tasks?" invite responses based on prior experiences and knowledge of how a task ought to be performed, rather than responses to the specific problem-solving situation. General questions about how to solve an imaginary situation are least likely to elicit responses closely linked to the cognitive processes under discussion (Ericsson & Simon, cited in Brown, 1987). Consequently, to provide valid information, questions should be specific to the problem-solving task. For example, instead of asking students what strategies they would use if reading a passage containing embedded main ideas, more valid information can be obtained by presenting students with actual passages containing embedded main ideas and asking them to describe specific steps they use to identify main ideas.

Interactions between context and a student's prior experience also confound the measurement of metacognition. Individuals do not demonstrate the same metacognitive difficulty or expertise in every situation (Meltzer, 1993). Performance on measures of metacognitive procedures depends on task complexity and may be heavily influenced by a student's prior experience with the task and familiarity with the type of information required by the task (Torgesen, 1994). Therefore, it is important to attend to measures, tasks, and familiarity of information before drawing research conclusions.

In summary, the points of difference in definition, theory, and measurement surrounding metacognition research suggest caution in interpreting findings. New fields of study such as metacognition are ripe for investigation but also hold enormous opportunity for misinterpretation and overgeneralization. Therefore, components and measures of studies designated as metacognitive require close analysis prior to drawing conclusions regarding implications for diverse learners.

With these caveats, we present the convergence of evidence regarding metacognition and its relation to reading comprehension. We attempt to unpack some of the unresolved issues noted earlier, fully realizing the risk of "oversimplification" (Brown, 1987) of this complex construct.

METHODOLOGY

Sources

For this chapter, we examined 8 secondary and 14 primary sources. In Table 12.1 (p. 354), we present a brief description of each source. Secondary sources included one book chapter (i.e., Paris et al., 1991) and seven articles (i.e., Billingsley & Wildman, 1990; Borkowski, 1992; Harris & Pressley, 1991; Johnston & Winograd, 1985; Swanson, 1989; Weisberg, 1988; Wong, 1992). Six of the secondary sources (i.e., Billingsley & Wildman; Borkowski; Harris & Pressley; Johnston & Winograd; Paris et al.; Weisberg) were descriptive narratives with research references. Two secondary sources (i.e., Swanson; Wong) were introductions to special journal editions devoted exclusively to metacognition.

Two of the primary sources were quasi-experimental (i.e., Cornoldi, 1990; Wong & Wong, 1986), nine were reports of interventions (i.e., Boyle, 1996; Chan, Cole, & Barfett, 1987; Chan, Cole, & Morris, 1990; Gaultney, 1995; Malone & Mastropieri, 1992; Palincsar et al., 1991; Rottman & Cross, 1990; Schunk & Rice, 1992; Simmonds, 1990), and three were nonexperimental, descriptive studies of learner characteristics (i.e., Chan, 1994; Hannah & Shore, 1995; Pintrich et al., 1994). Three additional sources provided background information about metacognition (i.e., Brown, 1987; Meltzer, 1993; Torgesen, 1994). Secondary and primary sources are delineated in Table 12.1 at the end of this chapter.

Participant Characteristics

In this chapter, we focus explicitly on diverse learners. We define diverse learners as students who, by virtue of their instructional, experiential, cognitive, linguistic, and physiological backgrounds, bring different and often specialized requirements to traditional instruction and curriculum. Selected secondary and primary sources included as participants students with diverse learning needs, or as defined by the sources, learners and students with reading-skills deficiencies, learning problems, or learning disabilities. The ability levels of participants ranged from *gifted, accomplished, and above-average;* to *average, normal, and good;* to *poor, remedial, low-achieving, and at risk.* Also included were students with learning disabilities and educable mental retardation. Participants were in general and special education, and grade levels ranged from elementary through secondary.

Summary of Methodology

Two reviewers independently identified and categorized general conclusions, learner characteristics, and instructional implications from each source. The findings from independent reviews were discussed and clarified at weekly group meetings. Next, two additional reviewers checked findings for each category for reliability. Finally, findings were entered into a database. The two primary authors of this chapter identified convergent areas of evidence for the relation of metacognition to reading comprehension and carefully reread, examined, and discussed secondary and primary sources for supporting information for each area of convergence.

Definitions

In general, metacognition refers to knowledge and self-regulation of one's own learning processes (e.g., Billingsley & Wildman, 1990). Some definitions include motivation as a third component (e.g., Borkowski, 1992; Johnston & Winograd, 1985; Pintrich et al., 1994; Swanson, 1989; see Fig. 12.1). To address definitional ambiguities, we separate discussions of metacognitive knowledge and self-regulation and attempt to clarify the dimensions of metacognition under investigation. We categorized studies by attending to the authors' descriptions of interventions in the study and the fit between their respective descriptions and definitions of metacognitive knowledge and self-regulation. We define components of metacognitive knowledge and self-regulation in the ensuing areas of convergence.

Additional terms used in this chapter are defined as follows. For clarity, we refer to these definitions throughout the chapter.

- *Skills:* Information-processing techniques that are automatic, whether at the level of recognizing grapheme–phoneme correspondence or summarizing a story (Paris et al., 1991). An "emerging skill" can become a strategy when it is used intentionally, and a strategy can go "underground" (i.e., internalized by a reader) and become a skill, when used automatically. The interchangeability of metacognitive strategies and skills poses problems when trying to determine whether an intervention is metacognitive. Although there is disagreement over the skill automaticity, we use the Paris et al. definition for this chapter.
- *Strategic readers:* Readers who select appropriate strategies that fit the particular text, purpose, and occasion (Paris et al., 1991).
- *Strategies:* Actions selected deliberately to achieve particular goals. Strategies are conscious, deliberate, "open to inspection," and can be evaluated. A strategy can go underground and become a skill when used automatically. There is controversy over the consciousness of strategies. We use the Paris et al. (1991) definition for this chapter. Further, we define two categories of strategies, cognitive and metacognitive.

  Cognitive strategies: A broad array of learner-based actions that help control attention, behavior, communication, emotions, motivation, and comprehension (Weinstein & Mayer, cited in Paris et al., 1991).

  Metacognitive reading strategies: Strategies that generalize across

many tasks, help readers' awareness of whether or not they comprehend what they are reading, and assist readers' decision of what
strategies to employ to aid comprehension (Weisberg, 1988).

- Task demands: Knowing what the reading task is (e.g., purpose or
criterion of the task) and how to do the task (Weisberg, 1988).

Overview of the Chapter

In this chapter, we present four converging areas of research evidence (see
Fig. 12.2). The first two areas support a relation between the knowledge
and regulation components of metacognition and reading comprehension.
Discussion of these two areas of convergence includes definitions of reading metacognitive knowledge and self-regulation as they relate to reading
comprehension, convergent evidence, and relations to normally achieving
and diverse learners.

The third area of convergence relates to motivation and use of
metacognitive knowledge and self-regulation including definitions and
classes of motivational beliefs and the convergent evidence. The fourth
area of convergence denotes emerging evidence regarding dimensions of
metacognitive instruction that enhance reading comprehension. The
discussion of this final area of convergence includes common instructional
dimensions across interventions and theories, relations to learners, and
unresolved issues (see Fig. 12.2).

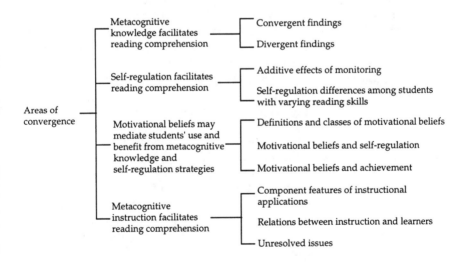

FIG. 12.2. Overview of a synthesis of research on the relation between
reading metacognition and reading comprehension.

General Areas of Convergence

The studies reviewed for this chapter provided evidence that reading metacognition is related to reading comprehension. Reading metacognition includes knowledge and self-regulation components. The four general areas of convergent evidence from this literature review are:

1. Metacognitive knowledge facilitates reading comprehension.
2. Self-regulation facilitates reading comprehension.
3. Motivation may mediate students' use of and benefit from metacognitive knowledge and self-regulation strategies.
4. Metacognitive instruction facilitates reading comprehension.

INTRODUCTION TO
AREAS OF CONVERGENCE 1 AND 2

Our review of the literature identified 23 studies in which the relations between reading metacognition and reading comprehension were investigated (i.e., Bergamo & Cornoldi, cited in Cornoldi, 1990; Boyle, 1996; Chan, 1994; Chan et al., 1987; Gaultney, 1995; Graves, cited in Weisberg, 1988; Weisberg & Balajthy, cited in Weisberg, 1998; Hannah & Shore, 1995; Idol, cited in Billingsley & Wildman, 1990; Idol & Croll, cited in Billingsley & Wildman, 1990; Malone & Mastropieri, 1992; Paris, Cross, & Lipson, cited in Paris et al., 1991; Pintrich et al., 1994; Schunk & Rice, cited in Paris et al., 1991; Taylor, cited in Paris et al., 1991; Palincsar et al., 1991; Pressley, cited in Harris & Pressley, 1991; Rottman & Cross, 1990; Schunk & Rice, 1992, Studies 1 & 2; Simmonds, 1990; Wong & Jones, cited in Billingsley & Wildman, 1990; Wong & Wong, 1986). Because of the complexity of metacognition, its various dimensions, and definitions, we applied several decision rules to aid our analysis and synthesis of findings. First we analyzed studies according to two areas of metacognition:

1. Metacognitive knowledge (awareness) and reading comprehension, and
2. Self-regulation and reading comprehension.

Relevant features of investigations and studies were classified as experimental ($n = 17$), quasi-experimental ($n = 2$), and nonexperimental ($n = 4$). Single-subject research designs and studies that involved manipulation of independent variables and randomization of participants were classified as experimental. Studies that involved manipulation of independent variables but not randomization of participants were classified as quasi-experimental. Studies that did not involve manipulation of independent variables nor randomization of participants were classified as nonexperimental.

Following classification of studies, we coded research findings as reliable or preliminary depending on the degree of experimental control. A study demonstrated adequate experimental control if: initial equivalence between groups was established; alternative explanations could be evaluated and ruled out; and the metacognitive variable was isolated as a within- or between-subjects variable while controlling other sources of variability. Significant findings from studies that met all experimental control conditions were coded as reliable evidence. Significant findings from studies that did not meet all experimental control conditions were coded as preliminary evidence.

To facilitate understanding, we identified metacognitive features in each study by matching the authors' descriptions with metacognitive definitions that emerged from our literature review. The metacognitive definitions are listed at the beginning of each area of convergence.

AREA OF CONVERENCE 1:
Metacognitive Knowledge (Awareness) Facilitates
Reading Comprehension

The knowledge component of reading metacognition is multifaceted and refers to one's knowledge or awareness of:

1. Self as a learner (Billingsley & Wildman, 1990; Palincsar et al., 1991);
2. Task demands (Billingsley & Wildman, 1990; Palincsar et al., 1991);
3. The relation between reading comprehension and critical reading variables such as text, prior knowledge, and reading strategies (Billingsley & Wildman, 1990);
4. How, why, and when to perform reading skills or strategies (Billingsley & Wildman, 1990); and
5. Resources, such as time, needed to perform cognitive reading tasks (Billingsley & Wildman, 1990).

The relation between metacognitive knowledge and reading comprehension was investigated in 18 studies. Eleven of the studies were primary (i.e., Boyle, 1996; Chan, 1994; Chan et al., 1987; Gaultney, 1995; Hannah & Shore, 1995; Pintrich et al., 1994; Rottman & Cross, 1990; Schunk & Rice, 1992, Studies 1 & 2; Simmonds, 1990; Wong & Wong, 1986) and 7 of the studies were reported in secondary sources (i.e., Idol, cited in Billingsley & Wildman, 1990; Idol & Croll, cited in Billingsley & Wildman, 1990; Pressley, cited in Harris & Pressley, 1991; Schunk & Rice, cited in

Weisberg, 1988; Taylor, cited in Paris et al., 1991; Weisberg & Balajthy, cited in Weisberg, 1998; Wong & Jones, cited in Billingsley & Wildman, 1990). In most studies, metacognitive knowledge was defined as knowledge of task demands and the relation between reading variables (e.g., strategies, prior knowledge) and reading comprehension. To a lesser extent, metacognitive knowledge was defined as knowledge of resources needed to perform certain reading tasks. Comprehension was measured via comprehension questions and oral and written recall of passages.

Convergent Findings

Metacognitive knowledge and reading comprehension were related significantly in 89% (n = 16) of the studies. The significant findings were reported in 11 experimental studies (i.e., Chan et al., 1987; Gaultney, 1995; Idol, cited in Billingsley & Wildman, 1990; Idol & Croll, cited in Billingsley & Wildman, 1990; Pressley, cited in Harris & Pressley, 1991; Rottman & Cross, 1990; Schunk & Rice, 1992, Studies 1 & 2; Schunk & Rice, cited in Weisberg, 1988; Weisberg & Balajthy, cited in Weisberg, 1998; Wong & Jones, cited in Billingsley & Wildman, 1990), 1 quasi-experimental study (i.e., Wong & Wong, 1986), and 4 nonexperimental studies (i.e., Chan, 1994; Hannah & Shore, 1995; Pintrich et al., 1994; Taylor, cited in Paris et al., 1991). The evidence for metacognitive knowledge facilitating independent reading comprehension is detailed and organized by type of evidence. Two additional studies included an examination of metacognitive knowledge but resulted in diverse findings (i.e., Boyle, 1996; Simmonds, 1990).

Reliable Evidence. Adequate experimental control was demonstrated in 3 of the 16 studies (i.e., Chan et al., 1987; Schunk & Rice, 1992, studies 1 & 2). In all three studies, initial equivalence between groups was established, common internal validity threats were controlled, and metacognitive knowledge was well isolated. That is, strategy instruction occurred with and without a metacognitive knowledge component. Overall, each study provided reliable evidence that comprehension differences between groups were a result of differences in metacognitive knowledge.

In the Chan et al. (1987) study, normally achieving students and diverse learners were taught to use a cross-referencing technique to evaluate the internal consistency of text propositions. The cross-referencing task required students to identify inconsistent sentences embedded within text. Metacognitive knowledge was manipulated as a between-subjects variable. Students were told that specific sentences were inconsistent because they were about topics that differed from other sentences and thus did not make sense. We classified this knowledge as metacognitive because it clarified the task demands of the cross-referencing technique by providing an operational definition of inconsistent text information.

Knowing the conditions that make sentences inconsistent should increase the likelihood of locating them in text, discerning their usefulness, and comprehending the full text. Chan et al. (1987) tested this hypothesis by randomly assigning 32 average readers and 32 students with learning disabilities, matched on reading level, to specific and general reading groups. Each group received two demonstrations on use of the cross-referencing strategy. In each demonstration, the instructor pointed out two inconsistent sentences embedded within a passage. Students in the specific instruction group also were given an explanation as to why sentences were inconsistent. After the training session, students were given four test passages, two of which contained two inconsistent sentences. Students indicated if they thought something was wrong with the passage; identified inconsistent sentences; and answered seven comprehension questions per passage, for a total of 28 questions.

Chan et al. (1987) found a moderate positive correlation between student performance on comprehension monitoring and comprehension measures. For example, students who correctly identified wrong passages, also tended to correctly identify inconsistent sentences and answer comprehension questions correctly. An instructional method by learner group interaction also was reported. When instruction was general, average readers performed better than students with learning disabilities on all measures. Conversely, students with learning disabilities outperformed regular education students on all measures when instruction was specific (i.e., included an explanation as to why sentences were inconsistent). These data indicated that diverse learners benefited more from specific instruction than from general instruction.

Schunk and Rice (1992) conducted two studies to investigate whether strategy instruction on main ideas would be more effective for remedial readers if knowledge about strategy usefulness was included. The main ideas strategy included five steps that required students to read the passage questions, read the passage to determine what it mostly was about, think about what details had in common, think about what would make a good title, and reread critical parts of the passage if they did not know the question answers. Metacognitive knowledge about the main ideas strategy was provided before strategy implementation and during two of the strategy steps. Before implementing the main ideas strategy, students were required to ask themselves, "What do I have to do?" and say the strategy step. We classified this knowledge as metacognitive because it required students to attend to the task demands of the main ideas strategy. In Step

4 of the strategy, students were told that determining a title would help them remember important ideas from the story. We classified this knowledge as metacognitive because it informed students of the relation between a reading strategy and reading comprehension. In Step 5 of the strategy, students were taught to reread the story if they could not answer the story questions. We classified this knowledge as metacog-nitive because it informed students when to use a self-regulation strategy.

Information on strategy usefulness differed between studies. In the first study, Schunk and Rice (1992) gave students feedback on the value of the main ideas strategy when they answered questions and implemented strategy steps correctly. For example, students who implemented the third strategy step correctly were asked, "Do you see how thinking about details in common helps you answer questions correctly?" Students who answered questions correctly were told, "You have been answering correctly because you have been following the steps." We classified this knowledge as metacognitive because it informed students of the relation between strategy use and reading comprehension.

The contribution of strategy-value feedback to main ideas strategy instruction was investigated by randomly assigning 33 fourth- and fifth-grade remedial readers to one of three conditions: comprehension instruction without the strategy; strategy instruction on main ideas; and strategy instruction on main ideas plus strategy-value feedback. After completing a comprehension pretest on main ideas, all students received 15 days of instruction. The test included 8 passages and 20 questions (1 to 4 per passage). Students in the strategy conditions were taught the main ideas strategy by using a model, lead, test instructional format and by a visual display of the strategy steps. They read passages daily and used the strategy to answer main idea questions. Additionally, students in the combined group also were given strategy-value feedback three to four times daily during independent practice times. Students in the comprehension-only group read the same passages and answered the same questions as the strategy students. After the 15-day instructional phase, all students completed a parallel form of the comprehension pretest. Six weeks after completing the posttest, students completed the pretest as a measure of skill maintenance.

Using pretest as a covariate, the authors reported significant differences between groups on post- and maintenance-comprehension measures. Students in the strategy-value feedback group answered significantly more post- and maintenance-comprehension questions than did students in the strategy- and comprehension-only conditions who performed comparably. Although strategy-only students performed significantly higher on the post- than precomprehension measures, their progress was not significantly greater than that of comprehension-only students. Overall, these findings indicated that strategy instruction was beneficial for remedial readers only when strategy-value feedback was provided. Alternatively, perhaps students in the strategy-value feedback group performed better on the comprehension tasks because they were reminded of the relation between strategy use and reading comprehension more frequently than students in the strategy-only group.

In the second study, Schunk and Rice (1992) taught students to modify the main ideas strategy so that it could be used for locating details. Specifically, students were told that if they changed a step in the main ideas strategy, they could use the strategy to locate details. Instead of thinking about what details have in common, students were told to look for key words. We classified this knowledge as metacognitive because it informed students of how to modify a strategy so that it was useful for different tasks.

The contribution of strategy-modification instruction to main ideas strategy instruction was investigated by randomly assigning 33 fourth- and fifth-grade remedial readers to one of three conditions: comprehension instruction without the strategy; strategy instruction on main ideas; and strategy instruction on main ideas plus strategy modification. Although sample size, grade, and learner characteristics were identical in each Schunk and Rice study, the students differed between studies. After completing a comprehension pretest on main ideas and details all students received 20 days of instruction. The test was comprised of 10 passages and 20 questions (1 to 4 per passage). During the first 10 days, students in the strategy conditions were taught the main ideas strategy using a model, lead, test instructional format and a visual display of strategy steps. They practiced using the strategy daily to answer main idea questions. Students in the comprehension only group answered the same questions but without the strategy. During the last 10 weeks, students in the combined group were taught to modify the main ideas strategy so that it could be used to locate details. They practiced using the strategy daily to answer story detail questions. Students in the other groups answered the same comprehension questions but without the strategy. After the 20-week instructional phase, all students completed a parallel form of the comprehension pretest. Six weeks after completing the posttest, students completed the pretest as a measure of skill maintenance.

Using pretest as a covariate, the authors reported significant differences between groups on the post- and maintenance-comprehension measures. Students in the strategy-modification group answered significantly more post- and maintenance-comprehension questions than did students in the strategy- and comprehension-only groups who performed comparably.

These data indicated that strategy instruction was beneficial for remedial readers only when strategy-modification instruction was provided. This finding is consistent with those reported in the first Schunk and Rice study (1992), and adds credence to arguments for inclusion of strategy usefulness information to strategy instruction provided to remedial readers.

Preliminary Evidence. The remaining evidence of metacognitive knowledge facilitating reading comprehension is considered preliminary for three primary reasons. First, 8 of the 16 studies did not demonstrate experimentally that comprehension differences between groups were attributable to metacognitive knowledge (i.e., Gaultney, 1995; Idol, cited in Billingsley & Wildman, 1990; Idol & Croll, cited in Billingsley & Wildman, 1990; Pressley, cited in Harris & Pressley, 1991; Rottman & Cross, 1990; Taylor, cited in Paris et al., 1991; Wong & Jones, cited in Billingsley & Wildman, 1990; Wong & Wong, 1986). Second, three of the studies were nonexperimental, descriptive studies (i.e., Chan, 1994; Hannah & Shore, 1995; Pintrich et al., 1994). Third, most of the evidence was reported in secondary sources and lacked sufficient detail for evaluating validity of findings (i.e., Idol, cited in Billingsley & Wildman, 1990; Idol & Croll, cited in Billingsley & Wildman, 1990; Pressley, cited in Harris & Pressley, 1991; Schunk & Rice, cited in Weisberg, 1988; Weisberg & Balajthy, Study 2, cited in Weisberg, 1988; Taylor, cited in Paris et al., 1991; Wong & Jones, cited in Billingsley & Wildman, 1990).

In the Rottman and Cross (1990) study, students were taught five Informed Strategies for Learning (ISL): evaluating the reading task; defining main idea; summarizing story elements; making inferences, and using prior knowledge. Metacognitive knowledge about the read-ing tasks was provided in three of the ISL modules and was manipulated as a within-subjects variable. In the first module, evaluating the reading task, students were told what they should know when they finished reading. We classified this knowledge as metacognitive because it clarified task demands of reading. In the third module, summarizing story elements, students were told that the summarization strategy would increase their comprehension. We classified this knowledge as metacognitive because it informed students of the relation between the summarization strategy and reading comprehension. In the fifth module, using prior knowledge, students were told that prior knowledge helps to understand written material and were told how to relate prior knowledge to text information. We classified this knowledge as metacognitive because it informed students of the relation between prior knowledge and reading comprehension. In all of the modules, students were given options for selecting and employing strategies. Although details were not provided, we classified this knowledge as metacognitive because it informed students when to use one strategy over others.

An ABA single-subject design was used to investigate effects of the ISL modules on reading comprehension and awareness of 18 third- and fourth-grade students with identified learning disabilities and attention deficit disorder. The baseline, treatment, and follow-up phases lasted 4, 5, and 2 weeks respectively. A new ISL module was introduced each week during three daily 45-minute instructional periods. During each instructional period, students were given instruction on the weekly ISL; time to think about the ISL covered that day; an opportunity to use the ISL as a basis for answering questions about a high interest passage; and feedback on selection and application options. Reading comprehension was measured weekly using orally presented comprehension questions from expository and narrative passages that students read aloud. Main idea, inference, and summarization questions accompanied each passage. Reading awareness was measured before and after the study using the Index of Reading Awareness and a strategy ratings task (Paris & Jacobs, cited in Rottman & Cross, 1990). The Index of Reading Awareness consists of 20 multiple-choice questions that assess students' awareness of variables that influence reading (e.g., knowledge of task goals, use of strategies). On the strategies ratings task, students use a 5-point Likert-like scale to indicate how they rate 25 different reading strategies. Possible responses range from *helps a lot* to *hurts a lot*.

Posttest performances were significantly greater than pretest performances on all but the summarizing story elements measures. Students' overall comprehension and performance on main ideas, using inferences, prior knowledge, and awareness measures were affected positively by the ISL interventions. However, as Rottman and Cross indicated, it is difficult to attribute the results to the ISL modules because a control group was not provided. Additionally, because of the unreliability of self-report measures, it is difficult to attribute the improved reading awareness to the ISL modules.

Rather than examining metacognitive knowledge as a component of strategy instruction, Gaultney (1995) examined the effect of prior metacognitive and content knowledge on strategy acquisition and literal, inferential, and free recall. Forty-five fourth- and fifth-grade males without learning disabilities, reading 1 year below grade level, and with knowledge of baseball were randomly assigned to one of four groups. The four groups were (a) strategy training using familiar content (baseball stories), (b) strategy training using less familiar content (sports, not baseball stories), (c) no training and familiar content (baseball stories), and (d) no training and less familiar content (sports, not baseball stories). Regardless of prior content knowledge and strategy instruction, males with higher prior metacognitive knowledge demonstrated significant improvement in literal recall from pretest to immediate and delayed posttests than students with lower prior metacognitive knowledge. Significant growth did not occur for inferential and free recall.

Prior metacognitive knowledge also played a role in strategy acquisition. Males with higher prior metacognitive knowledge demonstrated greater strategy acquisition than students with lower metacognitive knowledge. Counterintuitively, the males with lower prior metacognitive knowledge demonstrated a significant correlation between strategy use and free recall whereas the males with higher prior metacognitive knowledge did not. Gaultney (1995) hypothesized that competition with known strategies may interfere with implementation of newly acquired strategies.

In Phase 1 of a quasi-experimental study, Wong and Wong (1986) investigated whether diverse learners and normally achieving students differed in their knowledge of the relation between text variables and reading comprehension, and resources needed to study passages of varying difficulty. Vocabulary difficulty and text organization were the text variables. Time was the resource. Participants were 17 above average readers, 14 average readers, and 14 readers with learning disabilities.

Two sets of passages that differed on a critical text variable were shown to participants. The first set of passages differed in terms of vocabulary difficulty; vocabulary was easy in one passage, but hard in the other. The second set of passages differed in that text was organized in one passage but unorganized in the other. For each set, participants were told the amount of time two hypothetical students spent studying the passages. Specifically, one student spent the same amount of time studying each passage type. The other student spent more time studying passages with harder vocabulary and unorganized text. Participants were required to indicate which student would remember more of the passages, especially those with hard vocabulary and unorganized text, and to explain their answers. To facilitate responding, a schematic depiction of the hypothetical students' study behavior was placed before the participants, along with the set of passages. Each schematic depiction showed the amount of time each student spent studying each passage type.

Responses to the metacognitive knowledge tasks were evaluated using a 3 x 2 (Readers x Task) design. A main effect for readers was reported. Above average readers scored significantly higher than average readers and readers with learning disabilities on selection and explanation tasks. Above average readers were significantly more likely than average readers and readers with learning disabilities to (a) select the student who increased study time on difficult vocabulary and unorganized passages as the one who would remember more passage information, and (b) explain the relation between the text variables, passage comprehensibility, and study time.

Three nonexperimental studies provided preliminary evidence of a positive relation between metacognitive knowledge and reading comprehension (i.e., Chan, 1994; Hannah & Shore, 1995; Pintrich et al., 1994). We consider the evidence as preliminary because two studies (i.e., Hannah & Shore; Pintrich et al.) indicated a correlation rather than a causal relation between metacognitive knowledge and reading comprehension, and appear to disagree regarding the relation between metacognitive knowledge and learning disabilities.

In the three studies, metacognitive knowledge was defined as knowledge of (a) the person, task, and strategy variables in reading (Hannah & Shore, 1995); (b) metacognitive strategies for reading, particularly comprehension (Pintrich et al., 1994); and (c) cognitive reading and general learning strategies (Chan, 1994). Hannah and Shore measured metacognitive knowledge using a structured interview whereas Pintrich et al. and Chan measured metacognitive knowledge using multiple-choice or rating-scale questionnaires.

Participants in each study varied in their learning types. Participants included students (a) with and without learning difficulties (students scoring in the lower quartile of a standardized achievement test and with no intellectual disabilities) in Grades 5, 7, and 9 (Chan, 1994); (b) with and without learning disabilities in Grade 5 with the students with learning disabilities having IQ scores in the normal range with a mean of 98.4 and achievement scores at least two grades below the expected level (Pintrich et al., 1994), and (c) intellectually gifted (i.e., IQ of at least 130 on a full-scale comprehensive intelligence test and high achievement in at least one academic area with no discrepancies between IQ and achievement), intellectually gifted with learning disabilities (i.e., IQ of at least 127 on a standardized intelligence test or on the verbal or performance scale of the WISC–R and placement in a learning-disability program), students with learning disabilities (i.e., IQ between 90 and 115 and placement in a learning-disability group), and average-achieving students (i.e., perform at grade level and have never been in a program for exceptional children) in Grades 5 through 6 and 11through 12 (Hannah & Shore, 1995). Note that Hannah and Shore examined giftedness whereas Chan and Pintrich et al. did not.

In general, the three descriptive studies provided preliminary evidence of a positive relation between higher levels of metacognitive knowledge and reading comprehension without indicating any causal relations. We describe the evidence as preliminary because, although the studies generally related higher levels of metacognitive knowledge with reading comprehension, they also presented apparently contradictory evidence.

For example, Hannah and Shore (1995) associated lower levels of metacognitive knowledge and reading comprehension with lack of giftedness and not with learning disabilities, whereas Chan (1994) and Pintrich et al. (1994) associated lower levels of metacognitive knowledge and reading comprehension with learning difficulties. However, Chan and Pintrich et al. did not examine whether any of their participants had giftedness with their learning difficulties.

In a second example of apparent contradictions, Hannah and Shore (1995) found that younger students demonstrated significantly lower levels of metacognitive knowledge than older students, whereas Chan (1994) found no significant effect for age. One explanation for these apparent contradictory findings lies in the difficulties associated with measuring metacognitive knowledge. Hannah and Shore measured metacognitive knowledge using a structured interview requiring oral responses and rated student understanding of the person, task, and strategy variables in reading. On the other hand, Chan used a questionnaire requiring written responses to multiple choices and to a rating scale of the usefulness of strategies. Additionally, Chan used measures developed for the elementary and secondary levels. One explanation for the apparently contradictory results arises from the differing measures. We suggest that rather than contradict each other, the studies indicate a need for more careful descriptions of participants, more careful use of measures, and further investigation of the relations between diverse learners, intelligence levels, age, metacognitive knowledge and reading comprehension.

Additional preliminary support for the positive correlation between metacognitive knowledge and reading comprehension came from the secondary sources in this chapter. Metacognitive knowledge and reading comprehension were related significantly in all studies reported in secondary sources (i.e., Idol, cited in Billingsley & Wildman, 1990; Idol & Croll, cited in Billingsley & Wildman, 1990; Pressley, cited in Harris & Pressley, 1991; Schunk & Rice, cited in Weisberg, 1988; Taylor, cited in Paris et al., 1991; Weisberg & Balajthy, Study 2, cited in Weisberg, 1988; Wong & Jones, cited in Billingsley & Wildman, 1990). As reported for primary studies, metacognitive knowledge typically was defined as knowledge of the relation between reading variables and reading comprehension. For example, students were told that story mapping (Idol, cited in Billingsley & Wildman, 1990; Idol & Croll, cited in Billingsley & Wildman, 1990) and questioning strategies (Schunk & Rice, cited in Weisberg, 1988; Wong & Jones, cited in Billingsley & Wildman, 1990) increase comprehension. Metacognitive knowledge also was defined as knowledge of task demands. For example, students in the Pressley study (cited in Harris & Pressley, 1991) were told that mental imagery would enhance their memory of text information when images accurately reflected the text. Students in the Weisberg and Balajthy study (cited in Weisberg, 1988) were told how important facts contribute to content while unimportant facts do not. Various comprehension measures were used including comprehension questions, identification of main ideas and important facts, and inclusion of story mapping components in retells.

The population was specified clearly in only six of the secondary sources. Diverse learners were the target population in three studies (Idol & Croll, cited in Billingsley & Wildman, 1990; Schunk & Rice, cited in Weisberg, 1988; Weisberg & Balajthy, Study 2, cited in Weisberg, 1988) and diverse learners along with normally achieving learners in three studies (Idol, cited in Billingsley & Wildman, 1990; Taylor, cited in Paris et al., 1991; Wong & Jones, cited in Billingsley & Wildman, 1990). Diverse learners were defined as: learning disabled; low achieving; remedial readers; disabled readers; and less capable summarizers. Learner differences were reported in two of the three studies involving normally achieving and diverse learners (Taylor, cited in Paris et al., 1991; Wong & Jones, cited in Billingsley & Wildman, 1990). Taylor (cited in Paris et al., 1991) reported that skilled summarizers used text structure to help them identify main ideas but less skilled summarizers did not. Wong and Jones (cited in Billingsley & Wildman, 1990) reported that diverse learners performed better than normally achieving learners on a comprehension monitoring task. Moreover, the comprehension performance of normally achieving learners declined after using the self-questioning strategy (i.e., generating and determining answers to questions about passage main ideas). This finding indicated that the self-questioning strategy, although beneficial for diverse learners, was detrimental for normally achieving students.

Divergent Findings

Two of the 15 studies failed to report a significant relation between metacognitive knowledge and reading comprehension (i.e., Boyle, 1996; Simmonds, 1990). In the first study, Simmonds taught students a constraint-seeking questioning technique with four steps: (a) arrange items in the stimulus array into sets according to common characteristics, (b) order the array hierarchically and supply set names, (c) ask questions about the set in order, beginning with the most generic and proceeding to the least generic dimension, and (d) remove items according to the outcome of the questions. Students were given immediate feedback on whether their questions lead to rapid and accurate problem solutions. We classified this knowledge as metacognitive because it clarified task demands of the questioning technique.

Metacognitive knowledge was manipulated as a between-subjects variable. The effectiveness of the constraint-seeking questioning technique was investigated by randomly assigning 60 fourth- through sixth-grade students with learning disabilities to cognitive and cognitive-plus-verbalization instructional groups. The questioning technique was modeled for cognitive instruction students and taught explicitly to cognitive-plus-verbalization students during four 20-minute instructional periods that occurred over a 4-week period. Students in the cognitive-plus-verbalization group also were given immediate feedback on the quality of their questions and thus had multiple opportunities to receive metacognitive knowledge. All students completed alternative forms of a 20-question game before and after the training phase. The number of questions used to reach solution was the dependent measure.

The relative effects of the instructional strategies were evaluated using a 2 x 2 (Instructional Method x Testing Time) design. Using pretest as the covariate, the authors found no significant differences between groups on number of questions for reaching a solution at posttest. Students in both groups performed significantly better on the posttest than on the pretest. Because the study did not demonstrate that verbalization contributed to the efficacy of the cognitive modeling instructional approach, a statement about the effect of metacognitive knowledge on comprehension cannot be definitively made.

One plausible reason for this divergent finding is the nature of the instructional materials. Simmonds (1990) differed from reliable and preliminary studies in terms of instructional context. The constraint-seeking questioning technique was taught in the context of picture card games, whereas those investigated in other studies were taught in the context of reading. Simmonds' students were not required to use the questioning technique to gather information from reading material.

In the second study that did not report a significant relation between metacognitive knowledge and reading comprehension, Boyle (1996) compared the effects of a cognitive mapping strategy with taking notes or outlining on literal and inferential reading comprehension, and metacognitive knowledge. The participants were students with learning disabilities and educable mental retardation. Strategy instruction included teaching students the metacognitive knowledge when and why to use the strategy. Students in the cognitive mapping group demonstrated significant gains in literal and inferential reading comprehension on curriculum based reading measures whereas their matched pairs in the control group did not. However, there were no differences between groups on informal reading and metacognitive awareness measures. Additionally, students in the cognitive strategy group did not transfer the use of the strategy to the informal reading measure.

To explain the lack of transfer to the informal reading measure, Boyle (1996) suggested that teachers facilitate the transfer of a strategy to a new situation by encouraging students to modify the strategy when necessary and think "divergently about applying it to novel situations" (p. 96). To explain the lack of effect on metacognitive knowledge, we propose that the curriculum design was weak. Instruction occurred in only four lessons. Additionally, teachers provided no corrective feedback or reinforcement after the first lesson. Further research is required to determine whether longer and more carefully designed instruction increases metacognitive knowledge.

Summary

The relation between metacognitive knowledge and reading comprehension was investigated in 17 studies. With two exceptions, all studies reported a statistically significant effect or positive correlation between metacognitive knowledge and reading comprehension. Metacognitive knowledge frequently was defined as knowledge of task demands, and the relation between reading strategies and reading comprehension. Metacognitive knowledge seldom was defined as knowledge of self as a learner, or conditions when one strategy would be more appropriate to use than another.

The effects of various types of metacognitive knowledge (e.g., task demands, relation between reading variables and reading comprehension) on reading comprehension were not contrasted experimentally. Thus, it is unclear whether some facets of metacognitive knowledge are related more strongly with reading comprehension than others. Similarly, it is unclear whether various metacognitive knowledge facets when combined are related more strongly to reading comprehension than when featured individually. Answers to these questions would enhance our understanding of the relation between metacognitive knowledge and reading comprehension.

Additional areas that require clarification are the relations between learner types and metacognitive knowledge, prior metacognitive knowledge and strategy acquisition, and the specific role of increased metacognitive knowledge to improved reading comprehension. First, normally achieving students generally demonstrated more metacognitive knowledge than diverse learners. However, one study examined giftedness and found that gifted students with learning disabilities who were also poor readers demonstrated more metacognitive knowledge than normally achieving students. Second, in the relation between prior metacognitive knowledge and strategy acquisition, one study reported that diverse learners with higher rather than lower prior metacognitive knowledge demonstrated greater strategy acquisition. Finally, in the relation between increased metacognitive knowledge and improved reading comprehension, we cannot conclude that comprehension gains were solely attributable to increased metacognitive knowledge. In general, studies included metacognitive components in strategy instruction, but did not isolate the contribution of the metacognitive component to strategy acquisition or improved reading comprehension. In summary, evidence suggests a significant effect on reading comprehension when strategy instruction includes a metacognitive component, and positive correlation between metacognitive knowledge and reading comprehension. However, further research is required.

AREA OF CONVERGENCE 2:
Self-Regulation Facilitates Reading Comprehension

The self-regulation component of reading metacognition is multifaceted and refers to:

1. Coordinating metacognitive knowledge (Billingsley & Wildman, 1990), such as combining knowledge of task demands and resources needed to perform reading skills.
2. Planning (Billingsley & Wildman, 1990), such as selecting or scheduling comprehension strategies for a particular type of text, or predicting outcomes.
3. Monitoring reading behaviors (Paris et al., 1991), including evaluating understanding of text (Baker & Brown, cited in Chan et al., 1987), checking one's comprehension (Billingsley & Wildman, 1990), and evaluating outcomes against an efficacy criterion (Brown, 1987).
4. Identifying causes of one's comprehension failures while reading (Baker & Brown, cited in Chan et al., 1987), including incongruity with prior knowledge, text difficulties (e.g., internal inconsistency, incomplete information, syntactical errors, unorganized content), and failure to attend to reading.
5. Remediating reading failures (Baker & Brown, cited in Chan et al., 1987; Billingsley & Wildman, 1990), such as revising or rescheduling reading strategies (Brown, 1987) and employing "Fix-it" strategies (Weisberg, 1988).

The relation between self-regulation and reading comprehension was investigated in five studies. Two of the studies were primary (i.e., Malone & Mastropieri, 1992; Wong & Wong, 1986) and three of the studies were reported in secondary sources (i.e., Bergamo & Cornoldi, cited in Cornoldi,

1990; Graves cited in Weisberg, 1988; Taylor, cited in Paris et al., 1991). In most of the studies, self-regulation involved monitoring reading tasks. To a lesser extent, self-regulation involved planning, remediating reading failures, and adjusting study time for difficult passages. Comprehension was measured via story questions, summaries, and number of inferences and main ideas identified.

All of the studies provided partial evidence that self-regulation facilitates reading comprehension. The evidence is reported in two experimental studies (i.e., Graves, cited in Weisberg, 1988; Malone & Mastropieri, 1992), two quasi-experimental studies (i.e., Bergamo & Cornoldi, cited in Cornoldi, 1990; Wong & Wong, 1986), and two non-experimental studies (i.e., Hannah & Shore, 1995; Taylor, cited in Paris et al., 1991). Overall, the evidence indicating a causal relation between self-regulation and reading comprehension is preliminary. More than half of the studies did not demonstrate experimentally (or via correlation) that comprehension differences between groups were attributable to self-regulation. Moreover, significant findings were tempered by methodological and measurement limitations in one of the quasi-experimental studies (i.e., Wong & Wong), and were reported for only one of three primary measures in one of the experimental studies (i.e., Malone & Mastropieri). In the following discussion, the evidence for self-regulation facilitating reading comprehension is detailed and organized by type of investigation.

Additive Effects of Monitoring

Self-monitoring was investigated within the context of strategy instruction in two of the reviewed studies (i.e., Graves, cited in Weisberg, 1988; Malone & Mastropieri, 1992). The purpose of each study was to determine whether strategy instruction would be more effective for students with learning disabilities if a self-monitoring component was included. The instructional strategies and self-monitoring tasks differed between studies.

In the Graves study (cited in Weisberg, 1988), finding main ideas was the instructional strategy. Self-monitoring involved checking one's comprehension and remediating comprehension failures. Specifically, students were taught to (a) ask themselves, "Do I know what the story is about?" and (b) reread the story when they did not know what it was about.

The contribution of self-monitoring to main idea instruction was investigated by randomly assigning 44 students with learning disabilities to one of three instructional conditions: traditional comprehension, direct instruction of main ideas, and direct instruction of main ideas plus self-monitoring. Students in the combined group received opportunities to self-monitor and remediate their reading during eight training sessions. A week later, all students were tested on identifying passage main ideas. A main effect for instructional group was reported. Students in the combined group identified significantly more main ideas than students in the direct instruction of main ideas group, who in turn, identified significantly more main ideas than students who received traditional comprehension instruction. These data indicated that strategy instruction was enhanced by inclusion of a self-monitoring component.

In the Malone and Mastropieri study (1992), summarization was the instructional strategy. Three steps required students to determine who or what the paragraph was about, what happened, and to write a summary sentence using answers to Steps 1 and 2. Self-monitoring involved checking off summarization steps using a self-monitoring index card containing a Paragraph x Strategy-step matrix.

The contribution of self-monitoring to the summarization strategy was investigated by randomly assigning 45 students with learning disabilities to one of three instructional conditions: traditional comprehension, summarization, and summarization plus self-monitoring. All students received two days of instruction. Each day, students in the strategy conditions were taught to use the summarization strategy and were given an opportunity to use the strategy to write summary sentences on a line at the end of each passage paragraph. Students in the strategy plus self-monitoring group also were taught to immediately check off summarization steps when completed. All students practiced writing short answers to 12 questions about the training passages. Comprehension was measured using near-transfer, post, and far-transfer recall tests. For each test, students were required to write short answers to 12 questions about the test passage. The near-transfer test passage did not have prompt lines at the end of each paragraph. The posttest passage had paragraph prompt lines. The far-transfer test passage did not have paragraph prompt lines and was taken from a social studies, rather than reading text.

Students in the strategy groups performed significantly better on all three comprehension measures than students who received traditional comprehension instruction. Summarization plus self-monitoring students recalled significantly more information from the far-transfer passage than summarization students. Content complexity was a possible explanation for the differential finding. According to Malone and Mastropieri (1992), social studies content of the far-transfer passage was more complex than content of the post- and near-transfer tests. The authors posited that strategy instruction is only enhanced by a self-monitoring component when text material is complex.

Self-Regulation Differences Among
Students With Varying Reading Skills

The relation between self-regulation and reading comprehension among students with varying reading skills was investigated in two quasi-experimental studies (i.e., Bergamo & Cornoldi, cited in Cornoldi, 1990; Wong & Wong, 1986) and two nonexperimental studies (i.e., Hannah & Shore, 1995; Taylor, cited in Paris et al., 1991). The self-regulation strategy and skill level of participants varied between studies. For example, Taylor (cited in Paris et al., 1991) reported that skilled summarizers planned and monitored the accuracy of their summaries but that less-skilled summarizers did not.

Bergamo and Cornoldi (cited in Cornoldi, 1990) investigated whether good and poor comprehenders differed in monitoring, study time, and recall of plausible and implausible passages. The 21 good comprehenders had average or above-average oral reading skills. The 16 poor comprehenders had average oral reading but low comprehension skills. Half of the participants in each group were in second grade and half were in fifth grade.

Participants were required to read aloud five plausible and five implausible passages and rate the comprehensibility of each passage. Plausible passages had the word "not" embedded in core sections; implausible passages did not. Participants were required to recall the content of each passage, after receiving a story title prompt. The amount of time they spent studying each passage was recorded. The number of main ideas identified was the comprehension measure.

All participants rated implausible passages as less comprehensible than plausible passages, although poor comprehenders were less accurate in their monitoring. However, good and poor comprehenders differed in the amount of time they allocated to studying each passage type. Good comprehenders studied implausible passages longer than plausible passages, while poor comprehenders spent approximately the same amount of time studying each passage type. Moreover, good comprehenders recalled more critical passage points than poor comprehenders. These data indicated that poor comprehenders did not use their knowledge of passage comprehensibility to direct study behavior and perhaps, as a result, were less successful at remembering main ideas.

A second study investigated differences in error detection between types of learners. Hannah and Shore (1995) defined error detection as the verbal acknowledgment of inconsistencies in text or violations of prior knowledge embedded in the passages. Four learner types in Grades 5 and 6 and 11 and 12 participated in the study: gifted; gifted with learning disabilities; learning disabilities not gifted; and average. Similarly to the differences for metacognitive knowledge (see Area of Convergence 1, p. 307), Hannah and Shore found that in the area of error detection gifted students with learning disabilities were more like gifted than students with learning disabilities; older students out performed younger students; and error detection has a significant positive correlation with reading comprehension. Because gifted students with learning disabilities demonstrated more error detection than students without giftedness, Hannah and Shore hypothesized that gifted students with learning disabilities may possess metacognitive skills even though their scholastic achievement is deficient.

Hannah and Shore (1995) also reported differences between older and younger students. A visual examination of the error detection data indicated that younger students verbalized the detection of inconsistencies with prior knowledge but not violations of internal consistency. The Hannah and Shore results are limited by the number ($n = 6$) of participants in each group.

Wong and Wong (1986) investigated whether above-average and average readers and readers with identified learning disabilities differed in study time and comprehension of passages that varied in difficulty. Participants were required to study the same four passages used in the metacognitive knowledge tasks reported in the first study phase discussed in Area of Convergence 1 in this chapter. Specifically, they were told to study organized and disorganized passages for recall, and hard and easy vocabulary passages for a reading test. The amount of time participants studied each passage was recorded. Comprehension was measured via number of idea units recalled for organized and disorganized passages, and number of comprehension questions answered correctly for hard and easy vocabulary passages.

Only above-average readers studied disorganized passages significantly longer than organized passages. This finding is consistent with results from the metacognitive knowledge tasks reported in the first study phase and indicated that above-average readers applied knowledge of the relation between text organization and reading comprehension, and the resources needed to study passages of varying difficulty.Because students with learning disabilities did not demonstrate metacognitive knowledge of task variables, it is not surprising that they did not adjust study time.

Contrary to results from metacognitive knowledge tasks reported in the first study phase, only readers with learning disabilities studied hard vocabulary passages significantly longer than easy vocabulary passages. In agreement with the authors, we posit that this finding may indicate that students with learning disabilities had knowledge of the relation between vocabulary difficulty and reading comprehension, and the resources needed to study passages of varying difficulty, but they could not demonstrate or explain such knowledge. Alternatively, perhaps students with learning disabilities increased their study time of hard vocabulary passages because the words were harder to decode, or because hard passages were 69 words longer than easy vocabulary passages. It is unclear why above-average readers did not increase their study time for hard vocabulary passages given their metacognitive knowledge of the task variables. One explanation is the words were not difficult for the above-average readers and thus did not warrant additional study time.

Summary

The relation between self-regulation and reading comprehension was investigated in six studies. All studies reported a statistically significant relation between self-regulation and students' reading comprehension. Self-regulation involved self-monitoring most frequently; coordinating metacognitive knowledge less frequently; and planning, identifying causes of one's comprehension failures during reading, and remediating reading failures rarely or never. Overall, diverse learners benefited from strategy instruction that contained a self-monitoring component. Moreover, self-monitoring enhanced the efficacy of strategy instruction. In terms of learner differences, except for gifted students with learning disabilities, normally achieving students demonstrated more self-regulation skills than diverse learners.

The effects of various types of self-regulation (e.g., planning, monitoring, remediating reading failures) on reading comprehension were not contrasted in any of the reviewed studies. Thus, it is unclear whether some facets of self-regulation are related more strongly to reading comprehension than others. Similarly, it is unclear whether various self-regulation facets are related more strongly to reading comprehension when combined than when featured individually. Answers to these questions would enhance our understanding of the relation between self-regulation and reading comprehension. These conclusions are consistent with those reported in the metacognitive knowledge area of convergence.

We conclude our discussion of the relation between reading metacognition and reading comprehension by describing a study in which the effect of combining metacognitive knowledge *and* self-regulation was investigated (Palincsar et al., 1991). The purpose of the study was to explore the effects of different strategy instructional methods for students with varying reading skills. Partial evidence of a relation between reading comprehension and strategy instruction containing metacognitive knowledge and self-regulation was reported. However, the evidence is preliminary because adequate experimental control was not demonstrated. Method and content of instruction (including number and type of reading strategies) were manipulated between groups.

Several activities were used to promote *metacognitive knowledge*. For example, participants were required to identify problems they might encounter while reading and to identify possible resolutions. We classified this knowledge as metacognitive because it required participants to attend to variables that are related to reading comprehension. Similarly, participants were required to generate strategies that would help a robot who possessed adequate decoding but inadequate comprehension skills to become a good reader. We classified this knowledge as metacognitive because it required students to attend to strategies that are related to reading comprehension. Metacognitive knowledge also was promoted using vignettes describing strategies students used when preparing for various reading tasks. After each vignette, participants were required to:

1. Identify which hypothetical student would perform best on the reading task and explain their answers. We classified this knowledge as metacognitive because it required participants to attend to the relation between reading strategies and reading comprehension.
2. Explain when one strategy would be more appropriate to use than others. We classified this knowledge as metacognitive because it required participants to attend to conditions under which reading strategies are performed.
3. Identify information (e.g., prior knowledge) that would help them determine strategy appropriateness. We classified this knowledge as metacognitive because it required participants to attend to variables that are related to reading comprehension.

To promote self-regulation, participants were given expository passages and told the purpose for reading. Subsequently, they were required to choose, implement, and evaluate the effectiveness of one of the reading strategies that had been identified and generated during metacognitive knowledge activities. We classified these behaviors as self-regulatory because they involved planning and monitoring.

The effects of different strategy instructional methods for students with varying reading skills was investigated by randomly assigning approximately 39 third graders (divided into low, medium, and high reading triads) to one of three strategy instructional conditions: direct instruction, reciprocal teaching, and collaborative problem solving. All participants received 25 days of strategy instruction, with instructional time and text held constant across groups. In the direct instruction group, participants were taught summarizing, questioning, and clarifying strategies. In the reciprocal teaching group, participants were taught the same strategies and, in addition, taught how to make predictions. In the collaborative problem-solving group, participants were led through several student-controlled activities designed to promote strategy awareness *and* metacognitive knowledge and self-regulation of reading strategies. After the instructional phase, all students completed a criterion-referenced comprehension test.

All students performed significantly better on the postcomprehension measure than they did on the precomprehension measure. The amount of improvement was greatest for participants in the collaborative problem-solving group. Although the investigators partially attributed this finding to the metacognitive focus of collaborative problem-solving instruction, we believe method of instruction and number of strategies covered are alternative explanations. Overall, participants in the low reading group benefited significantly more from strategy instruction than those in the high reading group, regardless of instructional method.

Additional research on the relation between reading comprehension and strategy instruction containing metacognitive knowledge and self-regulation features is needed. For example, future research could investigate whether metacognitive knowledge and self-regulation in combination are related more strongly to reading comprehension than when featured individually. An investigation of this research question would have at least three features. First, the independent variable, that is, type of reading metacognition, would need to be manipulated within a minimum of three groups (e.g., strategy instruction plus metacognitive knowledge, strategy instruction plus self-regulation, and strategy instruction plus metacognitive knowledge and self-regulation). Next, key variables would need to be held constant across experimental groups (e.g., type of strategy instruction, metacognitive knowledge, and self-regulation). Finally, participants would need to be randomly assigned to experimental conditions.

CONVERGENT AREA 3:
Motivational Beliefs May Mediate Students' Use and Benefit from Metacognitive Knowledge and Self-Regulation Strategies

Some students fail even though they have knowledge that should help them succeed. This finding was illustrated in the Rottman and Cross (1990) study described in Area of Convergence 1 in this chapter. At a group level, children benefited from informed strategies for learning. However, data from a supplementary analysis revealed significant variability in the amount of comprehension improvement students made. One group did not improve at all. Ineffective use of knowledge is a possible explanation of why some students fail even though they have knowledge that should help them succeed. For example, although poor comprehenders in the Bergamo and Cornoldi (cited in Cornoldi, 1990) study rated implausible passages as less comprehensible than plausible passages, they did not use knowledge of passage comprehensibility to vary their study time of the passages. Johnston and Winograd (1985) used the term "passive failure" to describe this phenomenon.

Emerging evidence suggests that negative motivational beliefs may explain why some students fail to use knowledge effectively. For example, the subset of students in the Rottman and Cross (1990) study who failed to benefit from instructional strategies had average- to low-perceived competency, even though they had high reading and strategy awareness. The authors hypothesized that negative motivational beliefs may have minimized the effort that students devoted to strategies. Similarly, Bergamo and Cornoldi (cited in Cornoldi, 1990) hypothesized that poor comprehenders in their study may have believed they were incapable of comprehending the implausible passages and thus did not try. After examining several research perspectives, Johnston and Winograd (1985) concluded that "the key factor underlying the characteristics of passive failures seems to be the perception that responses and outcomes are independent" (p. 283).

Borkowski (1992) provided a theoretical explanation for the relation between motivational beliefs and self-regulation in his theory of metacognition. He argued that motivational beliefs develop over time as a function of how "refined" one becomes in strategic and executive processing. As processes become refined, positive motivational beliefs develop, including self-competency, strategic awareness, and attributing success to effort. When processes do not become refined, negative motivational beliefs develop, including feelings of incompetence and attributing success to luck. Borkowski also argued that motivational beliefs influence whether strategies will be selected and maintained in the future. Self-regulatory attempts that have resulted in feelings of self-competency are maintained while those that have resulted in feelings of incompetence are avoided.

Over time, motives underlying decisions to use strategies develop. Students who continue using strategies are motivated by a sense of the importance of being strategic. Students who avoid using strategies are motivated by a desire to avoid failure. According to Paris et al. (1991), students engage in avoidance strategies that lead to short-term success, require minimal effort, and offer protection against loss of self-esteem. Examples of strategies for avoiding failure include: withdrawal of participation; feigning interest or involvement; shifting blame from self to external factors such as noise, illness, task difficulty, bad luck; forgetting to take home necessary material for completing required tasks; reading wrong passages; procrastinating and not leaving enough time for completing tasks; and avoiding effort by lowering expectations or cheating.

The consequences associated with ineffective strategy use are serious. Over time, students experience greater academic failure because ineffective reading is exacerbated, and skills and content that develop as a result of reading remain unlearned (Paris et al., 1991). Moreover, time and energy devoted to avoidance strategies significantly reduce time available for learning effective reading strategies. Because negative motivational beliefs, in theory, contribute to ineffective strategy use, it stands to reason that negative motivational beliefs also influence achievement. The purpose of the third area of convergence is to describe empirical evidence of two relations: motivational beliefs and self-regulation, and motivational beliefs and achievement. Before detailing the evidence, we provide definitions and classes of motivational beliefs that emerged from our literature review.

Definitions and Classes of Motivational Beliefs

Motivational beliefs refer to personal beliefs about:

1. One's general competency (Borkowski, 1992; Rottman & Cross, 1990, also referred to as self-efficacy, self-esteem, and self-worth.
2. One's competency to perform specific reading tasks, such as applying strategies and achieving goals (Schunk & Rice, 1992; Johnston & Winograd, 1985).
3. One's ability to control or influence academic outcomes (Garner, cited in Paris et al., 1991; Johnston & Winograd, 1985; Swanson, 1989).
4. The causes and extent of academic successes and failures (Chan, 1994; Johnston & Winograd, 1985; Paris et al., 1991).
5. The benefits of using a strategy (Garner, cited in Paris et al., 1991; Schunk & Rice, 1992).

Positive Motivational Beliefs. Positive motivational beliefs are common among persons described as self-regulated learners, strategic readers, achieving students, and successful students. These normally achieving students tend to hold one or more of the following beliefs: I can control or influence academic outcomes (Weiner, cited in Paris et al., 1991); my academic successes and failures are caused by variables within my control, such as effort (Borkowski, 1992; Borkowski, Carr, Rellinger, & Pressley, cited in Paris et al., 1991; Diener & Dweck, cited in Johnston & Winograd, 1985); and I am capable of accomplishing reading tasks (Harter & Connell, cited in Paris et al., 1991; Weiner, cited in Paris et al., 1991). The latter belief may stem from knowledge of multiple strategies for learning effectively (Paris et al.).

In a descriptive study, Chan (1994) examined motivation beliefs related to attribution of academic successes and failures. Participants were 104 fifth-grade, 133 seventh-grade, and 101 ninth-grade students in Australia with and without learning difficulties. Students with learning difficulties were described as those with no intellectual disabilities who score in the bottom quartile on standardized achievement tests. Chan used written scaled measures to determine causal attributes and perceived competence.

As a result of the data analyses, Chan (1994) concluded that students without learning difficulties were more likely than students with learning difficulties to attribute school success and failure to factors under their personal control (i.e., effort, effective strategy use). Additionally, Chan concluded that as a group ninth-grade students were more likely to attribute success and failure to effort and strategy use than to ability and luck than were fifth- and seventh-grade students, thus suggesting a developmental pattern to positive motivational beliefs. In other words, Chan stated that students do not fully differentiate effort from ability, or strategy use from effort or ability until early high school. Chan suggested that the greater differentiation may reflect the greater awareness of the ninth-grade students of their personal control over learning outcomes. For perceived competence, Chan found no significant differences between fifth-, seventh-, and ninth-grade students.

Negative Motivational Beliefs. Negative motivational beliefs are common among persons described as passive failures or helpless students, and persons with reading difficulties, learning disabilities, poor comprehension skills, low self-worth, and a history of academic failure. These diverse learners tend to hold one or more of the following beliefs: I have little or no ability to accomplish reading tasks (Butkowsky & Willows, cited in Schunk & Rice, 1992; Lict & Kistner, cited in Schunk & Rice, 1992); I have little or no control over academic outcomes (Abramson, Seligman, & Teasdale, cited in Johnston & Winograd, 1985; Butkowsky & Willows, cited in Schunk & Rice, 1992; Lict & Kistner, cited in Schunk & Rice, 1992; Garner, cited in Paris et al., 1991); my academic successes and failures are caused by variables beyond my control (Cullen, cited in Chan, Cole, & Morris, 1990; Diener & Dweck, cited in Johnston & Winograd, 1985); I have little confidence that I will benefit from using reading strategies (Garner, cited in Paris et al., 1991; Schunk & Rice, 1992); and, I have low expectations that I will successfully complete given tasks (Johnston & Winograd, 1985; Paris et al.,1991). The latter belief may stem from inaccurate perceptions of the extent of academic successes and failures (Johnston & Winograd).

In the descriptive study described in the discussion of positive motivational beliefs, Chan (1994) found that students with learning difficulties were more likely than students without learning difficulties to attribute success to luck and failure to lack of ability, and demonstrate less confidence in their own control over success and failure in school tasks. For perceived competence, Chan found that students with learning difficulties scored significantly lower than students without learning difficulties in perceived cognitive and social competence, but not for perceived physical and general competence.

Motivational Beliefs and Self-Regulation

The relation between motivational beliefs and self-regulation was investigated in seven studies. Three of the studies were primary (i.e., Chan, 1994; Schunk & Rice, 1992, Studies 1 & 2) and four were reported in secondary sources (i.e., Borkowski, Carr, Rellinger, & Pressley, cited in Paris et al., 1991; Borkowski, Weyhing, & Carr; Rohrkempter & Como, cited in Paris et al., 1991; Diener & Dweck, cited in Johnston & Winograd, 1985). Partial evidence of a relation between motivational beliefs and self-regulation was provided in each of the studies.

Descriptive Research. The relation between motivational beliefs and self-regulation among normally achieving and diverse learners was investigated in three nonexperimental studies (i.e., Chan, 1994; Diener & Dweck, cited in Johnston & Winograd, 1985; Rohrkempter & Como, cited in Paris et al., 1991). The researchers defined motivational beliefs as attributions of academic outcomes. Diener and Dweck (cited in Johnston & Winograd, 1985) and Rohrkempter and Como (cited in Paris et al., 1991) defined self-regulation as student responses to challenging tasks. Chan examined strategy use. We categorized this as self-regulation. Normally achieving students were defined as achieving and successful students. Diverse learn-ers were defined as helpless students, students who did not understand what variables controlled learning outcomes, or students with learning difficulties.

Overall, Diener and Dweck (cited in Johnston & Winograd, 1985) and Rohrkempter and Como (cited in Paris et al., 1991) found that students who attributed academic outcomes to variables within their control (e.g., effort) showed greater persistence and strategy use (e.g., self-monitoring) on challenging tasks than students who attributed academic outcomes to variables beyond their control (e.g., luck). It is unclear whether the self-regulation differences were attributable to motivational beliefs, metacognitive knowledge (e.g., knowledge of fix-up strategies), or achievement, because none of these variables were controlled.

Chan (1994) examined strategy use by grade and by types of learners. She found that seventh-grade students reported significantly greater use of reading and learning strategies than ninth-grade students. However, she found no significant differences in reported strategy use by students with and without learning difficulties. Chan offered no explanations or hypotheses for these findings that on the surface appear to contradict the assumption that diverse students use fewer strategies than normally achieving students.

Correlational Findings. The relation between motivational beliefs and strategy use (self-regulation) was investigated in three studies (i.e., Chan, 1994; Schunk & Rice, 1992, Studies 1 & 2) described in Area of Convergence 2 in this chapter. Similar to the descriptive results of Diener and Dweck (cited in Johnston & Winograd, 1985) and Rohrkempter and Como (cited in Paris et al., 1991), Chan found a significant correlation between motivational beliefs and strategy use. Chan also found developmental patterns. She reported that seventh- and ninth-grade students who believe that they have personal control over learning outcomes (positive motivational beliefs) and who have high self-perceptions of cognitive competence were more likely to use reading and learning strategies. For fifth-grade students a significant correlation existed between belief in personal control and reading strategy use only, and perceived competence and reading and learning use.

Schunk and Rice (1992) investigated self-efficacy, which they defined as one's perceived ability to complete specific types of strategy questions. To evaluate self-efficacy, remedial readers read passages and then judged whether they could answer 20 strategy-type questions using a 10-unit interval scale that ranged from 10 (*not sure*) to 100 (*really sure*). Strategy use, the self-regulation variable in these studies, was defined as the number of strategy steps verbalized in correct order in both studies, and the frequency in which students performed each step in the second study. To determine the number of strategy steps verbalized in correct order, students were required to say aloud everything they read and thought about when given a passage and a question to answer. Up to 5 points could be earned on this measure. To determine the frequency in which students performed each strategy step, students were required to complete a self-report measure comprised of 5 scales that corresponded with strategy steps. Each scale had 10-unit intervals that ranged from 0 (*not used at all*) to 100 (*used a whole lot*).

Positive correlations between self-efficacy and strategy use were reported in both studies when strategy use was measured using the think-aloud task. Students who believed they were capable of completing the various types of strategy questions at the posttest also tended to verbalize more strategy steps in correct order on the post-strategy-use measure in Study 2 and on the maintenance-strategy-use measure in both studies. It is unclear why self-reported strategy use was not correlated with self-efficacy. One explanation is that students were inaccurate in their self-reports, rendering the measures unreliable.

Path Analyses. Chan (1994) also conducted path analyses to examine the influence of attribution beliefs and perceived cognitive competence on self-regulation (i.e., strategy use). To simplify the path analyses, Chan combined motivational factors to form two categories: personal control (the belief that success in school tasks is caused by effort and strategy use), and learned helplessness (the belief that success is caused by luck and failure by lack of ability). She reported developmental differences. For ninth-grade students, belief in personal control, learned helplessness, and perceived cognitive competence directly influenced reading strategy, with learned helplessness exerting a negative influence. For seventh-grade students, belief in personal control positively and learned helplessness negatively influenced knowledge of strategies, which then influenced strategy use, and perceived cognitive competence positively and directly influenced reading strategy use. For fifth-grade students, only perceived cognitive competence directly and positively influenced reading strategy use.

Self-Regulation Effects of Instruction Targeting Motivational Beliefs. The relation between motivational beliefs and self-regulation was investigated within the context of strategy instruction in two experimental studies (i.e., Borkowski, Weyhing, & Carr, cited in Paris et al., 1991; Schunk & Rice, 1992, Study 1) and one quasi-experimental study (i.e., Borkowski, Carr, Rellinger, & Pressley, cited in Paris et al., 1991). In addition to strategy instruction, students received instruction targeting motivational beliefs. The skill level of participants and content of motivational training differed between studies.

In the Borkowski, Weyhing, and Carr study (cited in Paris et al., 1991), students with reading disabilities, aged 10 to 14, were trained to use various summarization strategies. Some students also received attributional training on self-control. Although all students learned to use summarization strategies, only students who received summarization instruction and attributional training maintained their use of the strategies. These data indicate that motivational training enhanced long-term effects of strategy instruction.

In their first study, Schunk and Rice (1992) investigated whether strategy instruction on main ideas would produce more powerful self-regulation effects if feedback on the value of the strategy was included. We classified strategy-value feedback as addressing motivational beliefs because it focused student attention on the relation between personal actions and academic outcomes, an approach Johnston and Winograd (1985) recommended for changing negative motivational beliefs. Remedial readers were assigned to a comprehension-only, strategy-only, or strategy plus strategy-value feedback group. Strategy use, defined as the number of strategy steps verbalized in correct order, was assessed 6 weeks after the instructional period. A strategy-use main effect was reported. Students in the combined group verbalized significantly more strategy steps in correct order, than strategy-only students who in turn verbalized significantly more strategy steps in correct order than comprehension-only students. These data indicate that instruction targeting motivational beliefs enhanced long-term efficacy of strategy instruction on main ideas. This finding is consistent with findings reported by Borkowski, Weyhing, and Carr (cited in Paris et al., 1991) and adds credence to arguments for inclusion of information targeting motivational beliefs during strategy instruction for remedial readers.

In the Borkowski, Carr, Rellinger, and Pressley study (cited in Paris et al., 1991), achieving and underachieving students received training on the importance of effort in using strategies, in addition to receiving instruction on the utility of various strategies. Underachieving students generalized strategies after completing the training, despite their initial unwillingness to use strategies. The extent to which instruction on motivational beliefs increased the likelihood that students used the strategy is unclear because the authors did not manipulate the motivational belief variable.

Self-Regulation Outcomes Associated With Changes in Motivational Beliefs. With the exception of one study (i.e., Borkowski, Weyhing, & Carr, cited in Paris et al., 1991), positive self-regulation outcomes were associated with changes in motivational beliefs. For example, prior to training, underachievers in the Borkowski, Carr, Rellinger, and Pressley study (cited in Paris et al., 1991) did not attribute academic outcomes to controllable variables nor did they believe that strategies were useful. However, after completing the training, they changed their motivational beliefs and generalized strategies. In the first Schunk and Rice study (1992), remedial readers in the strategy plus strategy-value feedback group scored highest on the strategy-use measure. They also were the only students to believe that they could answer significantly more strategy-type questions on post-versus premotivational measures. Similar findings were reported in the second Schunk and Rice study. Of the three groups (comprehension-only, strategy-only, and strategy-plus-strategy modification), remedial readers in the strategy-plus-modification group scored highest on the think-aloud strategy-use measure and were the only students whose motivational beliefs increased significantly across the pre- and posttesting period.

Motivational Beliefs and Achievement

The relation between motivation and achievement was investigated in five studies. Four of the studies were primary (i.e., Chan, 1994; Rottman & Cross, 1990; Schunk & Rice, 1992, Studies 1 & 2) and one of the studies was reported in a secondary source (i.e., Kistner, Osborne, & LeVerrier, cited in Paris et al., 1991). Partial evidence that motivational beliefs influence achievement outcomes was provided in each study. For example, students in the Kistner, Osborne, and LeVerrier study (cited in Paris et al., 1991) who attributed failure to controllable causes made the greatest achievement gains over a 2-year period.

Post Hoc Findings. In the supplementary analysis conducted by Rottman and Cross (1990), remedial readers were divided into three groups according to reading awareness, strategy awareness, and motivational beliefs. Reading awareness was measured on an index consisting of 20 multiple-choice questions that assessed students' awareness and understanding of variables that influence reading, such as task goals, planful use of strategies, and effectiveness of activities. Student responses to each question were rated on a scale of 0 to 2 on conceptual awareness. Strategy awareness was measured by having students rate 25 strategies using a 5-point scale. A rating of 1 indicated that students believed the strategy would hurt a lot. A rating of 5 indicated that students believed the strategy would help a lot. The motivational belief targeted in this study was defined as general perception of competency and was measured using a 36-item, forced choice, perceived competency scale. Students judged whether items about scholastic competence, social acceptance, athletic competence, and global self-worth were true or false about themselves.

The three subgroups of subjects that emerged were classified as defensives, realists, and pessimists. Defensives had low to average reading and strategy awareness, but high perceived competency. Realists had low to average reading awareness, strategy awareness, and perceived competency. Pessimists had high reading and strategy awareness, but average to low perceived competency. An interaction between subgroup and testing time on number of main ideas identified was reported. Although defensives and realists identified significantly more main ideas on post- versus pretest, pessimists did not. The authors attributed this outcome to pessimists' failure to exert sufficient effort when using instructional strategies for learning, in an attempt to prevent a loss of self-esteem that could occur from a failed effortful attempt. This hypothesis does not explain why realists, who also had low motivational beliefs, made significant progress. Perhaps negative motivational beliefs decrease the likelihood that students will use knowledge effectively and thus limit achievement only when inaccurate. The authors were careful to indicate that findings were limited because they were based on post hoc rather than planned groupings.

Correlational Findings. The relation between motivational beliefs and comprehension was investigated in the two Schunk and Rice studies (1992). Positive correlations between self-efficacy and comprehension were reported in both studies. Students who believed they were capable of completing strategy-type questions at the posttest also tended to answer post- and maintenance-comprehension questions correctly. The opposite was true for students who did not believe they were capable of completing strategy-type questions.

Path Analyses. Using multiple regression, Chan (1994) examined the contribution of motivational beliefs and perceived competence to reading achievement. Again, Chan found a developmental pattern. For ninth-grade students, belief in personal control, learned helplessness, and perceived cognitive competence had no direct influence on reading achievement. Instead, their influence was mediated through their influence on use of reading strategies which, in turn, positively and directly influenced reading achievement. For seventh-grade students, a belief in personal control positively and learned helplessness negatively directly influenced reading achievement, while perceived cognitive competence had no influence on reading achievement. For fifth-grade students, learned helplessness negatively influenced reading achievement. Belief in personal control and perceived cognitive competence had no influence on reading achievement.

Achievement Outcomes Associated With Changes in Motivational Beliefs. Positive comprehension outcomes were associated with changes in motivational beliefs in both Schunk and Rice studies. Remedial readers in the strategy-plus-strategy usefulness groups answered significantly more comprehension questions on main ideas than remedial readers in the strategy-only and comprehension-only groups when pretest was used as a covariate. Only students in the combined groups demonstrated significantly increased motivational beliefs across the pre- and posttesting period.

Six weeks after the study, their motivational beliefs remained significantly higher than remedial readers in other groups 6 weeks after the study.

Summary

Nine studies were identified in which the relation between motivational beliefs and self-regulation or achievement were investigated. Motivational beliefs frequently were defined as personal beliefs about one's competency and the causes and controllability of academic outcomes. Motivational beliefs seldom were defined as personal beliefs about the benefits of using a strategy or the extent of academic successes and failures.

Overall, positive motivational beliefs were associated with effective strategy use, achievement gains, and normally achieving students, whereas negative motivational beliefs were associated with ineffective strategy use, lack of achievement gains, and diverse learners. Additionally, age appeared to be a factor in the development of motivational beliefs and in the influence of motivational beliefs on reading achievement. Self-regulation and achievement benefits from strategy instruction containing a motivational-belief component were demonstrated by diverse learners. Moreover, instruction targeting motivational beliefs enhanced long-term effects of strategy instruction. Negative motivational beliefs were altered by strategy instruction containing motivational beliefs or metacognitive knowledge components. Finally, positive motivational-belief changes were associated with positive changes in self-regulation and achievement.

Additional experimental research on the relations between motivational beliefs, self-regulation, and achievement, given knowledge, is needed. For example, future research could investigate whether negative motivational beliefs have to change in order for students to effectively use and benefit from knowledge. If the answer to this question is yes, subsequent research could investigate the most parsimonious approach to changing negative motivational beliefs. Finally, future research could investigate the amount of variability in achievement that is attributable to knowledge, motivational beliefs, and self-regulation using multiple regression procedures.

AREA OF CONVERGENCE 4:
Metacognitive Instruction Facilitates
Reading Comprehension

Until this point in the chapter, we separated discussions of metacognitive knowledge, self-regulation, and motivation to clarify the features of each and delineate each one's relation to reading comprehension. Our review revealed instructional commonalties that cut across metacognitive knowledge, self-regulation, and motivation interventions whether they were designed to increase metacognition directly or indirectly. For this area of convergence, we reunite metacognitive knowledge, self-regulation, and motivation to examine the role and features of instruction.

In this section, we focus on metacognitive instruction that enhanced reading comprehension rather than instruction that enhanced meta-cognition for two reasons: improved reading comprehension has tangible benefits for students, and many of the reviewed studies purported to increase metacognition, but actually measured reading comprehension as the outcome of instruction. In the following section, we discuss common instructional applications for metacognitive reading instruction that enhanced reading comprehension; the relation between metacognitive instruction and types of learners (i.e., normally achieving, diverse); and unresolved areas in metacognitive reading instruction.

Component Features of Instructional Applications

Because of several methodological limitations, we consider and treat evidence of instructional applications as preliminary. First, metacognition is a fairly new area of research. The construct itself is "fuzzy" with unclear boundaries and multiple components. Similar to any new area of investigation, metacognition is subject to a variety of interpretations. Second, most analyzed studies contained small numbers of participants, thereby limiting generalizations. Third, the metacognitive interventions included varying components and degrees of metacognition and cognitive strategies, making it difficult to determine whether enhanced reading comprehension was attributable to metacognitive components, cognitive strategies, or both.

Bearing in mind that evidence is preliminary, the following instructional dimensions appeared across interventions designed to directly or indirectly increase metacognition and reading comprehension:

- Reading context;
- Cognitive reading strategies;
- Metacognitive components;
- Explicit instruction;
- Modeling;
- Interaction;
- Increased student control;
- Guided practice; and
- Systematic feedback.

Reading Context. All but one of the primary metacognitive reading interventions (i.e., Simmonds, 1990) used narrative or expository text written specifically for the studies or text similar to those used in remedial programs (e.g., *Reading for Concepts*). The studies reviewed in the secondary sources also occurred in the context of reading passages. However, the secondary reviews did not usually provide sufficient information to identify the reading content specifically, that is, whether the passages were written for the interventions or taken from students' normal classroom materials.

Familiarity of content during initial instruction factored in strategy acquisition but not in improved free, literal, or inferential recall. When compared to students receiving strategy instruction using passages that contained unfamiliar content, students who received strategy instruction using familiar content demonstrated significantly more strategy use at immediate and delayed posttests. Even though familiar content significantly affected strategy use, there were no significant differences between the two instructional groups in free, literal, or inferential recall (Gaultney, 1995).

Cognitive Reading Strategies. Metacognition did not occur as an isolated component in any of the studies. Rather, metacognitive instruction occurred concurrently with instruction in one or more cognitive reading strategies. Instruction proceeded in one of two ways: Teachers taught a cognitive reading strategy directly, or teachers used prereading strategies (e.g., discussion, advance organizers) to either organize the new knowledge or link students' prior knowledge to new information. In general, interventions in which strategies were taught directly provided more lasting benefit than interventions in which teachers used but did not teach strategies (Billingsley & Wildman, 1990).

The most common cognitive strategies in the metacognitive interventions were procedures to *summarize* (Malone & Mastropieri, 1992; Palincsar & Brown, cited in Billingsley & Wildman, 1990; Rottman & Cross, 1990; Weisberg & Balajthy, cited in Weisberg, 1988; Wong et al., cited in Weisberg, 1998), *identify main ideas* (Graves, cited in Weisberg, 1988; Schunk & Rice, 1992, Study 2; Wong et al., cited in Weisberg, 1988; Wong & Jones, cited in Billingsley & Wildman, 1990), *promote visual imagery* (Chan et al., 1990; Clark et al., cited in Weisberg, 1988; Gambrell & Koskenen, cited in Weisberg, 1988; Pressley, cited in Harris & Pressley, 1991), and *map expository or story grammar elements* (Boyle, 1996; Idol, cited in Billingsley & Wildman, 1990; Idol & Croll, cited in Billingsley & Wildman, 1990).

Teacher-presented prereading activities that were assumed to induce self-regulation included discussing passages to facilitate interaction between readers' prior knowledge and incoming information (Paris et al.,

1991); evoking a network of relevant associations to prepare students for constructing the meaning of a text (Beck et al., cited in Billingsley & Wildman, 1990; Idol-Maestas, cited in Billingsley & Wildman, 1990); and asking questions that focused on the main character and goal of a story, while students skimmed the story to make predictions (Sachs, cited in Billingsley & Wildman, 1990).

Metacognition Components. Interventions included various combinations of metacognitive knowledge, self-regulation, and motivation. Some contained one component; others included several.

Nine studies taught the *usefulness of a strategy,* a metacognitive knowledge component (i.e., Borkowski, Carr, Rellinger, & Pressley cited in Paris et al., 1991; Boyle, 1996; Duffy et al., cited in Paris et al., 1991; Hansen & Pearson, cited in Paris et al., 1991; Palincsar & Brown, cited in Billingsley & Wildman, 1990; Pressley cited in Harris & Pressley, 1991; Rottman & Cross, 1990; Schunk & Rice, 1992, Study 1; Wong & Jones, cited in Billingsley & Wildman, 1990). Three of the studies taught usefulness of a strategy as a means to increase motivation; however, it is important to note that each operationalized metacognitive knowledge differently. In their first study, Schunk and Rice explicitly linked student achievement to accurate strategy use. In their second study, they operationalized knowledge as modification of one strategy (procedures to identify a main idea) to perform a different task (procedures to identify supporting details). Borkowski et al. (cited in Paris et al., 1991) told students the importance of using strategies, but the secondary review did not provide examples of the wording the investigators used.

Whereas usefulness of a strategy was the most common metacognitive knowledge component in the reviewed studies, *knowledge of task demands* was the second most common. Three studies addressed the relation of knowledge of task demands and reading comprehension (i.e., Chan et al., 1987; Rottman & Cross, 1990; Schunk & Rice, 1992).

The most common self-regulation component was *self-monitoring,* which included: reading comprehension or strategy use (Dewitz et al., cited in Paris et al., 1991; Malone & Mastropieri, 1992; Markman & Gorin, cited in Paris et al., 1991; Palincsar & Brown, cited in Billingsley & Wildman, 1990; Paris & Myers, cited in Paris et al., 1991; Schunk & Rice, 1992); reading comprehension using a self-questioning procedure (Billingsley & Wildman, cited in Billingsley & Wildman, 1990; Carnine & Kinder, cited in Billingsley & Wildman, 1990; Chan & Cole, cited in Weisberg, 1988; Clark et al., cited in Weisberg, 1988; Singer & Dolan, cited in Billingsley & Wildman, 1990; Wong & Jones, cited in Billingsley & Wildman, 1990); or identifying inconsistent information while reading passages (Baker, cited in Paris et al., 1991; Billingsley & Wildman, cited in Billingsley & Wildman, 1990; Chan et al., 1987).

In the Wong and Jones study (cited in Billingsley & Wildman, 1990) on self-questioning to monitor reading comprehension, eighth and ninth graders with learning disabilities and normally achieving sixth graders were taught to ask themselves the purpose for studying a passage (to answer questions that they would be given later); underline the main idea(s) in a paragraph; think of a question about the main idea; learn the answer to the question; and look back at previous questions and answers to see how each successive question and answer provided more information. Both Singer and Dolan, and Carnine and Kinder taught high school students (Singer & Dolan, cited in Billingsley & Wildman, 1990) or fourth-, fifth-, and sixth-grade low performers (Carnine & Kinder, cited in Billingsley & Wildman, 1990) to self-question based on story grammar elements (e.g., Who is the leading character? What is the character trying to accomplish? What stands in the way of the main character reaching the desired goal?). In teaching students to monitor for inconsistent text, Chan et al. (1987) pointed out an inconsistent sentence in text and explicitly explained that the sentence dealt with one topic whereas the story was about something else.

Explicit Instruction. Explicit instruction occurred in the majority of the interventions designed to increase metacognition directly or to induce metacognition indirectly (e.g., Boyle, 1996; Chan et al., 1987; Chan et al., 1990; Gaultney, 1995; Hansen & Pearson, cited in Weisberg, 1988; Harris, cited in Harris & Pressley, 1991; Markman, & Gorin, cited in Paris et al., 1991; Paris & Myers, cited in Paris et al., 1991; Pressley, cited in Harris & Pressley, 1991; Simmonds, 1990; Wong & Jones cited in Billingsley & Wildman, 1990). Explicit instruction was used differently, however, depending on whether metacognition was taught directly or induced. Direct interventions taught metacognitive components (e.g., the usefulness of a strategy, task demands) explicitly, whereas indirect interventions taught cognitive strategies (e.g., summarize, predict) explicitly with the assumption that the strategies would, in turn, enhance metacognition.

Modeling. Modeling is another instructional feature that occurred in the majority of interventions (e.g., Billingsley & Wildman, 1990; Borkowski, 1992; Boyle, 1996; Chan et al., 1987; Gaultney, 1995; Idol & Croll, cited in Billingsley & Wildman, 1990; Palincsar & Brown, cited in Billingsley & Wildman, 1990; Schunk & Rice, 1992, Studies 1 & 2; Simmonds, 1990). Teachers modeled by explicitly and overtly "thinking aloud" the steps for performing a strategy. In some studies, teachers also modeled why they performed the strategy. Schunk and Rice, 1992, Study 1, provided an example of the procedure. The teacher modeled each step of a 5-step comprehension strategy:

1. read the question,
2. read the passage to determine what it is mostly about,
3. think about what the details have in common,
4. think about what would make a good title, and
5. reread the story if you do not know the answer to a question.

At Step 4, the teacher modeled how to determine a good title using story details that had something in common, and that trying to think of a good title helps the reader remember important ideas in a story.

One issue concerning modeling is whether it alone is sufficient to benefit reading comprehension or whether modeling must be accompanied with explicit instruction. The evidence is mixed and may depend on the reading context, tasks, and students' ability. Simmonds (1990) found that modeling alone without explicit instruction was sufficient to teach students with learning disabilities a constraint-seeking questioning strategy. Modeling alone may have been sufficient because the strategy (constraint-seeking questions) was simple and easy to learn for 9- to 12-year-old students. Contrary to the finding by Simmonds, Chan et al. (1987) and Schunk and Rice (1992) found modeling-plus-explicit instruction or specific feedback to be more effective than modeling alone for diverse learners.

Interaction. A common assumption of metacognitive instruction is that interaction induces the social construction of metacognition (e.g., Palincsar, cited in Billingsley & Wildman, 1990). For example, teacher dialogue that includes how to do a task and providing feedback to students' responses facilitates understanding of the purpose of a task and execution of a strategy (Meichenbaum, cited in Harris & Pressley, 1991). Additionally, discussions between students provide opportunities for metacognitive exchanges and modeling (Palincsar et al., 1991). In the reviewed studies, interactions occurred between teacher and students (e.g., Hansen & Pearson, cited in Weisberg, 1988; Harris & Pressley, 1991), and target students and peers (e.g., Palincsar & Brown, cited in Billingsley & Wildman, 1990; Paris et al., cited in Paris et al., 1991). Through discussions, cooperative activities, and peer conferences, students interacted to determine goals for instruction; implement, evaluate, and modify strategy acquisition and use; discuss how a strategy could be applied in situations other than the reading lessons (e.g., Palincsar & Brown, cited in Billingsley & Wildman, 1990); and make the strategies concrete and sensible (Cross & Lipson, cited in Paris et al., 1991). Borkowski (1992) suggested that students rather than teachers play a major role in dialogue.

Increased Student Control. Billingsley and Wildman (1990) called increasing student control an important dimension of comprehension instruction. In many of the reviewed studies (e.g., Idol & Croll, cited in Billingsley & Wildman, 1990; Idol-Maestas, cited in Billingsley & Wildman, 1990; Palincsar & Brown, cited in Paris et al., 1991; Schunk & Rice, 1992), instruction occurred along a continuum of teacher versus student control. For example, instruction included three phases: teacher control usually by modeling; a bridge to gradually transfer control to students; and independent student application. Examples of teacher control included teachers modeling how to complete a story map (Idol & Croll, cited in Billingsley & Wildman, 1990; Idol-Maestas, cited in Billingsley & Wildman, 1990); predict, question, clarify, and summarize (Palincsar & Brown, cited in Paris et al., 1991); use a 5-step reading comprehension strategy (Schunk & Rice, Study 1); and ask *why* questions while reading (Gaultney, 1995). Examples of gradual transfer to student control included having students (a) read and provide information for a story map while the teacher supervised (Idol-Maestas, cited in Billingsley & Wildman, 1990); (b) model how to predict, question, clarify, and summarize with teacher input as needed (Palincsar & Brown, cited in Paris et al., 1991); (c) prove encouragement, feedback, and correction (Palincsar & Brown, cited in Paris et al., 1991); (d) verbalize and overtly perform five steps to a comprehension strategy under teacher guidance (Schunk & Rice, Study 1); and (e) progress from answering the *why* questions asked by the teacher to asking and answering *why* questions independently (Gaultney, 1995). Finally, students completed story maps (Idol-Maestas, cited in Billingsley & Wildman, 1990), applied the 5-step comprehension strategy (Schunk & Rice, Study 1), or asked and answered why questions (Gaultney, 1995) independently.

Guided Practice. Chan et al. (1990) concluded that students require adequate time and practice to increase metacognition. Guided practice provides students repeated opportunities to practice procedures of a strategy under teacher supervision. During the guided practice phase of the interventions examined, teachers (a) praised, prompted, or provided additional modeling, as appropriate (Idol & Croll, cited in Billingsley & Wildman, 1990; Palincsar & Brown, cited in Billingsley & Wildman, 1990; Paris et al., cited in Paris et al., 1991; Pressley, cited in Harris & Pressley, 1991); (b) faded prompts and increased the criterion level as students improved (Harris & Pressley, 1991); (c) referred to the appropriate strategy step (Schunk & Rice, 1992); (d) asked students to verbalize a strategy step (Schunk & Rice, 1992); or (e) provided practice using texts of increasingly difficult reading levels (Boyle, 1996) or increasing lengths (Pressley, cited in Harris & Pressley, 1991) and using expository materials rather than brief skill exercises (Paris et al., cited in Paris et al., 1991). Billingsley and Wildman suggested that teachers vary materials appropriate to students' reading levels and background knowledge so that students can concentrate on comprehension thereby minimizing the effect of decoding problems.

Systematic Feedback. Cross and Lipson (cited in Paris et al., 1991) concluded that diverse learners require considerable practice with feedback to increase metacognition. In addition, feedback should be specific, carefully planned, and timed (Billingsley & Wildman, 1990).

Several interventions contained feedback for strategy use during comprehension activities (e.g., Boyle, 1996; Harris cited in Harris & Pressley, 1991; Idol & Croll, cited in Billingsley & Wildman, 1990; Malone & Mastropieri, 1992; Palincsar & Brown, cited in Billingsley & Wildman, 1990; Paris et al., cited in Paris et al., 1991; Simmonds, 1990). Feedback specifically linked success in answering questions to strategy use (i.e., strategy-value feedback; Schunk & Rice, 1992) and included re-explanations and re-instruction as needed (Harris, cited in Harris & Pressley, 1991) In addition to teachers, peers provided feedback that included encouragement and corrections (Palincsar & Brown, cited in cited in Paris et al., 1991).

Another common feature was the timing and distribution of feedback. Across interventions, teachers provided feedback at different intervals. Students received feedback continuously (Palincsar & Brown, cited in Billingsley & Wildman, 1990; Simmonds, 1990): individually three- to four-times per 35-minute instructional period (Schunk & Rice, 1992), weekly for performance on comprehension tests (Palincsar & Brown, cited in Billingsley & Wildman, 1990), or at the end of strategy instruction to reinforce usefulness of a strategy (Wong & Jones, cited in Billingsley & Wildman, 1990). One study provided feedback only at the end of the first guided practice session (Boyle, 1996).

Relations Between Instructional
Components and Learners

Normally Achieving Learners. No definitive evidence emerged from this review to determine whether metacognitive instruction benefits or hinders normally achieving students. As a result of this synthesis, we suggest that the benefit of metacognitive instruction for normally achieving students may be dependent on metacognitive components, cognitive strategies, reading tasks, and ages of students.

The metacognitive component that appeared helpful for normally achieving and diverse learners alike is knowledge of the purpose of reading (Wong, Wong, & LeMare, cited in Weisberg, 1988). Another component, self-regulation, enhanced comprehension for some normally achieving learners, but not others. For example, on a reading comprehension measure, self-management plus summarization training was more effective than summarization alone for good junior college writers (Day, cited in Paris et al., 1991). However, self-questioning, another form of self-regulation, was not significantly different from rereading for 11-year-old average readers (Chan & Cole, cited in Weisberg, 1988). Furthermore, self-questioning when combined with a strategy to identify main ideas was not significantly different than the strategy alone for sixth-grade normally achieving students (Wong & Jones, cited in Billingsley & Wildman, 1990). In contrast to studies that indicated significant enhancement of reading comprehension, one study (Hansen & Pearson, cited in Weisberg, 1988) found that knowledge of strategy importance did not significantly enhance reading performance of normally achieving students, but significantly enhanced reading comprehension of diverse learners. More research and further analyses are required to impact the effect of metacognitive instruction on reading comprehension performance of normally achieving students.

Diverse Learners. The studies reviewed provided evidence that metacognitive instruction enhances reading comprehension for diverse learners. Additionally, the studies provided limited support that diverse learners may require instruction on "more" rather than less metacognitive components than average achievers and that such instruction will require greater attention to instructional features. The conclusion that diverse learners require *more* instruction may covary with student familiarity with text (e.g., more familiarity with narrative than expository) and task complexity (e.g., short-answer questions vs. retell).

In five studies, diverse learners benefited from metacognitive instruction while normally achieving students showed no significant benefit. For example, diverse learners, but not normally achieving students, benefited from instruction that included (a) purpose, usefulness, or importance of a strategy (Hansen & Pearson, cited in Weisberg, 1988; Wong & Jones, cited in Billingsley & Wildman, 1990); (b) self-questioning (Chan & Cole, cited in Weisberg, 1988); (c) knowledge of task demands and self-regulation (Chan et al., 1987); and (d) self-regulation (Chan et al., 1990).

Two types of studies provided support that more metacognitive components benefit diverse learners: studies that compared instruction on a strategy-plus-metacognitive component with the strategy alone, and studies comparing multiple metacognitive components with a limited number of metacognitive components. Four studies provided evidence that instruction on a cognitive strategy-plus-metacognitive component benefited diverse learners more when compared to strategy instruction alone. Instruction on a strategy to identify main ideas plus self-monitoring and remediation (Graves, cited in Weisberg, 1988), or self-questioning (Wong & Jones, cited in Billingsley & Wildman, 1990) was more effective than instruction on the main idea strategy alone for diverse learners. Teaching students to modify a main idea strategy to identify supporting details was more effective than teaching students to assist them in identifying supporting details without modifying a previously taught strategy (Schunk & Rice, 1992, Study 2). Finally, strategy instruction plus specific feedback linking reading comprehension achievement to strategy use was more effective than strategy instruction alone (Schunk & Rice, Study 1). Because of the combination of metacognitive components, it is difficult to discern whether systematic feedback, metacognitive knowledge (i.e., linking achievement to strategy use), or the combination of feedback and metacognitive knowledge was the component that made strategy instruction plus feedback more effective than strategy instruction alone.

A limited number of studies have been conducted to support the additive effects of metacognitive components for diverse learners. Specifically, students demonstrated more benefit from instruction in summarization plus knowledge of strategy use and self-monitoring than from instruction without the self-monitoring component (Malone & Mastropieri, 1992), and knowledge of task demands, self-regulation, and usefulness of the strategy than from instruction without the usefulness of the strategy component (Schunk & Rice, 1992, Study 1).

Evidence that diverse learners benefited from systematic attention to *instructional elements* came from two types of studies: comparisons of more and fewer instructional elements with diverse learners, and comparisons between diverse and normally achieving learners. The studies comparing more with less for diverse learners occurred in a variety of reading tasks. When monitoring narrative text for inconsistencies, modeling plus explicit explanation was more effective than modeling alone for 11-year-old students with learning disabilities (Chan et al., 1987). In a 5-step comprehension strategy that addressed the purpose of reading and identification of main ideas and supporting details to enhance comprehension, modeling plus specific feedback on the value of a strategy was significantly more beneficial than modeling without explicit feedback on post- and maintenance tests for fourth- and fifth-grade remedial readers (Schunk & Rice, 1992, Study 1).

Research also suggested that diverse learners required more elements of effective instruction than normally achieving students. For example, 11-year-old diverse learners benefited significantly from modeling plus explicit instruction when compared with modeling alone (Chan & Cole, cited in Weisberg, 1988). However, modeling alone was sufficient for 8-year-old normally achieving students.

Finally, the conclusion that diverse learners require *more* carefully designed metacognitive components may be *content specific*. For example, the effects of metacognitive components may depend on student familiarity with text. Malone and Mastropieri (1992) found that self-monitoring in conjunction with summarization instruction using narrative text did not benefit students with learning disabilities in Grades 6, 7, and 8. However, when summarization with self-monitoring was transferred to expository text, the students receiving self-monitoring instruction outperformed students receiving instruction in summarization only.

Additionally, the efficacy of instruction may vary differentially with the *task complexity* on the outcome measure. For example, Wong, Wong, and LeMare (cited in Weisberg, 1988) found that instruction regarding the purpose of reading was effective for a criterion measure but not for free recall for diverse learners. On the free recall measure, diverse learners who received explicit instruction regarding which passages to study in addition to metacognitive knowledge about the purpose for reading performed better than students not told which passages to study. Wong, Wong, and LeMare concluded that free recall may be too diverse a measure to use with students with learning disabilities.

When no metacognitive components were involved and the students were poor readers without learning disabilities, strategy instruction with no metacognitive components did not significantly benefit free, literal, or inferential recall (Gaultney, 1995). However, significant positive correlations between strategy use and outcome measures differed among the variables: type of recall (i.e., free, literal, inferential), type of content used for strategy training (i.e., familiar unfamiliar), type of content used in the outcome measure (familiar, unfamiliar), and time of test (immediate, delayed posttests). Students receiving strategy instruction using familiar content demonstrated significant positive correlations between strategy use and free recall whether the measures contained familiar or unfamiliar content or occurred during the immediate or delayed posttest. Students receiving strategy instruction using unfamiliar content demonstrated a significant correlation between strategy use and free recall only on the delayed posttest for both stories containing familiar or unfamiliar content. Interestingly, students receiving instruction in familiar content demonstrated a strong positive correlation between strategy use and literal recall only during the immediate posttest and only for stories that contained familiar content, and students who received strategy instruction using unfamiliar content demonstrated a significant positive correlation for inferential recall only during the delayed posttest and only for stories that contained unfamiliar content.

More research is required to determine the quantity and combinations of metacognitive components and instructional elements that effectively and efficiently produce long-lasting reading comprehension improvement for diverse learners. Additionally, research is required to determine what dimensions of reading comprehension benefit from metacognitive instruction.

Unresolved Issues

The ambiguities and variations that riddle metacognition research also add to potential confusion about best practices. What people do to improve reading comprehension under the "umbrella" of metacognition covaries between research studies, reading tasks, degrees of metacognition, and learner abilities, making it difficult to compare studies or reach clear conclusions. Although early research has provided fundamental knowledge of metacognition, what we do not yet know is the most effective or efficient balance between cognitive strategies, metacognitive components, and instructional techniques. Nor do we know the appropriate balance between teacher versus student control and direct versus indirect instruction (i.e., induced metacognition). The following discussion focuses on unresolved areas of metacognitive instruction.

Multiple Interacting Factors. Demonstrative of the complexities and unresolved issues in metacognitive instruction are the varying results in a study by Gaultney (1995) described previously in this chapter. Significant strategy use and correlations between strategy use and passage recall varied depending on multiple factors. For example, (a) students with higher prior declarative knowledge demonstrated significantly more strategy use than students with lower prior metacognitive declarative knowledge, (b) students with lower metacognitive declarative knowledge demonstrated significant correlations between strategy use and free recall at immediate and delayed posttests on passages with familiar content but only at delayed posttest on passages with less familiar content, (c) students with higher prior declarative metacognitive knowledge demonstrated a significant correlation between strategy use and free recall only if they had received strategy instruction using passages with familiar content and only on the delayed posttest on passages with familiar content. Because of the varied results, Gaultney concluded that strategic behavior is complex and probably influenced by multiple interacting factors including prior metacognitive declarative knowledge, content familiarity of the reading passages used in instruction, content familiarity of the passages used to measure reading comprehension, and time of the posttests (i.e., immediate, delayed).

Prior Metacognitive Declarative Knowledge. One factor not previously addressed in this chapter is prior metacognitive knowledge. The Gaultney (1995) study is the only study in this synthesis to include prior metacognitive declarative knowledge as one factor in strategy instruction. Although Gaultney's study was restricted to fourth- and fifth-grade male poor readers, she found (a) prior metacognitive declarative knowledge and not strategy instruction impacted passage recall, (b) students with higher rather than lower prior metacognitive declarative knowledge demonstrated significant strategy use during the posttests, and (c) students with lower rather than higher metacognitive declarative knowledge demonstrated more significant correlations between strategy use and free recall. Because of the varying results of strategy instruction in the Gaultney study and in studies comparing normally achieving and diverse learners, we feel that the effect of prior metacognitive declarative knowledge on strategy acquisition and reading comprehension requires further investigation.

Reading Context. Researchers and educators frequently recommend that metacognitive instruction occur in the context of authentic reading texts and tasks. To facilitate transfer, Harris and Pressley (1991) recommended that students practice with a variety of texts of varying lengths. In our review, we found that, while the reading tasks were authentic, most reading passages were adapted to simplify reading difficulty and reduce word recognition as a barrier to learning new strategies and increasing metacognition. Further research is required to determine whether initiating instruction with adapted passages and transferring to grade-level text is more effective and efficient for diverse learners than initiating instruction with grade-level text.

Cognitive Reading Strategies. At this time, it is impossible to identify which cognitive reading strategies, when included in a metacognitive reading intervention, most greatly enhanced reading comprehension. In his analysis of cognitive strategy instruction, Swanson (1989) found no best cognitive strategy to teach to diverse learners within or across domains. Rather, he noted that the type of expected learning outcome determines the rank ordering of importance of different strategies. Weisberg (1988) reported that cognitive strategies requiring greater reader interaction with text and greater depth of processing (e.g., generating summaries, construction graphic organizers or semantic maps) are more helpful than simply rereading as a fix-it strategy. Weisberg suggested that graphic organizers or semantic maps may provide greater benefit because they help students differentiate important from unimportant ideas and comprehend relationship among ideas. Additionally, because they make concepts and relations between concepts more visible, graphic organizers and semantic maps may prevent cognitive overload.

The specific cognitive strategy to include in metacognitive instruction most probably requires a critical analysis of the task, student needs and characteristics (Harris & Pressley, 1991), and the expected learning outcomes. For example, certain strategies are better suited to enhance comprehension of previously read information, whereas others are more appropriate for facilitating memory of words or facts.

Metacognitive Components. Two issues add to the ambiguity of metacognitive instruction. First, metacognitive research does not always match the rhetoric on metacognition. Second, the metacognitive components in interventions vary and range from none to several, making it difficult to determine which specific component or "how much" metacognition is sufficient to design effective efficient instruction for diverse learners.

Although metacognitive rhetoric recommends teaching where or when to use a strategy, the usefulness of a strategy, and motivation, only one study in this review (Rottman & Cross, 1990) included information about when to choose one strategy over another. On the other hand, nine studies supported teaching the usefulness of a strategy. In our analysis of the studies that included motivation, we found that the component described as motivational was often explicit instruction in a metacognitive knowledge component such as usefulness of a strategy. More research is required to elucidate essential features of effective metacognitive instruction and necessary emphases such as where and when to use a strategy or a motivation component. More research is also required to determine whether motivation is really teaching metacognitive knowledge (e.g., usefulness of a strategy, knowledge of self as a learner) intensely and sufficiently to change students' misrules about themselves as a learner or communicate the link between strategy application and achievement.

Interventions included a range of none to several metacognitive components in various combinations making it difficult to determine which components or combinations of components benefited reading comprehension. Interventions included: (a) self-regulation only (e.g., Chan et al., 1990), (b) a combination of metacognitive knowledge components (e.g., usefulness of strategy, task demands, usefulness of prior knowledge, when to use a strategy; Rottman & Cross, 1990), or (c) a combination of metacognitive knowledge and self-regulation (e.g., Chan et al., 1987).

Direct Instruction Versus Induced Metacognition. Another unresolved area in metacognitive instruction involves the theoretical issue of direct instruction versus induced metacognition. The question is whether students internalize and maintain metacognition when taught through a mediator or when required to induce metacognition themselves. Palincsar et al. (1991) examined this question in a study comparing three matched instructional groups: third graders ranging from first- through fifth-grade reading ability who received direct instruction in reading strategies; received reciprocal teaching in which students modeled strategies for each other; and generated their own reading strategies without explicit instruction (collaborative problem solving). On a reading comprehension measure, the students who generated their own reading strategies outperformed students who received direct instruction or reciprocal teaching. An analysis of the procedures revealed that direct instruction of reading strategies contained no metacognitive instruction. On the other hand, instruction designed to induce students to generate their own reading strategies used metacognitive components including knowledge of the purposes for reading, role of prior knowledge in determining one's approach to reading, and efficiency of different strategies. This leads us to propose that Palincsar et al. compared the degrees of metacognition in instruction (i.e., no components in direct instruction versus at least three in collaborative problem solving) instead of explicit strategy instruction versus induced strategies.

Another example of an intervention that is frequently cited as one that induces rather than directly teaches metacognition is reciprocal teaching (Palincsar & Klenk, cited in Borkowski, 1992). However, reciprocal teaching includes several metacognitive components, including attending to demands of each reading task (e.g., summarizing, clarifying, predicting), planning alternative approaches, selecting a reasonable choice, judging the success of performance as it unfolds, and finally trying a different approach if needed (Borkowski). We suggest that reciprocal teaching may increase reading comprehension, not by inducing metacognition, but because it contains metacognitive components.

Instructional Time. A sixth unresolved area is amount of time allocated for metacognitive instruction. Instructional time varied across studies, metacognitive components, and age and diversity of students. The shortest intervention, one that taught self-monitoring using a cross-referencing technique, occurred in one lesson (Chan et al., 1987). The longest intervention, lasting 6 months (Duffy et al., cited in Paris et al., 1991), involved educating teachers to provide more detailed explanations about reading strategies and resulted in increased student metacognition about their reading lessons. No reading comprehension results were reported. Three additional longer studies were: reciprocal teaching (Palincsar & Brown, cited in Paris et al., 1991; 20 days); a comparison of direct instruction, reciprocal instruction, and collaborative strategy building (Palincsar et al., 1991; 25 sessions, for 30 to 40 minutes each); and instruction in a self-questioning strategy to identify main ideas and summarize paragraphs (Wong et al., cited in Weisberg, 1988; 5.5 months).

Because of varied times for instruction, metacognitive components, instructional procedures, and types of measures, it is difficult to determine an optimal time to allocate for instruction. For example, shorter interventions (e.g., 1 lesson, 4 days) either did not improve reading comprehension (Gaultney , 1995) or include maintenance measures. Additionally, the 4-day study (Chan et al., 1990) did not benefit diverse students when scaffolded materials were faded, leading Chan et al. to conclude that, for diverse learners, scaffolding must be faded slowly and adequate time and practice must be provided for diverse students to master strategies. Rottman and Cross (1990) incorporated 5 weeks of instruction, but attempted to teach five strategies during that time. Because of weak effects for reading comprehension, they concluded that they taught too many strategies (5) in too short a time and that it would be better to teach fewer strategies and devote more instructional time to each.

On the other hand, the two Schunk and Rice (1992) studies were longer, 35 minutes a day for 15 days and 20 days respectively. The participants, students with reading deficiencies in Grades 4 and 5, maintained increased comprehension gains and motivation improvements on measures administered 60 days after completion of the interventions.

Bearing in mind that metacognition for normally achieving students develops slowly until students are in their teens (Garner & Alexander, cited in Harris & Pressley, 1991), we suggest that, for diverse learners, longer interventions may be more effective and longer lasting than shorter interventions. Ample time may be required for diverse students to experience sufficient modeling, guided practice in a variety of texts, and systematic feedback in order to develop metacognition and independent strategy use. Further research is required to more clearly define "ample time."

Summary

The reviewed studies provided evidence that metacognitive instruction enhanced reading comprehension of diverse learners. However, there was mixed support for the same benefit for normally achieving students. Metacognitive interventions consisted of multiple and varied metacognitive components and instructional features. The most frequent metacognitive components were knowledge of usefulness of a strategy, knowledge of task demands, and self-monitoring. Generally, metacognitive instruction occurred in the context of narrative and expository passages written for the intervention and concurrently with cognitive strategy instruction. The most common cognitive strategies were summarizing, identifying main ideas, using visual imagery, and mapping narrative or expository text. Instruction was explicit and incorporated modeling, interaction, increased student control, guided practice, and systematic feedback.

Because metacognitive instruction consists of multiple components, it is unclear how to translate research to practice. Future research is required to determine the most effective and efficient balance between cognitive strategies, metacognitive components, and instructional techniques. The balance may vary, depending on student ability and prior knowledge, text type, task demands, and cognitive strategies.

SUMMARY

Our review of the literature examining the relation between reading metacognition and reading comprehension resulted in four areas of convergence:

1. Metacognitive knowledge facilitates reading comprehension.
2. Self-regulation facilitates reading comprehension.
3. Motivation may mediate students' use and benefit from meta-cognitive knowledge and self-regulation strategies.
4. Metacognitive instruction facilitates reading comprehension.

Three outcomes were consistent across the first three areas of convergence. First, metacognitive knowledge, self-regulation, and motivational beliefs each are multifaceted variables. Second, diverse learners are significantly less likely than normally achieving students to demonstrate metacognitive knowledge, self-regulation skills, and motivation to use knowledge effectively. Third, diverse learners benefit from strategy instruction containing metacognitive knowledge, self-regulation, or motivational belief features. Because metacognitive instruction incorporates multiple and varied metacognitive components and instructional features, future research is required to identify parsimonious and effective instruction that maintains comprehension gains and improves motivation for diverse learners.

TABLE 12.1
Secondary and Primary Sources for a Synthesis of Research on the Relation Between Reading Metacognition and Reading Comprehension

Secondary Sources

Authors	Dimension of Metacognition	Participants	Purpose
Billingsley & Wildman (1990)	Knowledge; self-regulation	Accomplished readers, poor readers, at-risk students, remedial readers, students with LD, elementary, adolescents; secondary	Linked metacognitive theory and research to instructional practices that are designed to increase readers' control of comprehension processes
Borkowski (1992)	Self-regulation; beliefs about "self" as learner	Students with LD	Argued for a reciprocal relationship between self-regulated learning and beliefs about "self" as learner; discussed "working models" of metacognitive instruction and their roles in classroom teaching
Harris & Pressley (1991)	Knowledge; self-regulation	Students with LD and other learning problems	Argued that constructivism and explicit cognitive strategy instruction are not incompatible; illustrated the contribution of good cognitive strategy instruction to the education of students with LD and other learning problems

Johnston & Winograd (1985)	Self-regulation; motivation	Poor readers	Addressed relation between passive failure and reading comprehension, with implications for reading instruction
Paris, Wasik, & Turner (1991)	Knowledge; self-regulation; motivation	Strategic readers, young unskilled readers, remedial readers, students with LD, Grades 4, 5, 6, and 7	Described development of strategic readers, and changes due to mental growth, motivation, instruction, and social guidance
Swanson (1989)	Knowledge; self-regulation	Students with LD	Addressed the advantages of strategy instruction, and the components and principles of effective strategy use
Weisberg (1988)	Knowledge; self-regulation	Students with reading/learning disabilities	Reviewed influence of prior knowledge, text structure, task demands, and metacognitive strategies; concluded reading disabled students require explicit instruction
Wong (1992)	Self-regulation; cognitive process-based instruction	Students with LD	Clarified fundamental differences between cognitive process-based instruction and process training; discussed the relevance, possibilities, and difficulties in applying cognitive process-based instruction for students with LD

(continued)

TABLE 12.1
CONTINUED

Authors	Dimension of Metacognition	Subjects	Purpose
Primary Sources			
Boyle (1996)	Knowledge	20 LD, 10 with educable mental retardation; Grades 6, 7, and 8	Examined effects of instruction in a cognitive mapping strategy on (a) student independent use of the strategy, (b) literal and/or inferential comprehension, (c) metacognitive knowledge, (d) attitudes toward reading, and (e) comprehension on standardized measures; matched pairs group design
Chen (1994)	Knowledge; motivation	Grade 5: 18 with learning difficulties, 86 without learning difficulties; Grade 7: 43 with learning difficulties, 90 without learning difficulties; Grade 9: 25 with learning difficulties, 76 without learning difficulties	Examined the development of attributional beliefs with respect to ability, attributional beliefs, and strategy use and strategic learning; examined relationship among expectations of success, strategic learning, and reading achievement; group design
Chan, Cole, & Barfett (1987)	Knowledge; self-regulation	32 general education, age 8 years, 2 months; 32 with LD, age 11	Compared general and specific instruction in monitoring text for internal inconsistency; group design
Chan, Cole, & Morris (1990)	Strategy; self-regulation	39 average readers, Grade 3; 39 disabled readers, upper primary	Compared visualization instruction only, visualization instruction plus pictorial display, and read–reread; group design

Cornoldi (1990)	Knowledge; self-regulation	*Study 1*: Normal readers, poor comprehenders; Grades 2 & 5; *Study 2*: Good and poor comprehenders; Grades 2 & 5	*Study 1*: Examined whether metacognitive awareness is a cause of differences between good and poor comprehenders; *Study 2*: Examined good and poor comprehenders ability to judge difficulty and learning progress in memory tasks
Gaultney (1995)	Knowledge	45 poor readers; Grades 4 & 5	Examined whether prior metacognitive and domain knowledge facilitate the acquisition of a reading comprehension strategy; group design
Hannah & Shore (1995)	Knowledge	Grades 5 & 6: 6 gifted LD, 6 average-achieving, 6 LD; Grades 11 & 12: 6 gifted, 6 gifted LD, 6 average-achieving, 6 LD	Compared metacognitive knowledge, metacognitive skills, error detection, and comprehension of gifted, gifted LD, average-achieving, and LD; group design
Malone & Mastropieri (1992)	Knowledge; self-regulation	Students with LD; 13 Grade 6, 15 Grade 7, 17 Grade 8	Compared summarization instruction, summarization instruction with a self-monitoring component, and traditional instruction; group design
Palincsar, David, & Winn (1991)	Self-regulation	Heterogeneous; 2 classrooms; Grade 3	Reviewed six models of strategy instruction; compared Direct Instruction, Reciprocal Teaching, and Collaborative Problem Solving; matched triads group design

(Continued)

TABLE 12.1
CONTINUED

Pintrich, Anderman, & Klobucar (1994)	Knowledge; motivation	19 with LD, 20 without LD; Grade 5	Compared motivation and metacognitive knowledge of students with and without LD; examined relations between motivation and metacognitive knowledge; examined intraindividual differences in relations between motivation and cognition across groups of students with and without LD; group design
Rottman & Cross (1990)	Knowledge; self-competence	18 with LD; ages 8 & 9	Evaluated metacognitive reading program to improve awareness about reading and comprehension skills; trend analysis, cluster analysis
Schunk & Rice (1992)	Knowledge; self-regulation	Students with reading-skill deficiencies; Study 1: 33 Grade 4; 12 Grade 5; Study 2: 15 Grade 4, 18 Grade 5	Study 1: Compared instruction in comprehension strategy, strategy, and strategy-value feedback; group design; Study 2: Compared strategy instruction, strategy modification, and instructional control; group design
Simmonds (1990)	Knowledge	Students with LD; ages 9 to 12	Compared cognitive modeling, cognitive modeling and verbalization, and involving explicit instruction and feedback
Wong & Wong (1986)	Knowledge	Above average readers, average readers, students with LD; intermediate grades	Examined relation between expresses and applied metacognition

REFERENCES

Billingsley, B. S., & Wildman, T. M. (1990). Facilitating reading comprehension in learning disabled students: Metacognitive goals and instructional strategies. *Remedial and Special Education, 11*(2), 18–31.

Borkowski, J. G. (1992). Metacognitive theory: A framework for teaching literacy, writing, and math skills. *Journal of Learning Disabilities, 25,* 253–257.

Borkowski, J. G., Johnston, M. B., & Reid, M. K. (1987). Metacognition, motivation, and controlled performance. In S. J. Ceci (Ed.), *Handbook of cognitive, social, and neuropsychological aspects of learning disabilities* (Vol. 2, pp. 147–173). Hillsdale, NJ: Lawrence Erlbaum Associates.

Boyle, J. R. (1996). The effects of a cognitive mapping strategy on the literal and inferential comprehension of students with mild disabilities. *Learning Disability Quarterly, 19,* 86-98.

Brown, A. L. (1980). Metacognitive development in reading. In R. J. Spiro, B. C. Bruce, & W. F. Brewer (Eds.), *Theoretical issues in reading comprehension: Perspectives from cognitive psychology, linguistics, artificial intelligence, and education* (pp. 453–481). Hillsdale, NJ: Lawrence Erlbaum Associates.

Brown, A. (1987). Metacognition, executive control, self-regulation, and other more mysterious mechanisms. In F. E. Weinert, & R. H. Kluwe (Eds.), *Metacognition, motivation, and understanding.* Hillsdale, NJ: Lawrence Erlbaum Associates.

Chan, L. K. S. (1994). Relationship of motivation, strategic learning, and reading achievement in grades 5, 7, and 9. *Journal of Experimental Education, 62,* 319–339.

Chan, L. K. S. , Cole, P. G., & Barfett, S. (1987). Comprehension monitoring: Detection and identification of text inconsistencies by LD and normal students. *Learning Disability Quarterly, 10,* 114–124.

Chan, L. K. S., Cole, P. G., & Morris, J. N. (1990). Effects of instruction in the use of a visual-imagery strategy on the reading-comprehension competence of disabled and average readers. *Learning Disability Quarterly, 13,* 2-11.

Cornoldi, C. (1990). Metacognitive control processes and memory deficits in poor comprehenders. *Learning Disability Quarterly, 13,* 245-255.

Flavell, J. H., & Wellman, H. M. (1977). Metamemory. In R. V. Vail, & J. W. Hagen, (Eds.), *Perspectives on the development of memory and cognition* (pp. 3-33). Hillsdale, NJ: Lawrence Erlbaum Associates.

Gaultney, J. F. (1995). The effect of prior knowledge and metacognition on the acquisition of a reading comprehension strategy. *Journal of Experimental Child Psychology, 59,* 142–163.

Hannah, C. L., & Shore, B. M. (1995). Metacognition and high intellectual ability: Insights from the study of learning-disabled gifted students. *Gifted Child Quarterly, 39,* 95–105.

Harris, K. R., & Pressley, M. (1991). The nature of cognitive strategy instruction: Interactive strategy construction. *Exceptional Children, 57,* 392–404.

Johnston, P. H., & Winograd, P. N. (1985). Passive failure in reading. *Journal of Reading Behavior, 17,* 279-301.

Malone, L. D., & Mastropieri, M. A. (1992). Reading comprehension instruction: Summarization and self-monitoring training for students with learning disabilities. *Exceptional Children, 58,* 270–279.

Meltzer, L. J. (1993). Strategy use in students with learning disabilities: The challenge of assessment. In L. J. Meltzer (Ed.), *Strategy assessment and instruction for students with learning disabilities* (pp. 93–136). Austin, TX: Pro-Ed.

Palincsar, A. S., David, Y. M., Winn, J. A., & Stevens, D. D. (1991). Examining the context of strategy instruction. *Remedial and Special Education (RASE), 12*(3), 43-53.

Paris, S. C., Wasik, B. A., & Turner, J. C. (1991). The development of strategic readers. In R. Barr, M. L. Kamil, P. B. Mosenthal, & P. D. Pearson (Eds.), *Handbook of reading research* (Vol. 2, pp. 609–640). New York: Longman.

Pintrich, P. R., Anderman, E. M., & Klobucar, C. (1994). Intraindividual differences in motivation and cognition in students with and without learning disabilities. *Journal of Learning Disabilities, 27*, 360–370.

Rottman, T. R., & Cross, D. R. (1990). Using informed strategies for learning to enhance the reading and thinking skills of children with learning disabilities. *Journal of Learning Disabilities, 23*, 270-278.

Schunk, D. H., & Rice, J. M. (1992). Influence of reading-comprehension strategy information on children's achievement outcomes. *Learning Disability Quarterly, 15*, 51–64.

Simmonds, E. P. M. (1990). The effectiveness of two methods for teaching a constraint-seeking questioning strategy to students with learning disabilities. *Journal of Learning Disabilities, 23*, 229-233.

Swanson, H. L. (1989). Strategy instruction: Overview of principles and procedures for effective use. *Learning Disability Quarterly, 12*(1), 3–14.

Torgesen, J. K. (1994). Issues in the assessment of executive function: An information-processing perspective. In G. R. Lyon (Ed.), *Frames of reference for the assessment of learning disabilities: New view on measurement issues* (pp. 143–162). Baltimore: Brookes.

Weisberg, R. (1988). 1980s: A change in focus of reading comprehension research: A review of reading/learning disabilities research based on an interactive model of reading. *Learning Disability Quarterly, 11*(2), 149–159.

Williams, J. P., Brown, L. G., Silverstein, A. K., & deCani, J. S. (1994). An instructional program in comprehension on narrative themes for adolescents with learning disabilities. *Learning Disability Quarterly, 17*, 205–222.

Wong, B. Y. L. (1992). On cognitive process-based instruction: An introduction. *Journal of Learning Disabilities, 25*(3), 150–152, 172.

Wong, B. Y. L., & Wong, R. (1986). Study behavior as a function of metacognitive knowledge about critical task variables: An investigation of above average, average and learning disabled readers. *Learning Disabilities Research, 1*(2), 101–111.

Zimmerman, B. J. (1994). Dimensions of academic self-regulation: A conceptual framework for education. In D. H. Schunk & B. J. Zimmerman, (Eds.), *Self regulation of learning and performance: Issuers and educational applications* (pp. 3–21). Hillsdale, NJ: Lawrence Erlbaum Associates.

CHAPTER
13

Metacognitive Strategies: Instructional and Curricular Basics and Implications

Shirley V. Dickson
Vicki L. Collins
Northern Illinois University

Deborah C. Simmons
Edward J. Kameenui
University of Oregon

REVIEW OF CONVERGING EVIDENCE

One goal of reading instruction is to develop "thoughtful readers who plan selectively, monitor comprehension while reading, and reflect on process and content after reading" (Paris, Wasik, & Turner, 1991). This goal, however, appears unattainable for many students, students whom we choose to call diverse learners. When considering the multiple differences between successful and less successful readers, one differentiating factor aligns with the definition of "thoughtful readers." That factor is the knowledge and self-regulation of one's own learning processes—metacognition.

Compared to successful readers, diverse learners generally demonstrate metacognitive difficulties that cluster in two broad areas, insufficient knowledge and inappropriate application. The first broad area of difficulty, insufficient knowledge, manifests itself in a lack of knowledge of strategies, the value of strategies, and the effect of textual features (e.g., vocabulary, textual organization, coherence) on reading comprehension (Meltzer, 1993). At times, diverse learners may demonstrate knowledge of strategies and their value but demonstrate difficulty in the second broad area, inappropriate application. Inappropriate application includes failure to use a known strategy and may be due to a lack of motivation. Research evidence suggests the benefit of metacognitive instruction in helping diverse learners become independent readers.

While research supports the benefit of instruction in reading metacognition for diverse learners, much remains uncertain. Reading metacognition is an emerging construct with unclear boundaries and multiple components. Additionally, we do not yet know the most effective or efficient balance between the metacognitive components, cognitive strategies, and instructional techniques. Moreover, this balance may depend on the desired learning outcome and student familiarity with content, text structure (e.g., narrative vs. expository), and task complexity.

Even though metacognition is an emerging construct, the synthesis of research reported in the previous chapter on metacognition and its relation to reading comprehension resulted in the following areas of convergence:

- Metacognitive knowledge facilitates reading comprehension.
- Self-regulation facilitates reading comprehension.
- Motivation may mediate students' use and benefit from meta-cognitive knowledge and self-regulation strategies.
- Metacognitive instruction facilitates reading comprehension.

To derive curricular and instructional implications, we scrutinized the studies reviewed for the previous chapter on metacognition for convergence of teaching techniques. In our scrutiny, we found four patterns in the majority of the studies that provide guidelines for an instructional format. First, whether instruction was designed to induce or directly teach metacognition, instruction was explicit. Second, many of the reviewed studies purported to increase metacognition but measured reading comprehension rather than metacognition as an outcome of instruction. Third, metacognitive instruction occurred concurrently with instruction in cognitive reading strategies and in the context of reading narrative or expository text. Finally, instructional commonalties cut across interventions in metacognitive knowledge and self-regulation.

The four instructional patterns that we identified guide our presentation of instructional implications for diverse learners. First we present an explicit instructional format. Next, we focus on metacognitive instruction that enhanced reading comprehension rather than metacognition. We determined this focus not only because many of the studies measured reading comprehension rather than metacognition, but because reading comprehension has tangible benefits for students. Finally, we reconceptualize the concurrent instruction in metacognitive and cognitive components, and instructional commonalties according to six instructional principles developed by Dixon, Carnine, and Kameenui (1992).

In the following section, we delineate three instructional priorities, or big ideas relevant to metacognition, for instruction to enhance reading comprehension. To make the big ideas more explicit and employable, we discuss the principles of *conspicuous strategies, mediated scaffolding, strategic integration, primed background knowledge, and judicious review* and present examples of how they apply to instruction of the metacognitive components of knowledge, self-regulation, and motivation. The procedural principles, in combination with the content of the big ideas, illustrate how to translate research into practice. The following section should not be viewed as prescriptive, but rather as an application of principles to make tangible the details of instruction for students with diverse learning needs. To connect research and practice, we respond to two focal questions:

1. What are the research-based instructional priorities or big ideas in metacognition?
2. For the instructional priorities or big ideas in metacognition, what is the existing research evidence regarding curriculum design?

RESEARCH-BASED INSTRUCTIONAL PRIORITIES IN METACOGNITION: BIG IDEAS

Dixon et al. (1992) defined *big ideas* as concepts or principles within or across content areas that have the greatest potential for enabling students to apply what they learn in varied situations. In the area of metacognition, we identify two big ideas or instructional priorities for diverse learners:

1. Facets of metacognitive knowledge integrated with cognitive strategy instruction enhance reading comprehension and may increase motivation to use cognitive strategies and self-regulation.
2. Facets of self-regulation integrated with cognitive strategy instruction enhance reading comprehension.

Metacognitive Knowledge

The first big idea is that facets of metacognitive knowledge integrated with cognitive strategy instruction enhance reading comprehension and may increase motivation to use cognitive strategies and self-regulation. Metacognitive knowledge meets the criteria of a big idea because it demonstrates great potential for enabling students to apply cognitive strategies to varied situations. For example, the metacognitive knowledge of when or when not to use a cognitive strategy facilitates the application of the strategy in varied situations. Furthermore, the metacognitive knowledge of the value of a cognitive strategy may increase students' motivation to apply the strategy independently, and enhance self-regulation.

Twelve of the 13 reviewed studies on metacognition and its relation to reading comprehension reported a statistically significant effect of metacognitive knowledge on students' reading comprehension. Most frequently metacognitive knowledge was defined as knowledge of task demands, and the relation between reading strategies and reading comprehension. Although metacognitive knowledge significantly benefited reading comprehension, the instructional implications were not always unambiguous. For example, findings left unclear whether some facets of metacognitive knowledge are more strongly related to reading comprehension than others or whether various metacognitive knowledge facets when combined are related more strongly to reading comprehension than when featured individually. Furthermore, few studies compared cognitive strategy instruction alone with cognitive plus metacognitive components. Therefore, we cannot conclude that comprehension gains were solely attributable to metacognitive knowledge. The cognitive strategies most frequently investigated were summarization and main idea.

Besides enhancing reading comprehension, instruction in the metacognitive knowledge of the value of a strategy enhanced motivation. In the six reviewed studies that investigated motivation, motivational beliefs were defined as personal beliefs about one's competency and the causes and controllability of academic outcomes. For diverse learners, including metacognitive knowledge to enhance motivation (a) facilitated self-regulation, (b) enhanced achievement benefits of strategy instruction, (c) enhanced the long-term achievement benefits of strategy instruction, and (d) altered negative motivational beliefs. For example, poor readers who were given specific feedback (metacognitive knowledge) relating their personal use of a main idea strategy and academic success demonstrated higher self-efficacy and strategy use than poor readers receiving strategy instruction with no specific feedback or no strategy instruction (Schunk & Rice, 1992, Study 1).

Self-Regulation

The second instructional priority is that facets of self-regulation integrated with cognitive strategy instruction enhance reading comprehension. Similar to metacognitive knowledge, self-regulation meets the criteria of a big idea as it enables students to apply cognitive strategies in varied situations. For example, students who were taught to self-monitor and summarize using simple reading passages demonstrated greater reading comprehension on complex social studies passages than students who were taught the summarization strategy without the self-monitoring component.

In the five reviewed studies that investigated self-regulation, self-regulation was most frequently operationalized as self-monitoring. Self-regulation was less frequently operationalized as coordinating metacognitive knowledge and rarely or never operationalized as planning, identifying causes of one's comprehension failures during reading, or remediating reading failures. Similar to instruction in metacognitive knowledge, it is unclear what has the stronger relation to reading comprehension: specific facets of self-regulation such as self-monitoring, planning or self-questioning; combinations of self-regulation components rather than individual components; or combinations of self-regulation and metacognitive knowledge components.

Part of the vagary of the effectiveness of various combinations of self-regulation components and cognitive strategies may relate to the complexity of the reading passages or task demands. For example, for simple passages there was no difference in reading comprehension between students with learning disabilities who were taught a summarization strategy and those taught the summarization strategy with a self-monitoring component. However, when the same students read complex social studies passages the combination of the summarization strategy and self-monitoring benefited reading comprehension significantly more than the summarization strategy alone (Malone & Mastropieri, 1992).

The remaining five instructional principles (i.e., conspicuous strategies, mediated scaffolding, strategic integration, primed background knowledge, and judicious review) provide guidelines for instruction. The examples for each principle were taken from the procedures within the primary and secondary studies reviewed for the previous chapter on metacognition and its relation to reading comprehension. For clarity, the instructional guidelines are presented separately. In actual lesson plans, the teacher thoughtfully interweaves the instructional guidelines to frame effective instruction for diverse learners.

Rather than discuss the instructional implications for each *big idea* separately, we merge the discussions. Two factors make separate discussions of each big idea repetitive: Instructional commonalities frequently cut across instruction in metacognitive knowledge and self-regulation, and lessons that include metacognitive components frequently integrate metacognitive knowledge and self-regulation.

EVIDENCE OF CURRICULUM DESIGN
IN METACOGNITION

Conspicuous Strategies

Strategies are an organized set of actions designed to accomplish a task. Although there is controversy over the consciousness of strategies, we use the definition of Paris et al. (1991) that strategies are conscious, deliberate, "open to inspection," and able to be evaluated. We further define two categories of strategies. Cognitive strategies are a broad array of learner-based actions that help control comprehension (Weinstein & Mayer, cited in Paris et al., 1991). In order of frequency, commonly taught cognitive reading strategies were summarizing, identifying main ideas, and mapping expository or story grammar elements. Less commonly used cognitive strategies included identifying text difficulty, making inferences to understand stories, finding the theme of a story, question generating, clarifying, and predicting upcoming content.

Metacognitive strategies are strategies that generalize across many tasks, help readers' awareness of whether or not they comprehend what they are reading, and assist readers' decision of what strategies to employ to aid comprehension (Weisberg, 1988). The metacognitive strategies most frequently used in the reviewed studies were knowledge of the value of a strategy, knowledge of task demands, and self-monitoring. We consider knowledge of the value of a strategy as metacognitive knowledge and related to motivation; knowledge of task demands as metacognitive knowledge; and self-monitoring as self-regulation.

The metacognitive knowledge of the "usefulness of a strategy" becomes a metacognitive strategy because it helps students generalize the use of a cognitive strategy across varied settings. Examples of the knowledge of the usefulness of a strategy serving as a metacognitive strategy include teaching students that (a) the cognitive strategy of thinking of a good title for a passage helps the reader remember the important ideas in the story (Schunk & Rice, 1992, Study 1), (b) modifying a cognitive strategy to find main ideas helps you to find supporting ideas (Schunk & Rice, Study 2), (c) a summarizing strategy increases reading comprehension (Rottman & Cross, 1990), (d) prior knowledge helps readers understand written material (Rottman & Cross), and (e) relating prior knowledge to text information increases comprehension (Rottman & Cross). Teaching students how to modify a strategy is an explicit example of how metacognitive knowledge becomes a metacognitive strategy. Teaching students to modify a strategy broadens the usefulness of a strategy by making it applicable to more than one situation and aids students in deciding what cognitive strategies to use.

Similar to the knowledge of the value of a strategy, the knowledge of task demands becomes a strategy because it assists students in deciding what cognitive strategies to employ. Examples of knowledge of task demands include identifying the purpose for studying a passage (e.g., to answer questions that would be given after reading), taught as the first step in a 5-step comprehension monitoring strategy (Wong & Jones, cited in Billingsley & Wildman, 1990), and asking yourself "What do I have to do?" before performing each step of a 5-step main idea strategy (Schunk & Rice, 1992, Study 1).

Finally, the metacognitive strategy of self-monitoring helps readers' awareness of whether or not they comprehend what they are reading. Self-monitoring strategies include self-questioning, identifying inconsistent information in text, and monitoring reading comprehension or strategy use. One example of self-questioning involves story-grammar elements as students ask themselves "Who is the leading character? What is the character trying to accomplish? What stands in the way of the main character reaching the desired goal?" (Carnine & Kinder, cited in Billingsley & Wildman, 1990). Identifying inconsistent information in text includes cross-referencing as a strategy to identify sentences that contained topics not related to the other sentences in the passage (Chan, Cole, & Barfett, 1987). Monitoring reading comprehension includes (a) the last step in a 5-step comprehension strategy that has students check to see how each successive question and answer they generate provides more information (Wong & Jones, cited in Billingsley & Wildman, 1990), and (b) a student's check of story understanding and rereading to correct any lack of understanding (Schunk & Rice, 1992, Study 1). Monitoring strategy use includes teaching students when to use or modify a cognitive strategy (e.g., Rottman & Cross, 1990; Schunk & Rice, Study 2) and evaluating the success of strategy use (Palincsar, David, Winn, & Stevens, 1991).

Because metacognitive strategies were frequently taught concurrently with cognitive strategies, it is difficult to describe the metacognitive component of instrucation without also addressing the cognitive component. We endeavor as much as possible to address how the metacognitive strategies were made conspicuous to students. We found that in the majority of reviews studies, metacognitive strategies were made conspicuous through:

- Explicit statements,
- Modeling,
- Systematic feedback, and
- Interactions between teacher/students and students/students.

Mediated Scaffolding

Scaffolded instruction is an important feature of effective strategy instruction that encourages students to develop independence as teachers gradually release responsibility for strategies to the students (e.g., Billingsley & Wildman, 1990; Borkowski, 1992). By assuming initial control, the teacher directs attention to the task and appropriate strategies, controls frustration, decreases the risk of problem solving, and makes overt the discrepancies between a student's response and the use of a more appropriate strategy (Borkowski, 1992). In the reviewed studies, whether the goal of instruction was to directly teach or to induce metacognition, mediated scaffolding occurred through personnel, content, tasks, and materials. Initial instruction included stronger external scaffolding or support that was faded as students gained fluency or independence.

Personnel. Personnel scaffolding is the external support provided by teachers and peers through modeling, systematic feedback, or dialogue between teacher and students or among students. Teachers may use modeling, systematic feedback, and dialogue alone or in combination with each other.

In *modeling,* teachers think aloud as they demonstrate the performanc of a strategy. In the reviewed studies, modeling occurred in various forms: modeling a metacognitive strategy; modeling a cognitive strategy; or modeling appropriate use of dialogue.

Teachers generally modeled the metacognitive strategy concurrently with modeling a cognitive strategy. For example, for the cognitive part of the strategy, the teacher modeled by thinking and performing aloud how to read the question, read the passage to determine what it is mostly about, think about what the details have in common, think about what would make a good title, and reread if the answer to the question remained unknown. The teacher modeled the metacognitive knowledge of the usefulness of the strategy by thinking aloud that thinking of a good title (step 4 in the cognitive strategy) helps the reader remember important ideas in the story (Schunk & Rice, 1992, Study 1).

At times, teachers modeled only the cognitive strategy without also modeling a metacognitive component. When this occurred, they taught the metacognitive component using a different form of personnel scaffolding. The metacognitive component using a different form of personnel scaffolding. The metacoagnitive components of the lessons included the importance of accurate comprehension, the value of a strategy, when to use or not use the strategy, and selection of the appropriate strategy to use.

A third form of modeling to scaffold instruction in metacognition was teacher modeling of dialogue. Borkowski (1992) suggested that students rather than teachers play a major role in the dialogue. However, in the reviewed studies the teacher frequently first modeled the use of dialogue to make strategies conspicuous. Teachers modeled dialogue of the importance of using strategies, when to use a strategy, and selecting the appropriate strategy.

One question not addressed is when teachers should fade modeling. One recommendation is that the shift in responsibility from the teacher to student be gradual (Palincsar, Paris, Pearson, & Dole, cited in Billingsley & Wildman, 1990). Teacher modeling was minimal and faded quickly when specific feedback and dialogue were part of instruction (e.g., Palincsar et al., 1991). Following fading of modeling and the release of responsiblility to students, teachers generally provided additional modeling or explanation if students demonstrated difficulty applying the strategy or with comprehension.

One example of differing duration of modeling appeared in instruction to identify the theme of a narrative. Teacher modeling occurred over three lessons when the steps in the cognitive strategy were easier (i.e., "Who is the main character?" "What did he do?" "What happened?") and over five lessons for the more difficult questions ("Was this good or bad?" "Why was this good or bad?"). Because theme is difficult to identify, the teacher modeled for five of the nine lessons how answering the five questions led to the identification of the theme. For the five lessons, the teacher modeled two statements to help frame the theme:

(Main character) should have (should not have) _____.
We should (should not) _____.

Finally, the teacher modeled generalizing the theme by modeling responses to the questions "To whom would this theme apply?" "When would it apply—in what situation?" After responsibility was released to the students, if a student demonstrated difficulty with one of the questions or identifying the theme, the teacher provided additional modeling (Williams, Brown, Silverstein, & deCani, 1994, Study 1).

Modeling can be extended for students who appear to be unusually low performers or who have not responded well to other types of instruction. The earlier format was repeated in intact classrooms that contained only students who had been identified as having learning disabilities and who had not responded well to other types of instruction. In this case the modeled lessons were extended and responsibility was released to students more slowly than in the classrooms that contained normally achieving and diverse learners. The number of lessons to teach theme was extended from 9 to 12 (Williams et al., 1994, Study 2).

A second form of personnel scaffolding, *systematic feedback*, generally links strategy use with successful reading comprehension. For example, when students implemented a main idea strategy or answered comprehension questions correctly, teachers stated, "Do you see how thinking about details in common helps you answer questions correctly?" or "You have been answering correctly because you have been following the steps" (Schunk & Rice, 1992, Study 1). In other examples of systematic feedback, teachers and peers (a) encouraged and corrected the use of cognitive strategies (Palincsar & Brown, cited in Paris et al., 1991), (b) discussed the options for selecting and using strategies (Rottman & Cross, 1990), (c) gave students feedback on strategy use (Malone & Mastropieri, 1992; Palincsar et al., 1991; Rottman & Cross), (d) discussed whether the strategy was effective (Palincsar et al.), and (e) provided immediate feedback on the quality of questions in a constraint-seeking questioning technique (Simmonds, 1990).

The optimal use of feedback was not addressed in the reviewed studies. Feedback was provided (a) continuously (Palincsar & Brown, cited in Billingsley & Wildman, 1990; Simmonds, 1990), (b) 3 to 4 times each to individual students during a 35-minute instructional period (Schunk & Rice, 1992), (c) weekly for performance on comprehension tests (Palincsar & Brown, cited in Billingsley & Wildman), (d) once during the first practice of the strategy (Boyle, 1996), and (e) at the end of strategy instruction to reinforce the usefulness of a strategy (Wong & Jones, cited in Billingsley & Wildman, 1990).

A third type of personnel scaffolding to teach metacognition components is to use *interactions between teacher and students or students and students*. One form of interaction is question asking to initiate dialogue (e.g., Rottman & Cross, 1990; Williams et al., 1994). Teachers modeled asking and responding to questions before releasing responsibility for asking and responding to the students (Williams et al.). In other forms of interactions, students engage in discussions, cooperative activities, and peer conferences to (a) determine goals for instruction (knowledge of task demands; Rottman & Cross; Palincsar & Brown, cited in Billingsley & Wildman, 1990); (b) discuss the actions needed to reach the goals (Palincsar & Brown, cited in Billingsley & Wildman, 1990); (c) implement, evaluate, and modify strategy acquisition and use (Palincsar & Brown, cited in Billingsley & Wildman, 1990); (d) discuss how a strategy could be applied in situations other than the reading lessons (Palincsar & Brown, cited in Billingsley & Wildman, 1990); and (e) discuss when it is appropriate and inappropriate to use a specific strategy (Boyle, 1995). As in question asking, teachers frequently modeled the interaction before releasing responsibility to the students.

Content Scaffolding

A second method for scaffolding, content scaffolding, involves using content written at an easy reading level for the students; using content familiar to students; or teaching in stages from easier to more difficult steps of the strategy. Reasons for using materials written at an easier reading level include (a) content written at a high readability level in the initial stages of instruction may interfere with or delay strategy acquisition (Boyle, 1996), (b) decoding problems might interfere with comprehension (Carnine & Kinder; Wong & Jones, cited in Billingsley & Wildman, 1990), and (c) materials matched to the students' reading level increases the likelihood that the intervention procedures will be successful (Palincsar & Brown, cited in Billingsley & Wildman, 1990).

All but three of the primary metacognitive reading interventions used narrative or expository text written specifically for the study or text similar to those used in remedial programs (e.g., "Timed Readings," series by Jamestown Publishers, cited in Boyle, 1996; *Reading for Concepts*, published by Liddle, cited in Malone & Mastropieri, 1992). One technique for content scaffolding was to initiate instruction using easier text and increase the reading difficulty as instruction progresses. Students practiced twice on content written one grade level below their current grade level. Students followed this with two practices using passages written at their current grade level (Boyle). In another example, for students in fourth- and fifth-grade remedial reading classes, teachers initiated instruction using second-grade passages and proceeded to fourth grade passages as instruction progressed (Schunk & Rice, 1992). If the teacher used grade-level content, instruction included oral reading (e.g., Williams et al., 1994).

In a second form of content scaffolding, teachers used content familiar to students while teaching a new strategy. For students who had prior knowledge of baseball, teachers used baseball stories as they taught a self-monitoring strategy, asking "why" questions while reading. Students who learned the self-monitoring strategy while reading familiar content (i.e., baseball) asked more *why* questions when reading new, unfamiliar content than students who were taught the new strategy using content familiar to them (i.e., baseball) asked significantly more *why* questions than students who were taught the strategy using content not familiar to them (i.e., non baseball sports; Gaultney, 1995).

In a third form of content scaffolding, teaching in stages, instructors first teach the easier followed by the more difficult steps of the strategy. For example, the teacher first taught the cognitive strategy of mapping (i.e., linking main ideas) narrative and expository text. After two lessons, the teacher taught why the strategy is important, why it is important to comprehend accurately, and that using the strategy helps students improve comprehension. Finally, the students and teacher discussed when it is appropriate or not appropriate to use the strategy (Boyle, 1996).

Task Scaffolding

A third form of mediated scaffolding involves tasks. In task scaffolding, students initially practice on easier tasks, proceeding to more difficult tasks as instruction and practice continue. For example, initial practice involved simply verbalizing the steps of a mapping strategy TRAVEL (Topic, Read, Ask, Verify, Examine, Link; Boyle, 1996) or a main idea strategy (Schunk & Rice, 1992, study 1). In the second phase of instruction, students read a passage, verbalized the steps of the strategy, and applied the strategy to reading comprehension. In the final stages of instruction, students applied the strategy independently to reading a passage and answering comprehension questions.

In another example of task scaffolding, teachers use structured tasks to increase the sophistication of student responses. In the strategy to identify the theme of a story, the teacher used the questions for generalizing the theme (i.e., To whom would this theme apply?" When would it apply —in what situation?") to elicit more explicit and elaborated student responses (Williams et al., 1994).

Material Scaffolding

A fourth form of mediated scaffolding is the use of materials to remind students of the strategy steps before they independently apply the strategy. As in personnel scaffolding, the materials are gradually removed as students gain independence in strategy use. Material scaffolding was used for self-monitoring (metacognition) and for cognitive strategies.

For self-monitoring, students used a self-monitoring card to monitor their use of the summarization strategy. An index card contained a matrix with the columns labeled with reminders of the summarization strategy (i.e., "who or what," "what happened," "summary sentence") and the rows labeled with the numbers of the paragraphs. The matrix provided a space for students to check as they completed each step of the strategy for each paragraph. Lines drawn at the end of each paragraph further reminded students to self-monitor their use of the strategy (Malone & Mastropieri, 1992).

One common form of material scaffolding was a bulletin board display. Teachers made posters delineating the strategy steps or using a metaphor such as "Be a Reading Detective" to represent the strategy. "Be a Reading Detective" reminded students to examine clues about the passage topic, length, and difficulty. Teachers also incorporated the metaphor into daily lessons and on worksheets to remind students to use the strategy throughout the day. The metaphor was one of five in an intervention that taught five cognitive strategies in five weeks (Rottman & Cross, 1990).

Another form of material scaffolding is to provide students with cue cards listing the steps. For example, in the mapping strategy TRAVEL (Boyle, 1996) to find the main idea and details, the students had a cue card:

1. Topic: Write down the topic and circle it.
2. Read: Read a paragraph.
3. Ask: Ask what the main idea and three details are and write them down.
4. Verify: Verify the main idea by circling it and linking its details.
5. Examine: Examine the next paragraph and Ask and Verify again.
6. Link: When finished with the story, link all circles.

The cue card was removed after two instructional sessions and after students demonstrated that they could verbalize the strategy correctly for 3 out of 5 trials (Boyle, 1996).

Although material scaffolding appears to be effective, we require more guidelines. The following is an example of material scaffolding that initially benefited diverse learners, but had an adverse effect as it was faded. We do not know if the adverse effects of fading the scaffolds across four lessons was (a) a result of removing material scaffolding too quickly, (b) a lack of adequate instructional time and practice, (c) unique to the visualization strategy or type of material scaffolding used to teach the strategy, or (d) failure to be more explicit with the metacognitive component of instruction. We report it here as an example that we have more to learn about using and fading material scaffolding. In this example the cognitive strategy was a visualization strategy to make pictures in your mind as you read. The metacognitive component was the assumption that making pictures in your mind is a method for self-monitoring comprehension.

In Lesson 1, the teacher placed cardboard figures on a magnetic board; in Lesson 2, the teacher moved the characters to illustrate the sequence of events in the story; in Lesson 3, the magnetic figures were on the board with no movement; in Lesson 4 the white magnetic board was present with no figures on it. The effects of removing the scaffolded materials differed for average and diverse learners. The moving figures in Lesson 2 were effective for average and diverse learners, with the diverse learners as a group receiving a higher average score on reading comprehension than the average readers. However, in Lesson 3 when the teacher faded material scaffolding to still figures representing the story characters, the average learners demonstrated increased reading comprehension while the diverse learners demonstrated less reading comprehension than in Lesson 2 (moving figures). Furthermore, the diverse learners demonstrated the same reading comprehension as diverse learners (a) receiving strategy instruction with no material scaffolding, or (b) no strategy instruction. In Lesson 4 (white board, no figures), the reading comprehension of the average and diverse learners decreased from Lesson 3. The reading comprehension of the average readers decreased to the level of the average readers receiving strategy instruction with no material scaffolding or receiving no strategy instruction. For diverse learners, the results were more dramatic. The reading comprehension of the diverse learners decreased even more from Lesson 3 and was significantly less than that of diverse learners who received verbal instruction only or no strategy instruction (Chan, Cole, & Morris, 1990).

As we stated, the initial material scaffolding benefited diverse and average learners. The differing effects occurred as teachers faded the scaffolding. We interpret this to indicate that we have more to learn about material scaffolding. We also note that the intervention failed to make the metacognitive component overt to students.

Although we provide multiple examples of personnel, content, task, and material scaffolding, we cannot report on whether one method of scaffolding is more effective than another or whether using multiple scaffolds is more effective than using one scaffold. None of the reviewed studies compared the effectiveness of various scaffolds nor the additive effects of multiple forms of scaffolding.

Strategic Integration

Strategic integration refers to integrating content, skills, or concepts that mutually support each other, communicate generalizations, or transfer to areas further and further removed from the original area of instruction (Dixon et al., 1992). The strategic integration of skills that mutually support each other is addressed by the two instructional priorities or *big ideas* presented in this chapter. That is, instruction in metacognitive knowledge or self-regulation integrated with instruction in cognitive strategies enhances reading comprehension. In some studies, further integration occurred by combining instruction in multiple components of metacognition or cognitive strategies. Additionally, all but one primary study integrated instruction in metacognition and cognitive strategies with reading content. Finally, one of the reviewed studies reported that teachers were given suggestions for how to integrate the five taught strategies into their own teaching and other content areas, but the study gave no details (Rottman & Cross, 1990).

As indicated by the *big ideas* presented in this chapter, instruction in metacognition and cognitive strategies occurred concurrently. At times, instruction included multiple metacognitive or cognitive strategies. The metacognitive components included one or a combination of the following: (a) the importance of comprehending accurately, (b) the value of the strategy, (c) when to use or not use the strategy, (d) knowledge of task demands, (e) modifying a main idea strategy to identify details, (f) self-monitoring reading comprehension, and (f) cross-referencing to identify inconsistent information. The cognitive strategies included one or a combination of the following: (a) summarizing, (b) identifying main ideas, (c) identifying details, (d) using visual imagery, (e) mapping expository or narrative elements, (f) using inferences, and (g) integrating information while reading. In one study, cognitive strategies (i.e., summarizing, generating questions, predicting) were taught for concurrent use on one passage (Palincsar et al., 1991). In another study, multiple cognitive strategies were taught in succession (i.e., finding the main idea, modifying a main idea strategy; identifying text difficulty, identifying main ideas, summarizing, using inferences, and integrating information), and instruction included discussions of when to use the strategies (Rottman & Cross, 1990).

In all but one of the primary studies, instruction in metacognitive facets occurred using narrative or expository passages. As stated earlier, the initial instructional passages were generally written for the studies or were text similar to those used in remedial programs. Narratives from basals written at the students' grade level were used to teach the identification of theme. In the secondary studies, instruction in metacognition also occurred in the context of reading passages. However, not enough information was provided to describe the types of passages.

Primed Background Knowledge

Prior knowledge is generally considered to influence reading comprehension. In this section, we discuss prior content knowledge and prior knowledge of metacognition and cognitive strategies.

Prior Content Knowledge. Prior content knowledge may play a role in self-monitoring of reading comprehension as readers generate expectations of text, and use discrepancies between expectations and text as a signal for causes of the discrepancies (Winograd & Johnson, cited in Billingsley & Wildman, 1990). Furthermore, inadequate prior content knowledge may prevent diverse learners from monitoring their comprehension (Snider & Tarver, cited in Billingsley & Wildman, 1990). In the reviewed studies, teachers addressed prior knowledge of content in three ways. They used content the students were familiar with while teaching a new strategy; directly taught students to use prior content knowledge as a strategy; or elicited or pretaught prior content knowledge as part of the design of instruction.

In the first example of the use of prior knowledge, using familiar content while teaching a new strategy, teachers taught students a self-monitoring strategy, to ask *why* as they read. The boys who were taught using familiar content (i.e., baseball stories) asked more *why* questions when the strategy was transferred to unfamiliar content than boys who were taught the *why* strategy using unfamiliar content (i.e., non baseball sports stories). Besides facilitating the acquisition of a new strategy, prior knowledge of content also facilitated recall of the familiar content. In other words, boys with prior knowledge of baseball demonstrated greater recall of the baseball stories than did boys with no prior knowledge of baseball (Gaultney, 1995).

In the second example of the use of prior content knowledge, as a cognitive strategy, teachers directly taught the importance of prior knowledge for understanding text (Rottman & Cross, 1990). Additionally the teachers taught students to integrate their prior content knowledge with new information they read (Rottman & Cross, 1990). The study did not provide examples of how teachers did this. In a second example, the teacher and students discussed the role of prior content knowledge in determining one's approach to reading and selecting an appropriate cognitive strategy (Palincsar et al., 1991).

In the third example of the use of prior content knowledge, teachers used prereading activities to elicit what students already knew about a topic. In the first part of a five-part lesson on theme identification, the teacher discussed the topic of the story and its relevance to personal experiences. As the students read, the teacher asked questions that encouraged students to make associations between their own prior knowledge and the text information (Williams et al., 1994).

Prior Knowledge of Metacognition and Cognitive Strategies. One study ex-amined prior metacognitive knowledge as a variable in strategy acquisition and recall. Boys who demonstrated higher levels of prior declarative meta-cognitive knowledge (e.g., what strategy to use for remembering narrative versus expository text) before instruction demonstrated greater usage of the *why* strategy after instruction. Prior metacognitive knowledge did not appear to influence story recall (Gaultney, 1995). In this study teachers did not use prior metacognitive knowledge as part of their instruction.

No studies provided examples of teachers (a) directly teaching the importance of prior metacognitive knowledge as they did the importance of prior content knowledge or (b) eliciting prior metacognitive knowledge as they did content knowledge. However, teachers first taught a cognitive strategy and then used that strategy as prior knowledge to teach a metacognitive component. For example, teachers first taught a main idea strategy then used the main idea strategy as prior knowledge to teach the students how to modify the strategy to identify supporting details (Schunk & Rice, 1992, Study 2). In another example, teachers first taught the cognitive strategy of mapping (i.e., linking main ideas) narrative and expository text. Teachers then used the mapping strategy as prior knowledge to teach why the strategy is important, why it is important to comprehend accurately, that using the strategy helps students improve comprehension, and when it is appropriate or not appropriate to use the strategy (Boyle, 1996).

Judicious Review

Effective review is thoughtfully planned. That is, reviews of new skills and strategies are cumulative and integrated over periods of time (Dixon et al., 1992). In the reviewed studies, judicious review occurred as teachers taught new concepts intermittently between previously taught content, and integrated previously taught content into new content.

In the first example, in classrooms that contained normally achieving students and diverse learners, the teachers taught the theme "perseverance" in Lessons 2, 3, 4, 7, and 8 of nine lessons on nine different narratives. The intermittent themes were greed, cooperation, pride, and openness to experience (Williams et al., 1994, Study 1). In classrooms that contained only diverse learners and no normally achieving students, the teachers taught in 12 lessons and included perseverance again in Lesson 11 (Williams et al., 1994).

In the second example of judicious review, the teachers incorporated previously taught strategies into instruction in new strategies. In instruction that taught students five strategies in 5 weeks, Module 1 was a strategy on the difficulty of text. Module 2 was a main idea strategy. Module 3 incorporated the main idea strategy into a strategy to summarize stories to foster comprehension. Module 4 was on how to integrate information while reading. Module 5 incorporated the strategy from module 4 on how to relate text information into prior knowledge (Rottman, & Cross, 1990). In another example, students completed five lessons on a main idea strategy. In the next five lessons, students modified the main idea strategy to find details (Schunk & Rice, 1992, Study 2).

CONCLUSION

In summary, diverse learners appear less aware of metacognition than successful readers. Despite the metacognitive difficulties of diverse learners, research suggests that instruction containing metacognitive components enhances their reading comprehension. Specifically, our scrutiny of the primary and secondary studies reviewed for the previous chapter on metacognition and its relation to reading comprehension re-sulted in two instructional priorities or *big ideas* and examples of instruction that support five additional instructional design principles—*conspicuous strategies, mediated scaffolding, strategic integration, primed background knowledge,* and *judicious review.* We also found that instruction was generally explicit either for metacognition or cognitive strategies or both.

The two instructional priorities or *big ideas* that we identified involve metacognitive knowledge (e.g., knowledge of the value of a strategy or task demands) and self-regulation (e.g., self-monitoring). First, facets of metacognitive knowledge integrated with cognitive strategy instruction enhance reading comprehension and may increase motivation to use cognitive strategies and self-regulation. Second, facets of self-regulation integrated with cognitive strategy instruction enhance reading comprehension.

In our discussion of the remaining five instructional design principles, we reported that metacognitive knowledge and self-regulation become *conspicuous strategies* that help students generalize the use of cognitive strategies across varied settings, decide what cognitive strategies to use, or determine whether they comprehend what they are reading. *Mediated scaffolding* occurs when (a) teachers or peers provide modeling, systematic feedback, and dialogue; (b) initial instruction uses content written at an easy reading level, content that is familiar to students, or easier before more difficult strategy steps; (c) teachers initially present easier before more difficult tasks; and (d) teachers provide materials such as cue cards, check lists, or bulletin board displays to remind students of the strategy steps before they independently apply the strategy. *Strategic integration* occurs as teachers combine instruction in one or more metacognitive components with one or more cognitive strategies in the context of reading content. Examples of *primed background knowledge* include teachers (a) using familiar content to teach new strategies and metacognition, (b) teaching the importance of prior knowledge and how to integrate prior content knowledge with new information, and (c) using prereading activities to elicit what students already know about a topic while teaching a cognitive strategy. Additionally, teachers instruct students in a cognitive strategy, then use the strategy as prior knowledge for teaching metacognitive components. Finally, *judicious review* occurs by intermittently mixing new concepts between previously taught content and integrating previously taught strategies into instruction in new strategies. When interwoven, these six instructional principles frame explicit instruction in which teachers identify the metacognitive and cognitive strategies to be taught, model, and provide guided and independent practice. The interwoven six instructional guidelines enable diverse learners to experience success in their performance as they progress to being independent, thoughtful readers.

REFERENCES

Billingsley, B. S., & Wildman, T. M. (1990). Facilitating reading comprehension in learning disabled students: Metacognitive goals and instructional strategies. *Remedial and Special Education, 11*(2), 18–31.

Borkowski, J. G. (1992). Metacognitive theory: A framework for teaching literacy, writing, and math skills. *Journal of Learning Disabilities, 25,* 253–257

Boyle, J. R. (1996). The effects of a cognitive mapping strategy on the literal and inferential comprehension of students with mild disabilities. *Learning Disability Quarterly, 19,* 86–98

Chan, L. K. S. , Cole, P. G., & Barfett, S. (1987). Comprehension monitoring: Detection and identification of text inconsistencies by LD and normal students. *Learning Disability Quarterly, 10,* 114–124.

Chan, L. K. S., Cole, P. G., & Morris, J. N. (1990). Effects of instruction in the use of a visual-imagery strategy on the reading-comprehension competence of disabled and average readers. *Learning Disability Quarterly, 13,* 2–11.

Dixon, R. Carnine, D., & Kameenui, E. J., (1992). Curriculum guidelines for diverse learners. In *Monograph for the National Center to Improve the Tools of Educators.* Eugene: University of Oregon.

Gaulty, J. F. (1995). The effect of prior knowledge and metacognition on the acquisition of a reading comprehension strategy. *Journal of Experimental Child Psychology, 59,* 142-163.

Malone, L. D., & Mastropieri, M. A. (1992). Reading comprehension instruction: Summarization and self-monitoring for students with learning disabilities. *Exceptional Children, 58,* 270–279.

Meltzer, L. J. (1993) Strategy use in students with learning disabilities: The challenge of assessment. In L. J. Meltzer (Ed.), *Strategy assessment and instruction for students with learning disabilities* (pp. 93–136). Austin, TX: Pro-Ed.

Palincsar, A. S., David, Y. M., Winn, J. A., & Stevens, D. D. (1991). Examining the context of strategy instruction. Remedial and Special Education, 12(3), 43-53.

Paris, S. C., Wasik, B. A., & Turner, J. C. (1991). The development of strategic readers. In R. Barr, M. L. Kamil, P. B. Mosenthal, & P. D. Pearson (Eds.), *Handbook of reading research* (Vol. 2, pp. 609-640). New York: Longman.

Rottman, T. R., & Cross, D. R. (1990). Using informed strategies for learning to enhance the reading and thinking skills of children with learning disabilities. *Journal of Learning Disabilities, 23,* 270–278.

Schunk, D. H., & Rice, J. M. (1992). Influence of reading-comprehension strategy information on children's achievement outcomes. *Learning Disability Quarterly, 15,* 51–64.

Simmonds, E. P. M. (1990). The effectiveness of two methods for teaching a constraint-seeking questioning strategy to students with learning disabilities. *Journal of Learning Disabilities, 23,* 229–233.

Weisberg, R. (1988). 1980s: A change in focus of reading comprehension research: A review of reading / learning disabilities research based on an interactive model of reading. *Learning Disability Quarterly, 11*, 149–159.

Williams, J. P., Brown, L. G., Silverstein, A. K., & deCani, J. S. (1994). An instructional program in comprehension on narrative themes for adolescents with learning disabilities. *Learning Disability Quarterly, 17*, 205–222.

Author Index

Subject Index